He is the kind of man who
will get the job done.

that which

They were kind to her

They bought a different ms
than what they really needed.

Business English

HUBERT A. HAGAR

MARIE M. STEWART

E. LILLIAN HUTCHINSON

GREGG PUBLISHING DIVISION

and

Letter Writing

McGRAW-HILL BOOK COMPANY, INC.

New York, Chicago, San Francisco

Dallas, Toronto, London

PUBLISHED BY GREGG PUBLISHING DIVISION

McGraw-Hill Book Company, Inc.
Printed in the United States of America

Preface

The Importance of Business English. Teachers of English almost universally recognize the necessity for a special type of English instruction for students who are preparing for positions in business and industry. Familiarity with the "language of business" is now a *must* for every student who is preparing for a business career. Business English has, therefore, become an accepted course in nearly all secondary schools and colleges.

Student Attitudes Toward Business English. Experienced teachers of business English also know that, regardless of the student's previous training in English, many of those who enroll for business courses have become careless in their speech and writing habits. Many are often unfamiliar with words and terms frequently used in business. Some have forgotten the elementary principles of grammar, and relatively few have had training in the composition of business letters and reports. Then, too, a number of students may feel a certain antipathy toward further study of a subject in which they feel they are already proficient. Because of the special needs of students of business English, different, new, interesting, and challenging material must be provided.

In the preparation of this book the authors have kept these student attitudes and difficulties in mind. In addition to making the study of English interesting and challenging, they have maintained a proper relation and balance between the *corrective* and the *constructive* (or creative) type of instructional material.

Revision of a Popular Book. Parts I through V of *Business English and Letter Writing* represent a new edition of the extremely popular text, *The English of Business*. This book has been widely used in various types of schools for nearly forty-five years. Chief among the features that have contributed to the popularity of this book is the constant emphasis placed on the proper use of words and on the application of the rules of grammar, punctuation, capitalization, abbreviations, the use of figures, etc. These features have been retained.

New Materials. To this revision of *The English of Business* has been added an entirely new and complete section on business letter writing. These sections on English grammar and on letter writing make an effective combination for the business student, providing him with valuable training in the skills of business writing, so important in the business office.

Organization of the Book. *Business English and Letter Writing* is organized as follows:

Vocabulary. Part I is devoted to vocabulary testing and study. Then, when the student has become more word conscious, his attention is turned to remedial work in grammar (Part II). Each lesson in Part II, however, continues instruction and drill on vocabulary building.

Remedial Grammar. In the remedial presentation of grammar in Part II, the authors have assumed that all students have at least an elementary knowledge of the subject. Only those principles of grammar are presented that will help the student to detect errors in his own language and in the language of others, as well as in letters that he may later write or transcribe in the business office. No attempt is made to cover the fine points of grammar theory. The Reference Section of this book contains twenty-five useful "grammar refreshers," in addition to valuable reference material.

Punctuation and Style. Part III, which is devoted to punctuation and other details of style, is developed in far greater detail than are the preceding parts of the text because of the reference value of the material. The student will consult this section often both during and following his Business English course. Throughout, punctuation instruction is based on the grammatical structure of the sentence that is being punctuated. The student thus comes to see the errors that result from the "saltcellar" method of punctuating.

Effective Speaking. When the student has been given a background of correct word usage and sentence structure, he is introduced to the art of speaking effectively (Part IV). The ability to express oneself correctly and forcefully is a fundamental requirement for success in business. With individual needs of his class in mind, the teacher can adapt both classwork and assignments in order to make the work most helpful to the individual student.

Fundamentals of Writing. The section on the fundamentals of writing (Part V) is really a condensed treatment of rhetoric. An employee may possess original and often constructive ideas; but, if those ideas are not expressed in a forceful manner, they may be lost to the reader. Therefore, effective writing is a necessity for continued advancement in business.

Business Letter Writing. Part VI contains a complete treatment of business writing. The material is written in a friendly, readable style—the language of the marketplace—and the vocabulary is well within the range of the typical business student.

This part emphasizes not only the mechanics and techniques of effective business correspondence but also the reasons behind the writing of letters, thereby giving the student valuable guidance in the thinking and planning that are required in composing effective letters. Throughout this part, there is a continuing thread of emphasis on:

1. The sales-making possibilities inherent in all business letters.
2. The methods of building good will through business letters.
3. The reduction of letter costs.
4. The application of the principles of good human relations to the writing of business letters.
5. The techniques of accentuating the positive and subduing the negative.

Another departure from the traditional presentation is the unique lesson organization as a rounded teaching-learning unit, covering:

1. An introduction that provides motivation.
2. Simple, clear, practical presentation of subject matter.
3. Original illustrations of letter-writing principles.
4. A summary that "clinches" the learning.
5. Application in the form of practical assignments.

A separate Workbook, containing the same assignments that appear in Parts I, II, and III of the text plus much additional material, is available. The grammar refreshers, which appear in the Reference Section of this text, are also included in the Workbook. The Workbook is designed to save the student's time in copying long exercises from the text and thus conserve his energies for the constructive work of the lessons. Also, the substitution of print for longhand results in a further saving of time for both teacher and student.

The authors wish to express their deep appreciation to Mr. and Mrs. Lawrence E. Brooks for their co-operation in providing facilities for the preparation of the manuscript.

HUBERT A. HAGAR

MARIE M. STEWART

E. LILLIAN HUTCHINSON

Contents

ix

PART III. Punctuation, Capitalization, Abbreviation, and the Use of Figures

PART IV. *Effective Speech*

PART V. *Effective Writing*

PART VI. *Business Letter Writing*

Reference Section

PART I

Vocabulary Building

The unabridged dictionary is the most comprehensive reference book available. Form the habit of consulting it many times daily, not only for the spelling, pronunciation, and meaning of words, but also for the other types of information listed on page 1 of this text.

Building a Vocabulary; Getting Acquainted with the Dictionary

The Importance of Vocabulary Building

The connection between word knowledge and business success has been proved by scientific study. We have all wondered why one man with very little education has been able to advance to a high executive position and another man with, perhaps, a college degree has not been able to reach the top level of management. One of the answers is that the first man *continued* to educate himself by reading a great deal, by using his dictionary, and by listening attentively to people from whom he could learn. In order to read and listen intelligently, this man had to understand the *meaning of words*.

All over our country, great emphasis is placed on testing. Many of you will be required to take tests to obtain positions. Radio and television quizzes are very popular, and many magazines contain vocabulary and spelling tests. Even the newspapers print crossword puzzles, which are really vocabulary quizzes. In many cases, the tests may not be straight vocabulary tests; but a good vocabulary is necessary in order to pass the test. You see, a question cannot be answered correctly unless the words used in asking the question are understood.

Part I of this text has been planned carefully so that you will understand and use a vocabulary that will allow you to meet the competition that is growing ever more keen. Perhaps you would like to know why these particular words were selected for study.

←Webster's New International Dictionary, Second Edition, copyright, 1934, 1939, 1945, 1950, by G. & C. Merriam Co. Illustration reduced in size by permission of the publishers.

3

Word knowledge falls into three separate classes:

1. Speaking Vocabulary. When asked to give a definition of the word *vocabulary*, many people say that it means the words we use when we speak. This definition is not accurate. The words we use in talking comprise the largest part of our vocabulary, but we should and do understand many words that we ourselves would not use when speaking.

2. Writing Vocabulary. When writing even an ordinary personal letter, we are sometimes impressed by the fact that we have written words that we would not have used if we had been talking. That is an experience that everyone has, and it is proof that everyone possesses a writing vocabulary.

3. Reading and Listening Vocabulary. In our reading we frequently see words that we would not use were we speaking or writing, but we understand perfectly what those words mean. A good reading vocabulary is important for business people.

Suppose that you found on your desk some material to be typed and that attached to it was the note, "This is a preliminary outline." If you understood the meaning of *preliminary,* you would type one copy. If you did not know the meaning, you might type the outline in finished form, complete with the number of carbons required by your supervisor.

We must understand the meaning of words we hear, even though we ourselves would not use those words. How else can we follow oral directions? How else can we answer some of the questions that are asked? How else can we take an intelligent part in office conversation?

Your basic vocabulary should consist of words that are most frequently used in business, words that *you* will know and use, words that you will *understand* when used by others. The authors of this book believe that a thorough study of Part I will equip you with knowledge and understanding of the words needed to enable you to take your place as a contributing member of a business firm.

Getting Acquainted with the Dictionary

Take time now to get acquainted with your dictionary. Do not be like the woman who became so tired of whipping cream by hand that she bought one of those "newfangled" electric beaters. She was in a hurry; she did not have time to listen to the salesman; she did not bother to read the directions. The result was that only when the beater was worn out did she learn that in all those years she could have used the implement also to beat eggs, to mash potatoes, to mix cake batter—to do all spoon-and-arm work.

Latest editions of the standard dictionaries contain the following valuable information:

1. Abbreviations used in that particular edition
2. Abbreviations used in writing and printing
3. Correct English usage
4. Explanatory notes
5. Foreign words and phrases
6. Geographical and biographical proper names
7. Guide to pronunciation
8. New-words section
9. Rules for spelling
10. Signs and symbols

When studying words in the dictionary, learn:

1. Spelling
2. Pronunciation
3. Syllabification
4. Part of speech
5. Definition

In the lessons that follow, you will be asked to write original sentences. Construct these sentences so that there will be no doubt as to your understanding of the assigned words. Thereafter *use the words* whenever possible, in order that they may become a part of your vocabulary.

Suppose that you were asked to study the word *miscellaneous* and to write an original sentence containing the word. In *Webster's New International Dictionary*, for example, you would find the spelling, the pronunciation (mĭs ĕ lā'nĕ ŭs), the syllabification (mis-cel-la-ne-ous), the part of speech (adj.), and the following definitions:

1. Consisting of diverse things or members mingled without forming a system; . . . as, a *miscellaneous* collection.
2. Having various qualities; dealing with, or interested in, diverse topics or subjects; as, a *miscellaneous* writer.

For an illustrative sentence suppose that you write:

> It is a miscellaneous item.

This is a poor sentence because it does not show that you know the meaning of the word.

Consider the following sentence:

> This item of expense was not important enough for a separate account; so we debited the item to Miscellaneous Expense.

Now what is the picture? (1) You know that the item is so unimportant that it does not warrant a separate account. (2) You know that there must be more than one such unimportant expense, or this item would have a name of its own. (3) You conclude, therefore, that *miscellaneous* must be a term that is used to include very small or infrequent expenses.

From this point it is easy to carry the idea of *miscellaneous* from expense to any other topic. Whenever you hear or use the word, you will probably think of a collection of unrelated articles or items.

Assignment 1. Study the following words: *vocabulary, synonym, antonym, homonym, diacritical, biographical, typographical, archaic, obsolete, colloquial.* Use these words in original sentences.

Assignment 2. Read the following paragraph carefully and select the words you think are correct. Then with the aid of your dictionary *study* them—master the spelling, the pronunciation, the syllabification, the part of speech, and the definition of each word. Follow this procedure in all assignments concerning the correct use of words.

Excess, Access; Capacity, Ability

If you have (excess, access) to a typewriter, use this medium in preparing your homework. Your (capacity, ability) to operate the machine will thereby be increased; and your teacher, who is already burdened with (excess, access) drudgery, will, no doubt, be properly appreciative. Teachers, you know, are supposed to have limitless (capacity, ability) for work; but the fact of the matter is that the A-marking section of their hearts goes out to the pupil who relieves them of any (excess, access) work.

Assignment 3. Write original sentences that will prove your familiarity with *excess, access, capacity,* and *ability.*

LESSON 2

Vocabulary and Testing

It is now common practice for business firms to require applicants for positions to take tests that are designed to measure their thinking power. A sound vocabulary background is the foundation for most of these tests. Lessons 2-6, inclusive, combine vocabulary study and sample tests.

Study the list of words given below. Using the dictionary, learn the spelling, pronunciation, syllabification, part of speech, and meaning of each word.

abnormal	exit	idiotic	preliminary
abstain	exorbitant	illegible	premonitory
acquisitive	feasible	imaginary	progressive
altered	fluctuation	impartial	similar
artificial	fragile	indolent	slothful
client	genuine	indorse	sophisticated
concise	glib	morale	temperamental
consigned	gracious	pecuniary	vaulted
depreciation	guarantee	predatory	
emphasized	harried	predictable	

Assignment 1. ★ On a sheet of paper list the figures 1 to 10, inclusive, representing the ten numbered sentences that follow. After each figure write the letter that represents the word or group of words that you consider completes each sentence correctly.

Note: The star indicates that this assignment also appears in the Workbook prepared to accompany the text.

Example:

Pupil means most nearly: (*a*) bread, (*b*) aches, (*c*) knowledge, (*d*) student, (*e*) tuition. (*Answer: d.*)

7

1. You are told that a certain chair in the office is *fragile.* Will you: (*a*) be required to make the final payment on it? (*b*) take care lest the paint come off? (*c*) cut the legs off to make it lower? (*d*) use it only for office visitors? (*e*) treat it carefully because it might break?

2. The *morale* in our school is high. Is: (*a*) the tuition exorbitant? (*b*) the spirit exceptionally fine? (c) the equipment expensive? (*d*) the ceiling vaulted? (*e*) the enrollment large?

3. No applicant whose handwriting is *illegible* will be considered for a position with White & Sieve. You will have a chance of being employed by this firm if your handwriting is: (*a*) easily read, (*b*) individual in style, (*c*) full of curlicues, (*d*) small and feathery, (*e*) large and bold.

4. You characterize your employer as *impartial.* Is he: (*a*) temperamental? (*b*) harried? (*c*) bullying? (*d*) fair and just? (*e*) slothful and indolent?

5. You are a *progressive* young man. Are you: (*a*) advancing steadily? (*b*) always behind with your work? (*c*) overconfident? (*d*) too shy? (*e*) unable to work with the other members of the force?

6. *Feasible* is nearest in meaning to: (*a*) reliable, (*b*) capable, (*c*) practicable, (*d*) familiar, (*e*) predictable.

7. *Emphasized* is nearest in meaning to: (*a*) stressed, (*b*) finished, (*c*) began, (*d*) measured, (*e*) smashed.

8. *Consigned* is nearest in meaning to: (*a*) filed twice, (*b*) signified, (*c*) served, (*d*) delivered, (*e*) lifted.

9. *Preliminary* is nearest in meaning to: (*a*) preparatory, (*b*) predatory, (*c*) pecuniary, (*d*) salary, (*e*) premonitory.

10. *Concise* is nearest in meaning to: (*a*) concern, (*b*) terse, (*c*) smooth, (*d*) rough, (*e*) light.

Assignment 2. ★ Follow the directions given for Assignment 1.

1. *Exit* is most nearly opposite in meaning to: (*a*) entrance, (*b*) door, (*c*) fire escape, (*d*) go, (*e*) driveway.

2. *Artificial* is most nearly opposite in meaning to: (*a*) false, (*b*) positive, (*c*) painted, (*d*) healthy, (*e*) natural.

3. *Genuine* is most nearly opposite in meaning to: (*a*) general, (*b*) a kind of wine, (*c*) true, (*d*) false, (*e*) real.

4. *Gracious* is most nearly opposite in meaning to: (*a*) saintly, (*b*) surly, (*c*) charming, (*d*) sophisticated, (*e*) glib.

5. *Depreciation* is most nearly opposite in meaning to: (*a*) increase in value, (*b*) a form of tax, (*c*) reduction in value, (*d*) perfection, (*e*) necessary fluctuation.

6. *Altered* is to *changed* as *acquisitive* is to: (*a*) playful, (*b*) grasping, (*c*) questioning, (*d*) active, (*e*) accurate.

7. *Present* is to *absent* as *similar* is to: (*a*) unlike, (*b*) simple, (*c*) abnormal, (*d*) kind, (*e*) abstain.

8. *Doctor* is to *patient* as *lawyer* is to: (*a*) law, (*b*) nurse, (*c*) prosecutor, (*d*) client, (*e*) defense.

9. *Harsh* is to *gentle* as *imaginary* is to: (*a*) picturesque, (*b*) real, (*c*) idiotic, (*d*) impertinent, (*e*) dead.

10. *Indorse* is to *approve* as *guarantee* is to: (*a*) pledge, (*b*) barter, (*c*) pawn, (*d*) hide, (*e*) lock.

Assignment 3. In your notebook or on a separate sheet of paper, write an original sentence for each of the words in the following list.

abundance	apparently	audited	challenger
accommodate	arbitrary	autopsy	coincidence
adequate	ascertain	available	collision
adhere	assertion	calamity	command
adjourn	assumption	canceled	comparable
analysis	attributed	catastrophe	deference

LESSON **3**

Vocabulary and Testing (*Continued*)

Study the following list of words. Be sure that you know the spelling, pronunciation, syllabification, part of speech, and meaning of each word.

accede	contagion	grievance	proficient
accumulated	deficient	harmonious	prohibit
aggressive	deficit	incessantly	prosperous
approximately	demurrage	indulgent	reluctance
association	enterprise	infantile	reproval
beneficial	essence	interminable	resemblance
cherished	extravagance	permanence	severing
complement	flourishing	principal	surpass
compliment	gratifying	principle	suspense

Assignment 1. ★ Follow the directions for Assignment 1 on page 7.

1. In your office a most *harmonious* relationship exists. Do you: (*a*) sing well together? (*b*) work well together? (*c*) quarrel incessantly? (*d*) gossip about one another? (*e*) employ only relatives?

2. *Approximately* is most nearly opposite in meaning to: (*a*) almost, (*b*) grammatically, (*c*) gracefully, (*d*) exactly, (*e*) innocently.

3. *Beneficial* is nearest in meaning to: (*a*) forceful, (*b*) beautiful, (*c*) purposeful, (*d*) helpful, (*e*) harmful.

4. *Complement* is to *compliment* as *principal* is to: (*a*) primer, (*b*) prosperity, (*c*) privilege, (*d*) print, (*e*) principle.

5. To the lazy person, the working day seems *interminable*. Is the day: (*a*) bright and sunny? (*b*) seemingly never ending? (*c*) fast moving? (*d*) relaxing? (*e*) delightful?

6. *Proficient* is nearest in meaning to: (*a*) professional, (*b*) well skilled, (*c*) growing, (*d*) smug, (*e*) old-fashioned.

7. *Gratifying* is most nearly opposite in meaning to: (*a*) pleasing, (*b*) indulging, (*c*) displeasing, (*d*) tipping, (*e*) unyielding.

8. *Grant* is to *favor* as *accede* is to: (*a*) boast, (*b*) desert, (*c*) withdraw, (*d*) request, (*e*) surpass.

9. *Deficient* is nearest in meaning to: (*a*) sparkling, (*b*) flourishing, (*c*) lacking, (*d*) everlasting, (*e*) dangling.

10. *Prosperous* is most nearly opposite in meaning to: (*a*) fiction, (*b*) industrious, (*c*) favorable, (*d*) successful, (*e*) unsuccessful.

Assignment 2. ★ Follow the directions given in Assignment 1 on page 7.

1. Your employer tells you that you are not *aggressive* enough. Does he mean that: (*a*) you are rather untidy? (*b*) you must be more punctual? (*c*) you are too retiring? (*d*) your health is poor? (*e*) your mentality is not up to standard?

2. *Contagion* is to *disease* as *demurrage* is to: (*a*) objection, (*b*) withdrawal, (*c*) service, (*d*) freight, (*e*) suspense.

3. *Prohibit* is nearest in meaning to: (*a*) forbid, (*b*) protect, (*c*) allow, (*d*) beam, (*e*) show.

4. *Permanence* is most nearly opposite in meaning to: (*a*) instability, (*b*) hairdresser, (*c*) fortune, (*d*) grief, (*e*) lasting forever.

5. "Are you *severing* your connection with this company?" means that: (*a*) you are boasting about working here, (*b*) you are picturing us as severe with you, (*c*) you are having trouble cashing checks, (*d*) you are using your association with this company to further your private enterprises, (*e*) you are leaving our employ.

6. *Spending* is to *saving* as *extravagance* is to: (*a*) waste, (*b*) thrift, (*c*) grievance, (*d*) reluctance, (*e*) essence.

7. *Indulgent* is most nearly opposite in meaning to: (*a*) infantile, (*b*) male population, (*c*) strict, (*d*) humoring, (*e*) stupid.

8. If you knew that your company was operating at a *deficit*, would you: (*a*) ask for a salary increase? (*b*) hurry to the hospital? (*c*) expect to be busier than usual? (*d*) buy a hearing aid? (*e*) be on the lookout for another job?

9. *Accumulated* is nearest in meaning to: (*a*) spent, (*b*) amassed, (*c*) cherished, (*d*) contradicted, (*e*) discouraged.

10. *Deficit* is to *shortage* as *resemblance* is to: (*a*) court, (*b*) revenge, (*c*) likeness, (*d*) reproval, (*e*) continuance.

Assignment 3. In your notebook or on a separate sheet of paper, write an original sentence for each of the words in the following list.

comptroller	degrade	domination	equivalent
contingency	detach	eccentric	essential
correct	diligence	embarrassment	exaggerate
deceptive	delinquent	emergency	expect
deferred	discretion	endeavor	expedient
deflect	dissolution	equipped	extension

LESSON 4

Vocabulary and Testing (Continued)

Follow the same procedure that you followed in Lessons 2 and 3.

anonymous	facilitate	intermittent	sagacious
auxiliary	fascinate	itinerant	sanction
bovine	feline	liberal	sequence
chaotic	gratis	peruse	stationary
dauntless	hangar	pessimistic	stationery
deteriorate	humiliate	pliant	strategy
devastate	impressionistic	predicament	subsidiary
dilemma	impromptu	recreation	syncopated
dissipating	inefficient	remuneration	vibrant

Assignment 1 ★

1. If you were in a *dilemma*, would you: (*a*) run home with it? (*b*) consider yourself in a predicament? (*c*) be afraid of the savages? (*d*) close the door so that you could have some privacy? (*e*) fight your way out?

2. *Sequence* is nearest in meaning to: (*a*) following, (*b*) preceding, (*c*) consecutiveness, (*d*) introduction, (*e*) trimmings.

3. *Feline* is to *bovine* as *cat* is to: (*a*) streamers, (*b*) cow, (*c*) number, (*d*) strategy, (*e*) yearning.

4. *Stationary* is most nearly opposite in meaning to: (*a*) stationery, (*b*) mirthful, (*c*) jolly, (*d*) meek, (*e*) movable.

5. *Facilitate* is nearest in meaning to: (*a*) to make hard, (*b*) to make pliant, (*c*) to make better, (*d*) to make pleasant, (*e*) to make easy.

6. The chief clerk said that stenographers are as *itinerant* as peddlers. Did he mean that: (*a*) stenographers do not stay long in one position? (*b*) they have merchandise to sell? (*c*) they are in-

terested in bicycles? (d) they are lazy? (e) they have strong voices?

7. *Vibrant* is most nearly opposite in meaning to: (a) musical, (b) burning, (c) dead, (d) syncopated, (e) lively.

8. *Auxiliary* is to *power station* as *subsidiary* is to: (a) liquid, (b) mineral, (c) hangar, (d) formation, (e) company.

9. *Deteriorate* is nearest in meaning to: (a) degrade, (b) fas-cinate, (c) humiliate, (d) devastate, (e) degenerate.

10. You can expect additional *remuneration* beginning next week. Will you: (a) expect an increase in salary? (b) consider that you are dismissed? (c) expect to take on extra work? (d) look for a little more free time? (e) look for another job?

Assignment 2 *

1. *Sanction* is most nearly opposite in meaning to: (a) holy, (b) church, (c) disapprove, (d) sorrow, (e) donate.

2. *Intermittent* is to *continuous* as *disconnected* is to: (a) gay, (b) cereal, (c) disunited, (d) joined, (e) furious.

3. *Peruse* is nearest in meaning to: (a) trick, (b) purchase, (c) scrutinize, (d) pursue, (e) refuse.

4. You are asked to write a letter for a visiting salesman. Your employer says, "Of course, Miss Crowley, this work should be done *gratis*." Does he mean that: (a) you are not to use the company let-terhead? (b) the work will bring in business to your firm? (c) you are not to expect to be paid for this work? (d) you must be sure to use paper on which there is no printing? (e) this work will be more difficult than the work you are ordinarily asked to do?

5. *Dauntless* is to *cowardly* as *pessimistic* is to: (a) domestic, (b) impressionistic, (c) antagonistic, (d) futuristic, (e) optimistic.

6. *Impromptu* is most nearly opposite in meaning to: (a) un-prepared, (b) punctual, (c) inspiring, (d) failure to remember, (e) prepared.

7. After watching your work for a week, your immediate supe-rior tells you that you are *dissipating* your energies. Are you: (a) working too hard? (b) wasting your time? (c) taking too much out-door exercise? (d) using your time inefficiently? (e) indulging in too much recreation?

8. *Sagacious* is nearest in meaning to: (a) witty, (b) proud, (c) untrue, (d) liberal, (e) shrewd.

9. *Chaotic* is most nearly opposite in meaning to: (*a*) mute, (*b*) disorderly, (*c*) unfriendly, (*d*) orderly, (*e*) miraculous.

10. *Pliant* is to *flexible* as *anonymous* is to: (*a*) dauntless, (*b*) careless, (*c*) graceless, (*d*) nameless, (*e*) lifeless.

Assignment 3. In your notebook or on a separate sheet of paper, write an original sentence for each of the words in the following list.

foreign	ignoble	interchangeably	maintenance
forgotten	incurred	irrespective	marital
fruition	initiative	legitimate	multiple
function	insistent	liberation	mutually
hypocrisy	instill	lieu	obedient
identical	instinctively	literally	obstacles

LESSON **5**

Vocabulary and Testing (*Continued*)

Follow the same procedure that you followed in Lessons 2, 3 and 4.

abolish	discrepancy	incendiarism	munificence
appropriation	florid	integrity	precipitate
credulous	futile	judicious	profound
contemptuous	innovation	loathe	quibble
countenance	insolvent	mundane	unanimous

Assignment 1 ★

1. The decision of the committee was *unanimous.* This means that: (*a*) the members reached no decision, (*b*) the vote was very close, (*c*) the question was postponed to the next meeting, (*d*) there was no dissenting vote, (*e*) the decision was reached only after bitter argument.

2. The man was convicted of *incendiarism.* Did he: (*a*) exceed the speed limit? (*b*) forge a signature? (*c*) set fire to property? (*d*) cause a riot? (*e*) steal a horse?

3. Robert was *contemptuous* of the ability of the rest of the students. He: (*a*) envied them, (*b*) looked down on them, (*c*) admired them, (*d*) praised them, (*e*) neglected them.

4. Martin is known for his *integrity.* Does he: (*a*) brag too much? (*b*) appear honest in his dealings with others? (*c*) show off? (*d*) make high grades in school? (*e*) earn a big salary?

5. The auditor noted a *discrepancy* in the figures. (*a*) There was an error in the books. (*b*) The company made a great deal of money last year. (*c*) The figures were hard to read and illegible. (*d*) He could find nothing wrong. (*e*) His eyesight is failing.

6. *Countenance* is nearest in meaning to: (*a*) large desk, (*b*) happiness, (*c*) sadness, (*d*) serenity, (*e*) face.

7. *Munificence* is nearest in meaning to: (*a*) generosity, (*b*) holiness, (*c*) poverty, (*d*) honesty, (*e*) intelligence.

8. *Appropriation* is nearest in meaning to: (*a*) taxes, (*b*) money set apart, (*c*) Congressional action, (*d*) large navy, (*e*) suitable appearance.

9. *Insolvent* is nearest in meaning to: (*a*) rich, (*b*) indebted, (*c*) complacent, (*d*) secure, (*e*) impudent.

10. *Judicious* is nearest in meaning to: (*a*) solemn, (*b*) rash, (*c*) discerning, (*d*) impersonal, (*e*) creative.

Assignment 2 ★

1. *Abolish* is most nearly opposite in meaning to: (*a*) forgive, (*b*) establish, (*c*) destroy, (*d*) glorify, (*e*) punish.

2. *Innovation* is most nearly opposite in meaning to: (*a*) order, (*b*) novelty, (*c*) prize, (*d*) custom, (*e*) discovery.

3. *Precipitate* is most nearly opposite in meaning to: (*a*) cautious, (*b*) devoted, (*c*) rainy, (*d*) hasty, (*e*) early.

4. *Profound* is most nearly opposite in meaning to: (*a*) deep, (*b*) stern, (*c*) unhappy, (*d*) angelic, (*e*) shallow.

5. *Florid* is most nearly opposite in meaning to: (*a*) wet, (*b*) pale, (*c*) strong, (*d*) angry, (*e*) childish.

6. *Celestial* is to *heaven* as *mundane* is to: (*a*) country, (*b*) modern, (*c*) century, (*d*) earth, (*e*) commonplace.

7. *Cherish* is to *love* as *loathe* is to: (*a*) moan, (*b*) adore, (*c*) destroy, (*d*) croon, (*e*) abhor.

8. *Just* is to *impartial* as *futile* is to: (*a*) ridiculous, (*b*) useless, (*c*) contemptible, (*d*) hopeful, (*e*) wise.

9. *Robust* is to *sickly* as *credulous* is to: (*a*) faithful, (*b*) believing, (*c*) doubtful, (*d*) impoverished, (*e*) vigorous.

10. *Conduct* is to *guide* as *quibble* is to: (*a*) proclaim, (*b*) lead, (*c*) admit, (*d*) bicker, (*e*) decide.

Assignment 3. In your notebook or on a separate sheet of paper, write an original sentence for each of the words in the following list.

obstruct	prevaricate	reprimand	sacrificed
palatable	quotas	resignation	scruple
pernicious	recurrence	resources	smug
perseverance	reducible	reticence	solitary
personnel	reinstate	rotation	specifications
prestige	remittance	rote	statistics

LESSON **6**

Vocabulary and Testing (*Concluded*)

Follow the same procedure that you followed in Lessons 2-5, inclusive.

accruing	bewildered	incandescent	potential
acquit	competent	inquire	reimburse
antipathy	deceit	metropolis	superficial
assurance	dissension	opposition	surfeit
audacity	diversity	overture	vestige

Assignment 1 ★

1. Your employer says you are *competent*. Does he think that: (*a*) you talk too much? (*b*) you are a troublemaker? (*c*) you do your job well? (*d*) you are inclined to boast? (*e*) you are inaccurate?

2. If Joan spends more than $10 for decorations, Jack will *reimburse* her. This means that: (*a*) Joan will be repaid, (*b*) Jack will make a profit, (*c*) Joan will lose money, (*d*) Jack will be angry, (*e*) Joan will be promoted.

3. On the question of the new school building, there was a *diversity* of opinion. This means that: (*a*) the taxpayers thought it cost too much, (*b*) conflicting ideas were expressed, (*c*) everybody was in favor of it, (*d*) nobody was in favor of it, (*e*) nobody knew anything about it.

4. Jane showed a marked *antipathy* toward her work. Probably she: (*a*) likes it very much, (*b*) will be promoted soon, (*c*) dislikes what she is doing, (*d*) is frequently late, (*e*) has a great deal of responsibility.

5. The student gave the assignment a *superficial* reading. Did he: (*a*) read it thoroughly? (*b*) complain about the assignment? (*c*) read through it hurriedly? (*d*) review it? (*e*) forget all about it?

6. *Thought* is to *idea* as *vestige* is to: (*a*) age, (*b*) youth, (*c*) trace, (*d*) clothing, (*e*) evening.

7. *Dark* is to *gloomy* as *incandescent* is to: (*a*) shadowy, (*b*) luminous, (*c*) artificial, (*d*) unnatural, (*e*) old-fashioned.

8. *Beginning* is to *end* as *overture* is to: (*a*) middle, (*b*) opera, (*c*) music, (*d*) commencement, (*e*) postlude.

9. *Discord* is to *harmony* as *dissension* is to: (*a*) unanimity, (*b*) agreement, (*c*) wisdom, (*d*) adolescence, (*e*) idea.

10. *Minute* is to *vast* as *unique* is to: (*a*) immense, (*b*) diminutive, (*c*) real, (*d*) magnificent, (*e*) common.

Assignment 2 ★

1. *Surfeit* is nearest in meaning to: (*a*) surrender, (*b*) humble, (*c*) cowardly, (*d*) excess, (*e*) miniature.

2. *Metropolis* is nearest in meaning to: (*a*) city, (*b*) noisy, (*c*) village, (*d*) crowded, (*e*) modern.

3. *Accruing* is nearest in meaning to: (*a*) investing, (*b*) increasing, (*c*) losing, (*d*) forgetting, (*e*) earning.

4. *Audacity* is nearest in meaning to: (*a*) timidity, (*b*) inspiration, (*c*) equality, (*d*) boldness, (*e*) anxiety.

5. *Deceit* is nearest in meaning to: (*a*) decent, (*b*) orderly, (*c*) efficient, (*d*) fraud, (*e*) reality.

6. *Potential* is most nearly opposite in meaning to: (*a*) electric, (*b*) latent, (*c*) actual, (*d*) future, (*e*) clever.

7. *Opposition* is most nearly opposite in meaning to: (*a*) advice, (*b*) support, (*c*) argument, (*d*) bloc, (*e*) antagonism.

8. *Acquit* is most nearly opposite in meaning to: (*a*) judge, (*b*) plead, (*c*) set free, (*d*) condemn, (*e*) sentence.

9. *Bewildered* is most nearly opposite in meaning to: (*a*) bewitched, (*b*) charmed, (*c*) cautious, (*d*) admired, (*e*) enlightened.

10. *Assurance* is most nearly opposite in meaning to: (*a*) confidence, (*b*) belief, (*c*) firmness, (*d*) diffidence, (*e*) superficiality.

Assignment 3. In your notebook or on a separate sheet of paper, write an original sentence for each of the words in the following list.

securities	symbols	unimportant	venerable
stringent	technique	unparalleled	verity
substantial	trait	unruly	violation
supplementary	tremendous	utilize	visualize

LESSON 7

Look-and-Learn Words

How many good spellers do you think there are in this country? "Very few," you say; and you are right. Then, the office employee who can spell has an outstanding skill that is valued highly by businessmen, and you will be well on your way to the acquisition of spelling skill when you have mastered the Look-and-Learn words presented in these lessons.

If we know the sounds of letters, we can spell many of our words "by ear." For instance, when we hear the word *abnormal,* we hear *ab-nor-mal;* so we write it correctly. If all words were of this type and if we knew our sounds, we would all be proficient in spelling.

Spelling difficulty, however, is caused by the fact that many English words are spelled in a certain way for apparently no good reason. For example the word *accost* is spelled with two *c*'s, but *across* is spelled with one *c.* Why? The experts who are familiar with word origins (known as "etymologists") know, but most of us cannot figure out how many *c*'s there are in either of the words. We just have to *know* it.

And that brings us to the method we should use in studying our Look-and-Learn words. Since each word is a problem in itself, each word should be given individual attention. When studying the first word, *abbreviation,* we look and look at it. What is there about this word that we must remember? Obviously, we must get a mental picture of the two *b*'s. Again, when we look and look at *accountant,* we get a picture of the two *c*'s and of the *a* in the *ant.* Yes, this kind of learning takes time; but there is no quick and easy way to learn to spell these common puzzlers.

Even though you progress to the stage where you think you can spell, never guess at the spelling of a word. Remember:

When in doubt, consult a dictionary.

Class Procedure. Your teacher will assign for study as many of the following words as he thinks you should have for homework each night. After you have had an opportunity to study them, he will dictate the list of words to you. When the test has been corrected, you will write correctly on a separate piece of paper or in your notebook the words you misspelled. This will be your individual record of words that need extra study. Very probably at the end of Lesson 8, you will have had dictated to you all the words presented in Lessons 7 and 8. Such a test will show you how you compare with other spellers all over the country, for these are words that are most frequently misspelled.

Suggestion. Your teacher might like to appoint a Spelling Research Committee. The duty of the committee members will be to study the results of each test and list the misspelled words, together with the number of times that they were spelled incorrectly on any test. For instance:

Abbreviation	6
Across	10

The report might then be typed and posted on the room bulletin board. As a finishing touch to this little research, the committee members might form a panel to discuss the reason for the misspelling of each word.

Look-and-Learn Words

A	affiliated	arrears	beginning	carrying
abbreviation	allocated	arsenal	believe	centralized
accidentally	already	article	benefited	certainly
accordance	altogether	ascend	brevity	chemistry
accountant	analyze	ascension	brilliant	chief
accurate	**annihilate**	assignment	bulletin	choose
acknowledgment	antecedent	assistant		chose
acquainted	apologize	**athlete**	C	chosen
acquire	**apparatus**	authority	campaign	chronological
across	appearance	authorize	cannot	cipher
adaptability	approaches		capacity	classified
addressee	appropriate	B	capitalist	clothes
adjutant	argument	because	career	**clue**
admissible	around	becoming	careful	coarse
aerial	arrangement	before	carried	**coincidence**

colonel	convenience	**diphtheria**	enumerate	fourth
coolly	**corps**	disappear	environment	fulfill
coming	corrugated	disappoint	erroneous	
commensurate	course	disastrous	especially	G
commercial	**courtesy**	**discipline**	excellent	generally
commission	credentials	disillusion	excesses	**governor**
committee	criticism	division	executive	grammar
common	cylinder	doesn't	exhibited	grateful
community			existence	group
companies	D	E	expeditiously	H
comparative	dealt	**economical**	expendable	handicapped
compel	deceased	efficient	experience	handsome
competition	decide	eighth	extract	happened
competitor	deferring	elementary	**extraordinary**	happiness
compilation	definite	eligible		height
completion	democracy	eliminate	F	here
concealed	dependent	enemies	families	heretofore
conceding	descent	enforce	**February**	highest
concrete	description	engineer	field	hindrance
conferring	destroyed	enhance	finally	hyphen
conscious	determined	entertain	force	
conspicuous	develop	entirely	forcibly	I
control	device	entitled	forty	identify
controllable	devise	enveloping	forty-four	**illustrate**
				immediate

Assignment 1. While you are learning to spell the words in this lesson, be sure to check your pronunciation of the twenty words printed in boldface type.

Assignment 2. In your notebook or on a separate sheet of paper, list the words in this lesson that you do not use in conversation or in your writing. Include all words in your "reading and listening vocabulary" as well as all strange words. For each word on your list, include a synonym or a brief definition.

Assignment 3. In your notebook or on a separate sheet of paper, write at least twice all words that you misspelled in your final spelling test on the words in this lesson.

Assignment 4. ★ See Workbook.

Look-and-Learn Words (*Concluded*)

Follow the same procedure as for Lesson 7.

implement
impracticable
inasmuch
incidentally
incredible
indebtedness
indelible
independent
indicate
indispensable
individual
ingenious
innumerable
inquiry
installation
intelligence
intelligible
interrupt

K
known

L
laboratory
laid
layout
led
legible
liability
license

lieutenant
linoleum
literally
literature
logical
losing

M
mandatory
mathematics
maximum
maybe
mechanical
medal
medicine
meridian
merit
messenger
millionaire
miniature
misinterpretation
mobile
modifying
monotonous
mortgage
mosquitoes

N
necessary
nevertheless
nickel

nineteen
ninety
nonsense
numerical

O
obedience
occasion
occurrence
off
offer
opportunity
optimistic
ordinarily
organization
original
originator
outrageous
overrated

P
pamphlet
parentheses
particularly
passed
pastime
peculiarity
perform
permissible
piece

Pittsburgh
pleasant
politician
possess
possible
practical
practice
precede
precedence
prefer
preferable
prejudice
preparation
primary
priority
privilege
proceed
profession
prohibition
provision
pursue

Q
quantity
questionnaire

R
realize
reasonable
receive

receptacle
recipient
recognize
recollect
recommend
refer
reference
referring
registered
registration
relieve
remembrance
remittance
repetition
resources
responsibility
revenue
reversible
ridiculous

S
sabotage
saboteur
safety
salaries
schedule
scientific
seize
sense
separate

sergeant	status	their	U	valleys
shepherd	stressed	there	underwear	velocity
shipper	subdivision	thorough	undoubtedly	vengeance
siege	subordinate	to	unnecessary	villain
sincerely	superintendent	too	until	visible
site	superior	transferred	urgent	
solely	surname	transmission		W
sparingly	surprise	transmit	V	weather
specifically	**symmetry**	**tremendous**	vacancy	weird
specimen	T	two	vague	**whether**
squad	tariff		valid	

Assignment 1. While you are learning to spell the words in this lesson, be sure to check your pronunciation of the twenty words printed in boldface type.

Assignment 2. In your notebook or on a separate sheet of paper, list the words in this lesson that you do not use in conversation or in your writing. Include all words in your "reading and listening vocabulary" as well as all strange words. For each word on your list, include a synonym or a brief definition.

Assignment 3. In your notebook or on a separate sheet of paper, write at least twice all words that you misspelled in your final spelling test on the words in this lesson.

Assignment 4. ★ See Workbook.

LESSON **9**

Some Commonly Misused
Words and Phrases

All the Farther, All the Further. Read this sentence and listen to
it as you read:

> This is all the farther I can go.

If you are in the habit of using this expression, change at once to:

> This is *as far as* I can go.

A person who says "all the farther" or "all the further" is not observing accepted standards of English.

Where . . . at; Where . . . to; Where for That. Do you say:

> Where is she at?
> Where is she going to?
> Did you read in the paper where our company is going to give
> us a bonus?

You should say:

> Where is she? [Never use *at* with *where.*]
> Where is she going? [Never use *to* with *where.*]
> Did you read in the paper *that* our company is going to give us
> a bonus? [Never use *where* when you mean *that.*]

Like . . . as; Without . . . Unless; As for That. *Like* and *without* are prepositions and are followed by noun or pronoun objects.
As and *unless* are conjunctions and introduce clauses. A clause must
have a subject and a predicate. Do not use *as* when you mean *that.*

25

Wrong: You type like you were angry. [*You were angry* is a clause.]

Don't leave the office without you have your work finished. [*You have your work finished* is a clause.]

Please post those books like I showed you. [*I showed you* is a clause.]

I don't feel as I can do all this work. [*Not:* feel as; *but:* feel that.]

I don't know as I like your new assistant. [*Not:* know as; *but:* know that.]

Right: You type *as if* you were angry.

Don't leave the office *unless* you have your work finished.

Please post those books *as* I showed you.

I don't feel *that* I can do all this work.

I don't know *that* I like your new assistant.

Right: She looks like me. [*Me* is the object of *like.*]

Don't leave without finishing your work. [*Finishing your work* is the object of *without.*]

He acts like a pleasant person. [*Person* is the object of *like.*]

Place; -wheres. If you say *any place, every place, no place,* or *some place,* change to *anywhere, everywhere, nowhere, somewhere.* However, be sure that you do not add an *s* to the *where.*

Bertha told us to put the dictating machine *anywhere.* [*Not:* any place; *not:* anywheres.]

That letter is around here *somewhere.* [*Not:* some place; *not:* somewheres.]

Try to; Come to; Be Sure to. Avoid *and* after *try, come, be sure,* in such sentences as:

Try to do as you are told.

Be sure to change that ribbon today.

Come to see me about missing enclosures.

As . . . as; So . . . as. Use the correlatives *as . . . as* in making positive statements; *so . . . as* in making negative statements.

She transcribes *as* fast *as* I do.

She does *not* transcribe *so* fast *as* I do.

Awhile; A While; Sometime, Some Time. *Awhile* is an adverb meaning "for some time"; *a while* is a noun plus an adjective meaning "a short space of time." *Sometime* is an adverb meaning "at some

unspecified or indefinite time." *Some time* is a noun plus an a[c]
tive, the phrase meaning a part (little or considerable) of a s[pe]c[i]-
fied period.

> Rest *awhile* before you make up the payroll.
> Why don't you rest for *a while* before you start to make up the
> payroll?
> I will type those letters *sometime* this afternoon.
> I must find *some time* this afternoon to type those letters.

Either, Neither; Any, Anyone; No One, Not Any. *Either* and *neither* refer to one of *two* persons or things. *Any* or *anyone* and *no one* or *not any* should be used to refer to one of *three or more* persons or things.

> *Either* of the two girls will take your dictation. [Obviously *two*.]
> *Neither* of them will have to work tomorrow morning. [*Them* must refer to only *two* persons.]
> *Any one* learning to type is likely to have the same experience. [Refers to *three or more* persons.]
> *No one* of the group knows the combination to the safe. [*Three or more* in the group.]
> *Not one* of the operators went to the meeting. [There must be at least *three* operators.]

Between, Among. *Between* is commonly used when referring to *two* persons, places, objects; *among* when referring to *more than two*.

> *Between you* and *me*, I think he should apologize.
> The work was evenly divided *between* the *two* stenographers.
> The work was evenly divided *among* the *three* stenographers.

Between may also express the relation of one thing to each and all of several surrounding things; as:

> An agreement has just been reached *between* our company and the retailers, jobbers, and wholesalers handling our product.

Who, Which, That—relative pronouns. Use:

> *Who* when referring to persons
> *Which* when referring to places or objects
> *That* when referring to persons, animals, places, or objects

Who, that when referring to persons. Use *who* when the individual person or the individuality of a group is meant. Use *that* when a class, species, or type is meant.

> He is the man *who* knows how to use the bookkeeping machine. [The individual person.]
> He is the kind of bookkeeper *that* will advance rapidly. [Type.]
> People *who* shirk their obligations do not advance. [Individual persons.]

That, which introducing restrictive and nonrestrictive clauses. A restrictive clause is a dependent clause that cannot be omitted if the meaning is to remain clear. A nonrestrictive clause is a dependent clause that can be omitted without affecting the meaning of the main clause. The comma is used before a nonrestrictive clause; if the clause occurs in the body of a sentence, it is set off by commas. Use *that* to introduce a *restrictive clause, which* to introduce a *nonrestrictive clause.*

> I shall always remember the advice *that* you gave me yesterday. [*That you gave me yesterday* is essential to the meaning.]
> Machines *that* require frequent repairs are a poor investment. [*That require frequent repairs* is essential to the meaning.]
> Learn to use the teletype, *which* is a quick way of sending messages. [*Which is a quick way of sending messages* is not essential to the meaning.]
> Income tax reports, *which* make extra work for our Accounting Department, must go out tomorrow. [*Which make extra work for our Accounting Department* is not essential.]

Assignment 1. ★ Rewrite the following sentences, making corrections where necessary.

1. Don't do like I do; do like I say.
2. There seems to be a difference of opinion between the three executives.
3. Union Street is as far as the bus goes.
4. This duplicated report is not as clear as it might be.
5. Before making your decision, think awhile.
6. Where is the correction fluid at?
7. This is the report that I asked you to copy.
8. You must not change the spacing without you get instructions from Miss Willard.

9. Be sure and ask her about getting new supplies.

10. Neither of the four typewriters in our office is in condition.

11. I saw in the daily bulletin where we are not going to work Saturday.

12. The poor office boy has to go every place in the plant.

13. Girls which take office time to powder their noses are frequent visitors at the employment agencies.

14. Our school employment agency that is managed by Miss Brooks will list the name of any of our graduates.

Assignment 2. ★ Rewrite the following sentences, making corrections where necessary.

1. Come and see us some time when you are free.

2. My fountain pen, which I use only for shorthand, was returned to me speedily.

3. Where were you hurrying to this noon?

4. Just take any one of the two desks not in use.

5. I really cannot choose between the different makes of typewriters.

6. I like to work for a man who knows what he wants.

7. Show Mr. Bessette into the private office. He has been waiting for sometime.

8. There is absolutely nowheres in this office to keep an adequate supply of carbon paper.

9. Try and balance these accounts today.

10. Do not leave without accomplishing this task.

11. Is this all the farther you have gone toward striking a balance?

12. I am surprised that you did not wait for awhile before sending him his bill.

Address, Speech, Talk; Admission, Admittance

Note: In this exercise as well as in all following exercises concerning the correct use of words, follow the instructions given on page 6.

Seniors! Plans for graduation are now complete. Dr. Edward B. Sloane, of the Standard Business School, will give the commencement (address, speech, talk). (Admission, admittance) to the auditorium will be by invitation only. The usual (addresses, speeches, talks) of class officers will be omitted this year, to allow more time for Doctor Sloane's (address, speech, talk). Keep in mind the suggestions given this morning in the (address, speech, talk) by our principal. Remember that we are at the point of gaining (admission, admittance) to the ranks of proud alumni.

Assignment 3. Write original sentences containing *address, speech, talk, admission,* and *admittance.*

LESSON **10**

Some Commonly Misused
Words and Phrases (*Continued*)

Leave, Let. A well-known radio comedian owes much of his success to the misuse of *leave* and *let*. His hearers laugh at him, and your hearers will laugh at you—but not in the same way—if you use *leave* or *let* incorrectly. *Leave* means "to move away." *Let* means "to permit" or "to allow." Probably the easiest way to remember the correct use of these words is to use *leave* when motion away is involved and *let* in all other cases.

> Leave me alone. [Go away so that I can be by myself.]
> Let me alone. [Don't bother me.]
> Let us go to work now.

Else. Always use *nobody else's, somebody else's, anybody else's.*

> He thinks his position is more difficult than anybody else's.

Kind, Sort. These words are singular. Say *this kind* or *that sort.* If you feel that you must use the plural, be sure to have a plural noun and a plural adjective—*these kinds* or *those sorts.* Also, the articles *a* and *an* are unnecessary after *kind of* or *sort of. Kinda* or *sorta* are labeled as "corruptions" in the dictionary; they are used by illiterate persons.

> I rather like that kind of inkstand. [*Illiterate:* I kinda like, or sorta like, that kind of an inkstand.]

Badly. Do not use *badly* when you mean "a great deal" or "very much." Consider the sentence, "Beverly Brooks wanted to obtain the position badly." The implication is that Beverly wanted to get the position in some evil manner. "Beverly Brooks wanted very much to obtain the position" is correct.

Reason Is That. Use *reason is that* rather than *reason is because.* *Reason* means "motive," and *because* also indicates motive.

> The *reason* the stenographer failed *is that* she was poorly prepared in English.

Pretend. Say *pretend,* never *pretend like.*

> *Pretend that* you do not see her. [*Not:* Pretend like you do not see her.]

Almost, Most. *Almost* is an adverb meaning "nearly," "all but," "a little short of"; *most* is either an adjective or a noun meaning "greatest in number" or "the largest part."

> Business is *almost* at a standstill.
> *Most* of the office workers are idle.
> They have *almost* spent *most* of their savings.

Formerly, Formally. *Formerly* means "at some time in the past"; *formally* means "according to a set form" or "in a ceremonious way." "He was *formerly* inducted into the army" means that at some past time he was taken into the army. "He was *formally* inducted into the army" means that there was a ceremony attendant upon his entrance into the armed forces.

Got. *Got* means "obtained" and should be used in no other way.

> Lucy got the position. [Correct.]
> I have a new pen. [*Not:* I've got a new pen.]
> I must go now. [*Not:* I've got to go now.]

Both Alike. *Both* is superfluous.

> The typewriters are alike. [*Not:* The typewriters are both alike.]

Worst Kind or Worst Way. If you use *worst kind* or *worst way* when you mean "very much," you must provide a great deal of amusement for your associates. Consider the sentence, "David wanted to learn to typewrite in the worst way." David will surely meet with competition, for we already have too many people who typewrite in the worst way. Employers are looking for those who can typewrite in the best way. The sentence correctly written is: "David wanted very much to learn to typewrite."

Both, Each. *Both* means the "two considered together"; *each* refers to "number considered separately." "There is a calculator on both sides of the typewriter" is illogical. How could *one* calculator be on *both* sides? "There is a calculator on each side of the typewriter" is logical and correct.

Assignment 1. ★ Rewrite the following sentences, making corrections where necessary.

1. Leave us use the dictionary when we are doubtful about a word.

2. When conceited people fail, they always think it is somebody else's fault.

3. As far as I can see, they are both alike.

4. There is a dictionary on both large shelves in the library.

5. Most dictionaries include reference material as well as word explanations.

6. I am sorta partial to the person who checks his work.

7. Those sorts of machines are always in need of repair.

8. The reason you made that mistake is because you are not familiar with business reference books.

9. Specifications should always be formerly set up.

10. Mr. Allen was formerly a salesman with our company.

11. He was unsuccessful because he was kinda conceited.

12. He badly needed the services of a psychiatrist.

13. Those kind of people are doomed to failure.

Assignment 2. ★ See directions for Assignment 1.

1. Pretend like you do not notice the new clerk's nervousness.

2. She was so happy when she got this position.

3. She certainly needed it in the worst kind of way.

4. Let us give her all the help we can.

5. The average beginner is most always very nervous.

6. To her, everybody else's work seems to go smoothly.

7. What kind of an education do you think she has had?

8. Leave us remember that high ideals have a definite place in our business life.

9. You've got a good start when you recognize this fact.

10. It was formally believed that business could be successful only by using methods that bordered on the dishonest.

11. The reason for the change in opinion is that business now demands desirable personal qualities as well as skill.

12. Today our chosen lifework is as well regarded as anybody's else.

Anxious, Eager; Assure, Insure

Please let us go home. The fire engine has just turned down my street. I am (anxious, eager) to see whether it is my house that is burning. I have neglected to (assure, insure) it. I (assure, insure) you I am most (anxious, eager) to go with you today, but I shall enjoy myself only if I (assure, insure) myself that I have a roof over my head.

Assignment 3. Write original sentences, using *anxious*, *eager*, *assure*, and *insure*.

LESSON **11**

Some Commonly Misused
Words and Phrases (*Concluded*)

All Right. This phrase is correct. There is no such word as *alright* or *allright*.

Bring, Take. *Bring* denotes motion toward the speaker; *take* denotes motion away.

> *Bring* the papers to me.
> *Take* the letters to the next office.

But. *But* meaning "only" requires no other negative in the same sentence.

> I have but two more hours to work. [*Not:* I haven't but two more hours to work.]

Appreciate. While *appreciate* may be used to mean "to be aware," it is much overworked in this sense. *Appreciate* means primarily "to value, to be grateful for, to be sensitive to." If you mean "know" or "understand," say so. Appreciate people, their kindnesses, their favors, their patronage; but *understand* how people feel, *know* what their difficulties are.

Blame. Do not blame things *on*. Blame the person or thing directly; as:

> I am forced to blame you for that mistake. [Correct.]
> I am not going to blame the mistake *on* you. [Wrong.]

Line. This word is much overworked in the sense of a branch of business. Avoid using it.

35

He is in the wholesale dress business. [*Not:* He is in the wholesale dress line.]

Ought. Never use *had* with *ought*. For the negative, use *ought not to*. Always use *to* after *ought*. Never say *ought to of*—to use *of* instead of *have* is illiterate. *Should have* is preferable to *ought to have*.

You *ought* to be told what is expected of you. [*Not:* had ought.]
You *ought not* to bother your superior with unimportant details. [*Not:* hadn't ought.]
Many secretaries *ought to* and do take care of a multitude of petty details. [*Not:* ought and do.]
While at school you *should have* learned to use initiative. [*Not:* ought to of; *better than:* ought to have.]

Former, Latter. Use *former* and *latter* only when making a reference to *one* of *two* things. If there are *more than two*, use *first* or *last*.

Typewriters, calculators, and duplicating machines are important articles of office equipment, but the *first* is perhaps the most important. [*Not:* Typewriters, calculators, and duplicating machines are important articles of office equipment, but the *former* is perhaps the most important.]

First Two, Two First; Last Two, Two Last. Two persons or things cannot be first; so you should say *first two*, not *two first*. In like manner, say *last two*. You ask for the *last two* letters from Hall and Company, not the *two last* letters.

Never, Not. *Never* means "not ever; at no time; not in any degree, way, or condition." It is a strong word. *Not* is simply a word that expresses negation. *Never* is used all too frequently and incorrectly instead of *not*.

We have not received your check. [*Not:* We never received your check.]

Fix, Nice. These words are grouped here because they are correctly and incorrectly overworked to the point of boredom. *Fix* means "to make fast or firm"; as, "Your typewriter should be *fixed* to the desk." Avoid using *fix* to mean "to repair, to adjust, to prepare, to be in difficulty, to bring about a desired result by a wrongful act" (fixing an officer).

Nice means, basically, showing discrimination, which may be exact or finely drawn. "Through your vocabulary study it is hoped that you will acquire a *nice* sense of word usage." *Nice* also means "pleasant, agreeable"; and it is in this sense that the word is so overused. Some people see a nice picture, have a nice dinner, hope for a nice day, ask for a nice cut of meat, think the baby is nice, and have only one comment for everything—"very nice."

Individual.   Do not use *individual* when you mean "person." *Individual* means a single person or thing as distinguished from a group.

> She is an unusual person. [*Not:* individual.]
> Profits result from the efforts of the individuals among the personnel. [Correct.]

Have, Of.   Never use *of* for *have* in such expressions as: *could have, would have, should have, must have, may have, might have.* This error is considered grossly illiterate.

> You must have been told this many times. [*Not:* must of.]

Expect, Right, Guess.   *Expect* for *suppose, right* for *very,* and *guess* for *think* are colloquialisms. Avoid them whenever possible.

> I suppose that I shall have to make up that lost time. [*Not:* expect.]
> Mr. Bellamy expects a letter from his client. [Correct.]
> He receives a very good salary. [*Not:* right good.]
> I think I shall walk to the post office for the mail. [*Not:* guess.]
> Try to guess the number of paper clips there are in this box. [Correct.]

Inside of.   *Inside of* should not be used to mean *within.* You expect his answer *within* a week, not *inside of* a week.

Win out, Lose out.   You do not win or lose *out;* you simply *win* or *lose.*

Funny.   *Funny* means *laughable;* it does not mean "strange," "odd," or "queer." If you say that you saw a *funny* picture, then the picture caused you to laugh. If you mean that the picture is *odd,* say so.

Posted.   Do not say *posted* when you mean *informed.*

> Please keep me informed. [*Not:* Please keep me posted.]

Bank on. *Rely on;* do not *bank on.*

> I am *relying* on you to help me. [*Not:* I am banking on you to help me.]

Wait on. Do not say *wait on* when you mean *wait for.*

> Do not *wait for* me more than fifteen minutes. [*Not:* wait on.]

Assignment 1. ★ Rewrite the following sentences, making corrections where necessary.

1. Whether or not to ask for an increase in salary is a nice question.
2. I do not expect you to wait on me after five o'clock. I may be late.
3. You are right kind to wait that long.
4. I really appreciate your kindness.
5. I think his line is insurance.
6. If you do not work harder, you will lose out on your chance for advancement.
7. You hadn't ought to be so careless with that inventory.
8. Spelling isn't but one of my weaknesses.
9. Don't bank on me for any additional work today.
10. You should of sent the trade acceptance with the bill of goods.
11. If anything goes wrong with that Multigraph, blame it on me.
12. I guess I was the only clerk who used it yesterday.
13. However, I think it will work alright.
14. While you are on your vacation, I will keep you posted about changes here at the office.

Assignment 2. ★ See directions for Assignment 1.

1. Are you going to night school this year? Yes, I expect so.
2. I had to laugh because his expression was so funny.
3. We shall expect a reply from you inside of three days.
4. He is an unpleasant individual, and I dislike him.
5. Fix it with the boss so that I can have my vacation when you have yours.
6. I never heard you say you wanted your vacation during the month of September.
7. June, July, and August are good months for me; but I prefer the former.

8. You ought to of made your request earlier.

9. Please bring me the *World Almanac*.

10. You had ought to know where we keep our pamphlets and periodicals.

11. The two first references are "almanac" and "atlas."

12. I can appreciate how you feel when you forget to reverse the telephone charges.

13. Please take this money to the bank this morning.

14. It is funny that you have not learned how to make out a deposit slip.

Accept, Except; Advice, Advise

It seems to be very difficult for young people to (accept, except) the (advice, advise) of older people. Yet, who else (accept, except) a person of experience could be expected to (advice, advise) a beginner in the world of business? Anyone, young or old, who knows it all never learns. The wise person learns from the experience of others. He asks for (advice, advise) and is grateful to the one who (advices, advises) him. The beginner who insists on learning only by making his own mistakes can be automatically (accepted, excepted) from the list of those "most likely to succeed."

Assignment 3. Write original sentences, using *accept, except, advice,* and *advise*.

PART II

Grammar Review

No matter how capable and alert an employee may be, habitual errors in grammar will prove a real handicap to his progress in business. Customers, fellow employees, and executives—all will react unfavorably. Not all employees are so considerate in advising improvement as the one shown here.

LESSON 12

The Sentence

In previous lessons we have been dealing with words: their correct use, spelling, pronunciation, and similar factors. Now we are ready to consider the use of words in the *sentence*, the basis of all composition, both oral and written. An effective composition, no matter how simple or how complex, is nothing more nor less than the logical arrangement of properly constructed sentences.

A properly constructed sentence consists of two or more words used to express a complete thought. For instance, *Pupils study*, a very simple statement of only two words, qualifies as a sentence because these two words convey a complete thought.

Every sentence must have a subject and a predicate. In this sentence, *pupils*, about which something is said, is the subject; and *study*, which says something about the subject, is the predicate.

You will find it helpful to remember that the subject of a sentence is always a noun, a pronoun, or some expression used as a noun; also, that no predicate is complete without a verb. Simple sentences may also contain other qualifying words or phrases, sometimes called *modifiers*. Simple sentences may also contain two or more subjects and predicates connected by *and* or *or*. Examples:

1. Pupils study.
2. Ambitious students study diligently.
3. Students of English study books about English.
4. Success in business is based on ambition.
5. The desire for success comes first.
6. Ambition, without diligence, is daydreaming.
7. Hard, steady work turns daydreaming into reality.
8. Ambition and diligence are needed for success.

43

9. The wise person wishes for success and works for it.
10. The presence or absence of these qualities will win or lose for
you the business struggle.

The expressions *in business, on ambition, for success, without diligence, into reality, for it, of these qualities, for you* are called *phrases*—groups of related words that do not contain either a subject or a predicate.

In the eighth sentence we speak of *ambition* and *diligence;* therefore, the subject is compound. In the ninth sentence *wishes* and *works* are connected by *and;* therefore, we have a compound predicate. Point out the compound subject and the compound predicate in the tenth sentence.

Assignment 1. ★ Select the subjects and predicates in the ten sentences previously listed.

Compound Sentence. Compound sentences consist of two or more simple sentences of *equal rank* connected by the words *or, but, and,* or some other connecting word. For example:

1. You may go, but I shall remain.
2. You may go, or you may remain.
3. The workers had all gone home, and the building was closed for the night.

Complex Sentence. You have learned that compound sentences consist of two or more simple sentences of equal rank joined by *and* or some other connecting word. Another type of sentence, ordinarily known as the *complex sentence,* contains one main or independent sentence and one or more subordinate or dependent expressions called *clauses.* Although a clause contains a subject and a predicate, it does not express a complete thought when standing alone. For example:

Advancement comes to the worker who does his work well.

In this sentence, *who does his work well* is a clause. What is the subject of this clause? the predicate? Guard against writing a part of a sentence as a complete sentence. If you have any doubt as to whether a group of words is a sentence, just ask yourself whether or not a *complete* thought is expressed.

Assignment 2. ★   In the following paragraphs select the clauses and name the subject and the predicate of each clause. Select the phrases.

Would you be a power among your fellow men? Then learn how to use words, how to express yourself correctly. For some reason, the world is critical of the man or woman whose grammar is not up to standard. It may be that the idea behind the words is sound, even noble; but the message loses its effectiveness if it is poorly stated.

Life is a continuous process of selling. Every time you speak or write, you are selling yourself as a person. Determine now that you will master the elements of grammar contained in this textbook, so that your words will command attention and respect.

Assignment 3.   Write sentences containing clauses beginning with *who, whom, that, which, when, where, if, while, as, since.*

Normal and Inverted Order.   The subject of a sentence normally precedes the predicate; as:

The missing memorandum | was in the files.
   (Subject)   *(Predicate)*

This sequence is known as the *normal,* or *natural, order.* In many sentences, however, the subject is not stated first; as:

In the files was | the missing memorandum.
   (Predicate)   *(Subject)*

This sequence is known as the *inverted order.* Nearly all interrogative sentences (sentences that ask questions) are in inverted order. Many errors in grammar are made because of failure to distinguish the real subject or predicate in sentences arranged in inverted order. (These errors will be discussed from time to time.) Therefore try to acquire facility in changing sentences from inverted to normal order.

The following sentences are in inverted order. Change them to normal order.

Here is the president with his secretary.
Inside the outer office were the clients.
Who is the man with the brief case?

Assignment 4. ★ In the following sentences, change the order from inverted to natural.

1. May I ask your secretary to take my dictation?
2. At present we are not in a position to make a statement.
3. In the dead file were the lost letters.
4. Shall we begin by arranging the list alphabetically?
5. Each year the office receives a thorough renovation.
6. Who did you think he was?
7. By means of intelligent and concentrated study, the pupils learn to speak and write correctly.
8. In the supply cabinet will be found bottles of red ink.
9. For the position of receptionist, a pleasing personality is an outstanding requisite.
10. Whom do you wish to see?

Grant, Give, Accord; Affect, Effect

When your employer enters the office, you should (grant, give, accord) him the respect that is due his position. His opinion of you will be (affected, effected) by your courtesy. When he (grants, gives, accords) you work to do, be gracious. A pleasant, willing, cheerful manner is a distinct asset to the person who wishes to succeed. The (affect, effect) of such behavior on your employer will show in your pay envelope. You will also find that he will be more disposed to (grant, give, accord) you a favor should you make a request.

Assignment 5. Read the preceding paragraph carefully and select the words you think are correct. Study these words. Write original sentences designed to show that you are familiar with *grant, give, accord, affect, effect.*

LESSON **13**

Verbs

You have learned that the predicate of every sentence must contain a verb; that no sentence is complete without a verb. This makes the verb a very important "part of speech." Verbs are sometimes referred to as *action words;* but, as some verbs do not express action, a better definition is, "A verb is a word that asserts or implies action, a condition, or a state of being." For example:

He *moved* his desk nearer the window. [*Moved* asserts action.]
He *wishes to move* his desk nearer the window. [*Wishes* asserts action. *To move* implies action.]
I *was* in the office yesterday. [*Was* asserts condition or state.]
I *promised to be* in the office yesterday. [*Promised* asserts action. *To be* implies a condition or state.]

Principal and Auxiliary Verbs. According to rank, all verbs are either *principal* or *auxiliary.* Sometimes an assertion may be made by a group of verbs. Such a group of words is called a *verb phrase.* A verb phrase has one *principal* verb and one or more helping, or *auxiliary,* verbs; as:

The cost of living *has risen* rapidly. [Principal verb, *risen;* auxiliary verb, *has.*]
The report *has been read* by the entire office force. [Principal verb, *read;* auxiliary verbs, *has* and *been.*]
This correspondence *should be taken* to the purchasing agent. [Principal verb, *taken;* auxiliary verbs, *should* and *be.*]
He *was seen* at his home yesterday. [Principal verb, *seen;* auxiliary verb, *was.*]

The most common auxiliaries are:

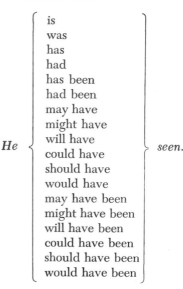

He { is / was / has / had / has been / had been / may have / might have / will have / could have / should have / would have / may have been / might have been / will have been / could have been / should have been / would have been } *seen.*

Assignment 1. ★ Select the principal and the auxiliary verbs in the following sentences:

1. He sells boots and shoes.
2. Have you written the letter?
3. Bring me the checkbook.
4. Your order has been received.
5. The clerk opens the mail each morning.
6. The mail was opened when the employer arrived.
7. Please send me your latest catalogue.
8. I will send you our catalogue as soon as it comes from the press.
9. Selling prices increase as costs advance.
10. Our selling prices must be increased as our manufacturing costs are constantly advancing.

Principal Parts. You have observed that some verbs express or imply *present* time (now). Others express *past* time (time fully passed). Still other forms, usually known as *past participles,* refer to time passed but connected with present time. These forms are usually called the *principal parts* of a verb. To express past time, most verbs add *d* or *ed* to the present-time (or present-tense) form. Most past participles are also formed by adding *d* or *ed*. Such verbs are called *regular* verbs. Other verbs have different forms for the past tense and the past participle. These are usually called *irregular* verbs. Examples:

	Present	Past	Past Participle
(*Regular*)	call	called	called
(*Irregular*)	go	went	gone

The misuse of these irregular verbs is the direct cause of many errors in speech and writing. Some verbs have two permissible forms for the past tense and two for the past participle. Sometimes the same verb is used for the present, past, and participle forms:

Present	Past	Past Participle
beat	beat	beat-beaten
burst	burst	burst

Only preferred forms are given in the following table, as you will want to learn the preferred or most acceptable forms. In studying this list, remember that the past-participle form is always used with an auxiliary and that the auxiliary is never used with the past-tense forms.

Present	Past	Past Participle
awake	awoke	awaked
be	was	been
beat	beat	beat
begin	began	begun
bid (to command)	bade	bidden
bid (to offer to pay)	bid	bid
bite	bit	bitten
blow	blew	blown
break	broke	broken
bring	brought	brought
burn	burned	burned
burst	burst	burst
catch	caught	caught
choose	chose	chosen
come	came	come
dive	dived	dived

Present	Past	Past Participle
do	did	done
drag	dragged	dragged
draw	drew	drawn
drink	drank	drunk
drive	drove	driven
dwell	dwelt	dwelt
eat	ate	eaten
fall	fell	fallen
fight	fought	fought
flee	fled	fled
fly	flew	flown
forget	forgot	forgotten
forsake	forsook	forsaken
freeze	froze	frozen
get	got	got
give	gave	given
go	went	gone
grow	grew	grown
hang (of criminals)	hanged	hanged
hang	hung	hung
hide	hid	hidden
know	knew	known
lay (to place)	laid	laid
leave	left	left
lend	lent	lent
lie (to recline)	lay	lain
light (to set on fire)	lighted	lighted
light (as of a bird)	lighted or lit	lighted or lit
pay	paid	paid
ride	rode	ridden
ring	rang	rung
rise	rose	risen
run	ran	run
see	saw	seen
set (to place)	set	set
set (as of the sun)	set	set
shake	shook	shaken
shrink	shrank	shrunk
sink	sank	sunk
sit (to rest)	sat	sat
slay	slew	slain

Present	Past	Past Participle
speak	spoke	spoken
spring	sprang	sprung
steal	stole	stolen
strike	struck	struck
swim	swam	swum
take	took	taken
tear	tore	torn
throw	threw	thrown
wake	waked	waked
wear	wore	worn
wring	wrung	wrung
write	wrote	written

Assignment 2. ★ Select the correct verbs in the following sentences:

1. This morning we (awoke, awaked) to see the ground white with frost.

2. After a good breakfast, she (ran, run) for the bus.

3. The office time clock broke just after Edith had (rang, rung) in.

4. She (saw, seen) at a glance that she was the last employee to arrive.

5. As she (came, come) into her office, her employer greeted her pleasantly.

6. Edith knew that she was dangerously close to being tardy, but she also knew that she had never (did, done) this before.

7. She (began, begun) to collect the materials she would need.

8. The first setback occurred when she found that the shift key on her typewriter was (broke, broken).

9. As the morning wore on and the strain increased, she was glad she had (ate, et, eaten) a substantial breakfast.

10. By twelve o'clock she had (sat, set) so long that she welcomed her noon respite.

11. Upon returning to the office, she (hung, hanged) her coat on a hanger and resumed typing.

12. At the end of the day she was gratified to see that the pile of work had (shrank, shrunk) to nothing.

13. Work completed, machine covered, desk tidied, she mentally (give, gave) herself a pat on the back and started for home.

14. To a busy person, it always seems that the time has (flew, flown).

Transitive and Intransitive Verbs. According to their relation to objects, all verbs are either *transitive* or *intransitive*. A transitive verb expresses *action* as passing from the subject to an object—in other words, a transitive verb requires an object to complete its meaning; as:

> The *customer paid* his *bill* promptly.
> The *bookkeeper sent* the *invoices* with the merchandise.
> I *shall meet him* tonight.
> I *invited him* to dinner.
> I *invited him and his wife* to dinner. [*Not:* he.]

An intransitive verb does not take an object. It may be complete in itself, or it may be completed by an adjective or by a noun or pronoun called a *predicate nominative* or a *predicate complement*.

> The new typewriter *arrived* today. [Complete in itself.]
> He *rose* from his chair. [Complete in itself.]
> I *shall work* tomorrow. [Verb phrase complete in itself.]
> It *was she* to whom he referred. [Predicate nominative.]
> Her assistants *were June* and *I*. [Compound predicate nominative.]
> She *seems lazy*. [Adjective.]
> He *feels bad*. [Adjective.]

Assignment 3. ★ Select the transitive and intransitive verbs in the following sentences:

1. Julia tore the carbon paper.
2. The new bookkeeper writes legibly.
3. The carbon paper tore easily.
4. Brown & White submitted a complete set of specifications.
5. The sales manager approved the requisitions.
6. Can you operate a typewriter?
7. Alice looked rested this morning.
8. The cost accountant sent Henry to New York.
9. That continued noise is disturbing.
10. The letters were in the bottom drawer.
11. You must teach Eleanor to use the bookkeeping machine.
12. I will go to Boston Thursday.

13. Please give these pencils to Mr. Culley.
14. A capable executive leads the way.
15. Please take these papers to Mr. James.
16. The office needs a good airing.
17. I very much prefer a noiseless typewriter.
18. I have never been late to work.
19. I shall see Mr. Adams this morning.
20. He made an appointment last week.
21. The attorney collected the money.
22. Mary wanted a position in the office.
23. The president presided at the meeting.
24. He writes books for publication.
25. He writes for pleasure.

Infinitives. The importance of the special verb form known as the *infinitive* will be apparent when we reach the study of the case of pronouns. One of the characteristics of the infinitive is that it never changes its form to agree with the person and the number of the subject; as:

> I like *to write.*
> He likes *to write.*
> They like *to write.*

An infinitive may usually be recognized by the sign *to,* although the sign is often omitted; as:

> We are pleased *to report* that your order has been filled.
> We should like *to have* this shipment (*to*) *go* out today.

Split Infinitive. A split infinitive is an infinitive in which the sign *to* is separated from the verb by a word or a phrase; as, "*to* clearly show"; "*to* in any way *improve* them." Careful writers avoid split infinitives (see Lesson 57, "Coherence").

Participles. You have already been introduced to the term *past participle.* Participles ending in *ing* are called *present participles.* Except those having irregular endings, participles may also be recognized by their endings; as:

> We are *filling* your order today.
> We *have filled* your order.
> Your order *was filled* yesterday.

Although infinitives and participles are essentially verbs, they may be used as nouns, adjectives, or adverbs; as:

> I enjoy *working* in the office. [Noun.]
> *Writing* letters is my favorite pastime. [Noun.]
> He seems *well informed*. [Adjective.]
> School is *to be closed* during the holidays. [Adjective.]
> He went *to work* for this company. [Adverb.]
> He enjoys *marching*. [Noun.]
> The boys are *marching*. [Adjective.]
> The boys came *marching* home. [Adverb.]

Gerunds. *Ing*-ending participles used as nouns are usually called *gerunds*. (The first, second, and sixth of the preceding sentences illustrate this statement.) Note that gerunds and participial adjectives do not express any idea of *time*.

Assignment 4. ★ Select the participles and infinitives in the following sentences and indicate whether they are used as nouns (gerunds), adjectives, or adverbs.

1. She likes to write.
2. Skating is her favorite sport.
3. He spent his entire day in dictating letters.
4. The young woman taking dictation is the president's secretary.
5. Using the typewriter is easier for some than for others.
6. Disappointed at the delay, the manager wrote him a sharp letter.
7. He seems well informed.
8. He came to help us.
9. She studies to improve her English.
10. If you are unable to supply all these books now, please send those you have in stock, and let us know when you will be able to send the rest.

Bravery, Courage; Character, Reputation

Never be afraid or ashamed to say, "I was wrong." This takes (bravery, courage), but your (character, reputation) will be strengthened by the inward knowledge that you have done right. The soldier who captures a machine-gun nest has a great (character, reputation) for (bravery, courage). To me, the real hero is the person of (character, reputation) who, with steadfast (bravery, courage), fights and wins daily spiritual and moral battles.

Assignment 5. Read the preceding paragraph carefully and select the words you think are correct. Study these words. Write original sentences designed to show that you are familiar with *bravery, courage, character,* and *reputation*.

LESSON 14

Verbs—Tense

Tense means "time" and is that modification of the verb that indicates the time of the action or being; as:

> I *do*.
> I *did*.
> I *shall do*.

Primary Tenses. There are three primary tenses, corresponding to the three divisions of time: *present, past,* and *future.*
The *present tense* indicates present action or being; as:

> I *bring*. [Simple form.]
> I *am bringing*. [Progressive form.]
> I *do bring*. [Emphatic form.]

The *past tense* indicates past action or being; as:

> I *brought*. [Simple form.]
> I *was bringing*. [Progressive form.]
> I *did bring*. [Emphatic form.]

The *future tense* indicates future action or being; as:

> I *shall bring*. [Simple form.]
> I *shall be bringing*. [Progressive form.]

Perfect Tenses. Three secondary, or perfect, tenses represent the action or being as *completed* in *present,* in *past,* or in *future* time.
The *present perfect tense* indicates action or being completed in the present time; as:

> I *have brought*. [Simple form.]
> I *have been bringing*. [Progressive form.]

The *past perfect tense* indicates action or being completed at or before some stated past time; as:

> I *had brought.* [Simple form.]
> I *had been bringing.* [Progressive form.]

The *future perfect tense* indicates action or being that will be completed at or before some stated future time; as:

> I *shall have brought.* [Simple form.]
> I *shall have been bringing.* [Progressive form.]

Tense Forms for Third Person Singular. The form of the verb changes in the present and in the present-perfect tenses when its subject is in the third person singular. In the present tense, third person singular, *s* is added to the verb; thus:

> I or you do; but *he, she,* or *it does.*
> I or you walk; but *he, she,* or *it walks.*
> I or you guess; but *he, she,* or *it guesses.*

In the *present perfect tense*, the auxiliary changes from *have* to *has;* thus:

> I or you have seen; but *he, she,* or *it has seen.*

Remember: Although *s* added to a *noun* is the sign of the plural, *s* added to a *verb* indicates the third person singular.

Assignment 1. ★ Select the correct verb in each of the following sentences and state whether it is singular or plural.

1. I *don't—doesn't* need to go.
2. You *don't—doesn't* need to go.
3. He *don't—doesn't* need to go.
4. She *don't—doesn't* need to go.
5. It *don't—doesn't* matter.
6. She *comes—come* to the office daily.
7. John and she *come—comes* to the office daily.
8. The noise of the bookkeeping machines *gives—give* me a headache.
9. All the clerks in our office *has been—have been* given a holiday.

10. Lack of co-operation *don't—doesn't* make a happy working life.

Agreement of Tenses. The verb in the subordinate clause should agree with the verb in the principal clause, unless the subordinate clause expresses a general or universal truth; as:

> Our employer *told* us that he *was* going to give us a salary increase. [He still intends to do so.]
> Mr. Ritchie *said* that he *was* going to Chicago tomorrow. [He still intends to go.]
> The broker *told* him that, with regard to security, Federal, state, and municipal bonds *rate* highest. [General truth.]
> In our economics course, we *learned* that prices *are* governed by the relation between supply and demand. [General truth.]

Use of the Present and Perfect Infinitives. The perfect infinitive (*to have been*) should be used only when action that has been completed before the time of the predicate verb is to be expressed; in all other cases the present infinitive (*to be*) should be used.

> The salesman is supposed *to be* punctual.
> The salesman was supposed *to meet* you here yesterday.
> Our salesman is supposed *to have completed* his calls last Monday.
> I am glad *to have been* of help to you during the war years.
> I am also glad *to be* of help to you now.

Assignment 2. ★ Select the correct forms in the following sentences:

1. Miss Cornell reported that the typewriter was (to be, to have been) repaired.
2. The auditor wrote us that he (is, was) going to visit us soon.
3. Miss Cornell reported that the typewriter was (to be, to have been) repaired yesterday morning.
4. I was obliged (to change, to have changed) some of the habits acquired at school.
5. During this rush, we feel very much the loss of Miss Bailey's services. She is said (to be, to have been) the best stenographer we ever had.
6. We were told (to clean, to have cleaned) the duplicating machine.

7. Miss Evans said that the Gulf Stream (affects, affected) the climate of New England.

8. Before he departed for his vacation, Samuel ought (to leave, to have left) us his summer address.

9. Eileen said that she (likes, liked) her new work.

10. I intended (to show, to have shown) him his error, but I decided that the matter was not important.

Assignment 3. Write five original sentences to illustrate the agreement of the verb in the subordinate clause with the verb in the principal clause; write three sentences to illustrate the use of the present infinitive; and write two sentences to illustrate the use of the perfect infinitive.

Council, Counsel, Consul; Concise, Brief

The United States (council, counsel, consul) took a (concise, brief) trip to the city where the (council, counsel, consul) was sitting. He was to act as (council, counsel, consul) for a fellow countryman. When the hearing was over, he had to write a (concise, brief) report to send to his superior in Washington.

Assignment 4. Use *council, counsel, consul, concise,* and *brief* in original sentences.

LESSON **15**

Verbs—Voice and Mood

Voice

Voice is the modification of the verb that shows whether the subject acts or is acted upon. There are two voices, the *active* and the *passive*.

A transitive verb is said to be in the *active voice* when it represents the subject of the sentence as the doer of an action. The action passes from the subject through the verb to an object; as:

Julia *filed* the letter.

Maryann *uses* the check protector.

A verb is in the *passive voice* when the subject is acted upon; as:

The letter *was filed* by Julia.

The check protector *is used* by Maryann.

Only transitive verbs—verbs requiring an object—are modified to indicate voice. Intransitive verbs—verbs not taking an object—are active; as, "Stenographers work." In the passive voice the subject is acted upon *by* someone. The *by* may be expressed or understood; as:

Peter *was given* a receipt. [By someone.]
He *was seen* at the desk this morning. [By someone.]

Mood

Mood is the modification of a verb that indicates the manner in which a verb makes an assertion. The three moods of the verb are the *indicative*, the *imperative*, and the *subjunctive*.

The *indicative mood* is used to express a fact or to ask a question; as:

> He went to the stock room.
> Were you at work yesterday?

The *imperative mood* is used to express a command or a request; as:

> Close the door.
> Please send us your check.

The *subjunctive mood* is used to express a thought as doubtful, as conditional, as a mere wish, or as a supposition that is contrary to fact; as:

> If I were in your position, I would try to make a better impression.
> I wish I were a court reporter.
> If the typewriter were unknown, business would be limited.

The tendency today is to use the indicative rather than the subjunctive; the subjunctive is therefore largely disappearing from English usage, both spoken and written, except in resolutions, votes of thanks, or other formal statements. The subjunctive of the verb *to be* causes the most difficulty. The past tense of the verb *be* is the subjunctive form employed in such cases. The student should have no real difficulty in mastering these forms, for they differ from the indicative only in the *first and third persons singular, past tense*, as you will see from this list.

Past Tense of the Verb "Be"

Singular		Plural	
Indicative	*Subjunctive*	*Indicative*	*Subjunctive*
I was	if I were	we were	if we were
you were	if you were	you were	if you were
he was	if he were	they were	if they were

The subjunctive mood is often introduced by *if, though, even though, although, unless, lest;* but these words are also used with the indicative and, therefore, cannot be depended upon as a sign for the use of the subjunctive. However, the conjunctive phrase *as if* must always be followed by the subjunctive mood; as:

She acted as if she *were* disappointed.
He looked as if he *were* wealthy.

Assignment 1. ★ Select the corect word in each of the following sentences:

1. If I (was, were) in your place, I would check those figures carefully.

2. He impressed upon me that, if it (was, were) not for the accuracy of bookkeepers, profits would turn to losses.

3. I wish he (was, were) with us today.

4. All through the years, I have realized that he (was, were) my very good friend.

5. He treated me as if I (was, were) his own brother.

6. I wish it (was, were) possible to do as much for him as he did for me.

7. (Was, Were) it not for him, I could not hold my present position.

8. If I (was, were) not so busy, I could do more for you.

9. I do not remember the time, however, when I (was, were) idle.

10. If I (was, were) you, I should always listen to those who are interested in guiding young people in the right direction.

Continual, Continuous; Co-operation, Corporation

No (co-operation, corporation) can operate at peak efficiency without the full (co-operation, corporation) of its entire personnel. (Co-operation, corporation) consists not so much of united effort in an emergency as of (continual, continuous), unfailing willingness to help in the small daily tasks. Do not grumble. Twenty per cent of your living time is spent at the office. (Continual, Continuous) complaining will rob you and those around you of the enjoyment of a part of life.

Assignment 2. Use *continual, continuous, co-operation, corporation* in original sentences.

LESSON **16**

Some Troublesome Verbs

Shall and Will. *Shall* and *will* are both signs of the future tense. The rules for their correct usage are as follows:

1. To express simply a future action or state, use *shall* in the first person and *will* in the second and third persons; as:

> I think I *shall* need the stencil machine this afternoon.
> You *will* probably have finished with it by that time.
> They *will* be waiting for the work.

2. To denote promise or determination, use *will* in the first person and *shall* in the second and third persons; as:

> Do not worry; I *will* finish that work this afternoon.
> You *shall* do your part if I have to stand over you all morning.
> They, also, *shall* be made to contribute.

3. In *questions* in the *first person,* always use *shall,* no matter what meaning is intended; and in *questions* in the *second or third person,* use the word that is expected in the answer; as:

> *Shall* I get the correction fluid for you?
> *Shall* we have time to complete the task?
> *Shall* you have your luncheon sent in today? [Questioner expects a statement of simple futurity; so the answer would be "I shall."]
> *Will* you have six stencils on my desk by two o'clock? [Questioner expects a promise; so the answer would be "I will" or "I will not."]
> *Will* he approve our using this stylus? [Questioner expects a statement of simple futurity; so the answer would be "He will" or "He will not."]

Shall he be required to have the duplicator repaired by tomorrow afternoon? [Questioner expects a promise; so the answer would be "He shall."]

Should and Would. *Should* and *would* follow the same rules as *shall* and *will;* that is, the uses of *should* correspond to those of *shall* and the uses of *would* correspond to those of *will;* as:

I *should* appreciate an early reply. [Futurity.]
You *would* be surprised to see what progress she has made. [Futurity.]
He *would* be glad to do that work for you. [Futurity.]
I *would* do you that favor if I were able. [Promise.]
You *should* make the effort if I were your employer. [Determination.]
I resolved that he *should* get the position. [Determination.]

Should is sometimes used to mean "ought to," but in this sense it has no connection with the idea of futurity or with the use of *would.* This use of *should* is not intended in the examples or exercises in this lesson.

May, Might; Can, Could. *May* and *might* imply permission; *can* and *could* imply ability or power; as:

When *may* I talk with you, Mr. Sheffield? [Permission.]
May I examine the shift on the new electric typewriter? [Permission.]
Yes, if you *can* come over here. [Power.]
I asked Mr. Sheffield if I *might* examine the shift on the new electric typewriter. [Permission.]
He said I *might* [permission] if I *could* [power] leave my desk.

Learn, Teach. *To learn* means to acquire knowledge; *to teach* means to impart knowledge to others; as:

We hope you will *learn* the English that will be useful to you in business.
Your instructors are well qualified to *teach* you English.

Assignment 1. Write six original sentences to illustrate each of the three rules for the use of *shall* and *will.* In three of the sentences show simple futurity, and in the other three show promise or determination.

Assignment 2. Write two original sentences to illustrate each of the following words: *should, would, can, may, could, might.*

Assignment 3. ★ Indicate whether *shall* or *will* is correct for each of the following sentences:

1. When (?) we expect to see you again?
2. They (?) be forced to sign the paper. My attorney will see to that.
3. You (?) probably see him tomorrow.
4. The stenographers (?) be glad to hear that Natalie has recovered from her illness.
5. (?) he be compelled to make way for me?
6. I (?) give him the message even at the cost of my position.
7. You (?) replace every letter you have removed from the files. Your slipshod methods have inconvenienced every stenographer.
8. (?) I report this to the office manager?
9. I (?) be glad to get the reference books for you.
10. (?) he be in the office this morning?
11. I think I (?) go shopping during my noon hour.
12. They (?) pay their obligation in full by the first of the month. The account is in the Small Claims Court.
13. (?) you return to the office this evening to finish the payroll?
14. You (?) find working conditions very pleasant in our office.
15. I (?) not be blamed for errors I do not make.
16. (?) you try to make an appointment with him today?
17. The girls (?) arrive early tomorrow.
18. The head bookkeeper is determined that you (?) work a full eight hours.

Assignment 4. ★ Select the correct word in each of the following sentences:

1. He (should, would) make a good bookkeeper for our firm.
2. Miss Brant tried hard to (learn, teach) me spelling rules.
3. We (should, would) be glad to give you further information.
4. (May, Can) I borrow a sheet of carbon paper?
5. I know you (should, would) be glad to be a member of the Chamber of Commerce.
6. (Might, Could) you use the automatic telegraph before you came to work for us?

7. I wonder whether I (might, could) ask you some questions about its operation.

8. We (should, would) prefer to give you our reply next week.

9. I said that I (should, would) substitute for you Tuesday.

10. (Can, May) I do all the work you require of a general clerk?

11. You (should, would) find it easy after a while.

12. (Can, May) I leave a message for Miss Forbes?

Lie, Lay; Sit, Set; Rise, Raise. The six little words *lie* and *lay*, *sit* and *set*, *rise* and *raise* are probably among the most troublesome in the language; but after a careful study of their meanings, you should be able to use them correctly. The principal parts and the precise meaning of each verb should be thoroughly memorized.

Present	Past	Past Participle	Meaning
lie	lay	lain	to recline
lay	laid	laid	to place
sit	sat	sat	to rest
set	set	set	to place
rise	rose	risen	to rise of its own power
raise	raised	raised	to cause to rise

The verb *set* has two other meanings in addition to its most common meaning, "to place." The verb also means "to start out on a journey" and "to go down, as the sun"; but when the verb has these meanings, it is seldom confused with *sit, sat, sat*.

Remember that: (1) *lay, set,* and *raise* are transitive verbs. Each of these verbs requires an object to complete its meaning. (2) *Lie, sit,* and *rise* are intransitive verbs, complete in themselves. The following illustrations may help you in the correct use of these troublesome words.

ACTIVE VOICE

Lie

I shall *lie* down this afternoon.

The papers *lay* on the desk yesterday.

Her pen *had lain* in full sight all morning.

Lay

I shall *lay* the papers on your desk.

I *laid* the matter before him.

She *had laid* it there when she came to work.

Sit

I shall *sit* here today.

I *sat* in this chair yesterday.

I *have sat* here long enough.

Set

I shall *set* the plant on the window sill.

I *set* the clock before I left.

I *have set* that clock for the last time.

Rise

You should *rise* when you give a talk.

John *rose* from his chair.

He *has risen* to the occasion.

Prices *are rising*.

Raise

You should *raise* the curtain when you want more light.

Henry *raised* the question of insurance.

The retailers *have raised* the prices of foodstuffs.

They *are raising* prices.

PASSIVE VOICE

The sketches *have been laid* in the drawer. [Correct, because someone laid the sketches in the drawer.]

The machine *was set* on the wrong table. [Correct, because someone set the machine on the wrong table.]

The roof *has been raised*. [Correct, because someone raised the roof.]

Remember: All verbs in passive voice are transitive.

Assignment 5. ★ Select the correct word in each of the following sentences:

1. (Lie, Lay) down, Fido.
2. The house (sits, sets) on a hilltop.
3. Please (rise, raise) your hand.
4. The table has been (sat, set) for two hours.
5. I (lay, laid) abed all day yesterday.
6. The river has (risen, raised) a full 6 inches.
7. I (sat, set) at the typewriter until I was stiff.
8. I have (risen, raised) the window; I hope you will not be cold.

9. The temperature in this room is (rising, raising).

10. (Lie, Lay) those parcels on the floor.

11. There was absolute silence as Mr. Harper (rose, raised) to speak.

12. I have (sat, set) the time limit for this job.

13. I want you to know that Mr. Carey is still (sitting, setting) in the outer office.

14. The check has (lain, laid) in Mr. Wood's private file for so long that I think he has forgotten it.

Assignment 6. ★ Follow the directions given for Assignment 5.

1. I (lay, laid) the carbon copies right there.

2. It is not necessary to (rise, raise) when your employer stops at your desk.

3. He has (lain, laid) down the rules for me.

4. Sally is (sitting, setting) the type now.

5. It is cooler in our office this summer than it was last summer; the ceiling has been (risen, raised).

6. Mr. Spears (sat, set) the requirements for all junior clerks.

7. He is (lying, laying) the foundation for increased efficiency.

8. (Sit, Set) your machine for double spacing.

9. I have (sat, set) still too long.

10. Mr. Lynch (rose, raised) an objection to the plan.

11. To the left of the typewriter (lay, laid) the copyholder.

12. It was (lying, laying) there yesterday, too.

13. We are gradually (rising, raising) our standards.

14. His coat and hat had been (lain, laid) on the divan.

15. In the president's office (lay, laid) the strongbox.

16. The office manager (lay, laid) down the procedure.

17. Elsie (lay, laid) down during her lunch hour.

18. Carbon paper should be (lain, laid) very carefully in the folder.

19. I (lay, laid) awake last night for three hours.

20. I hope our case will be (lain, laid) before the general manager.

21. She will (learn, teach) the lesson to the child.

22. I have (sat, set) in this place two hours.

23. He has (sat, set) the trap.

24. He (sat, set) a poor example.

25. When will the court (sit, set) again?
26. They are (sitting, setting) posts for the fence.
27. The hen is (sitting, setting) on her eggs.
28. He told her to (lie, lay) the child down.
29. Each one in favor of this motion (rise, raise) his right hand.
30. Do you think the river will (rise, raise)?

Balance, Remainder, Rest; Confessed, Admitted

Your bank (balance, remainder, rest) as given in the enclosed statement is now correct. One of our bookkeepers has (confessed, admitted) that he deliberately falsified your account. He subtracted the correct figures, but his (balance, remainder, rest) was incorrect. We (confess, admit) that the time allowed our employees to make up bank statements and to do the (balance, remainder, rest) of the work is short. This, however, does not excuse the person who, for some reason of his own, purposely struck the wrong (balance, remainder, rest).

Assignment 7. Write original sentences using *balance, rest, remainder, confessed, admitted.*

LESSON 17

Nouns and Pronouns—Number

Number is the distinction made in a noun or a pronoun in order to denote whether one or more than one object is meant; as:

| girl | girls | I | we |
| woman | women | he | they |

Rules for Forming Plurals of Nouns

1. The plural is regularly formed by adding *s* to the singular; as:

| store | stores | building | buildings |
| expediter | expediters | audition | auditions |

2. Singular nouns ending in *ch, sh, s, x,* and *z* form the plural by adding *es;* as:

inch	inches	tax	taxes
brush	brushes	chintz	chintzes
business	businesses		

3. Singular nouns ending in *y* preceded by a consonant form the plural by changing *y* to *i* and adding *es;* as:

| company | companies | lady | ladies |
| utility | utilities | industry | industries |

4. Singular nouns ending in *y* preceded by a vowel form the plural by adding *s* only; as:

| toy | toys | attorney | attorneys |
| day | days | turkey | turkeys |

5. Singular nouns ending in *o* preceded by a vowel form the plural by adding *s* only; as:

radio	radios	ratio	ratios
cameo	cameos	folio	folios
oratorio	oratorios	studio	studios

6. Some singular nouns ending in *o* preceded by a consonant form the plural by adding *es;* as:

mosquito	mosquitoes	cargo	cargoes
potato	potatoes	echo	echoes
motto	mottoes	hero	heroes

Exceptions: The following, however, take only *s:*

memento	mementos	zero	zeros
domino	dominos	solo	solos
dynamo	dynamos	piano	pianos
soprano	sopranos	lasso	lassos
proviso	provisos	canto	cantos
merino	merinos	albino	albinos

7. Some singular nouns ending in *f* or *fe* change the *f* or *fe* to *v* and add *es;* as:

shelf	shelves	self	selves
thief	thieves	life	lives
leaf	leaves	half	halves
knife	knives	calf	calves

Exceptions: Others form their plurals regularly; as:

proof	proofs	chief	chiefs
belief	beliefs	safe	safes
plaintiff	plaintiffs	gulf	gulfs
strife	strifes	grief	griefs

8. Some singular nouns form the plural by a vowel change instead of by the addition of a suffix; as:

woman	women	man	men
mouse	mice	tooth	teeth
goose	geese	foot	feet

9. A few plurals end in *en;* as:

brother	brethren	ox	oxen
child	children		

10. Letters, numerals, symbols, signs, and words regarded as words form their plurals by adding an apostrophe and *s;* as:

f.o.b.'s	the 70's	-'s
three A's	6's	the's

11. Compound nouns, either hyphenated or consisting of two separate words, pluralize the more important element; as:

court-martial	courts-martial	man-of-war	men-of-war
son-in-law	sons-in-law	major general	major generals
editor in chief	editors in chief	notary public	notaries public
senator-elect	senators-elect	personnel manager	personnel managers

When a compound is written as one word, the sign of the plural is always placed at the end; as:

handful	handfuls	cupful	cupfuls
stepchild	stepchildren	bookcase	bookcases
fisherman	fishermen		

Note: In a few words ending in *man* the plural is formed by adding *s*— not changing *man* to *men*—as these words are not compounds of *man;* as:

talisman	talismans
Ottoman	Ottomans
German	Germans

Note: A few compounds add the plural sign to both elements; as:

gentleman usher	gentlemen ushers
manservant	menservants
Knight Templar	Knights Templars

12. Proper names ending in *s* or an *s*-sound form their plurals by adding *es;* the others take *s;* as:

Brooks	the Brookses	Veal	the Veals
Byrnes	the Byrneses	Griffin	the Griffins
Fritz	the Fritzes	O'Brien	the O'Briens

Note: When the proper name is accompanied by a title, either the proper name or the title may be pluralized; as:

Mr. Palmer	Messrs. Palmer, the Messrs. Palmer, or the two Mr. Palmers
Mrs. Harrison	The Mrs. Harrisons or Mesdames Harrison
Miss Safin	Misses Safin or the two Miss Safins
Professor Bly	Professors Bly or the Professor Blys

13. Some nouns have two recognized plural forms with different meanings; as:

cloth	cloths	clothes (garments)
staff	staves	staffs
index	indexes (to books)	indices (symbols)
brother	brothers (blood relations)	brethren (members of a society)

14. Some nouns have the same form for the singular and for the plural; as:

means (instrument)	heathen (in collective sense)	wheat
salmon	Chinese	sheep
Japanese	corps	moose
vermin	odds	pains (meaning care)
politics	cod	deer

15. When accompanied by *numerals*, the following nouns usually have the same form in both numbers; in other usages *s* is added.

three thousand	four score years
four thousand strong	two dozen apples
two yoke of oxen	

16. The following nouns are always singular:

mumps (disease)	milk	mathematics
measles (disease)	molasses	music
statistics (science)	amends	whereabouts
economics (science)	news	civics

Note: Athletics, gymnastics, and *calisthenics* are more frequently plural than singular, because each is commonly understood to include several sports or exercises.

17. The following nouns are always plural—they have no corresponding singular form in the same sense:

antics	doings	proceeds	tidings
ashes	goods	remains	tongs
assets	grounds	riches	trousers
auspices	headquarters	scales (for	wages
belongings	hysterics	weighing)	winnings
blues	leavings	scissors	works
brains	means (income)	statistics (facts)	
credentials	premises	thanks	

18. **Plurals of foreign nouns.** Many nouns of foreign origin have been introduced into the English language. Some of them have been given English plurals; others still retain their foreign plurals. If in doubt with regard to the plural of a foreign noun, consult your dictionary. The following are most frequently used in business:

Singular	Foreign Plural	English Plural
analysis	analyses	
basis	bases	
crisis	crises	
parenthesis	parentheses	
terminus	termini	terminuses
datum	data	
memorandum	memoranda	memorandums
Madam, Madame	Mesdames	
Mr.	Messrs.	
alumnus	alumni	
alumna	alumnae	

Assignment 1. ★ Write the plurals of the following nouns.

analysis	calico	C.O.D.	foxhole
radius	bill of lading	curio	bailiff
formula	trousers	community	chimney
economics	defroster	Mr. Trumbull	datum
spoonful	Bailey	scissors	alumnus
high light	headquarters	Miss Powers	knife

Assignment 2. ★ Which of the following words are singular and which are plural?

oxen	odds	assets	tidings
children	mumps	credentials	trousers
means (instrument)	statistics	means (income)	winnings
politics	economics	proceeds	mathematics
wheat	milk	scissors	memoranda
deer	news	civics	

Aggravate, Irritate, Exasperate

Do you make excuses when you are taken to task for some mistake or omission? Do you know that this habit is (aggravating, irritating, exasperating) to an employer? You accomplish nothing by continually offering feeble excuses. You only (aggravate, irritate, exasperate) the situation. Such conduct, if persisted in, will eventually (aggravate, irritate, exasperate) your employer to the limit of his endurance; and he will then dispense with your services. If you are not at fault, say so in a pleasant, respectful tone. If you are at fault, have the courage to admit it and to promise that such a mistake will not occur again.

Assignment 3. Write a paragraph, using *aggravate*, *irritate*, and *exasperate* correctly.

LESSON 18

Agreement—Predicate with Subject

Many errors in English are made because two very important rules in connection with number are not observed.

Rule I. *A predicate must agree with its subject in number* (and person).

This rule is often violated because of the following difficulties:

1. The real subject is not recognized when a modifying or parenthetical phrase is placed between the subject and the predicate, or when the order is inverted; as:

> The *president,* as well as the three vice-presidents, *is going* to the convention Saturday. [*President is going.*]
>
> *One* of them *is going* to preside at the morning meeting. [*One is going.*]
>
> In the convention room *is* a *desk* for each of the ten delegates. [*Natural order: A desk* for each of the ten delegates *is* in the convention room.]

Remember that you are interested only in the real subject, which may be only one word or two or more words connected by a conjunction. In the latter case, we say the subject is *compound.* (See page 44.)

> *Janet,* as well as the other members of the office force, *is* having difficulty adapting herself to the new schedule. [*Simple subject: Janet*—singular; verb: *is having*—singular.]
>
> *Janet and Miss Withers,* as well as the other members of the office group, *are* having difficulty adapting themselves to the new schedule. [*Compound subject: Janet and Miss Withers*—plural; verb: *are having*—plural.]

Assignment 1. ★ Copy the following sentences, inserting *is, are, has,* or *have* as required.

1. Each one of us (?) always finished his work on time.
2. The office, together with the furnishings, (?) been cleaned.
3. On the shelves (?) the material you need.
4. His principal hobby (?) taking candid camera shots.
5. Every one of the girls (?) planning to remain after closing time tonight.
6. The news about the merger of the corporations (?) just reached our office.
7. Michael, with three other boys, (?) hired by Roberts & Roberts.
8. The girl of many caprices (?) not the secretary for me.
9. In the storerooms (?) a variety of supplies.
10. Various systems of filing (?) known to her.
11. Somewhere among those papers (?) the letter I asked you to get.
12. Not one of the Houston girls (?) her mother's business ability.

Assignment 2. Write ten original sentences, each containing a modifying or a parenthetical phrase between the subject and the predicate. Underline the simple subject and the verb.

Write two original sentences illustrating the agreement of subject and predicate when the order is inverted. Underline the simple subject and the verb.

2. The correct number of a collective noun used as a subject is not recognized. If the group or collection is considered as acting as a whole, the subject is singular; if the group or collection is considered as acting separately, the subject is plural; as:

> The *committee was* meeting with the strikers.
> The *committee were* disagreeing among themselves.

In the first example above, the subject is singular because *committee* is considered as a whole; it is acting as a unit. In the second example, the subject is plural because the individuals composing the *committee* are considered separately. The members of the group are disagreeing; so they are not working as a unit.

Collective subjects denoting a definite part, quantity, or amount, as *one-half, two-thirds, three-fourths, part, portion,* and similar words, usually demand a singular verb when they are followed by the preposition *of* and a singular noun and demand a plural verb when followed by the preposition *of* and a plural noun; as:

> *Nine-tenths* of our office *is* adequately lighted.
> In this modern age, *nine-tenths* of the offices *are* adequately lighted.

Some Exceptions:

> *One-half* of the hundred dollars *is* due.
> *Two-thirds* of the regiment *are* young men.
> *One-third* of the population *are* whites.
> *One-fifth* of the poor *have* repaired to their respective quarters.
> The *majority* of this species *are* confined to the northern hemisphere.

A *number, the number.* The expression *a number* has a plural meaning, and the predicate must be plural; the expression *the number* has a singular meaning, and the predicate must be singular.

> A *number* of letters *were* typed this afternoon.
> *The number* of letters typed this afternoon *was* gratifyingly large.

Assignment 3. ★ Select the correct word in each of the following sentences.

1. This group (shows, show) a very fine spirit of co-operation.
2. The jury (was, were) obviously busy with their own thoughts.
3. I cannot understand why parts of that paper (is, are) gone.
4. Our company (has, have) a fine policy with regard to promotions.
5. It is a fundamental principle of our democracy that the majority (rules, rule).
6. A large number of reference books (is, are) used by the advertising agent.
7. Half the shipment (was, were) damaged.
8. Three-quarters of the stenographers (is, are) poor in spelling.
9. The number of erasures (is, are) limited.
10. His audience (was, were) so small that he decided to postpone his lecture.

11. Part of the papers (was, were) on the desk and part (was, were) on the floor.

12. The jury (was, were) selected in short order.

13. The public (has, have) been known to criticize those who do not conform to convention.

14. The council (acts, act) on every petition brought before it.

Assignment 4. Write original sentences using the following words as subjects: *jury, class, club, group, two-thirds, board of directors, three-fourths, committee, minority, audience.*

3. The failure to recognize as plurals those plurals that do not end in *s* or *es*, such as the plurals of many foreign words; as:

> The *data were* of great value to Mr. Shelton.
> I know that the *memoranda were* in your desk yesterday.

If you are in doubt about the plural form of a word, consult your dictionary.

Assignment 5. ★ Copy the following sentences, inserting the correct word in each.

1. *is, are.* The Messrs. Smith (?) waiting to see you, sir.

2. *was, were.* The bases of his argument (?) logical.

3. *is, are.* The data (?) all assembled.

4. *is, are.* Parentheses (?) used when a comment or an explanation is inserted.

5. *is, are.* Bus terminuses (?) crowded at night.

6. *is, are.* Your analyses (?) based upon insufficient information.

7. *is, are.* I have already told you that the memoranda (?) to be filed.

8. *realizes, realize.* The wise alumnus (?) now that the training received at the Blank Business College is of great value.

9. *is, are.* The Misses Talbot and Wheeler (?) public stenographers.

10. *This, These—has, have.* (?) data (?) been carefully checked.

4. The correct number of subjects that are connected by conjunctions is not recognized.

a. Singular or plural subjects connected by *and* take a plural verb except:

(1) When the subjects denote the same person or thing.
(2) When the subjects are preceded by *each, every,* or *many a.*

> *Accuracy and speed are* both important.
> The *bills and* the *trade acceptances have* been given my attention.
> *Ice cream and cake is* my favorite dessert. [Exception 1.]
> *Many a young man and young woman has risen* in the profession.
> [Exception 2.]

b. Subjectes connected by *or, nor, either-or, neither-nor* demand that the verb agree in number and person with the nearer or nearest antecedent.

> Neither Peter *nor Paul is* able to write shorthand.
> Neither Peter *nor* the other *boys are* able to write shorthand.
> Neither the boys *nor Catherine is* able to write shorthand.
> Either the office boy *or* the file *clerks have* the work to do.

Assignment 6. ★ Copy the following sentences, making corrections wherever necessary. Give your reason for every correction you make.

1. Neither Esther nor the two boys was responsible for the smudge.
2. Neither Ann nor I am ready to start that job.
3. Every accountant, every stenographer, and every clerk are happy to be of service to you.
4. Either you or he are to be transferred to the wholesale office.
5. Answering the telephone and receiving callers are my duties.
6. The end and aim of my existence are to become expert in both duties.
7. Neither Frank nor David avails himself of his opportunities.
8. Many a boy and girl are seeking a position.
9. Neither Arthur nor Fred have arrived yet.
10. Mr. Brown said that neither you nor Virginia are to use the duplicating machine.
11. Frank and David avail themselves of all their opportunities.
12. Each pencil, paper, and pen are to be returned to the box.
13. Pie or cake or ice cream are the dessert choice today.
14. Neither Leo nor the twins does good work after lunch.

Assignment 7. Write:

1. Five original sentences in which singular or plural subjects are connected by *and.*

2. Three original sentences in which singular or plural subjects are connected by *or, nor, either-or,* or *neither-nor.*

3. Two original sentences in each of which a singular verb is used correctly with a compound subject joined by *and.*

4. Two original sentences in which compound subjects are preceded by *each, every,* or *many a.*

5. Three original sentences in which mixed singular and plural subjects are connected by *or, nor, either-or,* or *neither-nor.*

Avocation, Vocation; Amateur, Novice

Many a fine baseball player has lost his (amateur, novice) standing by accepting remuneration. It is a fact that in many cases the sport that was at first only (a, an) (avocation, vocation) has developed into (a, an) (avocation, vocation). To the (amateur, novice) who tries so sorely the patience of his partners, this may seem doubtful. It is not the purpose of this paragraph to advocate that the business person select a sport as (a, an) (avocation, vocation) with the idea that it will, with the acquisition of skill, become (a, an) (avocation, vocation); but considering leisure-time pursuits from the health angle, every office worker should have (a, an) (vocation, avocation) that permits him to spend time in the fresh air. What if he does try so many different activities that he remains (a, an) (amateur, novice) at them all? That is unimportant. The important thing is that he choose for (a, an) (avocation, vocation) some recreation that will give him pleasure and, at the same time, will promote mental and physical well-being.

Assignment 8. Write a paragraph using *avocation, vocation, amateur,* and *novice.*

LESSON 19

Agreement of Pronouns
with Antecedent

Now consider the second important rule:

Rule II. *A pronoun must agree with its antecedent in number* (and person).

An *antecedent* is the word for which the pronoun stands. In the sentence, "It is the efficient employee who succeeds," the word *employee* is the antecedent of the pronoun *who*.

Rule II is often violated because of the following difficulties:

1. The real antecedent of the pronoun is not recognized.

> *Not one* of those girls keeps her pencils sharpened.

So many times you hear this statement worded, "Not one of those girls keep their pencils sharpened," because the word *girls* is considered the antecedent of the pronoun. The real antecedent is the simple subject *not one*, and it must be followed by a singular pronoun.

2. The correct number of the antecedent is not recognized when the antecedent is plural in form, but in use is sometimes singular and sometimes plural. Such words were discussed in Lesson 17.

> The *means that was* used by the dishonest businessman carries *its* own punishment.
> His *means were* unlimited, and *they* justified his extravagance.
> *Statistics* has *its* place in every college curriculum.
> *Statistics* carry *their* own proof.

3. The correct number of the antecedent is not recognized because the antecedent is a collective noun.

This point was fully discussed in Lesson 18; so a repetition here is not necessary. The following examples illustrate the rule:

> The *jury* gave *its* verdict after deliberating for only an hour.
> The *jury* had evidently been expressing *their* opinions rather heatedly.
> *Half* the *office was* in *its* usual untidy condition.
> *Half* the *offices were* in *their* usual untidy condition.

4. The correct number of the antecedent is not recognized because the antecedent is composed of words connected by a conjunction.

This point was fully discussed in Lesson 18; so a repetition here is not necessary. The following examples illustrate the rules and exceptions:

> *She and I have our* own ways of obtaining information.
> The *Vice-President* and *General Manager has* completed *his* report. [One person holds both positions.]
> Either the secretary *or* the *treasurer* is to give *his* report.
> Neither the manuscripts *nor* the *news items are* to be taken from *their places* on my desk.

5. The correct number of the antecedent is not recognized because it is a foreign plural.

Foreign words commonly used in business were given in Lesson 17; so examples only will be given here.

> Please put the *parentheses* in *their* proper places.
> The *alumni* of State University *are having their* annual meeting Friday.

Assignment 1. ★ Select the correct word in each of the sentences given below and give the reason for your selection.

1. Surely some one of us (is, are) correct in (his, their) thinking.

2. The majority of the applicants (is, are) qualified to take (his, their) vocabulary tests.

3. Whoever passed those tests received (his, their) grades within three days.

4. Neither Allen nor Edward (gives, give) (his, their) services willingly.

5. The data for the financial report (has, have) been compiled, and (it, they) should be checked by the auditor.

6. If a stranger calls, treat (him, them) courteously.

7. Every one of those containers (is, are) filled with (its, their) own brand of ink.

8. Either Lawrence or Joseph must submit (his, their) resignation.

9. If anyone should telephone while I am at luncheon, ask (him, them) to leave (his, their) number.

10. Every stamp, every envelope, and every sticker (is, are) expected to be in (its, their) assigned place.

11. Not one of those men (has, have) the courage of (his, their) convictions.

12. Many a brilliant thinker and worker (is, are) too shy to express (himself, themselves).

13. The majority of the board of directors (is, are) determined to carry out (its, their) policy with regard to dividends.

14. Neither Barbara nor the boys (is, are) submitting (his, her, their) expense accounts.

15. The Lions Club will hold (its, their) meeting on Tuesday.

16. Every girl in the office (has, have) voiced (her, their) approval of the new machines.

17. The Fife and Drum Corps will make (its, their) first public appearance tomorrow.

18. The board of directors, who (is, are) all in town today, held (his, their) meeting this morning.

19. The purchasing agent's memoranda lay in (its, their) usual place.

20. Every clerk (has, have) applied (himself, themselves) today.

21. The production manager and his assistant (has, have) handed in (his, their) data.

22. It is always the girls who (is, are) blamed for losing the paper clips.

23. Every applicant must present specimens of (his, their) penmanship.

24. Half the machines (has, have) been moved from (its, their) original positions, and (it, they) should be returned immediately.

Additional Problems in Agreement

1. If a sentence begins with *there, there is, there are, there has been, there have been,* and similar expressions, the subject follows the verb; therefore the verb form that will agree in number with the subject should be chosen.

> There *is* one *letter* on the desk.
> There *are* two *letters* on the desk.
> There *has been* one telephone *call* this morning.
> There *have been* several telephone *calls* this morning.

2. Be sure to use a singular verb and a singular pronoun when referring to such indefinite words as *everyone, everybody, someone, somebody, either, neither, each, every, one, no one, anyone, anybody,* and *a person.*

> *Each* of us *has his* work to do.
> *Everyone is* to use *his* own typewriter.
> *Neither* of them *was* in *his* office.
> *Someone has* lost *his* memorandum book.

Caution: If *neither* is followed by *nor,* or *either* is followed by *or,* this rule may not apply. *Neither-nor* and *either-or* are correlatives. (See Lesson 28.)

> Neither the *files* nor the *desks have* to be moved. [*But:* neither the *file* nor the *desk* has to be moved. *Neither-nor* are correlatives used to connect the two parts of the compound subject.]
> *Neither* of the files *has* to be moved. [*Neither* is the subject.]

3. Should a clause be introduced by a relative pronoun, the verb and all pronouns in that clause agree with the *antecedent,* not with the relative pronoun. Usually the noun or pronoun immediately preceding the relative pronoun is the antecedent.

> Where can I buy one of those *erasers* that *have* a brush attached to *them?*
> He is the *one* who *is* to take the message.
> She is one of those *stenographers* who *think their methods* are always the most efficient.
> Mr. Brooks is a *man* who *requires his* secretary to be punctual.
> *I,* who *am* your friend, need your help now.

Assignment 2. ★ Write your choice of the correct word for each of the following sentences and give the reason for your choice.

1. There (is, are) two mistakes on this page.
2. This pencil is one that (has, have) no eraser.
3. Each of the boys (has, have) (his, their) own pencil.
4. (Is, Are) either of your parents at home?
5. She is one of those women who (likes, like) to monopolize the conversation.
6. There (was, were) ten applicants here yesterday.
7. Everyone will please tidy (his, their) own desk.
8. Neither the scoutmaster nor the scouts (has, have) knives.
9. Is he one of those men who always (says, say) exactly what (he, they) (means, mean)?
10. Surely everybody (knows, know) the answer to that problem.
11. Neither of the boys (was, were) accepted for the position.
12. Someone will lose (his, their) position when that becomes known.
13. Donald is one of those pupils who (thinks, think) (he, they) (knows, know) more than the teacher.
14. There (is, are) the new files.
15. I bought one of those lawn rollers that (does, do) not break the sod.

Discover, Invent; Emigrant, Immigrant

Every (emigrant, immigrant) who sets foot on Ellis Island must, consciously or unconsciously, be thankful that Columbus (discovered, invented) America. We owe our present status as a world power to a host of men—to Edison, who (discovered, invented) the incandescent lamp; to Whitney, who (discovered, invented) the cotton gin; to Howe, who (discovered, invented) the sewing machine. That our country is great is proved by the fact that, while we have many, many (emigrants, immigrants), we have comparatively few (emigrants, immigrants).

Assignment 3. Write a paragraph using *discover, invent, emigrant,* and *immigrant.*

Allusion, Delusion, Elusion, Illusion

Develop a sense of values. Decide for yourself what you want out of life. Many people labor under the (allusion, delusion, elusion, illusion) that wealth is the be-all and the end-all. It is no (allusion, delusion, elusion, illusion) of reality to say that wealth is important, but it is not all-important. I make this (allusion, delusion, elusion, illusion) to wealth simply because so many of us miss much that promotes happiness while we pursue the fleeting (allusion, delusion, elusion, illusion) of riches. Any wise elderly person will tell you that the happiness that comes from unselfish service is a worthwhile life objective.

Assignment 4. Write a paragraph designed to show that you understand the uses of *allusion, delusion, elusion,* and *illusion*.

Nouns and Pronouns—Person and Gender

Person

Person is that modification of the noun or pronoun that denotes the speaker, the person spoken to, or the person or thing spoken of.

1. The *first person* denotes the person or persons speaking; as:

Singular	*Plural*
I need a pencil	*We* need pencils.
I, Robert, need a pencil.	*We, Robert and I,* need pencils.

2. The *second person* denotes the person or persons spoken to; as:

Singular	*Plural*
You do good work.	*You* do good work.
Robert, you do good work.	*Robert and Marie, you* do good work.

The pronoun of the second person, *you,* always takes a plural verb. That is why you *always* say "you were." The person who says "you was" is illiterate.

3. The *third person* denotes the person(s) or thing(s) spoken of; as:

Singular	*Plural*
She does good work.	*They* do good work.
He does good work.	
It does make the work easier.	
Robert does good work.	

Note that the person of the noun *Robert* is indicated only by its use in the sentence, whereas the person of the pronoun is indicated by a change in the form of the pronoun.

Many times, errors in spoken English are caused by the incorrect use of the contraction for *do* and *not*. In the third person singular, the contraction is *doesn't*. Test yourself by saying the words separately. Consider the sentence, "It doesn't make any difference." Would you say, "It do not make any difference?" Then you would not say, "It don't make any difference." (See Lesson 14.)

Gender

Gender is the modification made in a noun or a pronoun in order to denote the sex of the object named.

The *masculine gender* denotes the male sex; as, *man, king, Mr. Bailey, he, him.*

The *feminine gender* denotes the female sex; as, *woman, queen, Miss Bailey, she, her.*

The *common gender* denotes an object of either sex, or it denotes a group that is possibly composed of both masculine and feminine members; as, *leader, congress, clerk, teacher, parent, they, us, someone.*

The *neuter gender* denotes want of sex; as, *desk, machine, table, typewriter, chair, it.*

Do not confuse *gender* with *sex*. Sex is a characteristic belonging to *living beings*, and gender is a modification belonging to all *nouns* and *pronouns*.

Ways of Distinguishing Gender. Nouns distinguish in three different ways the sex of the objects they represent:

1. By the use of different words:

Masculine	Feminine	Masculine	Feminine
Robert	Roberta	bachelor	maid
father	mother	sir	madam
drake	duck	son	daughter

2. By adding suffixes: (*a*) to masculine nouns:

Masculine	Feminine	Masculine	Feminine
host	hostess	heir	heiress
peer	peeress	tiger	tigress
executor	executrix	hero	heroine

(*b*) to feminine nouns:

Feminine	*Masculine*
bride	bridegroom
widow	widower

Note: Although the suffix *ess* may be used, correctly, to form the feminine gender of any noun (as *actor, actress*), yet the following words are ordinarily used to denote persons of either sex: *author, doctor, poet, editor, instructor.*

3. By forming compounds with distinguishing words: (*a*) as suffixes:

Masculine	*Feminine*
landlord	landlady
salesman	saleswoman

(*b*) as prefixes:

Masculine	*Feminine*
manservant	maidservant

4. By retaining the original endings of foreign words:

Masculine	*Feminine*	*Masculine*	*Feminine*
alumnus	alumna	fiancé	fiancée

Gender of Personified Nouns. The names of personified animals and objects may be either masculine or feminine without regard to sex, according to the characteristics that the animals or objects are supposed to possess; as:

> The cat is shedding *her* fur.
> The ship sailed majestically on *her* way.
> The sun shed *his* glory upon the earth.
> As dawn approached, the moon dimmed *her* radiance.

Gender of Collective Nouns. When a collective noun is considered to be singular, it is represented by a pronoun in the neuter gender; as:

> Each group must make *its* own rules.

Agreement with Antecedent. A pronoun agrees with its antecedent in person, number, and gender; as:

> Every *man* must be prepared to take *his* place in society.
> Every *woman* must be prepared to take *her* place in society.
> Social *activity* has *its* place in our way of life.
> Social *activities* have *their* place in our way of life.

A pronoun of masculine gender is used when the antecedent is a singular word used to imply a person of either sex; as:

> Everybody must provide *his* own fountain pen.

Note: Because in English there is no singular personal pronoun of common gender, a difficulty arises in some sentences; as, "Every boy and girl brought (*his, her, their*) books." The use of the word *his* would denote only the boys; the use of the word *her* would denote only the girls; the use of the word *their* would be incorrect. The only correct, although admittedly awkward, way to state the sentence is: "Every boy and girl brought his or her books." The same idea may be expressed more pleasingly by saying: "Every boy brought his books, every girl hers."

Assignment 1. ★ Copy the following exercise and underline the pronouns in the first person once; the pronouns in the second person twice; and the pronouns in the third person three times.

"A full day's work for a full day's pay" is my slogan, and for me it has been a very satisfactory rule of action. I believe that the person who slights his work or idles away his time lacks both good sense and character.

The law of supply and demand seems to govern the attitude of all too many workers toward their work. Many people, when jobs are plentiful, seize every opportunity to do nothing. The young man gives himself frequent rest periods in which to "catch up" on his smoking. The young woman freshens her make-up several times during the day and takes time to gossip with her friends. They belong among the foolish ones.

Consider such conduct from the point of view of good business policy. If you were the employer, how would you feel if you knew that certain of your employees were not using their time to the best advantage? You might feel that, under the circumstances, some work was better than no work. But when the time came to reduce the office force, whom would you retain and whom would you discharge? Employers are noted for their long memories.

Now let us consider the situation from its other angle—personal morale. The business person who has conscientiously done his or her best during every working day has a reserve of inner strength that can be drawn on again and again. He or she is the wise one. It is well to remember that, while it is true that we have to live with other people, it is also true that we have to live with ourselves.

Quiet, Quite; Compare, Contrast; Statue, Statute, Stature

If you were to (compare, contrast) the qualities possessed by outstanding figures in business, it would be (quiet, quite) possible that you would find strong determination and dogged persistence to be common to all. In the main, these men are (quiet, quite), just, and charitable. Many towns and cities owe to them their schools, libraries, parks. In gratitude for their various philanthropies, (statues, statutes, statures) have been erected in honor of such men. Should you have an opportunity to see any of these (statues, statutes, statures), note the lift of the chin, the tilt of the head. Note that few are men of short (statue, statute, stature). Then (compare, contrast) their bearing with that of the unsuccessful or the moderately successful people you see every day. The "look of success" counts for much in our struggle to progress, and you should cultivate it. Fortunately for us, no legislative body in our country has ever passed a (statue, statute, stature) forbidding self-development.

Assignment 2. Write original sentences, using *quiet, quite, compare, contrast, statue, statute,* and *stature.*

LESSON **21**

Nouns and Pronouns—Case

Case refers to the relation between a noun or a pronoun and other
words in the sentence, or to the variation in form that expresses such
relation. In English grammar there are three cases: nominative,
objective, and possessive. As the nominative- and objective-case
forms of nouns are the same, we shall limit our study to the proper
use of pronouns. No student who masters this chapter will ever say:
"Between you and *I*" and "I took *he* and his mother for a drive."

The first step in learning to use pronouns correctly is to commit
to memory the case forms as follows:

Nominative Forms	*Objective Forms*	*Possessive Forms*
I-we	me-us	my-mine-our-ours
you	you	your-yours
he	him	his
she	her	her-hers
it	it	its
they	them	their-theirs
who	whom	whose

Nominative Case

The most common nominative-case constructions are as follows:

1. Subject of a sentence:

> *John* and *I* study English.
> *He* studies English.
> *He* speaks correct English.
> *We* speak correct English.

2. Predicate nominative or complement:

It is *I*.
It was *he* who encouraged the workers.
It was *we* who were to blame.
It might have been *they*.
Who is he?

You will notice that the predicate nominative always names the same person or thing as the subject. The predicate nominative usually follows some form of the verb *to be*. These forms are as follows:

am	shall be	had been
is	will be	shall have been
are	should be	will have been
was	would be	should have been
were	could be	would have been
can be	might be	could have been
may be	have been	might have been
	has been	must have been

Note: Although "It's *me*" or "It was *him*" is sometimes permissible in spoken English, it should not be used in formal writing.

3. Complement of the infinitive *to be:* The complement of the infinitive *to be* is in the nominative case if the infinitive does not have a subject of its own:

I was thought to be *he*.
She was thought to be *I*.

Assignment 1.   Prepare five original sentences to illustrate each use of the nominative case discussed in this lesson. Whenever possible, use pronouns. Underline each word that is in the nominative case.

Assignment 2. ★   Name the rule that governs the italicized word in each of the following sentences.

1. It must have been *we* whom you heard last night.
2. There is no doubt about *who* will get the promotion.
3. He was thought to be *she*.
4. That is *they* over by the switchboard.
5. *I* should prefer to type a stencil.

6. *It* could be *he who* loses the pencils.
7. *It* may be *he,* or *it* may be *she.*
8. If *I* were *he, I* should be more careful.
9. Why did *you* think *it* was *we?*
10. *We* thought *it* was *they.*

Assignment 3. ★ In the following paragraph, select each word used in the nominative case; be prepared to tell which of the three uses of the nominative each word illustrates.

Speech is the most-used method of communication. We who have to earn our living must talk during our working hours and must also express our ideas and opinions during all other waking hours. We are constantly selling ourselves. We grant that appearance and personality are important, but a fastidious person who radiates personality will fail to promote himself if his speech is careless or grammatically incorrect. Many times we have had the urge to say something like, "Miss Cogan, you will never obtain a better position until you recognize the fact that your grammar is faulty." Of course, it is she who will suffer; but it is difficult to refrain from stretching out a helping hand when a cause of failure is so apparent.

Likely, Liable, Apt; Audience, Spectators

The curtain rose. Immediately all rustling ceased as the (audience, spectators) prepared to listen. The first number was a piano solo by John Griffin. Surely he must have been (a, an) (likely, liable, apt) pupil! The applause was so prolonged that it looked as if he were (likely, liable, apt) to give an encore. If he refused to play again, he would be (likely, liable, apt) to incur the displeasure of the (audience, spectators). There might be just such an ugly demonstration as was given by the (audience, spectators) at the basketball game last night.

Assignment 4. Write original sentences to illustrate the use of *likely, liable, apt, audience,* and *spectators.*

LESSON 22

Nouns and Pronouns—Case (Continued)

Objective Case

A noun or pronoun may be in the objective case as:

1. Object of a transitive verb:

> He called *him* and *me.*
> I invited *him* to dinner.
> I invited *him* and his *wife* to dinner.
> I saw *her* yesterday.
> I saw *her* and her *husband* yesterday.
> He wants to see *her.*

2. Object of a preposition:

> I talked with *him.*
> I talked with *him* and *Mary.*
> This confidence is strictly between *you* and *me.*
> I had dinner with *him.*
> I had dinner with *him* and his *wife.*

3. Subject or complement of an infinitive:

> I wished *him* to leave me.
> I told *her* to go to the cashier's window.
> They thought *him* to be me.
> They thought *her* to be *him.*
> They thought *us* to be *them.*

Note again that the complement of the infinitive *to be* is always in the same case as the subject. If the infinitive *to be* has a subject of its own, the subject is always in the objective case and the complement must, of course, be in the same case. In some sentences, the main verb and the infinitive have the same subject. In such sentences, the case of the subject, also the case of the complement, is determined by the main verb; as:

I was thought to be *he.*
She was thought to be *I.* (See page 94.)

Note that in the first sentence above the nominative pronoun *I* is the subject of the main verb *was thought;* also of the infinitive *to be.* As the complement is always in the same case as the subject, the complement in this sentence must be the nominative *he.*
Note the difference in the following sentences:

The receptionist thought *him* to be *me.* [The infinitive *to be* has an objective subject and an objective complement.]
The secretary was thought to be *she.* [The infinitive *to be* has a nominative subject and a nominative complement.]

Nominative or Objective

When a noun or a pronoun follows *than* or *as* in a statement of comparison and appears in an incomplete clause, the correct form may be ascertained by supplying mentally the words that are not expressed.

She works more rapidly than *I.* [She works more rapidly than I *work.*]
The new calculator pleases me more than *her.* [The new calculator pleases me more than *it pleases her.*]
Miss Dennehey is as co-operative as *we.* [Miss Dennehey is as co-operative as *we are.*]
I like him better than *her.* [I like him better than *I like her.*]
I like him better than *she.* [I like him better than *she likes him.*]

Self-Ending Pronouns

Myself, yourself, himself, themselves, and other *self*-ending pronouns. Case-conscious people who have not had the grammar training that you have had frequently use the *self* pronoun (called an *intensive* pronoun) when they are not sure of the correct case of the pronoun. "Mr. Taylor divided the work between Cecil and myself" should be stated "Mr. Taylor divided the work between Cecil and *me*." The *self* pronouns should be used to emphasize or to reflect nouns or pronouns *already expressed*.

> *I* will attend to that letter *myself*. [Emphasizing.]
> The *president himself* gave the order. [Emphasizing.]
> The *members* of the Senate voted *themselves* an increase in salary. [Reflecting.]
> The *girl* who can laugh at *herself* possesses the highest form of humor. [Reflecting.]

Appositives

When a noun or a pronoun is used as an *appositive*, the noun or pronoun must be in the same case as the word with which it is in apposition. (An appositive is a word or group of words used to explain a preceding word or phrase.)

> The culprits were the *stenographers, Lora* and *I*. [*Stenographers* is a predicate nominative—the appositives are in the nominative case.]
> Miss Davis told *us, Eugene* and *me*, the whole story. [*Us* is in the objective case—the appositives are in the objective case.]
> The *victims, he* and *I*, were soon released. [*Victims* is the subject of the sentence—the appositives are in the nominative case.]
> Mr. Black told *them, Elma* and *her*, to use the other door. [*Them* is in the objective case—the appositives are in the objective case.]

Note: In the use of restrictive appositives, such as *we girls* and *us boys*, errors are frequent. To check the correctness of such expressions, mentally omit the appositive and retain the pronoun. This is the correct pronoun to use.

> The sales manager sent *us* girls out of the office. [Omit *girls*.]
> *We* clerks are not overworked. [Omit *clerks*. Would you ever say, "Us are not overworked"?]

Assignment 1. Prepare four original sentences to illustrate each use of the objective case discussed in this lesson. Whenever possible, use pronouns rather than nouns. Underline each word that is in the objective case.

Assignment 2. ★ Select the correct word for each of the following sentences. Mention the grammar principles involved in each case.

1. Remember that this is just between you and (I, me).
2. The personnel manager called Alice and (I, me).
3. He wanted her and (I, me) to file application blanks.
4. Please excuse me. I thought you to be (he, him).
5. At first I did not believe it could be (he, him).
6. I should like to be (he, him).
7. The customer stared at the receptionist and (I, me).
8. Before (who, whom) must the culprit appear?
9. I failed to see (he, him) in the lobby.
10. You cannot expect to add like Mr. Walker and (he, him).
11. Why did you wish it to be (they, them)?
12. The new bookkeeper was believed to be (he, him).
13. Why did you say it was (I, me)?
14. I want both Mildred and (she, her) to be at work on time.
15. The purchasing agent was embarrassed when he realized that he thought Ann to be (I, me).
16. Mr. Irons will take John and (he, him) to the conference.
17. All the clerks left the office but Miss Gayle and (I, me).
18. Young bookkeepers like Robert and (he, him) need advice.
19. I saw (he, him) fall.
20. Many persons think them to be (we, us).
21. Who helped Julia and (she, her) clean the office?
22. I had been asked to help Julia and (she, her).
23. We were thought to be (they, them).
24. Let Helen and (I, me) tell them the good news.
25. Please reserve a place at your table for Hazel and (me, myself).
26. She is much taller than (me, I).
27. Both Nan and (myself, I) are trying to set your files in order, Mr. Brown.
28. The board of directors put the question squarely to the executives and (us, ourselves).
29. (We, Us) girls will be glad to work overtime tonight.

30. I consider (myself, me) lucky to have such a fine position.

31. Does Jean work as hard as (I, me)?

32. Mr. Torren put us, Sam and (I, me), in charge of the office.

33. Eileen did not do so well as (I, me).

34. Leave it to them, Mr. Allison and (she, her), to get the work done.

35. Mr. Lawler is a better accountant than (he, him).

36. Inaccurate typing annoys Miss Prynne more than (I, me).

37. Are you as efficient as (he, him)?

38. You always expect (us, we) clerks to do more than (they, them).

Angry, Mad; Reply, Response, Answer

In (reply, response, answer) to my question, Mr. Grosse became very (angry, mad). His outburst was so violent that I began to think him a little (angry, mad). In (reply, response, answer) to my appeal for aid, one of his friends talked to him and calmed him somewhat. The next day I wrote a letter asking him to state his reason for creating such a scene. I am still awaiting his (reply, response, answer).

Assignment 3. Write original sentences to illustrate the use of *angry, mad, reply, response,* and *answer.*

direct address — nom. case
who — subj of linking verb —
vbs of sense —

Nouns and Pronouns—Case (Continued)

(Who) Whom

The pronouns *who, whom, whoever,* and *whomever* are English stumbling blocks for many people. These pronouns follow the same rules as do the personal pronouns, and any difficulty you have previously experienced is because of lack of clear and definite information on each of these words. Who and *whoever* are nominative forms; *whom* and *whomever* are objective forms. –

Use of the nominative *who* as:

who
1. Subject of a sentence or clause: *nom. case*

   He is the man *who will do* the work.

2. Complement or predicate nominative:

   Who is it? [It is *who?*]
   Who is that gentleman? [That gentleman is *who?*]

3. Complement of the infinitive *to be* when it does not have a subject of its own.

   Who do you wish to be? [You do wish to be *who?*]

Use of the objective *whom* as:

1. Object of a transitive verb or of a preposition:

   Whom does he outrank in seniority? [He does outrank *whom?*]
   Whom do you wish to see? [You do wish to see *whom?*]

Before whom will you speak? [You will speak before *whom?*]
To whom do you wish to speak? [You do wish to speak to *whom?*]

2. Subject or complement of an infinitive:

Whom do you consider to be the better stenographer? [You do consider *whom* to be the better stenographer?]

3. Complement of the infinitive *to be* when it does have a subject of its own.

Whom did they take John to be? [They did take John to be *whom?*]

When *who, whoever, whom,* or *whomever* occurs in a clause, first isolate the clause. If the order is inverted, change to natural order.

William is an office boy who is honest.
Clause: *who* is honest
Who: subject of a clause

Be courteous to whoever comes to your desk.
Clause: *whoever* comes to your desk
Whoever: subject of a clause

Be courteous to whomever you may meet.
Clause: *whomever* you may meet.
· Natural order: you may meet *whomever*
Whomever: object of the transitive verb phrase *may meet*

She is one of those clerks whom everyone seems to like.
Clause: *whom* everyone seems to like
Natural order: everyone seems to like *whom*
Whom: object of the transitive infinitive *to like*

Sometimes confusion arises because a parenthetical clause, such as *I think* or *he says,* occurs within a clause introduced by *who, whom,* or *whomever.* Disregard this parenthetical clause when deciding which pronoun should be selected.

He is the man who I think will make the best executive.
Clause: who I think will make the best executive
Intermediate clause: I think

Clause with intermediate clause disregarded: *who* will make the best executive
Who: subject of a clause

Is that the man whom you said I should introduce to Mr. Ames?
Clause: whom you said I should introduce to Mr. Ames
Intermediate clause: you said
Clause with intermediate clause disregarded: *whom* I should introduce to Mr. Ames
Natural order: I should introduce *whom* to Mr. Ames
Whom: object of transitive verb phrase *should introduce*

Assignment 1. ★ Select the correct word in each of the following sentences and give the rules for your choice.

1. He is a customer (who, whom) we know to be reliable.
2. I cannot imagine (who, whom) you took me to be.
3. Lend my eraser to (whoever, whomever) asks for it.
4. Will you co-operate with (whoever, whomever) is selected for the position?
5. Will you co-operate with (whoever, whomever) I shall select?
6. The door opened and in walked Jane, (who, whom) we all thought was ill.
7. She wondered (who, whom) the next secretary would be.
8. He said that he would award the bonus to (whoever, whomever) he thinks is worthy of it.
9. (Who, Whom) did you say is to prepare the financial statement?
10. He praises (whoever, whomever) he admires.
11. Mr. John Larsen, (who, whom) I believe you know, called while you were out.
12. (Who, Whom) did he refer to by that last remark?
13. I am ready to employ (whoever, whomever) you think you can recommend.
14. Ruth wondered (who, whom) the personnel manager would choose.
15. (Who, Whom) did you think they were?
16. (Who, Whom) did you seem to be in your dream?
17. Mr. Davis requested (whoever, whomever) was dissatisfied to leave.

18. (Who, Whom) did he speak to just now?

19. Anthony Pike, (who, whom) I believe is a graduate of a business college, will assume his duties tomorrow.

20. He knows (who, whom) it is that I respect.

21. (Who, Whom) do you think I met in the elevator this morning?

22. I shall consult with (whoever, whomever) I believe will give me the best advice.

23. Mr. Bates is the man (who, whom) you want.

24. (Whoever, Whomever) leaves a typewriter uncovered at night will be discharged.

25. (Who, Whom) do you want to leave in charge of the office during your absence?

26. (Who, Whom) do you think is the logical choice?

27. We shall do our best work for (whoever, whomever) is chosen.

28. (Whoever, Whomever) it is will be acceptable to us.

Assignment 2. Write a sentence to illustrate each of the following:

1. *Who* as the subject of a sentence or a clause.
2. *Whom* as the object of a preposition.
3. *Whom* as the complement of the infinitive *to be.*
4. *Who* as the complement of the infinitive *to be.*
5. *Whom* as the subject of an infinitive.
6. *Whom* as the object of a transitive verb.
7. *Who* as a predicate complement.

Copy, Duplicate, Facsimile, Transcript

Here are your instructions for this morning:

Write to your school for a (copy, duplicate, facsimile, transcript) of your record.

Make a (copy, duplicate, facsimile, transcript) of this letter for my file.

Send Robert Bell a (copy, duplicate, facsimile, transcript) of our trade-mark.

Make out these ten receipts in (copy, duplicate, facsimile, transcript).

Assignment 3. Write original sentences to illustrate the use of *copy, duplicate, facsimile,* and *transcript.*

LESSON **24**

Nouns and Pronouns—Case (Concluded)

Possessive Case

A noun or a pronoun is in the possessive case when the word is used to show ownership. The possessive case of nouns is formed by the use of the apostrophe and *s*, according to the basic rules that follow. The possessive-case forms of the *personal pronouns* and of *who* do not require the apostrophe because each one of these pronouns has its own particular possessive form. Many errors in writing will be avoided if this caution is remembered. The pronoun *it* seems to be the chief troublemaker. *Its* is the possessive; *it's* is the contraction for *it is*.

> Every river must go *its* own way. [Possessive.]
> *It's* a known fact that only the superior person is considered for promotion. [Contraction.]

The possessive forms that cause difficulty are: *its, their, theirs, whose, hers, ours,* and *yours.* Remember: these forms do *not* take an apostrophe.

Basic Rules for the Formation of the Possessive Case

1. To form the possessive of *singular* nouns *not* ending in *s*, add an apostrophe followed by an *s*.

customer	customer's	world	world's
month	month's	Frank	Frank's

2. If a *singular* noun ends in *s* or an *s*-sound, add an apostrophe and an *s* if a new syllable is formed in the pronunciation of the possessive.

boss	boss's	Jones	Jones's
miss	miss's	Thomas	Thomas's
fox	fox's	witness	witness's

If the addition of *s* would make an *s*-ending word hard to pro-nounce, it is permissible to add the apostrophe only.

hostess	hostess'	Frances	Frances'
princess	princess'		

Note: Not all authorities agree on this exception.

3. The possessive of *regular plurals* is formed by adding only the apostrophe after the *s*.

lawyers	lawyers'	celebrities	celebrities'
sheriffs	sheriffs'	Negroes	Negroes'

Caution: In forming the possessive of a noun ending in *s*, the apostrophe must not be placed *before* that *s*.

> *Wrong:* Burn's, misse's   *Right:* Burns's, misses'

4. The possessive of *irregular plurals* is formed by adding the apostrophe followed by *s*.

freshmen	freshmen's	Englishwomen	Englishwomen's

5. The sign of the possessive is added at the end of a compound.

> somebody else's   bookkeeper-secretary's

6. Ordinarily, the apostrophe and *s* are not used to form the possessive of inanimate things. In most cases, an *of* phrase is preferred.

> *Right:* The cover of the book was soiled.
> *Wrong:* The book's cover was soiled.

Exceptions: The following exceptions have become established by usage: expressions of time or measure; as *a day's pay, two months' notice, a stone's throw;* and expressions implying personification; as *the heart's desire, the law's delay, winter's frown.*

Possessive of Two or More Nouns Used Together. When two or more nouns are used together, implying joint or common possession, the last noun only takes the possessive. When the nouns imply separate possession, both nouns take the possessive.

> Alice and *Jane's* town was flooded by the spring rains.
> *Alice's* and *Jane's* typewriters are in good condition.

Possessive before a Gerund. A noun or a pronoun that precedes a gerund should be in the possessive case. (A gerund is a verb form ending in *ing* used as a noun. See Lesson 13.)

> They can count on *my* doing the best I can.
> Count on *me* and on *my* doing my best.
> Count on *him* and on *his* doing his best.
> Count on *them* and on *their* doing their best.
> I disapprove of *your* using a worn-out typewriter ribbon.
> Can you imagine *John's* receiving a dismissal slip?
> Time must be allowed for the *train's* crossing.

Note: This principle is violated daily in the news columns of almost every newspaper in the country. It is seldom violated in the editorial columns or by our more closely edited magazines. Many of our best speakers also fail to observe this rule.

Assignment 1. ★ Write the singular possessive and the plural possessive of the following words: *secretary, bookkeeper, clerk, president, manager, girl, fox, woman, wife, child, brother, mouse, Englishman, father-in-law.*

Assignment 2. ★ Copy the following sentences, making whatever corrections are necessary.

1. Those firms are very careless about there outgoing mail.
2. I cannot imagine our being so careless.
3. I can check signatures and enclosures without a moment's delay.
4. The envelope's flap should be securely sealed.
5. When an error is made, it's sometimes difficult to find who's fault it is.

6. Sometimes the mistake is yours, and sometimes its mine.

7. Each task should have it's own established routine.

8. His mother's-in-law visit disrupted our entire schedule.

9. Their are no excuses to be made for the lazy.

10. Mr. Byrnes is very much interested in me attending night school.

11. The girls in our office have formed a girls' league.

12. Please return the carbon to it's place.

13. Those duplicated papers are our's.

14. Whose going to lunch?

15. Ones typewriting can be improved by practice.

Farther, Further; Alley, Ally

The (farther, further) you travel on the road of life the more convinced you will be that the quality of self-respect is a valuable (alley, ally). In order to merit the respect of others, you must have respect for yourself. That other "you" that is within you must be your critic. Never try to (farther, further) your own interests at the expense of another person. Do not waste time envying the fellow worker who seems to progress (farther, further) and faster than you do. (Farther, Further), do not betray yourself to the extent that you consciously make an unkind remark. If you are not true to yourself, you will find that you are in a blind (alley, ally) as far as business and social advancement are concerned. If you consistently follow the practice of treating others as you would be treated, you will be rewarded by finding an (alley, ally) in almost everyone you meet.

Assignment 3. Write original sentences, using *farther, further, alley,* and *ally.*

LESSON 25

Adjectives

An *adjective* is a word that limits or describes the meaning of a noun or a pronoun; as:

There are *ten* offices on this floor.
Please order a *black* ribbon.
Her manner was *impertinent*.

Those and Them. Use *those* if the word is to be followed by a noun; use *them* if the word is not to be followed by a noun.

I shall take *those* papers to Mr. Hale.
I shall take *them* to Mr. Hale.

Comparison. Most adjectives are inflected, or modified, to express different degrees of quality. This modification is called *comparison*.

There are three forms or degrees of comparison:

1. *Positive.* The positive degree expresses the simple quality of the word and is used when the object described by the adjective is not compared with any other object; as, *tall, wide, sweet*.

2. *Comparative.* The comparative degree expresses a higher or lower degree of quality than is expressed by the positive degree and is used when two objects are compared; as, *taller, wider, sweeter*.

3. *Superlative.* The superlative degree denotes the highest or lowest degree of quality and is used when more than two objects are compared; as, *tallest, widest, sweetest*.

The comparative and superlative degrees of adjectives are formed in three ways:

1. By adding *er* to the positive to form the comparative degree and *est* to the positive to form the superlative degree; as:

large	larger	largest
fine	finer	finest
friendly	friendlier	friendliest

2. By changing the form of the word completely; as:

much, many	more	most
little	less	least
good	better	best

3. By adding the words *more* or *less* to the positive to form the comparative degree and *most* or *least* to the positive to form the superlative degree; as:

delicate	more delicate	most delicate
efficient	more efficient	most efficient
trusting	less trusting	least trusting

Adjectives of one syllable are compared by adding *er, est;* adjectives of two syllables, by adding *er, est,* or *more, most, less, least,* depending on the difficulty of pronounciation (*more* or *most* formal, but *happier, happiest*); adjectives of three or more syllables, always by adding *more, most* or *less, least.*

Choice of Comparative or Superlative Degree. To emphasize a point already made: When referring to two persons, places, or things, use the comparative degree; when referring to more than two persons, places, or things, use the superlative degree.

This course is the *better.* [Must be only two courses.]
This course is the *best.* [Must be three or more courses.]

Adjectives That Cannot Be Compared. Some adjectives express qualities that do not admit of comparison. A few of these are:

supreme	unique	immaculate
right	correct	perpetual
round	perfect	complete
spotless	level	unanimous
dead	perpendicular	conclusive
eternal		

"Other" in Comparison. In comparing one particular person or thing with the group to which it belongs, the comparative degree is used and the word *other* is inserted; as:

> There are more office workers in New York than in any *other* city in the world.
> No *other* boy in the office is so industrious as Joseph.

If you do not use the word *other*, you are including in the comparison the person or thing compared. "There are more office workers in New York than in any city in the world" would mean that New York was being included in the group with which New York was being compared, inasmuch as New York is "any city in the world."

Double Comparison. Avoid double comparisons; as, *more kinder, more better, most cheapest.*

Omission of the Article. When two or more adjectives modify the same noun, the article should be repeated if the qualities belong to different individuals. The omission of the article indicates that only one person or thing is meant. Note the difference in meaning: *a black and a gold fountain pen* and *a black-and-gold fountain pen.*

Before nouns, the repetition of the article indicates separate persons or things; as:

> A stenographer and musician. [One person]
> A stenographer and a musician. [Two persons]
> The army and navy. [One service]
> The army and the navy. [Two separate branches of the service]

Compound Adjectives. When two or more words are combined *before* a noun to form one adjectival idea—to make a compound adjective—they should be joined by a hyphen or hyphens.

ten-story building	sixty-day period	first-class operator
air-conditioned theater	twenty-second floor	high-grade goods
well-known person	up-to-date methods	middle-aged man

Assignment 1. Write the comparative forms of the following adjectives: *cold, cheap, fast, lovely, circular, accessible, expensive, beautiful, dirty, anxious.* Be careful!

Assignment 2a. ★ Select the correct word in each of the following sentences and give the reason for your choice.

1. Did you get (those, them) checks for Mr. Beale?
2. Both bookkeepers are good, but Arthur is a shade the (better, best).
3. Agnes is the (faster, fastest) typist I know.
4. I need (those, them) envelopes now.
5. Please get (those, them) for me immediately.
6. Who has the (better, best) personality, Natalie or Sandra?
7. I am so glad I work in an (air-conditioned, air conditioned) office.
8. You can type a (clearer, more clearer) stencil than I.
9. Mr. Hammond's office is the (emptiest, most nearly empty) of furniture.
10. We have received several letters of application, but I think Miss Dunn's is the (neater, neatest).
11. That station does a great deal of (short-wave, short wave) broadcasting.
12. A strikeover is the (worse, worst) typing error that can be made.

Assignment 2b. ★ In the following sentences make corrections wherever necessary. Give the reason for each correction made.

1. Both jobs are so difficult that I cannot decide which is the hardest.
2. In some respects secretarial work is different from any kind of office work.
3. Ruth is the most efficient of all the girls.
4. It is too bad that your building is in such an out of the way location.
5. I hardly know which is most interesting, receiving callers or taking dictation.
6. Our firm has been in this business longer than any company in the city.
7. I have examined both machines, and I think you should purchase the smaller one.
8. Which name is prettier—June, Jean, or Joan?
9. This is the most unique letter setup I have ever seen.

10. Bertha has been granted a thirty-day leave.

11. After studying all the sketches, we decided that Marion's idea was the better.

12. Please do not order any more of them pencils.

13. George is a better operator than any man in the office.

14. Of them two duplicating machines, I believe the larger is the best for our purposes.

15. Our employer pays higher wages than any firm in the state.

Assignment 3.   Write original sentences, using the superlative form of each of the words listed for comparison in Assignment 1.

Little, Few; Healthy, Healthful

The (healthy, healthful) executive is the man who takes (healthy, healthful) exercise. It is a fact that (less, fewer) mistakes are made by the person who is physically and mentally (healthy, healthful). The executive has (less, fewer) trouble with his work when he feels right. There is (less, fewer) delay in making decisions, and (less, fewer) unwise decisions are made. It is important that he work and relax in (healthy, healthful) surroundings.

Assignment 4.   Write a paragraph using *little, few, healthy,* and *healthful.* If you wish, you may use the comparative or superlative degrees.

LESSON **26**

Adverbs

An *adverb* is a word that describes, explains, or limits a verb, an adjective, or another adverb; as:

1. Modifying a verb:

   Alice types *rapidly* and *accurately*.

2. Modifying an adjective:

   Alice is a *very* good typist.

3. Modifying another adverb:

   Alice types *remarkably* well.

Adverbs usually answer the questions when? where? how? why? how much? how little? or to what extent?

Classification According to Use.   According to use, adverbs may be classified as *simple* and *conjunctive*.

A *simple adverb* is used as a modifier only. Some of the most common are:

soon	quite	immediately
too	very	clearly
here	nearly	always

It is not *too* much to expect that a business person speak *correctly*. Employers are usually impressed by a person who talks *well*. Slovenly speech habits make promotion *almost* impossible.

A *conjunctive adverb* performs two services at the same time—it acts as a regular adverb in a subordinate clause and also connects the subordinate clause to the main clause.

Time passes quickly *when* one is busy.

As you did not keep your word, we will cancel the order.

We are sorry to be forced to take this course; *nevertheless,* we now have no use for your product.

Some of the most commonly used conjunctive adverbs are:

after	moreover	thus
as	then	when
before	therefore	while
however	since	yet

Assignment 1. Write five original sentences containing simple adverbs; underline each adverb. Write five original sentences containing conjunctive adverbs; underline each adverb.

Position of the Adverb. The adverb should always be placed as near as possible to the word that it modifies. In some instances the position of the adverb may even change the entire meaning of the sentence; as:

Only I have permission to sign Mr. Wood's name. [I am the only person who has this permission.]

I have permission *only* to sign Mr. Wood's name. [That is the only permission I have.]

I have permission to sign Mr. Wood's name *only.* [I do not have permission to sign the name of any other person.]

1 *also* changed the ribbon on that typewriter. [That makes at least two of us who changed the ribbon.]

I changed the ribbon on that typewriter *also.* [In addition to changing a ribbon on another typewriter.]

Also, I changed the ribbon on that typewriter. [Besides other work.]

Confusion in the Uses of Adjectives and Adverbs. A common error is the use of an adjective when an adverb is required. Adjectives can modify only nouns and pronouns; whereas adverbs can modify only verbs, adjectives, and other adverbs.

Whether to use an adjective or an adverb after such verbs as *appear, taste, feel, smell, look,* and *seem* is a perplexing question to many students. Usually such a verb is followed by an adjective because the word *describes the subject.* If the word refers to the *action of the verb,* however, the *adverb* should be used.

The carpet felt *soft*. [Adjective—describes the subject.]
This work looks *hard*. [Adjective—describes the subject.]
Edward felt *softly* about the desk. [Adverb—refers to action of the verb.]
That boy works *hard*. [Adverb—refers to action of the verb.]
I feel *fine*. [Adjective—describes the subject.]
I felt my way *carefully* through the hall. [Adverb—refers to the action of the verb.]

Assignment 2. Write original sentences using the words *appear, taste, feel, smell, look,* and *seem*. In the first six sentences follow these words by adjectives; in the last six, by adverbs.

Comparison of Adverbs. The rules for the comparison of adverbs are the same as those for the comparison of adjectives. See Lesson 25.

Sure, Surely; Real, Really. *Sure* and *real* are adjectives; *surely* and *really* are adverbs.

I was *sure* that I had filed that letter. [Adjective.]
Martha is a *real* file clerk. [Adjective.]
I was *surely* glad to find the original copy. [Adverb.]
She is *really* doing a fine job. [Adverb.]

Good, Well. *Good* is always an adjective. *Well* is an adverb except when it refers to health or making a favorable impression.

Robert does *good* work. [Adjective.]
Robert does his work *well*. [Adverb.]
Robert does not look *well* this morning. [Adjective.]
Robert looks *well* in that coat. [Adjective.]

Scarcely, Only, Hardly, But, Never. Adverbs such as these are negative in meaning; therefore no other negative should be used with them.

I have scarcely time to do my own work. [*Not:* I haven't.]
We use the script type only for Mr. Burnet's personal letters. [*Not:* We do not use.]
He could hardly wait for his secretary to answer the buzzer. [*Not:* He couldn't.]
He had but one request to make. [*Not:* He hadn't.]
Lucy has never done this kind of work. [*Not:* has not never.]

Assignment 3. ★ Select the correct word in each of the following sentences and give the reason for your choice.

1. I do my best work in a (real, really) quiet office.
2. Please send this telegram as (quick, quickly) as possible.
3. It is important that you dress (neat, neatly) at all times.
4. I shall (sure, surely) be with you tomorrow.
5. Your work seems (satisfactory, satisfactorily) in all respects.
6. His ideas sound (good, well) to the personnel director.
7. I am (real, really) sorry to leave your employ.
8. It is getting so dark you (can, cannot) hardly see the keyboard.
9. You cannot expect her to look (good, well) after such a long illness.
10. Why doesn't the executive (ever, never) use the front exit?
11. Mr. McGowan looks (real, really) tired.
12. The receptionist must have a voice that sounds (clear, clearly) on the telephone.
13. You (sure, surely) have been a success here.
14. Is the rug in Mr. Larsen's office a (real, really) oriental?
15. The new secretary's manner is (sure, surely) pleasing.

Assignment 4. ★ In the following sentences make corrections wherever necessary. Give the reason for each correction you make.

1. Please open the window. This room smells stuffy.
2. Filing is sure tiring for the girl who wears high heels.
3. Such an arrangement couldn't hardly satisfy the expediter.
4. We sure had a trying day at the office yesterday.
5. Even our best stenographers looked dejected.
6. They looked dejected about the office at all the letters that had to be rewritten.
7. Don't you feel good today?
8. I sure was frightened when I took my first dictation.
9. Elsie always arrives earlier than any employee we have.
10. Eileen and Marie can finish the work by noon easy.
11. I should say that they are sure to do so.
12. The good stenographer is only satisfied with a carefully placed letter.
13. Mildred's desk always looks neatly.

14. You should make a habit of saving money regular.

15. Do not stand idle by when your friends need assistance.

Assignment 5. The words at the end of this paragraph may be either adjectives or adverbs, according to their use. Use each one in an original sentence as an adjective; then in another sentence as an adverb. In each sentence, underline the illustrative word once and the word it modifies twice. *Fast, best, early, hard, high, just, late, long.*

Raise, Rear; Respectfully, Respectively

The children who are (raised, reared) with such care by kind parents should speak (respectfully, respectively) of and to these parents. Any normal person would prefer (raising, rearing) children to (raising, rearing) animals; but the thoughtlessness and selfishness evinced by some sons and daughters is a great disappointment. Parents want from their children love, honor, and gratitude (respectfully, respectively).

Assignment 6. Write original sentences using *raise, rear, respectfully,* and *respectively.*

LESSON **27**

Prepositions

A *preposition* is a connecting word that shows the relation between a noun or a pronoun and some other word in the sentence; as:

> The salesman asked *for* his itinerary. [*For* connects *itinerary* with
> *asked.*]
> The outline of his route was already *on* his desk. [*On* connects
> *desk* with *was.*]
> He obtained it *without* difficulty. [*Without* connects *difficulty* with
> *obtained.*]
> He made notes *in* shorthand. [*In* connects *shorthand* with *notes.*]

Note that the preposition in each of the following sentences shows
the relation of the box to the table.

> The box was *on* the table.
> The box was *above* the table.
> The box was *by* the table.
> The box was *beside* the table.
> The box was *under* the table.
> The box was *beneath* the table.
> He placed the box *upon* the table.

The noun or the pronoun following a preposition is called the *object* of the preposition and, as you already know, is always in the
objective case. A preposition and its object constitute a *prepositional
phrase.*

119

Some of the prepositions in common use are:

about	but (meaning "except")	off
above	by	on
after	except	over
among	for	to
at	from	under
before	in	up
below	into	upon
beside	like	until
between	of	with

The Correct Preposition. To avoid common language errors, study the following:

All. *Of* after *all* is incorrect unless followed by a pronoun.

All the bills are now paid. [*Not:* all of.]
All of us are guilty. [Correct.]

At, To. *At* means position; *to* means motion toward.

Mr. Rowland is *at* home today. [*Not:* to home.]
Mr. Rowland came *to* the office yesterday.

Behind, In Back Of. Use *behind* rather than *in back of. In front of*, however, is correct.

Mr. Higgins likes best to work *behind* closed doors. [*Not:* in back of.]
The letter with the latest date should always be *in front of* the other letters in the folder. [Correct.]

Beside, Besides. *Beside* means "by the side of"; *besides* means "in addition to."

The calculator was placed *beside* Edward's desk.
He thinks no one *besides* him can operate a calculator.

Both. Use *both of* only before pronouns.

Both men deserve an increase.
Both of them deserve increases.

From, Off. Use *from* when referring to persons. Never say *off of* or *off from*.

> I took the pencil *from* James.
> I took the pencil *off* the desk.

In, Into. *In* denotes position or place; *into* conveys the idea of motion.

> Mr. Jones is *in* his office.
> I saw Mr. Jones going *into* his office.

Inside, Outside. Do not use *of* with *inside* and *outside*. Do not use *inside of* when referring to time; use *within*.

> Alice had to wait *outside* Mr. Ryan's office. [*Not:* outside of.]
> If she does not finish those letters *within* an hour, please let me know. [*Not:* inside of.]

Than. Never use *than* as a preposition; it is a conjunction.

> *Wrong:* Mary is more accurate than me.
> *Right:* Mary is more accurate than I. [*Than* is a conjunction introducing the elliptical clause *than I am.*]

Upon, Onto. Use *upon* or *up on* rather than *onto*.

> Joyce had to climb *up on* the table to reach the reference books. [*Not:* onto.]

Words Requiring Certain Prepositions. Certain words require certain prepositions, the preposition depending on the meaning to be expressed.

abhorrence *of*	affinity *between*
abhorrent *to*	agree *to* (a proposal)
abide *by* (a decision)	agree *upon* (a course)
abide *with* (a person)	agree *with* (a person)
abound *in* or *with*	agreeable *to* (*with* is permissible)
accompanied *by* (a person)	angry *at* (things or conditions)
accompanied *with* (a gift)	angry *with* (persons)
acquit *of*	appropriate *for* (a charity)
adapted *to* (a thing)	appropriate *from* (an author)
adapted *for* (by nature)	attend *to* (listen)
adapted *from* (an author)	attend *upon* (wait)

bathe *in* (sea)
bathe *for* (cleanliness)
bathe *with* (water)
beneficial *to*
bestow *upon*
buy *from*
compliance *with*
comply *with*
confer *on* (give to)
confer *with* (talk to)
confide *in* (place confidence in)
confide *to* (entrust to)
conform *to* (in conformity *with* or *to*)
convenient *for* (a purpose)
convenient *to* (a person)
conversant *with*
correspond *to* or *with* (a thing)
correspond *with* (a person)
credit *for*
deal *in* (kind of business)
deal *with* (people)
depend *on*
dependent *on* (but independent *of*)
derogatory *to*
differ *from* or *with* (in opinion)
differ *from* (in likeness)
different *from* (preferred to *different than*)
disappointed *in* (what we have)
discrepancy *between* (two things)
discrepancy *in* (one thing)

dispense *with*
employ *for* (a purpose)
employed *at* (a stipulated salary)
employed *in, on,* or *upon* (a work or business)
enter *into* (agreements)
enter *upon* (duties)
enter *in* (a record)
enter *at* (a given point)
exception *to* (a statement)
familiarize *with*
foreign *to* (preferred to *from*)
identical *with*
inferior or superior *to*
⎰in regard *to*
⎱with regard *to* (interchangeable)
⎰as regards
martyr *for* (a cause)
martyr *to* (a disease)
need *of* or *for*
part *from* (friend)
part *with* (money)
plan *to* (infinitive sign *to*, not preposition *on*)
profit *by*
reconcile *to* (friend)
reconcile *with* (condition)
retroactive *to*
taste *of* (food)
a taste *for* (art)
thirst *for* or *after* (knowledge)
vary *from*

Redundant Prepositions. Do not use prepositions that are not needed; as:

Now, where did that girl go *to?*
Please take the wrapping off *of* that ream of paper.
Where is the eraser *at?*
I cannot help *from* asking all these questions.
His desk is opposite *to* mine.

See page 25.

Assignment 1. ★ Select the correct word in each of the following
sentences:

1. Important executives like Mr. Trumbull and (he, him) should
have private offices.

2. We parted (with, from) the other girls at the elevators.

3. Our old product is much inferior (to, than) the new one.

4. Do you agree (with, to) accepting her as a member of our
office family?

5. (At, With) whom was the secretary angry?

6. This duplicating machine is different (than, from) any other
I have used.

7. We must go (in, into) the conference room.

8. Our garage is (in back of, behind) the house.

9. In our office one of the girls does nothing (beside, besides)
filing.

10. It is bad policy to get an advance on your salary (from, off)
the cashier.

11. We buy our typewriter ribbons (off, from) Dunn & Dunn.

12. Joseph can be found anywhere except (at, to) his desk.

13. We accomplished a great deal while Mr. Travers was (at, to)
the conference.

14. All business people should be glad to conform (with, to) established policies.

15. Gracious compliance (with, to) established policies will be
appreciated by your employer.

Assignment 2. ★ In the following sentences make whatever corrections are necessary.

1. Do you plan on working late tonight?

2. Maria's office is in back of ours.

3. Where in the world were you going to when you met Mr.
Smith?

4. I would of posted the letters if you had asked me.

5. Would you like to go to lunch with Alice and me?

6. I'm so busy that I really don't know where I'm at.

7. Please go in Mr. Tucker's office and get all the signed letters.

8. You can borrow a dollar from Susan.

9. Florence dislikes very much to part from any of her carbon
paper.

10. Mr. Noyes would allow no stenographer but she to take his dictation.

11. In regards to your vacation, you may have a week either in August or in September.

12. Miss Kersey placed a guide card between each folder in the file.

13. Your increase in salary will be retroactive from January 1.

14. There is quite a discrepancy between your total and mine.

15. Your total should be identical to mine.

Assignment 3. Write original sentences, using the words listed below. Wherever possible, use pronouns as the objects of the prepositions. Five of the sentences must contain compound objects.

in	different from	between
from	at	deal with
off	to	part with
beside	inside	taste for
besides	angry with	convenient for

Correspondence, Correspondents, Corespondent;
Contemptuous, Contemptible

Jane Doe was named (correspondence, correspondents, corespondent) in that suit. She must be a (contemptuous, contemptible) person. We have had some (correspondence, correspondents, corespondent) with regard to the case from our Washington and New York (correspondence, correspondents, corespondent) who seem (contemptuous, contemptible) of the methods used by the defense attorney.

Assignment 4. Use *correspondence, correspondents, corespondent, contemptible,* and *contemptuous* in original sentences.

LESSON **28**

Conjunctions

A *conjunction* is a word used to connect words, phrases, or clauses; as:

> The letter *and* the envelope are on your desk.
> You will find them on the blotter *or* in the basket.
> They were there this morning, *but* I am sure they are not there now.

Conjunctions are usually classified into two groups, *co-ordinate* and *subordinate*.

A *co-ordinate conjunction* is used to connect words, phrases, or clauses of *equal grammatical value;* that is, a co-ordinate conjunction may connect two or more words, two or more phrases, or two or more clauses of the *same* rank. A co-ordinate conjunction should *not* be used to connect a word and a phrase, a phrase and a clause, or any other dissimilar combinations. Study the following examples carefully:

> Michael works quickly and quietly. [Conjunction connecting words.]
> He is in the office and at work before eight o'clock. [Conjunction connecting phrases.]
> He tries hard and he earns his salary. [Conjunction connecting clauses of the same rank.]

Now study the following:

> *Wrong:* Michael is honest, capable, and ought to be promoted.
> *Right:* Michael is honest, capable, and worthy of promotion.
> *Right:* Michael is honest and capable, and he ought to be pro
> moted.

125

Wrong: Our firm is noted for its excellent reputation and because it treats the employees fairly.
Right: Our firm is noted for its excellent reputation and for its fair treatment of employees.

Wrong: Our office is well ventilated and with plenty of light.
Right: Our office is well ventilated, and it has plenty of light.

The following are some of the most common co-ordinate conjunctions:

accordingly	however	otherwise
also	likewise	so
and	moreover	so that
as well as	neither	so then
besides	nevertheless	therefore
but	nor	thus
consequently	notwithstanding	wherefore
either	now	yet
hence	or	

But. The conjunction *but* should be used to express a contrasting or an opposing idea, however faint the contrast or opposition; as:

You are young, *but* I am old. [*Not:* and.]
Albert is neat, *but* Henry has the better personality. [*Not:* and.]
I will go with you, *but* I must finish this work first. [*Not:* and.]

A *subordinate conjunction* is used to connect clauses of unequal rank or grammatical value; as:

Please type this letter *whenever* you have some leisure time.
Eugene acts *as if* he were in a hurry.
While we are about it, we may as well cover all the machines.
Since we are junior clerks, we must expect to do routine work

The following are some of the common subordinate conjunctions:

after	because	inasmuch as
although	before	in case that
as	even if	in order that
as if	for	on condition that
as soon as	how	otherwise
as though	if	provided (*not* providing)

since	then	where
so that	though	whereas
supposing	unless	wherever
than	until	whether
that	when	while
till	whenever	why

Being that. This expression is incorrect. Use *since* or *as.*

Since the ability to speak well is so important, I think I shall devote more time to English grammar. [*Not:* Being that.]
The caller entered; and *as* I was nearest the door, I greeted him. [*Not:* being that.]

Prepositions Misused as Conjunctions. *Without, except,* and *like* should *not* be used to introduce dependent clauses. Each of these words is a preposition and should not be followed by a subject and predicate.

It looks *as if* it would be a good day tomorrow. [*Not:* it looks like.]
It looks *like* rain. [This is correct. There is no following subject and predicate.]
Don't make any changes *without* telling me. [*Not:* without you tell me.]
You may not leave *unless* I give you permission. [*Not:* except I give you.]

Correlative conjunctions are conjunctions that are used in pairs. They must connect *like* combinations; as, two or more words, two or more phrases, two or more clauses. Some of the most common correlatives are:

both—and	not only—but also
either—or	whether—or
neither—nor	

Note that *or* is used with *either* and *nor* with *neither.*
Correlatives must always be placed *immediately before* the combinations they connect; as:

I need *both* the originals *and* the carbons. [*Not:* I both need.]
You will work for *either* Mr. Allen *or* me. [*Not:* You will either work.]
You will go *either* to the post office *or* to the bank. [*Not:* You will either go.]

Wrong: Thomas has *not only* received offers from the broadcasting company for his short plays *but also* for his advertising copy. [Correlatives here connect unlike combinations.]

Right: Thomas has received offers from the broadcasting company *not only* for his short plays *but also* for his advertising copy. [Correlatives connect like combinations.]

Assignment 1. ★ Select the correct word or phrase in each of the following sentences and give the reason for your choice.

1. We went to school, (and, but) we did not study.

2. She works (as though, like) someone (were, was) driving her.

3. (Being that, As) this was her first experience, she made many mistakes.

4. The office is tastefully furnished, (and, but) you may not like the color of the walls.

5. You may not borrow my eraser (without, unless) you promise to return it.

6. This stationery is not to be used for either personal (nor, or) general office purposes.

7. (Being that, As) you are my best friend, I am telling you first about the vacancy.

8. I wish I could type fast, (as, like) she does.

9. That order will not be carried out (unless, except) you give clear directions.

10. I tried to help, (and, but) she refused to let me do so.

11. You cannot succeed (except, unless) you try.

12. The letter was mailable, (and, but) it was posted immediately.

13. (Being that, Since) I like to work with people, I am in the sales department.

14. Neither radio (or, nor) newspaper advertising will promote such a poor product.

15. (Excepting, Unless) you speak distinctly, you will not be understood.

16. You will never retain a position (without, unless) you learn to be more respectful.

Assignment 2. ★ In the following sentences make corrections wherever necessary and give the reason for each correction you make.

1. Writing advertising copy is more interesting than to work with figures.

2. The machine was not repaired, and the work progressed swiftly.

3. That department store has neither a good stock of dresses nor hats.

4. She is one of those women who talk either too much or too little.

5. The girls spent much of their time in talking and idleness.

6. The executive told us that we should learn the vocabulary of the business and to keep a shorthand notebook of these vocabulary words.

7. Being that I cannot write shorthand, I must decline to act as secretary.

8. Neither the office boy nor the porter has emptied the waste-baskets.

9. Finding a vacancy and to prepare for it took some time.

10. You ought not to leave without asking permission.

11. You look like you are ready to go now.

12. She is a tall girl with big ears, and she has an upturned nose.

13. He said that he would bring me the papers, but not to expect them this morning.

14. I expected him to be angry and that he would scold me.

15. Yesterday I met the head salesman, and whom you have often mentioned.

Assignment 3. Write five original sentences illustrating the use of co-ordinate conjunctions, five illustrating the use of the subordinate conjunctions, and five illustrating the use of the correlative conjunctions. In each sentence underline the conjunction.

Requirement, Requisition, Requisite; Lend, Loan

One (requirement, requisition, requisite) you should expect to meet when asking for a (lend, loan) at the bank is that you have collateral to cover the amount of the (lend, loan). The person who asks any banking institution to (lend, loan) him money when he knows that he does not have the (requirement, requisition, requisite) sound credit standing is wasting his time. It would be a procedure comparable to making out a (requirement, requisition, requisite) for the moon.

Assignment 4. Write original sentences, using *requirement, requisition, requisite, lend,* and *loan.*

Assignment 5. ★ *Comprehensive Grammar Test.* This comprehensive test will enable you to determine how well you have learned your grammar. The following grading scale will apply:

Perfect:	No errors
Excellent:	1 to 5 errors
Good:	6 to 15 errors
Fair:	16 to 25 errors
Poor:	More than 25 errors

1. The bell had already (rung, rang).
2. She never (did, done) that before.
3. She (hanged, hung) her coat on the hanger.
4. John took Emma and (he, him) for a ride.
5. It was (he, him) to whom they referred.
6. I invited (he, him) and his wife for dinner.
7. He (don't, doesn't) seem to care.
8. It (don't, doesn't) matter.
9. Henry and she (come, comes) to the office daily.
10. He said that this was the coldest day he (ever saw, had ever seen).
11. I intended (to have shown, to show) him his error.
12. If I (was, were) you, I should accept the position.
13. I wish he (was, were) here today.
14. I (will, shall) be happy to see you.
15. I (should, would) appreciate an answer to my question.
16. When (can, may) I talk with you? [Permission.]
17. We (should, would) prefer to postpone decision.
18. The table was (set, sat) for the party.
19. The book has (laid, lain) on the table all day.
20. He has (laid, lain) down the rules for us.
21. His coat and hat had been (laid, lain) on the couch.
22. The data (was, were) assembled for him.
23. Every one of the girls (is, are) planning to stay.
24. The jury (were, was) selected quickly.
25. The jury (was, were) busy with their personal problems.
26. Everybody (has, have) a day from which (he, they) (date, dates).

27. Neither Peter nor Paul (are, is) able to go.

28. Neither Peter nor the other boys (is, are) able to go.

29. Each paper, pen, and pencil (are, is) to be returned.

30. This is one of the most interesting games that (has, have) been played this year.

31. (We, Us) girls shall be glad to work overtime.

32. Give the money to (we, us) girls.

33. Jane is a better stenographer than (he, him).

34. Each group must make (their, its) own rules.

35. It was (us, we) who were at fault.

36. It's time for you and (he, him) to go.

37. It might have been (they, them).

38. I was thought to be (she, her).

39. She thought me to be (her, she).

40. If I were (him, he), I should be more careful.

41. I had dinner with (him, he).

42. I had dinner with (he, him) and his wife.

43. I invited (she, her) to dinner.

44. I invited (her, she) and her brother to dinner.

45. They thought us to be (they, them).

46. Remember, this is just between you and (me, I).

47. (Who, Whom) do you think I am?

48. (Whom, Who) do you wish to see?

49. (Who, Whom) is that man?

50. (Whom, Who) did you bring?

51. Will you vote for (whoever, whomever) is nominated?

52. She wondered (who, whom) the next secretary would be.

53. Mr. Smith is the man (who, whom) you want to see.

54. (Who, Whom) do you think is the logical choice?

55. Your contribution should be the equivalent of one (months, month's) wages.

56. Your contribution should be the equivalent of two (month's, months, months') wages

57. Emma and Jane's town (was, were) flooded.

58. Emma's and Jane's typewriters (are, is) in good condition.

59. What do you think of a (judge, judge's) running for President?

60. There is no doubt about the (meeting, meeting's) being a success.

61. Senator Smith is a member of the (committee, committee's) making a preliminary draft of the platform.

62. The (applicant's, applicants') interview required one hour. (One applicant).

63. The (applicant's, applicants') interviews required one hour. (Two applicants).

64. Count on (him, his) being here.

65. Please return the book to (its, it's) place.

66. No (boy, other boy) is so well liked as John.

67. The company is well known for (its, it's) up-to-date methods.

68. The company brought its methods (up to date, up-to-date).

69. He is the (strongest, stronger) of the two candidates.

70. I am (really, real) sorry to see you go.

71. I feel (bad, badly) because of his illness.

72. He (pondered, pondered over) the problem.

73. He placed the book (on, upon) the table.

74. We must go (in, into) the board room.

75. I wish I could type fast, (like, as) she does.

76. You look (like, as if) you are ready to go.

77. She did not seem (to particularly care, to care particularly) where I sent the key.

78. No gift certificate is (too, to) large or (too, to) modest; no delivery problem (too, to) difficult.

79. And I believe you will, (too, to).

80. We (will, shall) hurry the book to you so that you can start planning right away.

81. I (would, should) be delighted to come.

82. What has a businessman like (myself, me) got to say about Christmas?

83. I (ain't ate, haven't eaten) in there for a year.

84. They never have (nothing, anything) good to eat any more.

85. He didn't leave (no, any) money.

86. He (didn't, hasn't) come yet.

87. A number of changes (is, are) to be made next year.

88. None of the men (was, were) assigned to tactical operations.

89. He would have liked him (to have been, to be) there.

90. The patient seems to be (some, somewhat) better.

91. The story made a strong appeal to both (she, her) and Frank.

92. The union is right in trying to negotiate an (entirely, entire) new contract.

93. She must (of, have) lost her memory.

94. He didn't leave (no, any) forwarding address.

95. This is the first time I (have seen, saw) her do it.

96. This is the worst weather I (ever saw, have ever seen).

97. The loser will probably be (I, me).

98. You probably have some friends (whom, who) you like to remember at Christmas time.

99. Mr. Smith made an arrangement with Mrs. Bowman and (I, me).

100. In any case, it is the individual voter, you and (me, I), (who, whom) is sovereign in this country.

PART III

Punctuation, Capitalization,

Abbreviation, and the Use of Figures

HOME EQUIPMENT MANUFACTURING COMPANY

200 River Street

Rochester 5, New York

5/14/53

Mr. Geo. Perry
1,500 South Pleasant Street
Chicago, Ill.

Dear Mr. Peary,

Thank you for your order of Sept. 29 for two Modern
Air Cons our home air conditioning unit. Our representative Tom Keith also informs us that you would like to
open an account with us.

As this is the 1st time that we have had the pleasure
of recieving an order from you we are following our standard proceedure and asking you to fill out the enclosed
blank Application for Credit.

As soon as we receive the requested information and
have made the usual inquiries you will hear from us. No
doubt you, yourself, follow this same proceedure.

If in the meantime you prefer to have us ship the Air
Cons with bill please so inform us.

We assure you that we are anxious to serve you and
we hope that you will become a regular customer.

Very truly yrs,

Credit manager

Do you think that the stenographer who transcribed this letter will have much chance
of holding a job? How many slips can you detect?

LESSON **29**

The Period

At the End of a Sentence. 1. A period is used to mark the end of a sentence that makes a statement (a declarative sentence) or that gives a command (an imperative sentence).

> We apologize for our delay in writing you.
> Be sure to cover your typewriter before you leave the office.

2. Condensed (or elliptical) expressions—such as answers to questions or transitional phrases—are often used to stand for complete sentences. If a condensed expression is declarative or imperative, it is followed by a period.

> No.
> Next, your complaint.

This use of the period should be distinguished from the incorrect practice of writing subordinate parts of a sentence—clauses, for example—as complete sentences.

> Please ship collect, as we do not wish to wait while you investigate the enclosed credit references. [*Not:* Please ship collect. As we do not wish to wait while you investigate the enclosed credit references.]

Following Abbreviations. 1. An abbreviation is followed by a period; as, *Mr., M.D., amt.*

2. If an abbreviation falls at the end of a sentence, only one period should be used.

> The order is being shipped today C.O.D.

See Lesson 46 for a full treatment of abbreviations.

In Decimals. A period is used to separate a whole number from a decimal fraction; as, 8.5%, $15.10. Lessons 47 and 48 contain a full treatment of the rules for writing numbers.

Assignment 1. ★ Copy the following sentences, inserting periods where they are required and omitting any that are incorrectly included.

1. Mr S S Kennedy, the efficiency expert, will begin his analysis of our office procedure on May. 1
2. At noon, then
3. The thermometer registered 34°F..
4. A last-minute demand for gloves was noted. With suedes and double-woven cottons wanted.
5. Please call before noon
6. Our furnaces operated at 98, 3 per cent of capacity last year.
7. This dress has been reduced to $16,75.
8. The safe deposit vaults close at 3 p.m..
9. The secretary waited. Because Mr. Rice was in conference.
10. Mrs. Hall belongs to the D.A.R..
11. Not now
12. On July 6 Mr Bryan E Ross resigned

After Figures and Letters Indicating Subdivisions. The period is used after a figure or a letter designating a division or a subdivision in an outline. If the figure or letter is enclosed in parentheses, however, no period is necessary.

    I. Duties
      1. Officers
        a. Secretary
          (1) Recording
            and so on

For Emphasis. Three periods are often used for emphasis or before displayed items, especially in advertising copy.

    Who's got all-wool coats right now? . . . Stamford's, naturally . . . and are we proud of them? . . . Each and every model . . . long coats, jackets, strollers . . . all types for fall . . . Come to Stamford's.

We can give you the name of every available prospect for your merchandise
   . . . identified by line
   . . . classified by purchasing ability
   . . . classified as to size of concern

Where the Period Is Not Used. The period is *not* used:

1. After roman numerals, unless they are attached to enumerated items.

Vol. I   Chapter I

George V   I. Aims

2. After display heads, such as centered heads or titles of tables, charts, and so on.

CHAPTER VI
FILING FOR THE LAW OFFICE

3. After items in tabulated lists.

Study the following machine parts in the illustration:
Carriage
Carriage release
Paper rest

Typing Hints. Two spaces follow a period at the end of a sentence, but only one space follows a period after an abbreviation within the sentence. No space follows a period used as a decimal point.

As punctuation marks in telegrams are now transmitted without charge, periods should be used to indicate the ends of sentences in the message instead of the word "Stop," which was formerly used for that purpose.

Note: For the use of the period with closing quotation marks, see Lesson 38; with parentheses, see Lesson 41.

Assignment 2. ★ Copy the following sentences, inserting periods where they are required and omitting any that are incorrectly included.

1. Skip Chapter I. and begin to read on page 10

2. Please quote us your best prices on the following office supplies:

> Office paste.
> Black fountain-pen ink.
> Ink eradicator.
> Rubber bands.

3. Chapter X. of the book contains some comments on King George III. and the American Revolution

4. Please let us know how many copies are to be shipped to district managers in these cities:

> Cleveland.
> Cincinnati.
> Pittsburgh.
> Buffalo.

5. She began typing at the beginning of Section II. of the report.

6. The first page of the report was headed:

Chapter I.
Your Job and Your Future.

7. Special value in handbags   suited to the businesswoman
also offered to teen-agers   large assortment of leathers
all popular colors.

Assignment 3. ★ Type the following portion of an outline in correct outline form.

II Records essential to the management of a small business include A Cash receipts and payments. B Credit sales and purchases. C Annual summaries, especially: 1 Profit and loss statement, which is essential: a For income-tax purposes. b For borrowing money. c. For analyzing management of the business. 2 Balance sheet, which reveals: a What you own (assets) b What you owe (liabilities) c What you are worth.

LESSON 30

The Question Mark

To Indicate Questions. 1. A question mark should follow every direct question.

What qualifications does the applicant have for the position?

2. The question mark is *not* used after an indirect question.

The personnel manager asked what qualifications an applicant should have.

3. If a sentence contains a series of queries, the question mark follows each query; the separate items, however, are not capitalized. (For an exception, see item 2 under "First Words," page 201.)

Who is to make the decision? the office manager? the advertising manager? the sales manager?

4. A short direct question that follows a statement is preceded by a comma and followed by a question mark.

You will bring the book tomorrow, won't you?

5. A request or a suggestion placed in the form of a question for courtesy does not require a question mark.

Won't you fill in the form at the end of this sheet and mail it at once.
May we have your reply by return mail.

To Express a Doubt. The question mark enclosed in parentheses is used to express doubt or irony.

Mr. Roberts joined their staff in 1925 (?).
The machine was guaranteed (?) for one year.

141

Overuse of the question mark in this way to indicate humorous or whimsical allusions should be avoided.

> *Unnecessary:* They have given us a brief (?) explanation of the reasons for the change.

Note: For the use of the question mark with closing quotation marks, see Lesson 38; with parentheses, see Lesson 41.

Transcribing Hints. A common transcription error is to omit the question mark. The best way to avoid this error is to form the habit of inserting the shorthand symbol for the question mark in the notes. Then the mark will not be overlooked when transcribing. The rising inflection of the dictator's voice will indicate that one is needed.

Two spaces should follow a question mark at the end of a sentence, one space if within a sentence. No space should precede a question mark at the end of a sentence.

Assignment. ★ Copy the following sentences, inserting question marks where they are required and omitting any that are incorrectly included.

1. When was that picture sold.
2. What is his business paper products leather products furniture
3. May we call and discuss the matter with you.
4. He asked how I knew it was so?
5. You won't forget to send us a quotation on 250 yards of binding, will you.
6. Where was the report made
7. Have you worked during summer vacation after school during the Christmas holidays
8. May we add your name to our list of interested students.
9. He asked whether there would be an opening for a typist?
10. Will you please send us your specifications by April 1?
11. The school was opened to girls as well as to boys in 1840 ( ).

The Exclamation Point

To Show Strong Emotion. 1. A sentence that expresses deep feeling, satire, or surprise should be closed by an exclamation point. In business, the exclamation point is most frequently used in advertising material, to make enthusiastic claims.

> It will soon be here! The newest, strongest home safe that we have ever designed!
> The disclosure regarding the secret transactions of X Company astonishes me!
> No loitering on these premises! This means you!
> Who ever heard of such a thing!

2. The exclamation point may be used immediately after a single word or a short phrase. The sentence following is punctuated in the usual way.

> Stop! You are using the wrong size of letterhead.
> Well, now! Where do we go from here?

If the expression is only mildly exclamatory, however, it is usually followed by a comma or by a period.

> Of course, we cannot take the risk.
> Why, there's no end to the maze.
> Yes. I have the latest report.

3. The exclamation *oh* may be followed by either a comma or an exclamation point, depending on the emphasis required. It is capitalized only when it starts a sentence. The capitalized *O*, the sign of direct address, is seldom used in business.

> Oh! What a relief!
> But, oh, so sad!

143

To Indicate Irony. Disbelief, sarcasm, or surprise may be expressed by placing an exclamation point, enclosed in parentheses, immediately following a word within a sentence.

That is a justifiable (!) criticism.

As with the similar use of the question mark, this use of the exclamation point should not be overdone.

Typing Hints. The exclamation point is made by typing the apostrophe, backspacing, and typing the period. On some machines, the backspacing can be omitted if the space bar is held down while both characters are typed.

Two spaces follow the exclamation point at the end of a sentence, one space if within a sentence.

Note: For the use of the exclamation point with closing quotation marks, see Lesson 38; with parentheses, see Lesson 41.

Assignment. ★ Copy the following sentences, inserting exclamation points where they are required and omitting any that are incorrectly included.

1. Congratulations The judges have awarded your entry first place in the recent home-building contest.
2. Fair warning To see these suits is to buy one.
3. Well we start tomorrow morning.
4. What an idea?
5. She claims he paid only $25 for a genuine ( ) one-carat diamond ring.
6. That's a likely story—but oh how interesting.
7. His important ( ) conference was with an extra cup of coffee
8. A candy bar for 2 cents
9. This is your lucky day. Today you can buy beautiful silver at half price.

The Comma

The comma is used to indicate the smallest break in a sentence. Its purpose is to insure absolute clarity of the sentence. Note, for example, how the commas change the meaning of the following sentence.

> Our Chicago office reports the main office is leading all branch offices in sales.
> Our Chicago office, reports the main office, is leading all branch offices in sales.

Note also how a comma prevents the misreading of the following.

> Just the day before the meeting was called off.
> Just the day before, the meeting was called off.

The chief uses of the comma may be grouped thus:

> A. To separate the clauses of a compound sentence
> B. To separate the items in a series
> C. To set off nonrestrictive modifiers
> D. To set off parenthetic and explanatory elements
> E. To serve miscellaneous purposes

A. To Separate the Clauses of a Compound Sentence

1. A comma should precede the conjunctions *and, or, nor,* or *but* when these words separate the principal clauses of a compound sentence.

> We have ordered motors from you before, and they have always given satisfaction.

> We must have your check by the 15th, or we shall be obliged to
> close your account.
> The paper is not durable enough for so important a document,
> nor is it of the right size.
> A machine may cost $75, but in a month it may be difficult to
> realize $50 on it.

In applying this rule, distinguish between a sentence containing
true principal clauses, such as the sentences just given, and a sentence having a compound predicate or a compound subject. Compound predicates and compound subjects are not usually separated
by commas.

> We wired him at his hotel and asked him to call you. [Compound
> predicate.]
> The correspondence with the Northwood Company ana that with
> the Dover Company are to be transferred to a new file. [Com-
> pound subject.]

2. If clauses are very short, the comma may be omitted before the
conjunction.

> We wired him but we received no answer.

3. If either or both of the clauses are long or if they contain commas, separate the clauses by semicolons. (See page 165 for examples.)

4. A comma is *not* used between clauses that are *not* joined by a
conjunction. A period or a semicolon should be used. Commas may
be used between exceedingly short clauses.

> Divide a depreciation charge by the cost of the asset. Express the
> answer as a per cent. *Or:* Divide a depreciation charge by the
> cost of the asset; express the answer as a per cent. (*Not:* Divide
> a depreciation charge by the cost of the asset, express the
> answer as a per cent.)
> *But:* I ran, I taxied, I flew.

Assignment 1. ★ Copy the following sentences, inserting commas
where they are needed and omitting any that are incorrectly included.

1. At that point the speaker paused and one could have heard
the proverbial pin drop.

2. Is this your own work or did someone else suggest it to you?

3. Mr. Horten, who has been our special representative in the East, has been promoted to the new position of sales-training director, but Mr. Andrews, who wrote the sales manual, really has had more experience for the job.

4. The bell rang; and the light flashed.

5. Connoisseurs regard our Italian olive oil as the finest on the market, all first-class food stores carry it.

6. Not long after the postman came and there was the long-awaited letter.

7. Many of the students will attend the play tonight, they like comedies.

8. The bus stopped; the door opened.

9. Elizabeth works as a waitress during the day, and attends school at night.

10. The girl at the switchboard and Miss Abbott in the sales division, plan to go skating after work.

11. A guided tour will follow the lecture, meet at the rear of the hall.

B. To Separate the Items in a Series

1. When the last member of a series of three or more items is preceded by *and, or,* or *nor,* a comma is placed before the conjunction as well as between the other items.

> The dress makes up well in flannel, gabardine, or twill. [Series of words.]
> Our offices are located in New York, in Philadelphia, in Boston, and in Atlanta. [Series of phrases.]
> Type the letter, sign it in my absence, and enclose a self-addressed stamped envelope. [Series of clauses.]

Note: Long clauses in a series, however, are better separated by semicolons.

> Goods must be transported to the place where they are to be consumed; sometimes they have to be stored for a time; often they must be rearranged into shipping units; and the good must be culled from the damaged and spoiled.

2. If the items of a series contain commas, then semicolons should separate each of the items.

> The population of the city is made up of the following groups: native-born, 75 per cent; English, 5 per cent; German, 10 per cent; French, 2 per cent; Russian, 2 per cent; all others, 6 per cent.
>
> The house at 10 Main Street will be ready for occupancy October 1; the one at 75 North Avenue, which requires extensive alterations, on December 1; and the remodeled garage on Summit Avenue, on February 1.

3. When *etc.* closes a series, a comma precedes the abbreviation; if the abbreviation occurs in the middle of a sentence, a comma also follows it.

> There is a temporary embargo on butter, milk, eggs, ice cream, etc., both in and out of the city.

4. No comma should follow the last item of a series unless the sentence structure demands a comma.

> The four periods of prosperity, crisis, depression, and recovery comprise the business cycle. [*Not:* The four periods of prosperity, crisis, depression, and recovery, comprise the business cycle.]
>
> A jurist, an economist, and an explorer, each renowned for his contribution to social progress, were the afterdinner speakers.

5. When *and, or,* or *nor* is repeated after each member of a series, no comma is needed before the conjunction.

> Can you point out the difference between a certified check and a cashier's check and a treasurer's check?

6. No comma is required when a series consists of two items only.

> Do you plan to carry your money in traveler's checks or in cash?

7. In writing a weight, a capacity, or a measurement, do not separate the individual items in the quantity by commas because the quantity is regarded as one unit.

> 5 pounds 4½ ounces   3 hours 50 minutes 4 seconds
> 3 quarts 1 pint   7 feet 6 inches

8. No comma is used before the ampersand (&) in company names; as, *Brown, White & Company.*

9. When several adjectives modify a noun, a comma should be inserted between the adjectives if each adjective modifies the noun alone.

> You have been recommended as a progressive, wide-awake dealer.
> We never offer shopworn, defective merchandise for sale.

10. If the first adjective modifies the idea of the combination of the noun and the second adjective, no comma should be used.

> Modern air-conditioned coaches add to the comfort of summer travel.
> Enormous administrative expenses reduced the net profit to 5 per cent.

Assignment 2. ★ Copy the following sentences, inserting commas where they are necessary and omitting any that are incorrectly included.

1. Enclosed is your bill for heat water electricity and gas for the past month.

2. Henry Ford with his development of assembly-line production methods Luther Burbank with his great contributions to agricultural and horticultural science and Thomas Edison the so-called Wizard of Menlo Park were giants in our industrial and scientific development in the latter part of the nineteenth and the first part of the twentieth century.

3. A liberal allowance of such characteristics as loyalty enthusiasm persistency etc. is requisite for successful salesmanship.

4. To win the indorsement of the textbook committee, the text selected must be set in easily read type be illustrated attractively and purposefully and be bound in a durable cover.

5. You may obtain your passport by making application to the local office, or by writing direct to Washington.

6. Courses in business English, advanced shorthand and transcription, advanced typewriting, and an introduction to bookkeeping, are required in our secretarial course.

7. The library subscribes to five weekly magazines and seven monthly magazines and four daily newspapers.

8. On his vacation trip in June, Mr. Reilly plans to cruise up the St. Lawrence, or to go by train to the Canadian Rockies.

9. Her latest novel is a beautifully written interesting story of pioneer life in the Northwest.

10. After July 1 the company will be known as Wallace, Bond, & Company.

11. Find the area of a circle the diameter of which is 5 yards, 2 feet, 5 inches.

12. The treatment is in line with the latest, scientific discoveries.

13. According to reports, Mr. Wallace is to become president of Wallace, Reid, & O'Conner.

14. The shipment weighs just 18 pounds, 10 ounces.

15. I have just bought a dark-blue broad-brimmed hat.

16. I think that gray streamline car is Mr. Norton's.

LESSON **33**

The Comma (Continued)

C. To Set Off Nonrestrictive Modifiers

Subordinate Clauses. A subordinate clause that *follows* the main clause is sometimes set off by commas, sometimes not, depending on the meaning of the sentence.

1. Nonrestrictive (also called "nonessential") clauses are set off by commas.

> Mr. Anderson, who has had twenty years' experience in the shoe business, will join our staff on January 1.
>
> We are sending you our new catalogue, which will give you an idea of the many new items that we are featuring.
>
> In the South, where temperatures are milder, there is no demand for the heavier line of coats.
>
> We received their bid this afternoon, after the time for filing bids had expired.
>
> The results of the test mailing are disappointing, as you prophesied they would be.
>
> I am glad to rewrite the ad, since you feel it is unsuitable.
>
> We suggest that you call in about two weeks, when we expect our new stock to be in.
>
> We are allowing you our usual discount, although the discount period has expired.
>
> We must have the job by the 27th, so that we can proceed with the balance of the work on the 1st.
>
> Sales in Chicago increased, while those in Los Angeles remained stationary.

2. Restrictive (also called "essential") clauses are *not* set off by commas.

> The salesman who joined our staff on January 1 has had twenty years' experience in the shoe business.

> The catalogue that we are sending you will give you an idea of the many new items that we are featuring.
> In sections where temperatures are milder there is no demand for the heavier line of coats.
> We received their bid after the time for filing bids had expired.
> The results of the mailing are as disappointing as you prophesied they would be.
> The ad has been rewritten since the new prices went into effect.
> We will write you when our new stock is received.
> I will wait while you check the report.

Each of the foregoing sentences resembles a sentence in the group illustrating nonrestrictive sentences. Do you see how the inclusion of a comma affects the meaning?

Note: Careful writers make a distinction between the use of *that* and *which*. Restrictive clauses are introduced by *that,* nonrestrictive by *which.* See the second sentence in the illustration of Rule 1 and of Rule 2.

3. An inverted clause—that is, a subordinate clause that *precedes* its principal clause—is followed by a comma.

> If you care to write me on this matter, I shall be very grateful indeed.
> After you have read the enclosed brochure, we are sure that you will wish to order the set.
> Because we have the same interests at stake, we can co-operate fully.
> When you decide to make similar arrangements, we will send our representative to see you.

Assignment 1. ★ Copy the following sentences, inserting commas where they are required and omitting any incorrectly included.

1. The report which did not come to me until long after the meeting proved to be without foundation.

2. If she comes to work late once more the supervisor will discharge her.

3. When the book is finally published his responsibility will be over.

4. We find it almost impossible to accede to all the sample-copy requests, that we receive.

5. I shall be very grateful, if you care to write me on this matter.

6. When a ship comes into view at sea the top of the mast appears first.

7. Evidently, she wished me to discontinue the subject, that seemed to embarrass her.

8. We are sure you will want the job, after we have explained your duties.

9. The circulation of these magazines which is enormous makes it possible to produce them cheaply.

10. She plans to go home, if he comes before six.

11. We find it almost impossible to accede to all the sample-copy requests which this fall are heavier than they have ever been.

12. If a person-to-person call is made the complete name of the person to be reached should be given to the operator.

13. Are you always the first to leave, when the bell rings?

14. We are sure you will wish to order the set, after you have read the enclosed description of it.

Phrases. *Participial and Infinitive Phrases.*

1. Nonrestrictive participial and infinitive phrases should be set off by commas.

> The former receptionist, knowing the job as she did, made many
> helpful suggestions.
> The customer, extremely irritated by the many delays in shipping
> his order, canceled it.
> We all then breathed a sigh of relief, the job having been com-
> pleted.
> The material is reversible, to mention just one advantage.

2. Restrictive participial and infinitive phrases should *not* be set off by commas.

> The clerk operating the switchboard has had several years' experi-
> ence in an office.
> The crop planted last spring promises to be unusually large.
> I regretted the decision after having made it.
> It makes me very nervous to see such waste.

3. Like an inverted clause, an inverted phrase is followed by a comma.

> Speaking before a special committee, the treasurer outlined his
> reasons for the expansion.

Encouraged by the excellent response to the ad, the advertising manager inserted it for a second month.

Having forgotten for a moment the previous unfortunate experience, he ordered a year's supply of stationery.

To tell you the truth, I'd forgotten the appointment entirely.

To meet the unusual demands, we have doubled our staff.

4. An introductory *prepositional* phrase may or may not be followed by a comma, depending on its length.

In the spring we plan to open a new store. [Short phrase.]

With the addition of the new wing, the house will cost more than we had planned. [Long phrase.]

Assignment 2. ★ Copy the following sentences, inserting commas where they are required and omitting any incorrectly used.

1. Starting from scratch he built a newspaper empire that was an important factor politically in the whole Southwest.

2. The record clerk discouraged by her inability to strike a balance was on the point of tears.

3. Throwing discretion to the winds he invested his entire personal fortune in the venture.

4. In keeping with this goal we have exerted every effort to produce the best goods possible.

5. The X Company looking forward to a greatly increased South American market requires several Spanish-speaking stenographers.

6. To hold our trade we must give better service.

7. Speaking quietly and effectively he persuaded the customer to buy the shipment.

8. The door leading into Mr. Ray's office was closed.

9. It is my sad duty to announce the resignation of our president.

10. The words appearing in red ink fairly shout their message.

11. You should have made three carbon copies to give each committee member a copy.

12. On Friday, we shall celebrate our tenth anniversary.

The Comma (*Continued*) ·

D. To Set Off Parenthetic and Explanatory Elements

Certain words or groups of words interrupt the flow of the sentence in which they occur; that is, they are not necessary to the grammatical completeness of the thought that the sentence is intended to convey. Such interrupting words or groups of words are known as parenthetic, or interrupting, elements.

Two commas are needed to set off an interrupting element when it occurs within a sentence—one before and one after the interrupting element.

1. A parenthetic, or interrupting, element may identify, or be a substitute for, a preceding word, phrase, or clause. Such interrupters may be words, phrases, or clauses.

> The employment, or personnel, manager has recommended that the applicant be employed. [A word.]
> We have turned the matter over to our advertising department, located in Cincinnati, for attention. [A phrase.]
> The most recent office bulletin, the one that covers rules regarding overtime, was duplicated on the new machine. [A clause.]

This rule applies to the punctuation of degrees, titles, and other explanatory terms following a person's name and to *Inc.* and *Ltd.* in company names.

> The most recent book on the subject is by John Carter, Ph.D., who is a former member of the faculty of Blank University.
> The course will be taught by Doctor Hubbard, professor of business education.
> Edward Garfield, Jr., was elected president of the board.
> Make the check out to William H. Seton & Company, Inc., please.

Exception: If an identifying term is unusually closely connected with the major term, so that the sense would not be complete without the added identification, no comma is used.

> I *myself* prefer to take dictation with a fountain pen.
> My sister *Eileen* works for the same company.
> The year *1952* witnessed great conflicts.
> The film pictures the life of Richard *the Lionhearted.*

2. Some interrupting phrases or clauses are inserted to qualify, contrast, or amend some part of the sentence. Such elements should be enclosed in commas.

> The incident, so far as I am concerned, is closed.
> When a person buys low-priced clothing, the effect, not the durability, is often the most important consideration.
> Reorders, after all is said and done, are what count.
> The actual percentage of loss is as large as, if not larger than, it was before the "improvement" was made.

Note: In sentences like the last one, the full intervening expression, not just a portion of it, must be enclosed in commas.

> *Wrong:* The actual percentage of loss is as large as, if not larger, than it was . . .
> The actual percentage of loss is as large as if not larger, than it was . . .

3. Names and other words and phrases used in direct address should be set off by commas.

> It is my privilege, members of the radio audience, to introduce . . .
> We regret, Mr. Emerson, that we still are unable to grant your request.
> No, sir; I just cannot do it.

Assignment 1. ★ Copy the following sentences, inserting commas where they are needed and omitting any that are incorrectly included.

1. The Empire State Express one of the finest trains in the country runs between New York and Buffalo.
2. Bob I'm afraid the plan won't work.

3. There is no more important question in this whole field of politics my friend than this matter of taxation.

4. Mr. Carroll one of Mr. Reed's most efficient auditors will be in charge of the audit.

5. The great hope of preventing or at least controlling future wars lies in the United Nations.

6. Miss Rollins the new transcription supervisor has very high standards.

7. Has the life of Alexander, the Great, ever been featured in a motion picture?

8. P. S. Hunt & Company Inc. announces with pride the appointment of its chief engineer Mr. Edward Murray Jr. as consultant for the new City Planning Bureau.

9. Her brother, Jack, was one of the new students in the course.

10. The address list must be checked very carefully not just inspected casually if the revision is to be of any use.

11. The correct form is *all right* not *alright*.

12. The new secretarial chairs are not absolutely necessary but most desirable.

Transitional Expressions. Some short parenthetic elements show the relationship of the thought that is to follow to the thought that has gone before. These elements may be single words, phrases, or short clauses. Commas should set off such elements.

Words. Some of the single words most commonly used in this way are:

accordingly	first	naturally	personally
actually	fortunately	next	respectively
afterward	further	nevertheless	say
again	hence	no	so
also	however	notwithstanding	still
apparently	inclusive	now	then
besides	indeed	obviously	theoretically
consequently	meanwhile	originally	therefore
conversely	moreover	otherwise	thus
finally	namely	perhaps	yes

Besides, we do not approve of their methods.
Finally, there is the matter of discounts.
This last merchandise, however, is not up to our standards.
So, put the enclosed card in the mail today.
Meanwhile, we must ask you to abide by our decision.
The Senior model and Junior model, further, are priced at $10 and $7, respectively.
The parcel-post charge will amount to, say, 27 cents.
Theoretically, this is the last shipment.

Many of the words in the foregoing list are capable of two constructions. When the word is a connective, as in the sentences above, it is set off by commas; but when the word is used as a simple adverb, no comma is required.

Theoretically sound, the plan is still impracticable.
However poor the service is, we feel it is better than none.
We are again faced with the problem of a depleted staff.

Phrases and Short Clauses.   Some of the phrases and short clauses most commonly used in introduction and parenthetically are:

after all	for example	in the first place
as a matter of fact	for instance	in turn
as a rule	for the most part	of course
as I see it	for the time being	of necessity
as it happened	I believe	oftener than not
as it were	if any	on the other hand
as you know	in addition	strictly speaking
at any rate	in any case	that is
at last	in brief	to begin with
at least	in fact	to be sure
better yet	in other words	to say the least
by chance	in reality	without doubt
by the way	in short	

Our reasons, in brief, are as follows: . . .
In the first place, we haven't enough stock on hand.
The difficulties are, in fact, almost insurmountable.
There is, in addition, the consideration of time.
We can lower the price and still make a profit, without doubt.
We can lower the price, I believe, and still make a profit.

Competition, as you know, is the life of trade.

To be sure, we prefer the new stock if we can get it.

Strictly speaking, this item should be charged to selling expense.

Notes: 1. For the punctuation of *long* enumerations introduced by such phrases as *for example* or *namely,* see Lesson 36.

2. See also Lessons 40 and 41.

Assignment 2. ★ Copy the following sentences, inserting commas where they are needed and omitting any that have been incorrectly included.

1. I am sure moreover that he is trustworthy.

2. The competition between the two companies as you know has been acute for many years.

3. The invention of radar was without doubt one of the most important developments in the history of aviation.

4. He is not I believe the Mr. Smith for whom you are searching.

5. The slight improvement we all realize is only temporary.

6. We cannot however send you the catalogue immediately as it is not yet off the press.

7. However gratifying our attendance may be at the next meeting it will no doubt fall short of the goal we have set.

8. Again there is the problem of space which was discussed at a previous meeting.

9. Charts I and II show the sales trend for the years 1952 and 1953 respectively.

10. No I cannot do that job so well as you think I can.

11. Personally I consider him unfitted for the job. To begin with his health is very undependable; in the second place he is inclined to be theoretical not practical.

12. Consequently he failed the final examination and had to take the course again.

13. He was, in spite of this failure a studious and intelligent young man.

14. The next time he will I believe be better prepared.

The Comma (*Concluded*)

E. Some Miscellaneous Uses

To Indicate Omissions.   Commas are used to indicate the omission of a word or words that are clearly understood from the context.

> We are gratified to inform you that in May our sales jumped 15 per cent; in June, 20 per cent; and in July, another 20 per cent.
> To err is human; to forgive, divine.
> Something has been added. What, we are not sure.

Repeated Expressions.   Commas are used to separate words or phrases that are repeated for emphasis. (See also page 191.)

> Never, never draw a check before filling in the stub.
> The recommendation is nonsense, nonsense, I repeat.

For Clarity.   A comma is often used to separate parts of a sentence that might be erroneously read together.

> Inside, the factory was fitted with all the latest equipment. [*Misleading:* Inside the factory was fitted with all the latest equipment.]
> In the file below, the letters are arranged geographically. [*Misleading:* In the file below the letters are arranged geographically.]

See also the illustrative sentences at the beginning of Lesson 32.

In Numbers.   1. The comma is used to separate thousands, millions, billions, and so on, in numbers of four or more digits,

3,874	35,500	$1,500,000

except in years, page numbers, house and telephone numbers, serial numbers, and decimal fractions.

the year 1953   Caledonia 3420
page 1230   policy No. 4658693
7450 Northern Boulevard   5.57206

2. Two unrelated numbers should be separated by a comma.

In 1952, 1,732 persons requested free samples of our soap.

Assignment 1. ★ Copy the following sentences, inserting commas where they are required and omitting any that are incorrectly included.

1. Margaret was enthusiastic about her job really enthusiastic.
2. There were 2264 employees in 1952 according to the report.
3. Halfway down the block was filled with a mob of curious idle people.
4. A subterranean garage accommodating 2000 cars is to be built at an estimated cost of $1000000 to $1250000.
5. We have found your index cards most satisfactory. Please ship us 3000 with round corners and 2000 with diagonal-cut corners.
6. The decimal fraction .6,875 is equivalent to the common fraction $11\frac{1}{16}$.
7. Henry will major in English; Edward in history.
8. In the first month of 1952 2642 tractors rolled off the assembly lines.
9. The index of the gigantic volume ended on page 1,560.
10. That is a splendid idea; a splendid idea.

In Letter Parts. *Dates.* In a date, the items should be separated by commas.

May, 1953   April 1, 1953   Friday, February 13, 1953

In a sentence, a comma also follows the year.

Please cancel our order of April 16, 1953, for two portable typewriters.

In Addresses. Parts of an address are separated by commas.

65 Court Street, Westfield, Massachusetts
270 Madison Avenue, New York 16, New York

Note that a comma does *not* precede a postal-zone number. In a sentence, a comma also follows the state name.

> If you will write to the sales office in Camden, New Jersey, you will receive promptly the information you require.

After Complimentary Closings.   A comma always follows a complimentary closing (unless the extreme open style of punctuation is used).

> Yours sincerely,

Some Miscellaneous "Do Not's."   1. Do not separate the subject and the predicate of a sentence by a single comma. This is one of the most common errors in the use of the comma. A *pair* of commas or none should be used.

> Her beautiful typing at once attracted the attention of the supervisor. [*Not:* Her beautiful typing, at once attracted the attention of the supervisor.]
>
> Their financial statement, in our opinion, warrants our increasing their line of credit. [*Not:* Their financial statement in our opinion, warrants our increasing their line of credit.]

2. Likewise, do not separate a verb and its object or complement by a single comma.

> *Object:* I am returning to you record for the plaintiff in the case of Jones vs. Smith. [*Not:* I am returning to you, record for the plaintiff in the case of Jones vs. Smith.]
>
> *Complement:* His references proved to be incomplete and unenthusiastic. [*Not:* His references proved to be, incomplete and unenthusiastic.]

Note: For the use of the comma with quotation marks, see Lesson 38; with parentheses, Lesson 41.

Typing Hints.   One typewriter space follows a comma unless the comma appears in a figure.

Assignment 2. ★   Copy the following sentences, inserting commas where they are required and omitting any that are incorrectly included.

1. The correct address for this customer is 2000 Hartford Road Baltimore 3 Maryland not Belmore Ohio.

2. Mr. Henry Ladd was employed as accountant by our company from June 30 1939 to January 1 1953 when he retired.

3. May we congratulate you again on this new achievement. Cordially yours. James T. Barton.

4. The end of the war was in August 1945 not June 1944.

5. Change the mailing list thus: Harold Jones 1684 Perry Street Davenport Iowa.

6. The order received in August 1952 was for 2000 cases not 200.

7. If you have the facilities in your plant it may be possible for you to take over a number of these printing jobs Yours sincerely David Wells

8. Knitting classes meet at 10:30 a.m. on Thursdays, sewing classes meet at 2 p.m. on Wednesdays.

9. That his record is beyond reproach, is taken for granted.

10. The serious nature of their complaint without question, necessitates an investigation.

11. The new employee appeared, nervous and high strung.

12. Notice that Pittsburgh Pennsylvania is spelled with an *h*.

Assignment 3. ★ This assignment reviews the rules given in Lessons 32-35, inclusive. Copy the following sentences, inserting commas where they have been omitted and removing any that have been incorrectly inserted.

1. Thank you Madam for your patience in waiting.

2. It is useless for us to discuss further the advantages of this publication as an advertising medium its high quality being a sufficient guarantee.

3. I was well acquainted with the architect, who designed this building.

4. Oleomargarine which is a compound of vegetable fats and oils is used by many as a substitute for butter.

5. Try to learn if you can when he left the building who was with him and where they went.

6. The annual meeting of the stockholders of the Somerset Gas Company will be held at the office of the Company at 29 East High Street Miami 29 Florida on Tuesday July 14 1953 at eleven o'clock.

7. Last spring we recommended you will remember that you order 2 gross of our popular hose.

8. When taxes are reduced these goods will be priced much lower as you will readily understand.

9. We will send our representative to see you, and to straighten out the matter.

10. The two companies co-operate fully, because they have the same interests at stake.

11. A business transaction to be truly satisfactory should benefit the producer the seiler and the customer.

12. It seems to me that these are the arguments, that should convince you of the soundness of the scheme.

13. Yours is a legitimate, though somewhat unusual excuse.

14. If as you imply by what you say in your letter the fault is ours you may rest assured that we will rectify the mistake even if it means a loss to us.

15. There is indeed no other explanation.

16. That is an example of dishonest scheming advertising. No reputable retail store would use such methods.

17. What day in the year 1945 do you consider the most significant? I, myself, think it was May 8.

18. You will find that the booklet contains a wealth of practical, building information.

19. Thousands of persons have discovered how easy it is to make payments with our checks and most important how much time is saved.

20. He complains that his secretary is slow, and inefficient.

21. A report made public by the committee June 2, shows gross inefficiency at all levels of the bureau.

22. The revised manuscript consequently, is not entirely satisfactory Mr. Jimsen.

LESSON **36**

The Semicolon

The semicolon is used when the parts of a sentence require a stronger mark of separation than the comma would provide.

In Compound Sentences. 1. The semicolon is used to separate the clauses of a compound sentence when a connective is not used.

> Mrs. Henry received a bequest of $50,000; her daughter received only $2,000.
> Do not make this investment in a hurry; sleep over the matter.

2. When one or both of the main clauses of a compound sentence contain one or more commas, a semicolon should separate the clauses. (See page 146.)

> Now that we are partners, Mr. Prescott, our interests are identical; and we can talk things over with great frankness.
> We felt no hesitancy in accepting your application for membership; but, although we have sent you two statements, no payment has been received.

3. When either of the clauses of a compound sentence is very long, a semicolon rather than a comma is used to separate the clauses.

> We feel somewhat embarrassed in making the following request of a customer who has been so prompt in paying his account for so many years; but this record is the very thing that leads us to feel that our last statement has either gone astray or has been overlooked.

4. The semicolon is used to separate the clauses of a compound sentence when the clauses are connected by a conjunctive adverb (see Lesson 26). Frequently used conjunctive adverbs are:

165

accordingly	besides	indeed	therefore
after	consequently	likewise	thereupon
again	further	moreover	when
also	furthermore	nevertheless	while
as	finally	otherwise	
before	however	since	

Incoming mail may contain checks and currency; *consequently,* open all mail carefully.

Please bring this customer's account up to date; *also,* prepare a statement of account as of June 30.

The samples of material you sent are of excellent quality; *however,* the designs do not please me.

Miss Hughes understands bookkeeping; *furthermore,* she can operate a calculating machine.

5. Usually, the *one-syllable* adverbial connectives *hence, still, then, yet, thus,* and *so* are not followed by a comma unless special emphasis is required.

Several dishes in the shipment were received broken; *so* we are presenting our claim for the damage.

Knowing yourself is the starting point in looking for a job; *so,* start taking inventory of your characteristics.

They arrived half an hour late; *yet* they heard most of the lecture.

Joan completed her temporary assignment; *thus* ended her first job.

Assignment 1. ★ Copy the following sentences, paying particular attention to the correct use of semicolons.

1. We are glad to offer you this opportunity to buy direct from the factory this will save you the salesman's usual 10 per cent commission.

2. The speaker had planned exactly what he would say consequently he held the attention of the audience and made his points.

3. The Japanese beetle is not especially troublesome in its native country however in America it is a very destructive insect.

4. On the other hand nearly 40,000 people are killed yearly as a result of automobile accidents, and the number injured runs into a still larger figure.

5. Our present policy regarding transfers has been criticized as unfair, so we are making a change in our rules.

6. Management recognizes the principle of economic regionalism, but many businesses are unable to apply that principle fully for the exceedingly simple reason that it is well-nigh impossible for any manufacturer to know really who buys at retail.

7. We know that you will be interested in this type of job, your training has prepared you for it.

8. It is tiresome to follow these directions, so I am using my own methods.

9. Accordingly we plan to order an additional 10,000 cards this year to meet the increasing demand, and we may place additional orders in six months if sales continue to be brisk and the export picture brightens.

10. It was unusually skillful defense of his actions, but, as you know, we had been prepared for something like that.

11. I know you have had difficulty in making the adjustment before, however, in this case I hope you will be able to get along with all the employees.

Before Words That Introduce an Explanation or an Enumeration.
1. A semicolon is used before:

as	for instance	that is
for example	namely	that is to say

when these words or phrases introduce explanations and enumerations. A comma follows the word or phrase.

Affinity for dyes is usually determined by the porosity of a fiber; for example, wool dyes well and evenly because the wool fiber has a high affinity for dyes.

The most common typing error is the striking of an adjacent letter for the letter desired; as, a k for an l, a v for a b, and so on.

2. If the enumeration occurs *within* a sentence, there are two ways of punctuating the sentence: (1) place a comma before the introductory word or phrase and after the enumeration; or (2) place a dash in both places (see also Lesson 40).

(1) Many industries, for example, the automobile industry, are important consumers of textiles in various forms.

(2) Many industries—for example, the automobile industry—are important consumers of textiles in various forms.

3. When the phrase *such as* introduces an enumeration, it is *not* followed by a comma. A comma *precedes* the phrase when it introduces an element in apposition.

> Many of the materials we require, *such as* aluminum, steel, and copper, are in short supply.

No punctuation precedes *such as* when it introduces a restrictive element.

> Materials *such as* aluminum, steel, and copper are in short supply.

Typing Hint. Only one space follows a semicolon.

Assignment 2. ★ Copy the following sentences, paying particular attention to the correct use of semicolons. Also correct any other faulty punctuation.

1. Place all the bills face up that is with the portraits on top.

2. An agreement not to prosecute a criminal for example a thief if he returns the stolen property is considered a contract against public policy.

3. It's easy to concentrate if you try, that is it's easy for some people.

4. Tell me how you use your spare time, for instance, tell me what your plans are for this evening.

5. One major problem arises in cases of this type, namely, the increasingly large turnover of employees.

6. A claim such as yours will be given favorable attention.

7. By using prepared foods such as frozen fruit juice and instant coffee breakfast can be ready in about five minutes.

Note: For the punctuation of semicolons with quotation marks, see Lesson 38; with parentheses, Lesson 41.

LESSON 37

The Colon

The chief use of the colon is to indicate anticipation; that is, it follows a statement that arouses a feeling of expectancy and is followed by the words that explain the statement.

Before Listed Items. 1. The colon is used before items that are listed. Sometimes such items are tabulated; sometimes they follow one another in sentence form. Such expressions as the following usually precede the colon.

as follows:	thus:
the following:	these:

The most important factors to be considered in selecting filing equipment are the following:
1. Durability
2. Safety from fire
3. Adaptability
4. Convenience
5. Price

To make neat corrections, the typist needs the following tools: a piece of blotter, a typewriter eraser, a piece of artgum, and an erasing shield.

Among the disadvantages of the co-operative are these: (1) The number of patrons may be limited if the co-operative sells only to member-owners. (2) The co-operative may be inefficiently managed. (3) If the members do not trade exclusively at their co-operative, the volume of sales will not be large enough to justify the maintenance of the co-operative.

Note: See page 172 for reason for capitalization of items following the colon in the preceding sentence.

2. Sometimes the introductory word or phrase is merely implied, in which case the colon is used just the same.

> There are three important styles: the book-unit, the rotary, and the cabinet types.
> For sale: two 8-room houses.
> Several questions must be answered in the affirmative: Will the principal be safe? Will the return be satisfactory? Will it be easy to borrow on the investment? Does the investment meet your needs?

3. If the sentence in which the introductory phrase occurs is a complete sentence, and especially if the phrase occurs early in the sentence, a period instead of a colon follows the sentence.

> Your cashbook balance may not agree with the actual cash balance for one of the following reasons, which are here enumerated in the most convenient order for rechecking purposes.
> 1. ....
> 2. ....
> 3. ....
>   and so on

Likewise, if the sentence containing the introductory phrase is followed by another sentence, a period, not a colon, follows the first sentence.

> If you do the family buying, keep the following rules in mind. By heeding them, you can help "stretch" your income. (1) Take a shopping list with you. (2) Examine each article carefully before buying it. (3) Consider the cost of upkeep and of repairs of substantial items.

4. No colon is necessary if a list is informally introduced. A verb usually precedes such informally introduced items.

> The duties of the general clerical worker usually include filing, typing, record keeping, and often opening mail.
> The parts of the business letter are the heading, the date, the inside address, . . .

Assignment 1. ★ Copy the following sentences, inserting colons where they are needed or substituting correct punctuation for any incorrectly used colons. Correct any other faulty punctuation. *From now on, be on the lookout for punctuation errors of all types.*

1. Essential secretarial traits may be mentioned here without comment tact initiative discretion courtesy and poise.

2. A stenographic job may be either of two things a waiting shelf or a steppingstone.

3. The three wage systems that are most commonly used today are the following: Most of the computing required in preparing payrolls under any of the systems is simple arithmetic.

    a. The day wage system.
    b. The straight piecework wage system.
    c. The differential piecework wage system.

4. During World War II the following foods were rationed sugar coffee meats fats butter canned fruits canned vegetables.

5. In this job you will need the following skills typing, shorthand, and the ability to use an adding machine quickly and accurately.

6. There are three rules to follow. Move quickly, follow directions, remain calm.

7. For Christmas I'm giving her: a cookbook, a pair of stockings, and a rhinestone bracelet.

8. On the desk were: pencils, a fountain pen, and a notebook.

9. We hope that you will give these questions your thoughtful attention before answering them.

    What do you plan to be doing in five years?
    How do you plan to accomplish your aims?
    What are you doing about it now?

10. He reads constantly, all kinds of books, travel, poetry, history biography, economics, philosophy, and psychology.

11. Straighten the paper in your typewriter in this way (1) move the paper release slightly to loosen the paper (2) straighten the paper using both hands (3) release the paper release.

12. For each book published the proofreader must read and release galley proof page proof foundry proof and sometimes plate proof.

Before an Explanatory Sentence. The colon is used to separate two complete sentences when the second sentence explains, illustrates, or supplements the first sentence.

> The printed folders are very unsatisfactory: the illustrations are dingy and the printing uneven in color.
>
> Everything is ready for the mailing: the letter has been duplicated, the envelopes have been addressed, and the circulars have been folded.
>
> Make no mistake about it: long after you've spent those extra dollars, you will remember the added pleasure your purchase gave.

Capitalization after a Colon. Usually the first word of a complete sentence that follows a colon is not capitalized because the meaning of the sentence is so closely connected. If the material following the colon demands emphasis, however, or if it is introduced as a formal rule, the first word after the colon may be capitalized.

> The idea is this: Practice the first row until you can type it smoothly; then the next row until you can type that smoothly also.
>
> Here is an easy way to multiply by 75: First multiply by 100 and divide by 4; then multiply the result obtained by 3.

Before Quotations. 1. A long direct quotation is preceded by a colon.

> A booklet distributed by the telephone company reads: "The human element must be considered in telephone operating— the public is human, the operators are human."

Short quotations are preceded by a comma.

> Just over his desk hung a sign, "Genius at work!"

2. No colon is used before an indirect quotation.

> He said that the stock market rallied this afternoon.

(See page 201 for rules on the use of capitals in quotations.)

After Salutations and Complimentary Addresses. 1. The salutation of a business letter should be followed by a colon.

Gentlemen:	Your Excellency:
My dear Mr. Dennis:	To Whom It May Concern:

Note that no dash follows the colon.

2. Likewise, in reports of addresses or meetings, the complimentary address of a speaker is followed by a colon.

Mr. President:	Members of the Radio Audience:
Ladies and Gentlemen:	Fellow Club Members:

In Expressions of Time and in Proportions. 1. The colon is used between hours and minutes when they are expressed in figures; as, 5:30 p.m. (In railroad timetables a period is ordinarily used instead of a colon in such cases.)

2. A colon is used to represent the word *to* in proportions; as 5:1.

Note: For the use of the colon with quotation marks, see Lesson 38; with parentheses, Lesson 41.

Typing Hints. In typed matter, either one or two spaces may be left after a colon within a sentence. Most typing texts instruct the student to leave two spaces after a colon.

No space precedes or follows a colon in an expression of time. One space precedes and follows a colon in a ratio.

Assignment 2. ★ Copy the following sentences, giving particular attention to the correct use of the colon.

1. Dear Mrs. Holm
   We are sorry that your account with us is not yet in balance.
2. This is a good suggestion plan your work before you start it.
3. The letter read, "Never have I read such irresponsible accusations. Please cancel my subscription at once."
4. Our plane is scheduled to leave La Guardia Airport at 8 30 tomorrow morning and to reach the Chicago Municipal Airport at 10 50, Chicago time.
5. The Christmas letter from the president to all the employees of the company concluded "It is a pleasure to commend a job well done and to thank the employees on behalf of their partners in the business, the stockholders and the management."
6. Do not confuse bookkeeping with accountancy the bookkeeper enters items in his journals the accountant studies those entries and makes recommendations on the strength of them.

7. He asked me, how long I had been waiting for the bus.

8. The ratio of three to two is also written as 3,2.

9. To the Stockholders of XYZ Company
   The year 1952 has marked a new high in problems for both management and the consumer.

10. No product better exemplified our slogan "More goods for more people at less cost."

11. Here's a suggestion for you make use of our investment service.

LESSON **38**

Quotation Marks

To Enclose Direct Quotations. 1. The exact words of a speaker or a writer are enclosed in double quotation marks.

"All the news that's fit to print" is the slogan of a famous newspaper.

The letter contained just one sentence: "We are now ready to discuss a new lease with you."

2. When the words of a speaker or a writer are indirectly quoted, they are *not* enclosed in quotation marks.

A famous newspaper is proud of its claim that it prints only news that is fit to print.

The letter contained just one sentence stating that they were ready to discuss a new lease with me.

3. It is not necessary to enclose well-known proverbs or very familiar quotations in quotation marks.

We have always been great believers in the theory that a stitch in time saves nine.

Ordinarily, familiarity breeds contempt—but not familiarity with Bond's Letter-Writing Service.

With Other Marks of Punctuation. *Period and Comma.* 1. A period is *always* placed inside the closing quotation mark, whether the quotation is a single word, a phrase, a clause, or a sentence.

The Weather Bureau's forecast for tomorrow reads, "Fair." [One word.]

He replied, "By tomorrow night." [A phrase.]

175

The secretary was told to select the stationery "that seems the most appropriate." [A clause.]

Somewhere near the end of the sheet, insert this sentence: "Do not destroy this instruction sheet; keep it for reference." [A sentence.]

2. Also, where a comma and a closing quotation mark fall at the same point in a sentence, the comma *always* precedes the closing quotation mark.

"The rate of production is increasing," Mr. Crawford said.

In the first paragraph, after the word "taxes," insert this statement. . . .

Assignment 1. ★ Copy the following sentences, giving particular attention to the correct use of quotation marks.

1. She replied, "I will call again tomorrow".
2. We're all as "busy as bees."
3. Send all letters air mail Mr. Wagner said.
4. Tom said I don't know how to pronounce that word.
5. The instructor continued Both Mary and Agnes have made exceptional records.
6. The stock market suffered another sinking spell yesterday, the financial sheet reports.
7. Our sales manager voiced his belief Our production is suitable for domestic trade only.
8. Some industrialists state that there is a definite hardening in current prices.
9. The letter began This is confidential.
10. The first sentence stated that the letter was confidential.
11. I asked him "where he was going."
12. Remove all unnecessary papers from the file was my instruction.
13. Miss Marshall asked me whether I could work overtime.
14. My favorite quotation is Laugh and the world laughs with you; weep and you weep alone.
15. The interviewer's first question was whether "I was a good speller."
16. Naturally, I answered "I think so".

Question Mark, Exclamation Point, Semicolon, Colon. 3. When the quoted sentence is a question, the question mark *precedes* the closing quotation mark.

> The letter began, "What of the future?"
> "What of the future?" the letter began.

When the *entire sentence* is a question, the question mark *follows* the closing quotation mark.

> Just what do you mean by "fiscal year"?
> Did Mr. Warner really say: "This report must be on my desk at four o'clock"?

4. Likewise, an exclamation point *precedes* the closing quotation mark when the exclamation point is a part of the quotation.

> "Attention, please!" boomed a voice over the loud-speaker.
> A voice boomed over the loud-speaker, "Attention, please!"

An exclamation point *follows* the closing quotation mark when the exclamation point is *not* a part of the quotation.

> They gave the timeworn excuse, "He's in conference"!

5. A semicolon or a colon always *follows* the closing quotation marks.

> The person or corporation that is being sued is known as the "defendant"; the one that is bringing the suit, as the "plaintiff."
> The following are usually listed under "Assets": Cash, Furniture, Equipment, and Accounts Receivable.

Assignment 2. ★ Copy the following sentences, paying particular attention to the correct insertion of quotation marks.

1. Does one say Three and four is seven or Three and four are seven?
2. The interviewer asked What experience have you had for this position
3. Call for Mr. Jackson cried the bellboy
4. The bellboy cried Call for Mr. Jackson.
5. Is this word spelled with one or two *m*'s she asked.

6. Can you type accurately the supervisor inquired

7. The receptionist asked Will you call again

8. Will you guarantee this watch for five years the customer asked

9. And this time no excuses the foreman shouted

10. He called Stop the show

11. The witness characterized the defendant as "emotionally unstable" but as we all recognized he was prejudiced

12. All these expenditures may well be included under the budget heading of "Welfare and Development" advancement health recreation charity and gifts.

Interruptions in Quotations.   Any expression, such as *he said,* that indicates the source of the quotation is punctuated as follows:

1. If the expression *precedes* the quotation, the expression is followed by a comma if the quotation is short; by a colon if the quotation is long or formal (see page 172).

2. If the expression *follows* the quotation, a comma and the closing quotation mark follow the quotation.

> "Careful spending is the keynote of today's customer habits," the sales analysis ended.
> "Responsible Real Estate Broker would like to invest in a small management business," the ad read.

In case the quotation ends with a question mark or an exclamation point, these marks are used before the closing quotation mark instead of a comma.

> The sign, "Dangerous Curve Ahead!" could not have been overlooked.
> "When will the group meet again?" he asked.

3. If the expression *interrupts* the quotation, in most cases the expression is set off by commas. Neither the interrupting element nor the continuation of the quotation begins with a capital letter.

> "Neither the manufacturer nor our jobber," ran the letter, "can supply the goods in time to fill the order."

If, however, a semicolon or a period would naturally fall at the point where the interruption occurs, the semicolon or the period is placed *after the interruption.*

"Our sales staff should be enlarged," he recommended; "our show-rooms should be modernized."

"Our sales staff should be enlarged," he recommended. "Also, our showrooms should be modernized."

Assignment 3. ★ Copy the following sentences, paying particular attention to the correct use of quotation marks.

1. Always make it a practice counseled the auditor in charge of the job to report exactly what you find.

2. When a bank certifies a check, says this book, it assures that sufficient money is on deposit to meet the obligation and guarantees payment of the check.

3. Where is the correspondence with Mr. Baker Betty asked.

4. It can't be lost she exclaimed.

5. Yours is an exacting job, Miss Mitchell, he interrupted, but you handle the details competently.

6. The report goes into detail on the Christmas sales campaign, the manager added, but the Easter promotion is almost neglected.

Omissions from Quotations. 1. Words omitted from quoted passages are indicated by three periods—four at the end of a sentence. Such omissions are called "ellipses."

Mr. Lloyd continues: "This backspace-centering method . . . would not be used . . . on other ruled forms."

2. When the omission occurs at the beginning of a quoted portion, the first word of the quotation is not capitalized unless it so appears in the original material.

The Office Manual states: ". . . an alphabetized list of names of persons or offices that are frequently called should be prepared."

Quotations Within Quotations. 1. A quotation within a quotation is enclosed in single quotation marks (typed by striking the apostrophe key).

Memo to Branch Sales Managers: "Please play up the following new slogan in talking with all prospects, 'It's not only fun to own a Miller but also a great distinction.'"

2. Should a quotation appear within the single-quoted matter, revert to double quotation marks for the inner matter.

> Our Chicago office writes us as follows in response to the complaint: "Our adjustment clerk reports, 'The mere fact that a package is marked "Fragile" is not sufficient to guarantee safe transportation unless the goods are packed carefully.' "

3. Note that the closing period comes inside both quotation marks. An interrogation mark or an exclamation point may fall between the single and the double quotation marks, however, depending on the circumstances.

> The stenographer asked, "Shall I mark this cablegram 'Deferred Rate'?"
> The correspondence supervisor returned the letter, saying, "I suggest adding, 'May we expect you tomorrow at ten?' "

Portions of Quotations. 1. When a few words of a comment are incorporated as a grammatical part of a sentence: (*a*) no comma precedes the quotation, (*b*) the first word is not capitalized (unless it is a proper noun or a proper adjective), and (*c*) only the exact words are quoted—that is, any rearrangement of the author's original words is not included within the quotation marks.

> So this is the way they "co-operate in every way possible."
> He said he would leave the decision to "one of the top men" in the company. [Probably the exact words were: "I shall leave the decision to one of the top men in *our* company."]

2. One pair of quotation marks is used for the entire matter quoted; that is, do *not* enclose each sentence of an extract in separate quotation marks.

> The bookkeeper gave us this suggestion: "In adding a long column of numbers, you may find it helpful to divide the figures into two or more columns. Add each section separately. Then add the two or more subtotals, to obtain the sum." [*Rather than:* The bookkeeper gave us this suggestion: "In adding a long column of numbers, you may find it helpful to divide the figures into two or more columns." "Add each section separately." "Then add the two or more subtotals, to obtain the sum."]

If, however, the sentences are not parts of a single extract, quotation marks should enclose each sentence.

Here are some slogans that have been suggested for our product: "We know they're the best. Don't you?" "The one-way product —from factory to you." "We haven't a better suggestion—there isn't any."

3. *Etc.* following a quotation should not be included within the closing quotation mark.

"We, the people of the United States, in order to form a more perfect Union," etc., is the beginning of the Preamble to the Constitution of the United States.

Assignment 4. ★ Copy the following sentences, paying particular attention to the correct use of quotation marks.

1. Notice especially the manufacturer's statement Our new radio-phonograph combinations feature a method of reproducing sound from records without "chatter".

2. The letter from the public accountant who audited the end-of-year financial statements closed with the customary paragraph "In our opinion the accompanying balance sheet and related statement of income and earned surplus present fairly the position of, etc."

3. The president of the club spoke to us as follows

"Fellow Members If we are to make a success of our program this year we must all work together." "Our aim which is widely known is worthy of our best efforts." "It is an aim to be proud of." "Let us work toward it hopefully earnestly and cheerfully".

4. "Yes, it's an interesting job she agreed. "But what do you think when Mr. Arnold calls you in at 4:15, gives you four long letters, and says "Please see that these are mailed today" '.

5. His piecemeal directions were, "Give this letter to Miss Brown". Mail this report first class". "Make reservations for me on the Mayflower Express tonight".

6. We have seen no evidence of their boasted "Twenty-four-hour service."

7. The following is an excerpt from the standard fire insurance policy: "If fire occurs, the insured shall give immediate notice of any loss . . . . . . make a complete inventory of same . . ."

8. According to the candidate, "his opponent could not defend any of his claims."

9. He replied that "their company is no longer manufacturing this machine."

LESSON **39**

Quotation Marks (Concluded)

Expressions Defined. Words and phrases that are accompanied by their definitions or introduced by such expressions as *so-called, known as, termed, marked, entitled, signed, the word,* and similar phrases are enclosed in quotation marks.

> This is an example of their so-called "hands-off policy."
> A contest in a court of justice is termed "litigation" by attorneys.
> The notice was signed simply, "The President."
> The words "principal" and "principle" are often confused.

Note: In printed matter, words that are accompanied by their definitions are frequently italicized instead of quoted. In typewritten manuscripts of material that is to be set in type, therefore, such words should be underscored, the signal for setting in italics.

Emphatic or Peculiar Terms. Quotation marks are used to enclose words that have some special significance.

1. Technical or trade terms presumably unfamiliar to the reader.

> Each letter in the series is "tailor-made."
> In order to correct the error, the photo-offset printer will have to make an entirely new "flat."

Technical or semitechnical terms familiar to the reader need not be quoted.

> ceiling price　　　　　gadgets　　　　　streamlined mode'

2. Humorous or ironical terms.

> This is "confidential"—to a thousand people.
> The lock is "guaranteed" to wear out in a year!

182

When you've tried every sort of "expert" with no satisfaction, call
on us.

3. Slang or poor grammar purposely used in order to lend color
or reader interest.

We are proud of our "top-drawer" trade.
Our machinery is just "hummin'" along.
That is a "tell-all" story.

4. Translations of foreign words.

Laissez faire means "noninterference."

Assignment 1. ★ Copy the following sentences, paying particular
attention to the correct use of quotation marks.

1. Young boys are not the only ones who have 'hollow legs.'
2. The forward part of a ship is known as the forecastle.
3. The symbol for per cent is %.
4. Notice that company is to be capitalized throughout this report whenever the word refers to our company.
5. It would be much better in this case to use the English trans-
lation of *modus operandi*—manner of operating.
6. Such misrepresentations are merely matters of opinion and
are considered "puffing".
7. This new locomotive will make it possible to eliminate 'push-
ers' up the westbound grade.
8. Such exhibitions of lack of self-control will hardly make him
solid with the chief.
9. *Nom de plume* means pen name.
10. Her best 'friend' started most of the rumors.

Titles of Publications

1. *Book* titles:

   a. In *letters*, either handwritten or typed, book titles are usually enclosed in quotation marks.

   "Business Mathematics" is available in several editions.

   b. In material that is to be *set in type* later, such as the manuscript of a book, an article, or an advertisement, the title
   should be underscored but *not* quoted.

2. Titles of *magazines, newspapers,* and *annuals:*

> *a.* In *letters,* these titles are simply capitalized.
>
> We are advertising our new lathe both in the Manufacturer's Record and in the Sun.
>
> *b.* In material that is to be *set in type,* magazine and newspaper titles are underscored.

3. Titles of the following type are also enclosed in quotation marks:

> *a.* Divisions of books, as titles of *chapters, parts, sections, lessons, tables.*
>
> Part II, "Keeping Fit," contains two chapters only. The first is "Your Health."

Note: The words *Preface, Contents, Index, Appendix* are not quoted.

> *b.* Articles, Essays, Lectures, Sermons.
>
> "Why Not Let Them in on It?" is an intriguing title for an essay. Doctor Graham's topic was "How to Measure a Man."
>
> *c. Poems, Plays, Musical Compositions.*
>
> Kipling's "If" bears many a reading.
> By many, "Hamlet" is considered the greatest play ever written.
>
> *d. Paintings, Sculptures.*
>
> Recent accessions to the Industrial Arts Museum are an oil painting, "Youth's Vision," and a statue, "The Welder."
>
> *e. Mottoes, Toasts.*
>
> "There's always room at the top," long my own personal motto, is also my toast to you tonight.

Names of Ships.   Names of ships are enclosed in quotation marks.

The "Normandie" had a tragic history.

Assignment 2. ★   Copy the following sentences, paying particular attention to the correct use of quotation marks.

1. Did you see the ad of the vacation cruise on the steamship Santa Clara? The ad was in Holiday and the Evening Sun.

2. Have you read The Tale of Two Cities? I asked Yes he replied and I enjoyed it tremendously.

3. Marian typed the Preface for the new novel Winds Blow North.

4. The chapter on Judging Cotton Fibers contains practical suggestions.

5. How do you like the title of my graduation essay. How I Expect to Apply My Business English Course in My First Job?

6. The one table, Airline Distances Between Principal Cities of the United States, is worth the price of the book.

7. Though first performed in 1885, The Mikado is still popular.

8. Mr. Reed sails April 8 on the Queen Mary and will return June 4 on the Queen Elizabeth.

9. I found the information I wished in this month's Today's Secretary.

10. The principal speaker on the program had the topic The Future of Advertising.

11. The chaplain will speak on What Does the Golden Rule Mean to You?

12. There's great truth in Poor Richard's maxim, Keep thy shop, and thy shop will keep thee.

13. Winslow Homer's Northeaster portrays the surf dashing on the rocky coast of Maine.

Typing Hints. 1. Quoted material that will run four or more typewritten lines may be arranged in either of the following ways:

a. Type the extract single spaced in a shorter line length than that used for the balance of the material. Do *not* enclose the extract in quotation marks.

b. Type the extract in the same spacing and line length as that used for the balance of the material, placing a quotation mark at the beginning of each paragraph of the extract and a closing quotation at the end of the *last* paragraph only. Change any quotation marks within the extract to single quotation marks.

The authors of *The Consumer's Economic Life* suggest the following rules for a buyer.

"1. Know the quantity and quality of the goods you are buying.

"2. Find out the price per unit, and buy according to your needs.

"3. Discuss matters of quality and quantity with the storekeeper, as it may be to your advantage to buy in large quantities if you have storage facilities."

2. In typing dialogues or conversations, each speaker's remark appears as a separate paragraph, even though the remark is very short.

"Which feature of our new refrigerator should we play up?" asked the sales manager.
"The built-in freezer locker," said salesman A.
"I think more persons are interested in the moist cold compartment," ventured salesman B.

But in plays or in court testimony, where the name of the person speaking is given, no quotation marks are required.

Miss Kern. A Mr. Shuman to see you. He did not state his business.
Mr. Tyron. Show him in, please.
Miss Kern. Just step in, please, Mr. Shuman.

3. In typing poems, place quotation marks at the beginning of each stanza and at the end of the last stanza. The quotation marks at the beginning of stanzas should "clear" the left margin—the first letter of the quoted line should align with other lines.

4. For the method of indicating omissions from quoted extracts, see Lesson 38.

5. In copying quoted matter, follow the style of the extract *exactly* in the details of punctuation, spelling, capitalization, hyphenization, use of figures. This rule is especially important in copying legal papers.

6. In copying brief letters and telegrams, follow the plan described in Paragraph 1, page 185. A quotation mark precedes the date line, but not the complimentary closing nor the signature line. The closing quotation mark follows the signature.

In copying a long letter, a better plan is to copy the letter on a separate sheet headed "Copy," thus doing away with the use of quotation marks.

7. No space should be left between the quotation marks and the material enclosed, nor between single and double quotation marks.

8. In typing a list, any quoted items should "clear" the left margin.

Did you receive our designer's sample color schemes—two for your living room and three for your bedroom? [Sentence requires a question mark.]

What a gift for a bride—or for yourself! [Sentence requires an exclamation point.]

2. When the material that is set off by dashes within a sentence requires either a question mark or an exclamation point, that mark is retained before the second dash. (No other marks are ever retained.)

Their cashier—what did you say his name is?—entered an incorrect total on the deposit slip.

Here are pure-silk ties—yes, think of it!—for as little as $2.50.

3. No other mark of punctuation is used before the opening dash.

Introducing Enumerations or Illustrations. 1. The dash may be used *instead of a semicolon* before certain words or phrases that introduce an enumeration, an explanation, or an illustration. (See page 167.)

When you have complicated tabulation jobs—for example, payrolls, personnel analyses, market surveys, property records—call on us.

Cash transactions include cash receipts—that is, cash taken in—as well as cash disbursements—that is, cash paid out.

2. The dash is often used *instead of a colon* when the introductory word is implied only.

The box for petty cash contains coins of all denominations—pennies, nickels, dimes, quarters, and half dollars.

Department stores are so called because they are divided into various departments—men's clothing, household furniture, yard goods, jewelry, and many others.

It is far wiser to eat good plain food—plenty of fruit, vegetables, and dairy products—than to follow diet fads or seek health in capsules or bottles.

This use of the dash is especially common in advertising and sales letters, for enumerating the qualities of merchandise.

Do you want to know more about your camera—how to take better pictures, what's new in equipment and techniques?

All the style features of the fall season—the new sleeve, the latest drape, the correct skirt length—all in one model.

Assignment 1. ★ Copy the following sentences, paying particular attention to the correct use of the dash. Also correct any other faulty punctuation you notice.

1. She typed the report and what a long report it was, too,—in less than an hour.

2. Check your tally of bills by counting them and adding them as you count 20, 40, 60 and so on until you have completed the package.

3. Each of the words omitted and there are several is most important.

4. Which type of money order do you mean postal express or telegraph?

5. It is often said I am not sure how true the statement is that the real music lovers are found in the top balcony of the opera house.

6. In order to do actuarial work that is work pertaining to the calculation of insurance risks a person should have special training in mathematics.

7. We have bargains in every department notions linens accessories china.

8. He likes all sports fishing hunting golf tennis skiing.

9. We hope to visit many foreign cities, London, Paris, Rome, to mention a few.

10. It is the love of learning, or is it the love of good grades,—that marks the real student.

For Summarizing Preceding Particulars. The dash is used before a statement that summarizes preceding details. Such statements are usually introduced by *all* or *these*.

The plain weave, the twill weave, and the satin weave—these are the three basic weaves for fabrics.

The monotonous checking operations, the tiresome copying and recopying, the constant addition of new material—all were forgotten when the finished report was so enthusiastically received.

Indicating an Abrupt Break or a Repetition. 1. A dash is used to show a break in thought or an afterthought. Such sentences occur often in advertising letters.

On the other hand, the budget of the purchasing department shows—but we won't go into that now.

He just walked in and asked for an increase in salary—and got it.

2. The dash is used to indicate hesitancy, faltering speech, or stammering. Such sentences are found chiefly in reports of conversations or of speeches.

Yes, I think I should like to go—in fact, I know I should—when do we start?

3. A word or phrase that is repeated for emphasis may be set off by a dash. (See also page 160.)

Sam, you've made a fine record—a very fine record, indeed.

"Early to bed and early to rise makes a man wealthy, healthy, and wise"—wise if his rising brings him to Smith's.

Indicating Omissions. A long dash (made by typing three or four hyphens) is used to indicate the omission of words or parts of words that are undesirable to print in full, as in confidential correspondence.

I am told by Mr. S——— that the C——— Company will reorganize after January 1.

Before Name of Author of a Quotation. A dash is used before the credit line (name of an author, title of the work, or both) that follows a direct quotation.

The many values of business law to the student who plans a business career are of equal significance in the lives of all students, irrespective of the courses of study followed.—R. *Robert Rosenberg*

The business of being a consumer is as important as your pocketbook.—*The Consumer's Economic Life*

The credit line may be dropped below the extract.

'Tis education forms the common mind;
Just as the twig is bent the tree's inclined.
Alexander Pope

Typing Hint. 1. The dash is made by striking the hyphen twice, with no space before, between, or after the hyphens.

2. Place the dash at the end of a line rather than at the start of a new line.

Assignment 2. ★ Copy the following sentences, paying particular attention to the correct use of the dash.

1. Canning drying smoking pickling freezing all are methods of preserving food.

2. "There is no inborn knowledge about human nature any more than there is about chemistry or bookkeeping." *Practical Business Psychology.*

3. Her talk her constant talk distracted us all.

4. Typing and shorthand these are the two basic skills for the office worker.

5. I'm sure you'll find her a charming girl charming and very pretty, too.

6. The train leaves from the lower level of the Grand Central Station from the lower level notice.

7. Try it just once! that's all we ask Mr. Scott.

8. The device is very light,—it weighs only 5 ounces.

9. Mr. King added and bluntly I must confess that he was 'terribly anxious' about the whole matter.

10. "The American system of law, founded on the Constitution of the United States, is patterned after the system used in England". *The Legal Secretary*

11. Through the "grapevine", I have learned that Miss C— will leave the Company on January 1.

12. The house is worth about let me see I should say $10,000.

LESSON **41**

Parentheses

With Explanatory Matter. The chief use of parentheses is to enclose matter that is introduced in a sentence or in a paragraph by way of explanation.

Lessons 34 and 40 described the use of commas and dashes for enclosing certain types of explanatory matter. The third method of enclosing such matter—by the use of parentheses—should be chosen when the explanation or comment is independent of the chief thought of the sentence; that is, when it could be omitted without affecting the essential meaning of the passage.

> The person named in a will by the testator (the person who made the will) to carry out its provisions is known as the "executor."
>
> At the top of the second page of a typewritten letter, type the first line of the inside address, the date (month abbreviated), and the page number.
>
> Portland (Maine) reports a low temperature record for this date.

For References. 1. Parentheses are used to enclose the name of an authority for a statement.

> The population of the United States has grown from a total of 3,929,214 in 1790 to a total of 150,697,361 in 1950. (U. S. Bureau of the Census.)
>
> Good will: The favor or advantage in the way of custom which a business has acquired beyond the mere value of what it sells. (Webster.)

2. References and directions are enclosed in parentheses.

> The steps in the retail selling process have already been discussed (see page 57).

Insert the carbon pack in your machine (be sure that paper edges are even) and start typing on line 10.

For Confirming Figures. In legal work, and sometimes in financial work, parentheses are used to enclose figures that verify a spelled-out number. (See page 226 for illustrations of this rule.)

In Enumerated Items. 1. Figures or letters used to enumerate items that are arranged in sentence form should be enclosed in parentheses.

> Mark the carbons as follows: (1) for the department ordering the material; (2) for the Receiving Department, for checking when the material arrives; (3) for the Bookkeeping and Accounting Department.
>
> The new Office Manual should include regulations on: (a) office hours, (b) vacations, (c) absences, (d) overtime.

2. Parenthetically enclosed letters and figures are also used before certain indented steps in outlines. No period follows the closing parenthesis mark in this case. (See page 138 for an illustration of an outline.)

Occasionally when there are many gradations in an outline, a single parenthesis mark (the closing one) may follow a letter or a number in order to provide another "level" of division, thus:

$$1. \ldots\ldots\ldots\ldots\ldots$$
$$a) \ldots\ldots\ldots\ldots$$
$$(1) \ldots\ldots\ldots$$
$$(a) \ldots\ldots\ldots$$

and so on

Assignment 1. ★ Copy the following sentences, inserting parentheses where they are required and correcting any faulty punctuation you notice.

1. The bank may refuse to honor pay the check when it is presented for payment.

2. The following topics will be discussed: 1 the population 2 the political party in control 3 the recent bond amendments.

3. A foreclosure is a proceeding which bars or extinguishes a mortgagor's right of redeeming a mortgaged estate. Webster.

4. Wherefore, plaintiff demands judgment against defendant in

the sum of two hundred dollars $200, together with the costs of this action.

5. This food has an alkaline nonacid reaction in the body.

6. The check for one thousand dollars $1,000 was cashed after the treasurer had indorsed it.

7. His intransigence (uncompromising attitude—stood in the way of his making friends easily.

8. The speaker stressed three points: 1 the importance of the Y.M.C.A. to the individual 2 the importance of the Y. to the community and 3 the importance of the Y. in promoting world understanding and peace.

9. If you wish to make your language effective, you will have to train and exercise your judgment in choosing one good word after another. (Clarence Stratton.)

10. Please fill out the card do not write in the ruled box and return it in the enclosed envelope.

With Other Marks of Punctuation. *Parentheses Within a Sentence.* If a sentence requires punctuation at the point where a parenthetical remark is inserted, the following rules apply.

1. No mark of punctuation is ever inserted *before* the opening mark of parenthetically enclosed material that occurs within a sentence.

> Because of the delay (they claim it was unavoidable), we are much embarrassed. [*Not:* Because of the delay, (they claim it was unavoidable) we are much embarrassed.]

2. A comma, a semicolon, or a colon, as the case may require, is inserted *after* the closing parenthesis mark.

> If you will call before eleven tomorrow (Main 7800), we shall be able to make a definite appointment for you.
> Much as we should like to do so, we cannot consider your recommendation until after July 1 (the beginning of our fiscal year); therefore, please write us again after that time.
> Please select one of the following colors (they are all that the bindery has to offer): gray, blue, red.

3. If the expression enclosed in parentheses is a question or an exclamation, the question mark or the exclamation point precedes the closing parenthesis mark.

At this point I recommend (do you follow me?) that we revert to our old policy.
The task before us (and it's some task!) is clear.

4. The first word of the parenthetical material is capitalized only if it is a proper noun, as in the first sentence illustrating Rule 2. The first word is not capitalized even if the enclosed material is a complete sentence. See the last sentence illustrating Rule 2, and the two sentences illustrating Rule 3.

Parenthesis at End of Sentence.   1. When a parenthetical remark that falls at the end of a sentence is part of the sentence, the closing punctuation is placed *after* the closing parenthesis mark.

We specialize in up-to-date office equipment: desks, chairs, tables, files (all makes).
Would you be interested in our introductory offer of twelve treatments for $25 (regularly $3.50 a treatment)?
Only $5 (tax included)!

Should the parenthetical matter at the end of a sentence demand an exclamation point or an interrogation point, that point is placed inside the closing parenthesis and a closing sentence punctuation mark is placed outside.

I was delighted to receive an increase in salary (and it was retroactive to January 1!).
They have moved to Chester, Pennsylvania (or is it Vermont?).

2. If the matter follows a completed sentence—

a. The parenthetical matter begins with a capital and closes with its own closing punctuation mark.
b. The sentence preceding the parenthetical matter ends with its own closing punctuation mark.
c. No further punctuation follows the closing parenthesis mark.

No further action was taken on the Cass matter. (See the enclosed annual report for details.)

Typing Hints.   1. Opening parenthesis mark.

a. After this mark—no space.
b. Before this mark: one space when the parenthetic material

comes *within* a sentence; two spaces when the parenthetic
matter follows a sentence and starts with a capital and closes
with its own sentence punctuation.

2. Closing parenthesis mark.

   a. Before this mark—no space.

   b. After this mark: one space when the parenthetic matter
comes within a sentence; two spaces when the parenthetic
matter is itself a complete sentence and another sentence
follows.

Brackets

Brackets are not used extensively in business correspondence; but
they are sometimes required in reports or manuscripts, especially in
reports of meetings. The chief use of brackets is for enclosing a correction or an insertion in a quoted extract.

> "The ship carried 550 men, women, and children [press services
> put the number at 800 to 900] from various ports."
> I'm not going to begin my speech with a story about two Irish-
> men. [Laughter.]

Typing Hint. The typewriter keyboard carries no character for
the bracket. If a piece of typewritten work demands brackets, the
best plan is to leave a space at the points where the characters should
appear and then insert the brackets by pen after the paper has been
removed from the machine.

Assignment 2. ★ Copy the following sentences, giving special attention to the correct use of parentheses.

1. For reliable news bulletins, listen to Edward Brand, newscaster
on WXRQ, (1200 on your dial) at 9:30 p.m. every day except
Saturday.

2. Market quotations today include lamb chops, (shoulder) 95
cents; beans, (snap) 25 cents a pound; and oranges, (Florida) 50
cents for 5 pounds.

3. Beginning June 1, the World Airline offers the following new
flights: (nonstop) 4 to Los Angeles, California, 2 to San Francisco,
California, 2 to St. Louis, Missouri and 10 to Chicago, Illinois.

4. On legal documents not more than one letter should be erased in the written-out form of a sum of money (as, "four hundred dollars.")

5. Many times during the day the bookkeeper will be required to pay out sums that are too small to be handled by check. (Checks should not, as a rule be issued for amounts under $1).

6. Mr. Clark has expressed a preference for Model A-22 (Doesn't he mean A-202)?

7. I don't need to remind you ladies and gentlemen of the outstanding contribution that Mr. Thomas has made to this company. You are all well aware of it Great applause

8. The store repaired my radio free of charge (can you believe it)

9. Now it's my pleasure and it's a great personal pleasure! to introduce Senator Cook.

The Apostrophe

In Forming Possessives. The most important use of the apostrophe is for forming the possessive case of nouns and certain pronouns. These rules were given in Lesson 24.

In Contractions. The apostrophe is used to indicate contractions —shortened forms of one or two words; as, *nat'l* for *national, don't* for *do not,* and *o'clock* for *of the clock.*

The apostrophe must be placed at the exact place where letters have been omitted (*aren't,* not *are'nt*), and no period should be placed after a contraction (unless the contraction comes at the end of the sentence).

The same shortened form is sometimes treated as an abbreviation and as a contraction (for example, *dept.* and *dep't*). The abbreviated form is usually preferred, for it is easier to type a period than to shift for an apostrophe.

Contractions are used most frequently in advertising matter and in informal writing. They are not suitable for dignified correspondence and writing.

Some words formerly written with apostrophes are now recognized as complete words; for example, *phone, cello.*

In Forming Plurals. The apostrophe is used to form the plurals of letters, figures, symbols, and words used as words. (See Lesson 17.)

In Coined Verbs. Sometimes unusual verbs are coined from letters or abbreviations. The past tense and the present participle of such verbs are formed by adding an apostrophe and *d* and *ing,* respectively, to the verb.

O.K., O.K.'d, O.K.'ing
X out, X'd out, X'ing out

cap., cap.'d, cap.'ing

Omission of Figures. The apostrophe is used to indicate the omission of the first figures of a date; as '53 (for *1953*).

As a Single Quotation Mark. See Lesson 38 for the use of single quotation marks.

Typing Hint. *No space* precedes an apostrophe that appears within a word or at the end of a word. A space follows the apostrophe only when the apostrophe comes at the end of a word that is within a sentence.

Assignment. ★ Copy the following sentences, inserting apostrophes wherever they are required.

1. The cashier said, "Lets divide the coins evenly."
2. But then, after all, its not likely that shell go.
3. At Miss Conovers request we are mailing you a circular describing our new steam iron.
4. Her handwriting is very illegible because she never crosses her ts or dots her is.
5. I shouldnt have received this invitation, for Im not a member of the class of 50 nor was I affiliated with the Mens Club.
6. The 8s and 3s on this page are blurred.
7. The childrens department is on the second floor and the girls on the third.
8. The special shipment should have gone out last night, for Mr. Spencer OKd it yesterday afternoon.
9. He picked up the 'phone and dialed Marvins number.
10. Do you often visit at your grandfathers home?
11. Do'nt forget to call me before you leave.
12. Its not important to be first, but it is important to be right.

LESSON **43**

Capitalization

There are two fundamental reasons for capitalizing words: (1) to emphasize them, and (2) to add to the clarity of the material in which the words occur.

Advertising material carries a much larger proportion of capitalized words than does ordinary business correspondence because of the desire to make certain words and features as emphatic as possible.

> Just ask for our Saddle-stitched Strap Oxford with Ribbed Rubber Sole.

Legal matter also capitalizes many words that would not be capitalized in ordinary correspondence. (See page 212.)

It is impossible to include rules that will cover every problem of capitalization, but the following rules cover most of the problems that arise in the business office. It should be remembered that authorities differ on certain rules of capitalization. The business student, however, should know and be able to apply one set of rules consistently.

First Words. The first word of each of the following types of material should be capitalized: (1) sentences, including quoted sentences; (2) independent questions within other sentences; (3) groups of words used as sentences; (4) lines of poetry; (5) items in outlines.

> (1) Many of our most successful businessmen started out as office boys.
> The sales manager said, "Your excellent sales approach won favorable comment."

Note: Indirect quotations are not capitalized.

> The sales manager said that his excellent sales approach won favorable comment.

(2) I am faced with a real problem, Is it wise to change jobs at this time?

(3) Indeed, yes.

(4)   Be noble! and the nobleness that lies
In other men, sleeping, but never dead,
Will rise in majesty to meet thine own.

(5) See page 138 for an example.

Proper Nouns and Adjectives. A proper noun or adjective—that is, the name of a particular person, place, or thing, or an adjective referring to that name—is capitalized.

Nouns	*Adjectives*
North America	North American
Lent	Lenten
Elizabeth	Elizabethan

1. Popular descriptive names that are used in place of actual names of persons or places are capitalized.

> the Great Emancipator (Lincoln)
> the Wizard of Menlo Park (Thomas A. Edison)
> the Garden State (New Jersey)
> the Sunshine City (St. Petersburg, Florida)
> the Twin Cities (St. Paul and Minneapolis, Minnesota)

2. Certain names are no longer identified with the original proper names from which they were derived—that is, they have acquired a common-noun meaning. Such derived nouns are not capitalized.

bessemer steel	mason jar
bunsen burner	murphy bed
georgette crepe	morris chair
klieg lights	wilton rug

3. Words that are ordinarily common nouns are sometimes capitalized when they refer to specific persons or things.

> We are going to California by way of the Canal. [Meaning the Panama Canal.]

The policy of the Club in this matter is consistent.

In all its fifty years, the Company has not lost an executive by resignation.

We take pleasure in recommending you for membership in the Association.

Assignment 1. ★ Copy the following sentences, capitalizing all words that should be capitalized.

1. before you decide, answer this question honestly, "what would i do under these circumstances?"

2. can you tell me who it was who was known as the great dissenter?

3. we have just received some interesting new patterns in china and a full line of morocco leather goods.

4. you must begin to work with plaster of paris immediately because it hardens rapidly.

5. not if i can help it!

6. this newspaper is a member of the associated press.

7. the association voted to sponsor the annual harvest festival.

8. the company takes pleasure in announcing that employees will receive their usual christmas bonus.

9. kansas is known as the sunflower state.

10. only you can answer the question, is it worth taking a chance?

11. breathes there a man, with soul so dead,
    who never to himself hath said,
    "this is my own, my native land!"

Personal Names. Special problems of capitalization arise in some personal names.

1. The prefixes *O'* and *Mc* are always followed by a capital letter without extra spacing.

O'Neil   McDermott

The prefix *Mac* may or may not be followed by a capital, according to the style used by the owner of the name.

MacNamara   Macmillan

2. When foreign names begin with *d, da, de, della, di, du, la,*

le, van, von, the elements are capitalized if only the surname is used: as *Du Pree, Le Bron, Von Thaden.*

When a given name or a title precedes the surname, the elements are *not* capitalized; as *Alberto de Lara, Mademoiselle la Salle, Heinrich von Berg.*

Note: Some persons having names of this type do not adhere to these general rules. In such cases, of course, the owner's preference is followed.

Personal Titles. 1. Professional, business, executive, civic, military, religious, and family titles *preceding* personal names are capitalized.

Professor Edward M. Seton	Chairman Graham
Chief Justice Earl Warren	Captain John H. Willard
Senator J. William Fulbright	The Reverend Alan L. Wright
Commissioner George A. Arkwright	Aunt Ellen

2. When these titles *follow* names, however, the following rules apply:

a. In the inside address of a letter, and on an envelope, a title following a name is capitalized.

> Mr. Paul C. Owens, Comptroller
> Wells Manufacturing Company
> Atlanta 8, Georgia

b. Titles of high Government officials and of Congressmen are capitalized when they follow a name.

> Andrew W. Mellon, Secretary of State under three Presidents, was a patron of the arts.

Titles of Government officials of lesser rank and titles of state, county, or city officials are not usually capitalized when they follow a name.

> Walter F. Murray, mayor of Dunkirk, said that he had been advised . . .
>
> . . . ., chairman of the Appropriations Committee, reported . . .

c. Other titles following names are not usually capitalized.

> Miss Dorothy Rockwell, vice-president of the American Newspaper Guild, could not attend the meeting.

Mr. Frederick L. Daniels, executive director of the Brooklyn Bureau of Social Service, will be consulted in the matter.

3. Abbreviations of academic degrees are capitalized.

the Reverend George Arthur Chase, D.D.

4. A title that refers to a specific person and is used in place of a personal name is capitalized.

The Governor issued his annual Thanksgiving Day proclamation.
The Chief Executive will hold his press conference at 3 p.m.
Please suggest a suitable gift for Mother and Dad.
Your Honor   Mr. Chairman

But when such words occur without personal names or are not used in place of a name, they are *not* capitalized.

My brother has just become a director of his company.
Our present rector, like his predecessor, is a native of Canada.

5. In the minutes of meetings and in bylaws, rules, and reports of societies and institutions, the titles of the office holders are usually capitalized.

The Secretary's minutes were read and approved, as was the Treasurer's report.

6. The hyphenated elements *ex-* and *-elect* when joined to titles are not capitalized.

Mayor-elect Boyd will give the speech of welcome.
For many years Herbert Hoover held the distinction of being the only living ex-President of the United States.

Neither are the unhyphenated *former* and *late* capitalized when used with titles.

The late President Roosevelt began his first term in the midst of the country's worst depression.
Yes, former Secretary of State Hull is a native of Tennessee.

Assignment 2. ★ Copy the following sentences, paying particular attention to the correct use of capitalization.

1. i prefer to leave any recommendations for changes in the club's financial policy to treasurer-elect sherman.

2. the governor announced that he would not be a candidate for re-election.

3. the following committeemen have declared themselves in favor of the legislation: karl m. le compte, emmet o'neal, and wesly a. d'ewart.

4. please send me the exact title of doctor law's new textbook.

5. mrs. evalyn walsh mclean, the former owner of the famous hope diamond, was noted for her lavish social entertainments.

6. the annual campaign for destroying ragweed in the city was announced by herbert block, health commissioner.

7. please add this address to your stencil list:
    miss elizabeth french, personnel director
    wynn department store
    minneapolis 10, minnesota

8. mr. milton weeks, assistant to the vice-president in charge of sales, prefers our shoes to all other makes.

9. the late david lloyd george, former prime minister of great britain, lived to be eighty-two years of age.

10. miss la blanc wishes this purchase charged to her account.

11. robert rhoades, c.p.a., is the author of a new accounting text.

12. i wish to make a correction in the treasurer's report.

13. one of the notable events of 1952 was president-elect eisenhower's trip to korea.

LESSON 44

Capitalization (*Continued*)

Names of Organizations. 1. The names of firms, companies, associations, societies, commissions, committees, bureaus, boards, departments, schools, political parties, conventions, fraternities, clubs, and religious bodies are capitalized.

the Silver Manufacturing Company	the Advertising Department
Chicago University	the Bureau of Home Economics
the Republican National Convention	the Democratic Party
the Parent-Teacher Association	the Child Welfare Committee
the Elks	the Protestant Episcopal Church

2. When *the* precedes the name of an organization, the article is not capitalized unless it is part of the recognized official name of the organization.

The National City Bank of New York

Names of Governmental Bodies. 1. Names of countries, of international organizations, and of national, state, county, and city bodies and their branches are capitalized.

the Union of South Africa	the State Department
the Security Council of the United Nations	the National Labor Relations Board
	the United States Circuit Court
the Dominion of Canada	the Public Service Commission
the Senate	the United States Army
the Cabinet	the United States Weather Bureau

2. Shortened forms of governmental names are capitalized when they are used as substitutes for the complete names.

the House	the Department [referring to some
the Army	one department]

207

3. The words *federal, government, union, nation, commonwealth, province,* and *constitution* are capitalized when they are used as shortened forms of full names and as references to specific countries.

the United States Government
the Government (referring to either
    the United States Government or
    a specific foreign government)
a Federal agency

the states of the Union
under the Constitution
the British Commonwealth
the Province of Quebec

But, when these words are used merely as common nouns, they are not capitalized.

A government of the people, by the people, and for the people
A nation of over 150,000,000 people

Assignment 1. ★ Copy the following sentences, capitalizing all words that should be capitalized.

1. the purchasing department of the ajax manufacturing corporation has devised some unusual purchase-order forms.

2. he is an important member of the influential committee on admissions of north-south college.

3. the very fact that he is a member of the society of mechanical engineers indicates his professional standing, for the society has high standards.

4. the appointment of john hughes as vice-president of the lewis publishing company was announced yesterday by mr. charles bartel president of the bartel company of which the lewis company is a subsidiary.

5. most of the new members of the house of representatives voted against the bill.

6. the secretary of state explained the state department policy in his radio address.

7. our club constitution was revised by the executive committee.

8. i have written the bureau of internal revenue for a refund on my last year's federal income-tax payment.

9. the nation's traffic fatalities have reached alarming proportions.

10. the information in this booklet is based on statistical data gathered by the bureau of the census of the department of commerce.

11. can you quote the first sentence of the federal constitution?

12. the work of the civil service commission was greatly expanded during the war years.

13. the house, ignoring state department warnings, passed the bill.

Names of Places. 1. Names of geographic localities, streets, parks, and buildings are capitalized.

the North Pole	the Shenandoah Valley
the Mississippi River	Central Park
the Green Mountains	the Grand Canyon
New York Harbor	Main Street
North Africa	the Globe Building

2. The word *city* is capitalized only when it is part of the corporate name of a city.

Long Island City   the city of New York

The word *state* is capitalized when it follows the name of a state.

New York State   the state of New York

3. As in names of organizations, *the* is capitalized only when it is a part of the official name of a place.

The Hague [*but:* the Netherlands]
The Dalles (Oregon) [*but:* the Dalles region]

Points of Compass. 1. Capitalize the points of the compass when they refer to definite localities.

We are opening an office in the South.
The Far North suffered a severe blizzard.

2. But when such words indicate mere points of the compass or directions, they are not capitalized.

We are going north for skiing.
The design has an oriental suggestion.
The new sales territory includes southern Texas.

Names of Commercial Products. Names of commercial products are capitalized.

Star Radio	Gold Bar Butter
Griffith Shoe Polish	Pepso Toothpaste
Warner Hats	Martin's Coffee

Some trade names are so commonly used that they are considered common nouns. Out of courtesy to the manufacturers of the products, however, such brand names should be capitalized.

Kodak	Vaseline
Victrola	Mimeoscope

Assignment 2. ★   Copy the following sentences, paying particular attention to the correct use of capitalization.

1. the population of the far west grew as a result of the war and postwar boom.

2. in 1940 kansas city, missouri, had a population close to 400,-000.

3. many so-called cedar chests are made from southern pine.

4. many sections of the middle west suffered from disastrous floods.

5. beaumont park is a few minutes walk from the first presbyterian church.

6. how far west does the bus line go?

7. the second tallest building in new york city is the chrysler building at lexington avenue and 42d street.

8. when we flew south to buenos aires, we crossed the equator.

9. we stopped in yellowstone park to see the geyser old faithful on our way to the province of british columbia.

10. please add three cakes of ivory soap to my order.

11. eight presidents were born in the state of virginia.

LESSON **45**

Capitalization (*Concluded*)

Names of Months, Weeks, Days. Names of the months and of weeks, days of the week, holidays, and religious days are capitalized.

June	New Year's	Easter
Friday	Fire Prevention Week	the Day of Atonement

Historical Events and Documents. The names of important historical events, of movements, of periods, and of specific treaties, bills, acts, and laws are capitalized.

World War II	the Declaration of Independence
Battle of the Bulge	the Treaty of Versailles
the Industrial Revolution	the Social Security Act
the Dark Ages	the Wagner Labor Relations Act
the Machine Age	*but* the twentieth century

Races, Peoples, Languages. The names of races, peoples, tribes, and languages are capitalized.

Negroes	Indians	Latin
Filipinos	Caucasians	

Titles of Literary Works. The main words in the titles of literary, musical, and art compositions are capitalized. Articles, conjunctions, and short prepositions are not capitalized. A long preposition, however—one of six or more letters—is capitalized.

Sentences containing various types of literary titles appear in Lesson 39.

The above rule of capitalization is also applied to the individual words that make up a compound word that appears in a title.

Characteristics of Well-Known Brands
Results of Twenty-One Investigations
How to Lose That Down-in-the-Mouth Expression

211

Parts of Letters. 1. The first word and any title in a salutation are capitalized.

Dear Sir: Dear Father Flynn:
Dear Mr. Brown: Right Reverend and dear Sir:
My dear Mr. Brown: Your Excellency:

2. Only the first word of the complimentary closing is capitalized.

Yours truly,   Most cordially yours,

3. For the capitalization of titles in inside addresses and in envelope addresses, see Lesson 43.

4. A business title that appears under the signature line of a letter is capitalized.

Sincerely yours,

. . . .
Advertising Manager

5. The word *Subject* or *Attention* preceding the body of a letter is capitalized.

Capitals with Various Marks of Punctuation. For the rules governing the use of the capital after various marks of punctuation, see the following pages:

1. Following a colon, page 172.

2. Following an opening quotation mark, page 201.

3. Beginning a direct question incorporated in a sentence, page 201.

4. With an opening ellipsis, page 179.

Capitalized Abbreviations. See Lesson 46.

Legal Work. 1. In legal documents many words are capitalized that are ordinarily written in small letters; as, references to the parties, the name of the document, special provisions, and spelled-out amounts of money.

The said premises are also leased upon the further Covenants and
Conditions:
1. That the Tenant shall take good care of the apartment and
fixtures, etc.
In consideration of the sum of One Dollar . . .

School Courses and Subjects. 1. Names of subjects are not capitalized unless they contain proper nouns or proper adjectives.

biology	history
grammar	American history
English grammar	shorthand
business English	psychology

2. Names of courses of study are capitalized.

the History of Business Administration
International Law
Shorthand I

Assignment. ★ Copy the following sentences, paying particular attention to correct capitalization.

1. when you use the informal type of salutation, dear mr. scott, choose a correspondingly informal complimentary closing, as sincerely yours or cordially yours.

2. turners mens shop is running an ad in the morning world on friday, reading remember dad on fathers day, june 15.

3. and remember mother knows best—and for the laundry the best is eureka soap.

4. our course in advanced secretarial procedures includes far more than a study of shorthand, typewriting and bookkeeping.

5. probably the first white man to venture into montana was chevalier de la verendrye, who learned of the land from the indians. on new years day 1743 he sighted the snow-capped mountains and called the region "land of the shining mountains.

6. our school play, called a time-honored custom, is a hilarious comedy.

7. the subject of professor hendersons lecture is the psychology of salesmanship in the postwar world.

8. at the top of the page we wish to add the nebraska state motto equality before the law.

9. did you read the letter of protest on the new traffic regulations that appeared in the thats my opinion column of the evening ledger.

10. you will find an interpretation of the federal regulations on income-tax evasion clearly set forth in the new manual by stephen van horn certified public accountant.

11. prior to world war ii, japanese was taught in very few colleges.
12.

mr. david sage,
465 east 48th street
new york 17, n. y.

my dear mr. sage

many persons have spoken to me of the talk on "legal problems under the antitrust laws" that you gave recently at the young businessmens club.

would it be possible for you to repeat the talk saturday april 21 before the association for merchants and credit men.

we usually pay $25 for such speeches. would that amount be satisfactory.

sincerely yours,

. . . .
chairman of the program committee

LESSON 46

Abbreviations

An abbreviation is a shortened form of a word, used chiefly to save space. The simplest form of abbreviation consists of the first letter of a word; for example, *C.* for *Centigrade, p.* for *page, N.* for *North.* For clarity, additional letters are sometimes added; as, *vol.* for *volume, Inc.* for *Incorporated.* Other abbreviations are formed by omitting certain letters of the words; as, *mdse.* for *merchandise, shpt.* for *shipment.* The abbreviations of a few commonly used words are based on the Latin form of the word; thus, *lb.* for *pound* is an abbreviation of *libra,* the Latin form; *a.m.* for *forenoon* is an abbreviation of the Latin phrase *ante meridiem,* meaning "before noon." For the difference between an abbreviation and a contraction, see Lesson 42.

Most dictionaries contain recognized lists of abbreviations. These lists should be consulted for the correct forms.

When an abbreviation consists of the abbreviations of several single words, the period follows each unit in the abbreviation; as, *C.O.D.* for *cash on delivery,* and *r.p.m.* for *revolutions per minute.*

Abbreviations should be used sparingly in business letters and in formal composition of any kind—reports and manuscripts of books and of articles. In scientific and technical work, in tabular work, and in informal and interoffice correspondence, however, many terms are ordinarily abbreviated.

Personal Names. Christian names should be spelled out. If, however, the writer's signature indicates that he prefers an abbreviated or a contracted form, that form should be used; for example, *Geo., Chas., Thos., Sam'l, Wm., Jno.*

Notice, however, that certain shortened first names are not always

215

abbreviations and therefore require no periods. Follow the signer's style for *Ed, Ben, Fred, Sam, Alex, Will.*

Spell out a person's given name rather than write an initial to represent the name unless the owner signs with only an initial; for example, write *Kenneth S. French* rather than *K. S. French.*

Personal Titles. 1. The following titles are *always abbreviated* when they precede a personal name, either with or without Christian name or initial.

Mr.   Messrs.   Dr.   Mrs.   St.

Miss is not an abbreviation and therefore does not require a period.

Exception: In salutations of letters, it is considered more courteous to spell out *Doctor;* and some authorities extend the full form to all cases where the surname only is used.

Dear Doctor Grier:
The address of welcome was delivered by Doctor Strong.

2. Other civil, educational, religious, military, and naval titles are always spelled out when the *surname only* is used.

Governor Baldwin	President McCall	Captain Winter
Professor Loomis	General Arnold	Father Flynn

When the title precedes a *full name,* however, practice differs. In formal usage, such titles should always be spelled out; and many writers prefer to spell them out under all circumstances. In business correspondence, technical writing, tabulations, or wherever brevity is desirable, abbreviated forms are commonly used.

Lt. (jg) S. Henry Barton	Prof. Martin J. Blake
Col. Harold Otis	Supt. Alfred C. Locke

3. The following titles are always abbreviated when they follow personal names.

Esq.	academic and religious degrees (M.A.,
Jr.	Ph.D., M.D., S.T.D., etc.)
Sr.	

Note: If *Esq.* follows a name, no other title, as *Mr.* or *Dr.*, should precede the name.

Peter Grinnell, Esq.   Dr. Peter Grinnell

4. *Honorable* and *Reverend* are titles of respect and dignity used in addressing government officials of any rank and clergyman, respectively. The titles are preferably spelled out except in addresses, lists, and notices. *The* should always precede the titles in formal usage; it may be omitted in addresses, lists, and notices.

Either a given name or a title must intervene between either *Reverend* or *Honorable* and the surname.

The Honorable John W. Snyder   The Reverend George Clarke
The Honorable Mr. Snyder   The Reverend Doctor Clarke

Firm Names. Do not abbreviate the words *Company, Corporation, Association, Brothers, Railroad, Railway, Manufacturing,* or other parts of a firm name unless the company's letterhead or other published material shows this to be the official form. The following actual firm names show variations in these details.

Chas. H. Bohn Co.   Maryland Glass Corporation
Monotype & Linotype Composition   Union Pacific Railroad
Corp.

Names of Associations and Government Agencies. Abbreviations are increasingly used instead of the full names of various organizations that are often referred to; for example:

1. Professional and trade associations or charitable organizations.

A.B.A.	American Bankers Association
A.A.A.	American Automobile Association
A.L.A.	American Library Association
C.O.S.	Charity Organization Society
N.E.A.	National Education Association
Y.M.C.A.	Young Men's Christian Association

2. Government agencies. The initials of the words in the names for these agencies are usually written close, with no periods.

SSB	Social Security Board
NLRB	National Labor Relations Board
TVA	Tennessee Valley Authority

3. Labor organizations. Apply Rule 2.

| CIO | Congress of Industrial Organizations |
| TWU | Transport Workers Union |

Assignment 1. ★ Copy the following sentences, abbreviating or spelling out wherever necessary.

1. Memo to Miss. Farrell: Please get some red ink tomorrow. —C. B.

2. Here is a message from Doctor Chas. Greene, the noted educator.

3. Write to the Milton Publish. Co., and theyll send you the book.

4. Ladies and gentlemen, we are fortunate tonight to have two distinguished guests on our program, Gov. Smythe and Gen. Hamilton.

5. The Rev. Dr. Henry Dalton presented the diplomas to the graduating class.

6. Two names are to be added to the letterhead—those of Thomas Webster, junior, and Everett Willard, Certified Public Accountant.

7. May we call your attention to an opinion expressed by Dr. Dwight Weston, Medical Adviser to the Chester C.O.S.?

8. Dear Dr. Huston;

At the annual meeting of the Board of Directors of the N. Y. Zoological Soc., your name was presented as one of those persons to be made honorary members of the society. . . .

Yrs. Truly

. . . . .

Exec. Sect.

9. The Hon. John Faulkner will present the trophies.

10. Each of the unions represented is affiliated with the C. I. O.

11. Doctor Robert English, Esq., served as a Lt. (jg.) in the U. S. navy during World War II.

12. Gov. Lewis and the Hon. Judge Reilly were the speakers at the rally sponsored by the NAM.

13. The letter was addressed to Mister Jno. Williamson, Esquire., care of Young Men's Hebrew Assn.

Geographical Names. 1. The names of cities, counties, states and possessions, provinces, and countries should be spelled out in sentences.

> Baltimore, Maryland
> Greenwich, Fairfield County, Connecticut
> London, England

In lists, and sometimes on envelopes, names of states and United States possessions may be abbreviated. The abbreviations recommended by the Post Office should be used; thus:

State	Abbreviation	State	Abbreviation
Alabama	Ala.	New Jersey	N. J.
Arizona	Ariz.	New Mexico	N. Mex.
Arkansas	Ark.	New York	N. Y.
California	Calif.	North Carolina	N. C.
Colorado	Colo.	North Dakota	N. Dak.
Connecticut	Conn.	Oklahoma	Okla.
Delaware	Del.	Oregon	Oreg.
District of		Pennsylvania	Pa.
Columbia	D. C.	Rhode Island	R. I.
Florida	Fla.	South Carolina	S. C.
Georgia	Ga.	South Dakota	S. Dak.
Illinois	Ill.	Tennessee	Tenn.
Indiana	Ind.	Texas	Tex.
Kansas	Kans.	Vermont	Vt.
Kentucky	Ky.	Virginia	Va.
Louisiana	La.	Washington	Wash.
Maryland	Md.	West Virginia	W. Va.
Massachusetts	Mass.	Wisconsin	Wis.
Michigan	Mich.	Wyoming	Wyo.
Minnesota	Minn.		
Mississippi	Miss.	*Territories and*	
Missouri	Mo.	*Dependencies*	
Montana	Mont.	Canal Zone	C. Z.
Nebraska	Nebr.	Hawaii	T. H.
Nevada	Nev.	Puerto Rico	P. R.
New Hampshire	N. H.	Virgin Islands	V. I.

Exception: The names of the following states and possessions should not be abbreviated:

Idaho	Maine	Alaska
Iowa	Ohio	Utah

2. The words *Fort, Mount, Point,* and *Port* in names are not abbreviated.

Fort Knox	Point Pleasant
Mount Desert	Port Royal

3. The words *Street* and *Avenue* and similar designations in street addresses are preferably spelled out. Where it is necessary to save space, as in lists, and sometimes on envelopes, these words may be abbreviated as follows:

Avenue	Ave.	Park	Pk.	Square	Sq.
Boulevard	Blvd.	Place	Pl.	Street	St.
Building	Bldg.	Road	Rd.	Terrace	Terr.

Note: Always adopt a uniform style of abbreviation in cases like this. Do not vary the abbreviation, nor spell out in some cases and abbreviate in others.

Days and Months. Names of days of the week and of months of the year are spelled out.

Thursday, April 17   April 17, 1953

In narrow columns or other places where space is at a premium, the following abbreviations may be used, however.

Sun.	Thurs.	Jan.	Sept.
Mon.	Fri.	Feb.	Oct.
Tues.	Sat.	Mar.	Nov.
Wed.		Apr.	Dec.
		Aug.	

May, June, and *July* should not be abbreviated.

Terms of Measure. 1. Names of the common units of weight, length, capacity, area, volume, temperature, and time are ordinarily spelled out.

50 pounds	4 square miles	80 degrees Fahrenheit
7 yards	10 cubic feet	3 dozen
1 gallon	30 days	

In technical work and on invoices, however, where measurements occur frequently, such terms are usually abbreviated. Standard abbreviations should be used. Each trade and profession has its authorized list, and lists are included in most dictionaries.

2. Compass directions occur most frequently in technical and real estate work, in which the directions are abbreviated according to the following style: *N., NE., NNE.,* and so on. In single occurrences, however, compass directions are spelled out.

The plot is at the northeast corner of Main and Henry Streets.

Assignment 2. ★ Copy the following sentences, abbreviating any words that should be abbreviated and spelling out any abbreviations that are incorrectly used.

1. In most states a bushel of oats is considered to weigh 32 lbs.
2. Do you mean Ft. Dodge Ia or Ft. Dodge Kans?
3. Ted is leaving Tues. April 1 for Winnipeg, Man.; afterward he plans to go to Victoria, B. C.
4. I'll be gone two or three wks, possibly a mo.
5. Is the book scheduled for publication in Feb. or Mar.?
6. Rochester, N. Y. is N. of N. Y. C.
7. I think that a bu. of peaches weighs about 40 lbs., although it feels more like a ton when you have to carry it even a few yrds.
8. Our Canadian office is located at 50 Bloor St., Toronto 5, Ont., Can.
9. My vacation starts Fri. Jly. 15.
10. Enter the following stock requisition presented by the repair dept.: 2 dozen stenographic notebooks, 1 gross pencils, 1 dozen 1-qt. bottles red ink, 10 dozen penholders.
11. Is it true that 1 gal. of water weighs 8⅓ lbs.?
12. The U. S. govt. uses the long ton of 2240 lbs. in fixing the duty on mdse. that is taxed by the ton.
13. Arnolds dep't store is showing some excellent dark-blue rayon at $1.50 a yd. Please get me 5½ yds.
14. Not once during the month did the temperature go over 75 deg.
15. There are 128 cubic feet in a cord of wood.
16. The state of Nebr. was admitted to the union on Mar. 1, 1867.

Other Words Always Abbreviated. The following expressions are always abbreviated:

1. *A.D.* and *B.C.* in year dates. Notice that *A.D.* precedes, and that *B.C.* follows, the year.

> The Middle Ages are generally considered to have begun in A.D. 400
> Julius Caesar was assassinated in 44 B.C.

2. *Am., p.m.,* and *m.* in statements of time.

> 10:05 a.m.   5 p.m.   12 m. (noon)

Small letters are preferred for these abbreviations. The word *o'clock* should not be added, nor should the abbreviations be used without figures.

> I will report at 9 a.m. (*Or:* I will report at nine o'clock.)

3. The abbreviation *No.* when followed by a numeral, except at the beginning of a sentence.

> Enclosed is policy No. 39462547.
> Number 3 moves up to first place.

The abbreviation *No.* is correct only when accompanied by a numeral.

> It is impossible for me to remember my Social Security number. (*Not:* No.)

Cases in Which Periods Are Not Used.   Certain letters, symbols, and shortened forms are not followed by periods.

1. Chemical symbols.

> Na (sodium)   O (oxygen)   Fe (iron)

2. Mathematical symbols; as, *tan, log, cos.*
3. *Per cent,* which is really an abbreviation of *per centum.*
4. Ordinals; as, *1st, 2d, 4th.*
5. Letter designations of radio stations; as, *WNBC, WQXR.*
6. *IOU* and *SOS,* which are not abbreviations.
7. Letters used instead of a name to designate a person or a thing; as, *Miss A, Class B, Grade C,* and so on.
8. Contractions. (See Lesson 42.)

9. Names of certain organizations. (See pages 217-218.)

10. Certain shortened forms that have become accepted as correct—as *ad* for *advertisement*, *gym* for *gymnasium*, and *phone* for *telephone*.

Plurals of Abbreviations.   1. The plurals of most abbreviations are formed by adding *s* to the singular form.

yds.   lbs.   depts.

But many abbreviations are the same in both singular and plural.

oz. for both *ounce* and *ounces*   deg. for both *degree* and *degrees*
in. for both *inch* and *inches*   ft. for both *foot* and *feet*
min. for both *minute* and *minutes*   sec. for both *second* and *seconds*

2. The plural of an abbreviation that consists of letters is formed by adding an apostrophe and *s* to the abbreviation. (See also Lesson 17.)

C.P.A.'s   C.O.D.'s

3. The plurals of a few single-letter abbreviations consist of the same letter doubled.

p. for *page*   f. for *and the following page*
pp. for *pages*   ff. for *and the following pages*

Capitalization and Hyphenization.   Abbreviations follow the capitalization and hyphenization of the full words.

D.C.   District of Columbia   kw.-hr.   kilowatt-hour
G.O.P.   Grand Old Party   ft.-lb.   foot-pound
B.t.u.   British thermal unit

Typing Hints.   1. When an abbreviation consists of more than one initial letter, no extra space separates the letters; as in *B.C.*, *a.m.*, *C.P.A.*; but in a series of abbreviations (usually abbreviations of honorary degrees), a comma and a space should separate the individual abbreviations.

President Henry S. Ross, Ph.D., LL.D.

2. When an abbreviation occurs within a sentence, one space separates the period after the abbreviation from the word that follows.

3. Abbreviations should never be divided at the end of a line.

> *Wrong:* The contents of the packing case is stated as 9 cu.-
> ft.

Assignment 3. ★ Copy the following sentences, using words for any abbreviations that should have been spelled out and using abbreviations for any words that should have been abbreviated. Also, change the form of any incorrect abbreviation.

1. Box number 3 weighs 10 lbs.
2. The soil of Lancaster Co., Pa., is noted for its fertility.
3. Can you tell me the difference, legally, between a purchase fob factory and one fob destination.
4. An I.O.U. is not a promissory note.
5. Would you believe that Fri. June 13 proved a lucky day for me?
6. The Graybar Bldg. on Lexington Ave. in N. Y. City is a large office building.
7. Cheops the builder of the greatest pyramid in Egypt lived about BC 2,900.
8. Did you see the ad. of Wilson & Coles furniture sale in the Sun. Banner. The sale was also broadcasted over station W.S.T.U.
9. On sheet 1 list the Ph.D.s and on sheet 2 the D.D.s.
10. Does anyone in the room hold ticket number 15 the master of ceremonies called?
11. Shes not at all sure whether Dr Murray meant 9 am or 9 pm.
12. The sales conference of the Blare Co. is scheduled for 9 am oclock in the Jno. Marshall Bldg.
13. What is the license No. of your car the policeman asked?
14. This is license no. 624-326.
15. You must obtain the OKs of both CPAs in the accounting dep't.
16. Station W.N.B.C. also carried the ad. for Carlson's dep't store.
17. The bill was paid on the 1st., according to my letter.
18. The sales of Grade C. canned fruit are about 5 per cent. higher than a year ago.
19. The book contains 450 p.
20. The elephant is the symbol of the G O P.

LESSON **47**

The Use of Figures

When Numbers Are Expressed in Words. In business letters, numbers are more often written in figures than in words. The cases in which *words* are used are:

1. Numbers below ten when the numbers appear individually in sentences.

> The directors have named an executive committee of eight members.

Note: In social correspondence and in general reading matter, numbers below 100 are usually expressed in words.

2. Numbers starting sentences, no matter how large.

> One hundred ten boarded-up tenements are to be remodeled.
> Ten thousand seven hundred twenty-two persons are reported to have left the farms of our state for cities during the last ten years.

Usually, it is possible to reconstruct such sentences as those and so avoid the awkwardness of spelling out large numbers.

> The remodeling of 110 boarded-up tenements is planned.
> It has been reported that 10,722 persons left the farms of our state for cities during the last ten years.

In statistical and technical work this rule is sometimes disregarded and the sentence is begun with the figure.

Note: Some authorities insert the word *and* in large written-out numbers; thus: "one hundred and ten." As the word is not used in writing large amounts of money on checks, or in other business usages, it seems preferable to treat all cases the same way.

3. Round or indefinite numbers.

> About five hundred of the students are veterans.

In spelling out round numbers over a thousand, use the form *fifteen hundred*, not *one thousand five hundred*.

4. Ordinal numbers, except in certain technical work. (But see "Dates," page 228, and "Street Numbers," pages 228-229.)

> He will come into his inheritance on his twenty-first birthday.
> Can you tell what large cities are near the 90th meridian west of Greenwich?

5. Numbers in legal documents. Usually the figures, enclosed in parentheses, follow the words.

> The twenty-five (25) per cent is to be paid in thirty (30) days.
> I give and bequeath unto my son, Charles Stanton, the sum of ten thousand dollars ($10,000).

Such parenthetic figures should follow immediately the numbers they represent, not be placed at the end of a phrase.

> In addition, fifty thousand dollars ($50,000) in cash on the delivery of the deed . . .

In some attorneys' offices, the use of figures in parentheses is restricted to amounts of money only.

6. Fractions standing alone.

> Because of the current conditions, our supply of goods is only about one-half of normal.

In spelling out mixed numbers, the word *and* is used to separate the whole number from the fraction.

> 5½   five and one-half
> 5.1   five and one-tenth

When Numbers Are Written in Figures. 1. Figures are used for expressing numbers over 10 when such numbers appear individually in sentences.

> By the end of the year we expect to have 75 items in the series.

2. When numbers occur frequently, as in enumerations or statistics, all numbers should be written in figures, even when they are round numbers or below ten.

> Of the more than 200 members of the graduating class, 59 plan to become nurses, 65 secretaries, 8 dietitians; the remainder have not made known their plans.

3. The style of spelling out *million, billion,* and so on in extremely large numbers is becoming increasingly popular as an aid to clarity; as, *20 million houses; 5 billion dollars.* This style, however, cannot be used when the number contains uneven amounts of thousands and hundreds; as, *20,755,200 houses, $5,410,500,000.*

Assignment 1. ★ Copy the following sentences, using figures for the numbers that should be written in figures and spelling out the numbers that should be spelled out.

1. The truck driver delivered about 200 pieces of mail to the green mountain inn on Monday.
2. The property consists of 3 parcels, 1 containing a bldg. and the other 2 vacant.
3. 150 choice hotel rooms will be available for the 25th Convention of the Association.
4. The commercial artist who has won the contract has had only 2½ years experience.
5. Slater University conferred seven hundred fifteen degrees at its one hundred second commencement.
6. Their new brick plant has a capacity of twenty-five million bricks.
7. Im sure that 20 years ago good coats could be bought for about ½ their present prices.
8. The replies to the last mailing may be classified thus one hundred fifty-eight were from teachers, seventy-five from clergymen, forty-two from editors, and approximately one hundred from college students.
9. 112 students attended the organizational meeting.
10. About one thousand five hundred copies are to be rebound.
11. At the end of the thirty days (30) the note for twenty-nine dollars ($29) will come due.

Dates.   1. In business correspondence, the day of the month should be written in figures; as, *March 10.*

Note that the ordinal endings *st, th, d* (use the form *d* instead of *nd* or *rd*) do *not* follow the figure for the day.

When the day *precedes* the month, however, the ordinal endings are used; as, *the 10th of March,* or *on the 10th.*

Note: In Army and Navy correspondence, as well as in letters from foreign countries, the day appears before the month; as, *10 March 1953.*

2. In social correspondence and formal documents, the day of the month is often spelled out.

> the tenth of March
> the tenth day of March
> March the tenth

3. The year should be expressed in figures in business correspondence; as, *1953.*

The styles *3/10/53* or *3-10-53* are not recommended, even in informal memorandums, for they are easily confused.

4. In legal documents, years are usually spelled out thus:

> one thousand nine hundred and fifty-three

In other formal matter, such as reports or invitations, the year is usually written thus:

> nineteen hundred and fifty-three

House, Street, and Zone Numbers.   1. In business correspondence, house numbers are always expressed in figures; as, *270 Madison Avenue.* In social and formal correspondence, such numbers are often spelled out.

> Mr. and Mrs. John Greene
> At Home
> Five Crescent Place

Neither the number sign (#) nor the abbreviation *No.* is necessary before a house number or a rural route.

2. In business correspondence, names of numbered streets should

be spelled out when the numbers are below ten; written in figures when ten or above.

Fifth Avenue   West First Place   East 125th Street

Note: Many prominent newspapers spell out large-numbered streets. As figures are more quickly read, especially on envelopes, figures are preferred in business.

Practice differs regarding the use of the ordinal suffixes in numbered street names expressed in figures. The practice of omitting them seems to be growing because of the resulting increased readability on envelopes.

3. Postal-zone numbers immediately follow the name of the city and are expressed in arabic figures. A comma follows, but does not precede, the number; as, *New York 17, New York.*

Ages and Time. 1. A person's age should be spelled out when only the number of years is given.

> In our company any employee who becomes sixty-five years of age is eligible for a pension.

When an age is given in years, months, and days, however, figures are used.

> At the time of the accident, the insured's age was 45 years 7 months and 5 days.

Note that no commas separate the parts of such expressions.

2. Spell out the time of day when a shortened form or the word *o'clock* is used.

> I have made your appointment for one o'clock.
> Can you come at half past one?

But when the exact time is given or *a.m.* or *p.m.* is used (see also page 173), use figures.

> The mails close at 5:15.

It is not necessary to include two ciphers when the exact hour is mentioned except in tabulations—usually railroad schedules.

> Lock the door promptly at 5 p.m.

3. Usually isolated numbers representing periods of time—years, months, days, and so on—follow Rule 1 on page 225 and are spelled out.

> Your subscription expires in two months.

But periods of time mentioned in connection with terms of discount or interest rates are usually written in figures, for clarity.

> If you will pay for the goods in 10 days, they will cost you just $126.
> What is the accurate interest on $375 for 75 days at 6%?

4. The names of centuries and of decades are spelled out; as, *the gay nineties; the nineteenth century.*

5. Years of graduation and well-known years in history are usually written in two figures preceded by an apostrophe; as, *the class of '47; the blizzard of '88.*

Assignment 2. ★ Copy the following sentences, using figures for numbers that should be written in figures and spelling out numbers that should be written in words.

1. The special dispatch, which is dated June 5th, 1953 reads as follows: "Starting the 23rd of July . . ."

2. Mutual Airlines announced that they would operate 3 eastbound and 3 westbound flights a week from Duluth to Manila beginning the 2nd of May.

3. The Chickering Fur Co. will sponsor a new program of popular music over station s.m.x. at 8:00 p.m. beginning 4/1/53.

4. Please note that on June first my address will change from 270 1st Ave., N. Y., 16, to RFD # 1, So. Royalton, Vt.

5. The Senate adjourned at 6:10 p.m. today and will reconvene at 11.00 a.m. tomorrow.

6. Under the federal social security act passed by congress in 1935 retired workers receive monthly benefits from the government when they are 65 years of age or over.

7. His bookkeeping methods surely do not belong to the 20th century.

8. Can you tell me how to find the due date of a ninety-day note dated April eighteen?

9. The maximum length of term of the trade acceptance is

ninety days on all except agricultural paper, which is allowed to run six months.

10. The note will fall due in sixty days; that is, on March tenth.

11. The letter, dated March 4th, arrived on the 9th.

12. Members of the class of twenty-nine are having their reunion Oct. 16.

13. You have 2 hours for this examination.

14. When Dick earned the scholarship, he was only fifteen years and nine months old.

15. The meeting, scheduled for 10:00 a.m. Tuesday, was postponed to Thursday at three o'clock in the afternoon.

LESSON 48

The Use of Figures (Concluded)

Money. In business, amounts of money, whether dollars, cents, or foreign denominations, are ordinarily written in figures.

| $45 | $5.50 | 5 cents | £5 4s. 6d. | 2 francs |

In formal and social correspondence and in general matter, amounts of money are often spelled out in words.

In legal documents, amounts of money are often spelled out and written in figures as well. (See Lesson 47.)

Dollars. 1. When an amount of money consists of dollars alone— that is, when no cents are included—no ciphers nor decimal point should be used.

$10 (*not* $10.00 *nor* $10.)

In tabulations, if any amount in a column contains cents, then ciphers should be added to amounts that do not contain cents, to even up the columns.

$19.07
8.45
14.00
.04

2. In a series, the dollar sign should be repeated with each amount of dollars.

Hall and stair carpeting at $3.88-$5.73 a yard.
New fall blouses at $5, $7.50, and $10.

3. For one method of writing extremely large amounts of money, see Rule 3, page 227.

Cents. 1. Amounts of cents that appear individually in a sentence are written in figures followed by the word *cents.*

Take 50 cents from petty cash for the office boy's carfare.

2. The symbol ¢ is often used in technical matter containing many amounts below $1.

The Connelly Contracting Company's last bill contained a charge for 250 cement blocks at 10¢ and 4 bags of cement at 50¢.

3. The dollar sign and the decimal point are used with amounts under $1 if the amount occurs in a series of other amounts made up of dollars and cents.

Just today I spent $4 for stamps, $2 for a box of stencils, and $.30 for filing cards.

Decimals. 1. Decimals are always expressed in figures; as, *7.5; 0.65.* The cipher before the decimal point in the second decimal indicates that the writer has not overlooked the fact that this amount is less than one whole number.

2. In very accurate work, a cipher is placed at the end of a decimal to indicate that the computation has been carried out to a certain number of places, the remainder being dropped. Thus, *0.4760* indicates that the computation was carried out to the fourth place.

In columnar work, ciphers may be added to make all figures contain the same number of decimal places if extreme accuracy is not essential.

0.2500	*instead of*	0.25
0.1620		0.162
8.2000		8.2
3.3333		3.3333

3. Commas are never used in decimals. *Correct:* 5.374920.

Percentages and Proportions. 1. Percentages should always be written in figures. The figure is followed by the expression *per cent* where the percentages do not occur too frequently.

There are several methods of calculating interest, but the 6 per cent method is the simplest to learn.

Note: Some authorities prefer the one-word form *percent.*

2. The % sign is used after the figure in statistical or accounting work where percentages occur frequently.

> Of the total income, 40% was paid for wages, 20% for taxes, 16⅔% for repairs and maintenance, 12⅔% for miscellaneous expenses, and 10⅔% to stockholders.

3. The % sign should be repeated after each of several percentages occurring in succession, but the expression *per cent* follows the last figure in a series.

> We offer discounts of 5%, 10%, and 33⅓%.
> Our discounts range from 5 to 33⅓ per cent.

4. Fractional percentages are usually written as common fractions; as, *5½ per cent, 33⅓%*. In technical work, fractional percentages are usually expressed decimally; as, *5.5 per cent, 33.333%*.

5. Proportions and ratios are expressed in figures. (See also page 173.)

Assignment 1. ★ Copy the following sentences, using figures for numbers that should be written in figures and spelling out numbers that should be written in words.

1. One of our prominent citizens has contributed five thousand dollars toward a new stadium for our high school.

2. The Service Trust Co. has been appointed trustee for two million dollars of the Line Transportation Co. 40-yr. 2⅞ per cent debentures due Mar. 1st 1993.

3. Special sale of summer cottons, 65¢, $1.00, and $1.25 a yd.

4. Rents in this building have been increased 5, 10, 25, and in a few cases 33⅓%.

5. Please send me the following items advertised in todays Record, charging them to my acct.: one jar Lady Fair cold cream at $1.00; two bottles sun tan oil at 75 cents; one box Lady Fair face powder at $2.50.

6. On a power run the ship made a speed of 110% of her rate of speed.

7. At age 25 Irving Baker took out a three thousand dollar endowment policy for 20 years. He carried it for ten years and then dropped it.

8. The Higbee Shop carries an unusual assortment of barbecue and outdoor grill equipment, ranging from $3.50-42.00 in price.

9. I wouldn't have his job for $5000000.

10. The city sales tax on your purchase amounts to four cts.

11. The total of column 2 is 5,325.8,465.

12. Living costs have increased 10 per cent to 15 per cent.

Weights and Measures. In business and industrial usage, weights, measures, dimensions, distances, degrees, capacities, and market quotations are written in figures.

5 pounds	4 gallons	corn at 1.72½
2 feet 6 inches	70 degrees Fahrenheit	
2⅔ yards	7 kilowatts	

In general work, isolated measurements are often spelled out. For the punctuation of such measures as *2 pounds 14 ounces,* see page 148.

Political and Military Divisions; Sessions of Congress. Certain names that are composed of numbers should be spelled out:

1. Political divisions:

> Seventh Congressional District
> Seventeenth Assembly District
> First Ward

2. Military divisions:

> First Army
> Seventh Division
> Seventy-Seventh Regiment

3. Sessions of Congress; as, the *Seventy-Ninth Congress.*

Literary References. References to numbers of pages, chapters, volumes, paragraphs, sections, illustrations of books, reports, and other literary matter should preferably be in figures, for clearness.

In footnotes and bibliographical material, such references are usually abbreviated.

[1] Irene Place and Charles B. Hicks, *College Secretarial Procedures,* Chap. 9, Unit 3, Assign. 69.

Lerner, Julie. "A Bookkeeping Exercise That Is Different," *Business Edu cation World,* April, 1940, pp. 669-670.

Arabic and Roman Numerals. As arabic figures are more clearly read by most people, roman numerals should be used for the more infrequent cases, such as the chief divisions of literary material.

Miscellaneous Uses of Figures. 1. When one number follows another, the numbers should be separated by a comma.

> In 1952, 61,637,951 votes were cast in the presidential election.
> Please send us 5 gross of item No. 187, 3 gross by parcel post special delivery.

If two numbers form one item, however, the first member is usually spelled out unless it is so large that it is clumsy, in which case it is written in figures and the second is spelled out.

two 5-cent stamps	125 three-cent stamps
ten 30-inch strips	210 five-pound boxes

2. For the method of writing numbers representing a sequence, see Rule 2, page 227.

3. For the use of commas in large figures, see Lesson 35.

4. For the formation of plurals of numbers, see Lesson 17.

Accuracy Essential. Figures must be typed with absolute accuracy. If figures are misstruck, there is usually *nothing* in the context to tell the tale. The complications that may result defy description—they might easily lead to loss of business or money, or even to a lawsuit!

When typing fractions that do not appear on the typewriter keyboard, it is clearer to use the style 5/16 than 5-16. Also, it is clearer not to use the hyphen between the whole number and the fraction in mixed numbers; as, *4 5/16.*

Assignment 2. ★ Copy the following sentences, using figures for numbers that should be expressed in figures and spelling out numbers that should be written in words.

1. Rising two hundred and fifty feet out of the water, the lofty rock serves as a watchtower at the extremity of the mainland.

2. You'll have no trouble if you follow these directions: Enter the grand concourse of the Grand Central Station. Walk to gate seven and enter platform seven. Walk along this platform until you come to car 255 of the twentieth century limited. The porter will take you to compartment thirty seven. When you awake the next

morning, you will be looking out on the fields of the middle west.

3. The freighter lost her propeller nine hundred miles east of Cape Sable.

4. The 6-story bldg. occupies a site 59 feet, 6 inches by 107 feet, 4 inches.

5. This ship sailed 210,000 miles as a transport and carried 125,-000 American troops.

6. As converted, the four-hundred-thirty-foot vessel is a one-class ship, with accommodations for three hundred fifty passengers, or thirty more than she carried in prewar service.

7. The property includes forty seven acres and a group of one-story buildings.

8. The 1st session of the new Congress will convene January 3rd.

9. The house I live in is in the 17th congressional district, but the houses directly across the street are in the 18th district.

10. If you have no ten-cent stamps, five two-cent ones will do.

11. The financial news appears on pages thirty–thirty-two.

12. Yesterday afternoon at precisely 2.30 125 of the 500 booklets were delivered.

13. For this test review pp. thirty-eight—fifty-nine in Chapter 2.

14. Mr. Camfield bought 6 2-pound boxes of candy for members of the staff.

15. Harry made the two hundred twenty mi. journey by train in 4 hrs. 6 min.

16. In 1952 125,243 subscribers were added to the mailing list.

17. The alderman from the 3rd ward was in favor of the measure, but the bill was defeated by a vote of eleven to seven.

Assignment 3. ★ Punctuate and capitalize the following letters correctly.

1.

29 main st

chicago 10 Ill

june 14 1953

dr t d smith
    62 elm street
        hoboken 4 n j

my dear dr smith

may i write to commend your fine letter to the hoboken post concerning the condition of our highways that is our streets drives and boulevards when you say this disgrace must be remedied i am in hearty accord with you have you appeared before the board of aldermen on the matter they meet next friday can you be there

sincerely yours,
elbert t crawford
president realtors association

2.

sept 14th 1953

the martin j delman company
1416 parkside drive
springfield ill

gentlemen

we have taken over the insurance business of the john young company gary indiana and we find that your policy number 1495837 will expire tomorrow we are sending this letter to you by special delivery as we know you will not want to be without protection

the renewal premium on this policy will be $18.50 if you would like to have coverage for three years you will save a considerable sum as the premium is only $45.80 for the longer period perhaps this saving has not been called to your attention may we have your instructions by air mail or wire

we shall hold your policy until the day after tomorrow

yours truly
reynolds & roberts
henry rowland manager

3.   73 knoll street
                                           boston, 31, mass.
                                           july 14th, 1953

dr. james t. laurence phd
director of admissions
benjamin franklin college
plymouth, mass

dear dr. laurence

im very much interested in enrolling with the freshman class for the new term beginning in september. When i visited the campus in apr. miss downs suggested that we apply for admission directly to you.

my high school principal is sending you the transcript of credits. i believe that my grades and courses meet your standards. for liberal arts students.

please send me a catalogue and any forms or registration blanks that may be necessary.

                                           yours truly
                                           lee 1 mcmillan

PART IV

Effective Speech

The value of a pleasing, well-modulated voice cannot be estimated. In telephone conversations especially, the listener's impression is founded solely on the tone and quality of the speaker's voice.

LESSON 49

The Voice—Tone

One of the greatest selling instruments at our command is the human voice. Few persons know that every time they talk they are putting on a sales performance.

When selling an idea or a product, the salesman concentrates on methods of approach, on selling points, on closing the sale. Little does he realize that voice control would make his techniques more productive.

How many of us are aware of the fact that every time we talk we are selling ourselves? An unpleasant voice has been known to prevent a boy or a girl from being a social as well as a business success. Take time to study some very popular person of your acquaintance. You will find that there is something attractive about his voice. Since he probably has had no voice training, he may be what we would call a "natural"; but even he could increase his advantage by study and practice of the elements that make for an effective voice. Let us study this lesson with the purpose of insuring that the sounds we utter will work for, not against, us.

Tone is the sound we hear when a person speaks. Have you any idea how your own voice sounds? Ask your classmates to close their eyes while you say, "Good morning, Mrs. Nelson. How are you today?" Now ask what impressions were created by your words and tone. This experience may prove to be a revelation for some of you, and that is good! We shall gain most from a study of tone elements —pitch, quality, and energy—only when we are convinced that we need such study and can profit from it.

Pitch. Every musical composition is written in a certain key, and every person speaks in a certain key. No composer ever wrote a successful song in a very high key. Such a song would never sell, for a series of high-pitched sounds is unpleasant to the ear. If your

243

voice is pitched too high, you will not be able to sell yourself. A voice that is pitched too low will also destroy any conscious or unconscious sales effort.

If you can sing the notes of the musical scale, you can pitch your voice wherever you desire. The winning voice has a key or pitch in the middle range—neither too high nor too low. Listen to yourself as you talk. If your voice is high, try to bring down the pitch. If it is very low, try to raise the pitch. Start your practice now, for you will have to work if you want results.

Inflection. When working to attain a desirable midrange pitch, we must remember that we do not say *all* our words on that one key. There must be variety, or inflection, induced by saying some words and syllables in higher tones and others in lower tones. The voice without inflection is monotonous, dull, uninteresting.

Do you know any person to whom you dislike to talk because he bores you? Talk to him again and listen critically to his tone, not his words. It may be that you tire quickly of his conversation because he talks about subjects that are not of interest to you, or it may well be that the lack of voice inflection makes you want to get away as fast as you can.

And now listen just as critically to your own voice. Be sure that there are enough up-and-down variations from your basic key so that the sound of your voice will not bore *your* hearers. Who wants to be a bore?

Quality. The voice may be well pitched and free from monotony, but it may still be unpleasant because it does not sound round and full. We would then say that the quality is poor.

Before we can judge the quality of our own voices, we must recognize poor tone quality in the voices of other people. Listen until you have heard a voice that you would call thin. Then listen until you hear a voice that seems to come from the nose instead of the mouth. See whether you can hear a voice that is coarse and rough, that seems to be rooted in the chest. Now, listen to yourself.

If your tone quality is poor, do you want to do something to improve it? Assuming that you do, study carefully the following section. It was written especially for people like you.

We should understand that at the back of the throat is our voice box. Breath hits this box and should be pushed straight out into the

air. If your voice has a nasal quality, then you shoot your breath
from the voice box up into the nasal passages. If your voice is rough
and coarse, you hold your breath in the voice box.

Breath properly directed is the first step toward good tone quality,
but there are other things that we must learn. Let us work to open
our mouths and drop our jaws on the "long" words—words containing long, rounded vowel sounds, such as *our, home, go.* There is a
practice question that has been used by so many speech teachers
that it has become a joke. The words, however, provide excellent
practice in jaw dropping. Practice saying aloud, "How now, brown
cow?"

The tongue and the lips must also be used to produce fine tone
quality. Keep your lips rigid and almost closed and say *boom,
please, quiet, fragile, merchandise, valuable.* Repeat and use all the
lip movement you need. A marked difference, isn't there?

With your tongue held in the bottom of your mouth, say *their,
try, limited, tough.* Repeat and use your tongue forcefully. Note the
improvement in quality.

Try saying the following words in concert; then work on them
alone at home.

Dropped Jaw

charge	dark	grown	quality
closing	doubt	honor	responsible
compromise	found	mind	satisfy
co-operation	gold	operate	shadow
cordial	great	power	stop

Limber Lips

boyhood	friend	passive	spread
British	march	register	strike
business	merger	reservation	triumphant
formulate	mimeograph	river	view
freedom	office	shore	where

Active Tongue

actually	daughter	loudest	through
calculator	expediter	salesperson	ticklish
clothes	learn	seized	tonight
coldest	little	technique	yellow
dust	looseness	thousand	yield

Tone quality will be good if we push our breath from the voice box directly out through the mouth, and if we use correctly and freely our lips, tongue, and jaw. Keep practicing!

Energy. Voice energy is controlled by the amount of breath that is brought up from the lungs to the voice box. The farther you want your words to reach, the more breath you use. Shouting is unnecessary as well as impolite. If you have taken vocal lessons, you know that your teacher worked incessantly on your breathing. The boy or girl who is interested in becoming a good talker must work just as hard.

Suppose that you want to emphasize a single word in a sentence. Don't yell that word; just use more breath to push it out. Say aloud the following sentences, using extra breath on the italicized words.

> *I* told you to come here.
> I *told* you to come here.
> I told *you* to come here.
> I told you to *come* here.
> I told you to come *here*.

You did not have to shout the word in order to emphasize it. You were able to convey a different meaning every time you stressed a different word. You did it all by using more breath on the italicized words than you did on the other words.

Control of your breathing will allow you to create impressions. If you use much more breath than you need, you will push out a crude, boisterous sound. If you are a lazy breather and if you have little inflection, you will sound bored and a little tired of the world. You may even sound condescending. If your breathing is jerky, you will sound nervous or excited.

When we are under pressure or angry or fearful, our breathing is affected; and we betray the fact that our emotions are out of control. Therefore, whenever we become nervous or angry, we shall know enough to draw a few deep breaths to relax our breathing mechanism. Then, when we talk, we shall be able to conceal the fact that we are emotionally disturbed.

Let us work to acquire the ability to use enough breath to be heard. We have an ideal practice situation here in school, for every recitation; and every answer to a question presents an opportunity to use all the breath that is needed to reach *everyone* in the room.

Assignment 1. You happen to go by the entrance to your office just as a caller comes in. The visitor wishes to see Mr. Smith, who has let it be known that he is in conference. Convey this information to the caller and use your knowledge of pitch, quality, and energy to give the following impressions:

1. You are in a hurry, and the caller is interrupting your work.

2. Receiving callers is not your business. YOU are a bookkeeper.

3. Old Smith is using the same old gag—in conference. The caller may believe it, but you don't. You know he is in there reading a newspaper.

4. You knew that someday you would be caught! You always feared that you would be placed in a position where you would have to meet the public.

5. You are a show-off, and you very much want to amuse that certain girl or boy who is working at the nearest desk.

6. You have been trained to use your voice correctly. This caller might have a big order for your company, and you would like to impress him with the warmth of the people with whom he will deal. Don't overdo it.

Assignment 2. Select two of your school cheers. Show how a small group that knows about pitch, quality, and energy can make more noise than a large group that does not have this knowledge.

Assignment 3. Type a business letter addressed to your teacher. In the letter state your major tone weaknesses, your analysis of the causes, and your plan for improvement.

Assignment 4. Use the information given in the letter assigned for Exercise 3 as material for a talk. When you finish, ask your classmates for suggestions.

LESSON **50**

The Voice—Diction

The person who is characterized as using good diction pronounces his words correctly and fashions every sound distinctly. There is no place in business for the boy or girl who is slovenly in speech. Time is wasted when words or messages have to be repeated. Enemies of good diction are:

Omission and Misuse of Consonants. Final *t*, final *d*, and final *g* in the syllable *ing* are often ignored. Listen to hear whether you have this fault. Did you study shorthand "lashear," or do you plan to study it "nekshear"? Have you "foun'" it hard to follow instructions? Have we been having "mil'" weather? Are you careful about "cleanin'" your machine?

Sometimes consonants are omitted in the body of words or between words. Say:

quantity	gentlemen	recognize
government	hundred	clothes
February	Indian	let her
candidate	library	give me
didn't	perhaps	

The final *ng* sound is difficult for some people to master. Are you given to dreaming-*guh*? Say *hang* and listen. Do you say *han-guh*? You should hear only one sound. Now say *hanger* and *hanging*. The *er* and *ing* sounds should be separate, distinct, clear. Practice saying:

ringing	tongs	strong
long	young	among
bringing	eating	kingdom
sang	tongue	banging
		fling

The *th* sound is a stumbling block for those who have not learned to press the tip of the tongue against the edge of the upper teeth. Say:

these	thank	wealth
them	this	length
those	that	health
through	the	death
there	thread	month
theater	breadth	both
		with

Omission and Misuse of Vowels. Say the following words aloud and listen to discover whether you hear all the vowels:

cruel	municipal	lion
cabinet	metropolitan	general
real	literature	veteran
ivory	quietly	excellent
capital	original	temporary
ridiculous	analyze	sophomore
federal	especially	positive
accidentally	family	preferable
history	definite	regulate
separate	operation	terrible
stereotyped	indirectly	variable

In some sections of the country, the *er* and the *oi* sounds are transposed. Consider the sentence: "Do you oin very much woiking for the Moiphy Erl Company?" Now repeat the sentence, using the correct sounds.

When a word begins with a vowel followed by a double consonant, the initial vowel sound is short. Many speakers make the mistake of giving the long sound to the vowel. Say:

efficient	offensive	erroneous
official	efface	occasional
effect	elliptical	officious
opponent	oppress	

Note that this error usually occurs when the initial vowel is *e* or *o*.

Mispronunciation. You should be careful to know and to use correct pronunciation. Here are a few of the common errors. Study the list, and then watch *your* pronunciation.

exhilerator	for	accelerator
accumerlate	for	accumulate
akeret	for	accurate
accrost	for	across
annooity	for	annuity
artchitect	for	architect
athaletics	for	athletics
attackted	for	attacked
attawrney	for	attorney
authoritively	for	authoritatively
avenoo	for	avenue
becuz	for	because
bronical	for	bronchial
bergular	for	burglar
kin	for	can
karmel	for	caramel
ketch	for	catch
chimley	for	chimney
colyume	for	column
kewpon	for	coupon
doncha	for	don't you
drownded	for	drowned
aig	for	egg
esculator	for	escalator
extra ordinary	for	extraordinary
fillum	for	film
garaj	for	garage
genuwine	for	genuine
Eyetalian	for	Italian
itinery	for	itinerary
maintainance	for	maintenance
maisure	for	measure
mischeevious	for	mischievous
misherble	for	miserable
Noo York	for	New York
wunst	for	once
peculerly	for	peculiarly
prespire	for	perspire
punkin	for	pumpkin
puncheration	for	punctuation
regerlar	for	regular
wrench	for	rinse
secertary	for	secretary

shoulda or should of	for	should have
tremenjous	for	tremendous
wotcha	for	what did you
wen	for	when
ware	for	where
wich	for	which
wile	for	while
wye	for	why
willyuh	for	will you
yaller	for	yellow
yeah	for	yes

Overworked Words and Expressions. The well-trained business person has sufficient command of the English language to make it unnecessary for him to resort to such annoying speech mannerisms as: current slang—*sure, swell, loads,* and others; meaningless phrases —*you know, see what I mean, listen, wotcha callit;* fillers—*and-ah, ur-ur-ur.*

Assignment 1. If there is a voice-recording machine in your school, have a record of your voice made. Play the recording during class time and ask for help in discussing speech defects.

Assignment 2. If possible, bring to class a voice recording made by a professional. Be prepared to lead a discussion of the speaker's tone and diction.

Assignment 3. Without mentioning names, list some common voice faults of the members of your class. Be prepared to give a short talk on this material. Make constructive suggestions.

Assignment 4. Select a radio commentator to whom you frequently listen and be prepared to tell the class your opinion of his performance. Use the following as a guide:

1. What kind of person do you think he is? Why?
2. Is his voice pleasant? If so, what makes it pleasing?
3. Does he slur his words? Does he pronounce his final consonants?
4. Has he any objectionable speech habits, as: *and-a; ur-ur;* slang; overworked phrases?
5. Why do you listen to him rather than to some other commentator?

LESSON **51**

The Talk—Choice of Subject

Purpose. A successful talk is given with a definite purpose in mind. The speaker may wish to inform, to convince, or to entertain. It is possible that he may plan a combination of two or three aims. Your first step in choosing a subject is to decide the reason for giving your talk. When you have made your purpose clear to yourself, you know why you are going to speak. The next step is to select suitable material.

Consider the Audience. The audience is the customer; you are the salesman. Your talk must be geared to the buyer. It would be well to think about the following factors.

1. *Age.* The age group into which your audience falls is important to you. A subject that would interest people of middle age would very probably not appeal to teen-agers. If at a dinner given by the office force you should sit between the president of the company and your boon companion, you could not hope that the same topic would necessarily interest both. If, during the same day, you were to talk to a group of cub scouts and to a group of eagle scouts, you would probably talk on different subjects. If you used the same subject, you would vary the approach and the language.

2. *Sex.* A subject of interest to men is not always of like interest to women. Choose carefully your topic for a talk to be given to an audience composed of both sexes. This audience factor is important. Just try to talk to a boys' club on the subject of permanent waves!

3. *Experience, Background, Interests.* Experience, background, and interests are tied together very closely, for out of experience and background come the interests. Imagine talking to the student body of a large city school on the subject of automatic milking machines! Or trying to interest the members of the accounting department in

speed techniques in transcription! Or explaining to a freshman home-economics class the mechanics of the atom bomb! Your talk must be within the comprehension and interests of your audience. The subject should be deliberately chosen with the intention of evoking the "I see" or "Oh, yes" reaction. Lack of understanding will promote boredom.

Consider Your Own Interests. To inform others, you must be informed. To convince others, you must be convinced. To interest others, you must be interested. It is necessary that you know what you are talking about, that you be interested, and that you want to interest your audience.

Consider the Time Allotment. The subject you would choose for a five-minute talk might be entirely different from that for a fifteen-minute talk. Let us suppose that you wish to speak to your employer about a change in your lunch hour and also about an increase in salary. You ask for a conference, and he says that he can give you five minutes of his time. Which topic would you discuss with him?

While practicing a talk, let us remember that we should always plan to exceed our time allotment by at least two minutes. When we give a talk before an audience, we are keyed up, nervous; and that causes us to increase our tempo. Therefore, unless we allow for this recognized tendency, we shall find ourselves finished before time.

Limit the Subject. Whether you have been assigned a subject or whether you are to choose your subject, do not try to cover too much ground. Select what you think is an interesting phase and concentrate on that aspect of the whole topic. Suppose you choose to talk about airplanes. It would be impossible as well as unwise to attempt to cover this subject in one talk. If you would elect to talk about the latest developments in passenger models, you could do justice to the topic.

Arousing Interest. When you are in the throes of selecting the subject of a talk, you must give some consideration to those aspects of the subject that will appeal to people. Regardless of the age, sex, or experience of your audience, certain elements of a subject will win and hold the interest. A good talk includes some of these elements.

An audience will be interested in that which is—

1. *Amusing.* Everyone enjoys a good laugh at the proper time and place. Are there possibilities for humor in your subject? Is the humor consistent with good taste?

2. *New or Different.* Will your topic give your hearers something unusual to think about? Are you sure they have enough preliminary knowledge to be able to make the transition from the known to the unknown?

3. *Necessary to Happiness.* Human beings are interested in anything that pertains to their personal health, financial progress, possessions, families, loyalties. Can you appeal to one or more of these?

4. *Indicative of Conflict.* Nearly all novels have as a main or subsidiary theme a struggle of some kind. The hero may battle the elements, another person, economic conditions, established institutions, or some other force—but he is in there fighting, from page 1 to the end of the book. Will your talk in some way include the overcoming of obstacles?

5. *Not Self-Evident.* Most of us like an opportunity to do a little guessing. This is the type of interest that is carried to extremes by the mystery-story addict. Will your topic keep the audience a little, but only a little, in doubt as to the outcome of some situation?

6. *Living, Moving.* A good talk will make the audience see, visually or/and mentally. Will your topic provide you with an opportunity to paint word pictures? Can you use concrete verbal examples? Can you assemble material objects that will help you to make your points? For instance, can you have a diagram drawn on a blackboard and use it for the purpose of illustrating? Can you show small-scale models? Can you exhibit the actual product? From birth to death, human beings like to look at something. That is why the theater holds its own in spite of radio; that is why people will continue to buy ringside seats in spite of television. They want to be right there to see the real blows and to hear the real grunts.

Social Application. The principles you have studied in this lesson can be used in your business and social life. The brilliant conversationalist is the person who can lead *other* people to talk well. The boy or girl who is unsuccessful socially is the person who talks about himself or herself. The so-called "good mixer" knows how to draw out his associates by introducing topics of interest to *them.*

Assignment 1. Prepare a list of five topics about which you think you would be able to talk. Present this list to the class and state fully the reasons for selecting each topic.

Assignment 2. Choose one of the topics you listed for Assignment 1 and give a short talk on this subject.

Assignment 3. Select the title of a talk to be given to a Girl Scout troop; your own classmates; the sales force of a publishing house; the members of a stenographic pool working for a helicopter manufacturer; your local chapter of a national organization of business and professional women.

Assignment 4. You have been asked to be on a radio panel that will discuss "My Life at (your own) High School." Tell the class: what type of audience you expect to reach; how long you will talk; what phase of the topic you plan to cover; why you chose this phase.

Assignment 5. Prepare the talk on the topic selected in Assignment 4.

Assignment 6. You are attending a tea given by your business club to a group of businessmen in your city. You have been assigned to be host or hostess to the president of the largest local manufacturing concern, a man who looks to be about fifty years of age. List some of the conversational topics that might interest him. Prepare questions or observations that you think would lead him to want to talk.

LESSON **52**

The Talk—Organization

Now that you have chosen your subject and have in mind the various techniques that go toward making a good talk, it is time to think about the organization of your material. First, you must have an outline. Broadly speaking, every talk contains the following three sections:

    I. Introduction
    II. Body of the talk
    III. Closing sentences

Body of the Talk. We shall start with the second section, the body of the talk. A more polished introduction and closing will be possible if you have first developed the principal part of the talk.

Think about the subject until you have selected what you think are the main points. Suppose you have decided upon three important phases. Your outline will look like this:

    II. Body of the talk
        A. First important point
        B. Second important point
        C. Third important point

It will probably be necessary for you to do some reading about your topic. As you read and as you think about the matter, you will make notes. It might be a good idea to have separate sheets of paper, each labeled with one of the headings you expect to use. On each sheet write all notes pertaining to that heading.

Now take time to review the main points. Is the order you have chosen chronological? Is there logical progression? Are you sure you have selected the distinctive points? Revise if necessary. Do not be disturbed if you find that the final list bears no resemblance to the original.

You are ready to assemble the supporting facts. Take the sheets containing the revised headings and the notes you have made. From the maze of notes, select those that best express the thoughts you wish to convey. These are also subject to subsequent change. Fill in your outline thus:

II. Body of the talk
    A. First important point
        1. First supporting or related thought
        2. Second supporting or related thought
        3. Third supporting or related thought
        4. Fourth supporting or related thought
    B. Second important point
        1. First supporting or related thought
        2. Second supporting or related thought
        3. Third supporting or related thought
        4. Fourth supporting or related thought
    C. Third important point
        1. First supporting or related thought
        2. Second supporting or related thought
        3. Third supporting or related thought
        4. Fourth supporting or related thought

Introduction. Whether or not you have been introduced and the subject of your talk has been mentioned, you should state your topic in the opening sentence. Otherwise, it will take the audience so long to find out what you are talking about that many of your best points will be lost.

Plan the opening sentences so carefully that your first words will gain the immediate attention and interest of your listeners. They have paid you the compliment of coming to listen to you, and it is your obligation to keep them from falling asleep.

You may wish to amplify the opening sentence. Possibly you would like to tell the audience why you chose the topic or why you enjoy speaking to that particular group; you may wish to tell some amusing incident connected with the choice of subject. Then you will surely say something that will be a connecting link between the introduction and the body of the talk. Your outline for the introduction will be:

I. Introduction
   A. Opening sentence
   B. Related thought
   C. Transition thought

Caution: Never apologize in your introduction.

Closing Sentences. Last impressions are likely to be lasting impressions; so do not neglect the preparation of your final paragraph. Your purpose here is to round off your subject gracefully, to leave the audience with a feeling of satisfactory completion. You may end with an apt quotation, a poem, or a story. You may summarize your talk. You may repeat the introductory theme. You may indicate future trends relative to the topic. In any case, when you have thought through this section, fill in your outline.

III. Closing sentences
   A. Transition from body of talk to closing
   B. Concluding words

The Complete Talk. The outline is finished, and from it you will write your talk. Try to use your own speaking words and style. You have no intention of memorizing this material, but you are eager to give an outstanding performance. You must have the over-all picture in order to judge whether or not the result is good. Memorize only the first and the last sentences—the first sentence to help you through those first nervous seconds, the last sentence to insure an effective finale. Watch the delivery of that last sentence lest you give the impression of rattling it off in order to dash for your chair.

Read the speech aloud several times and listen critically. Then practice saying it with the aid of the outline. Ask members of your family or some of your friends to listen to you and criticize. Be satisfied only when you think your words will impel the audience to say, "That was a splendid talk."

To use or not to use the outline while speaking is a question that frequently arises. Some speakers memorize the outline and do not use it while talking. Other speakers know the outline, but prefer to look at it while they talk. Possibly the best compromise would be to memorize the outline and then have it available either in card form or in a small notebook for reference should the need arise. This might ease any nervous tension attendant upon the fear of forgetting.

General Principles to Be Observed

1. State the subject of the talk in the opening sentence.
2. State the main point in each section of the body of the talk; then develop the statement.
3. Stick to the point. Do not wander.
4. Stress points by repeating in a different form.
5. Never criticize or scold the audience.
6. Refrain from using sarcasm or irony.
7. Remember that jokes are like dynamite. They are effective if used correctly, but they may have disastrous results if used incorrectly. If a joke is told, be careful not to offend. Tell a joke only for the sake of making a point or of illustrating a point. Be sure to build up the telling in such a way that the audience cannot miss the point.
8. Use apt illustrations, but be sure that they do not obscure that which you wish to stress.
9. Do not overtalk your welcome. Many a talk would have been eminently successful had the speaker stopped five minutes earlier.

If you are one of two or more speakers and have been assigned a definite time limit—say, fifteen minutes—for your talk, do not exceed the time limit. If necessary, ask the chairman to give you a one-minute warning.

Introducing a Speaker. Introducing a speaker is an important duty and one that you may sometime be called upon to perform. You should know, then, that an introduction ought to be short and simple and that it should include the following:

1. Some gracious remark that will make the speaker feel that he is warmly welcomed.
2. Statement of the subject of the talk.
3. Brief, very brief, summary of the speaker's background or special interests that will show that he is well qualified to talk on his chosen subject.
4. Presentation of the speaker by name. The announcement of the name of the speaker is usually left to the very last because it serves as a signal for the speaker to begin his talk.

Assignment 1. Be ready to introduce some one of your classmates when he gives the talk assigned in Assignment 2.

Assignment 2. Prepare an outline for a talk on any subject with which you are very familiar. Write the outline on the board and go over it, point by point, with the class.

LESSON 53

The Talk—Delivery

Personal Preparation. It is of vast importance that you select with care the clothing you intend to wear. Somewhere in your wardrobe you have a costume in which you feel that you look "right." Attend to your personal grooming. See that all accessories are firmly attached. The boy whose hand strays repeatedly to the knot of his necktie is obviously ill at ease and makes a poor impression. The feeling of being well dressed promotes self-confidence.

Posture. The speaker has a decided advantage over the writer, for the writer has only words at his command. The speaker has both words and facial expression and posture with which to interpret the words to the audience.

Stand with your weight evenly distributed on both feet, leaning slightly forward. The hip-out-of-joint effect, caused by an uneven distribution of weight, is most unfavorable. Accomplished speakers use a change of position when they wish to round off a thought, to indicate a break. If you wish to take a step to change your position, take it deliberately, purposefully. Do not sidle or shuffle. Provide variety by moving shorter and longer distances, always at an angle toward the audience.

Lift the chin enough so that you can look squarely at your hearers, be they two or a hundred.

The conventional position for arms and hands is to let them hang loosely from the shoulders, a little to the fore. Of course, if you were to maintain this position throughout your talk, you would give the impression of tenseness. Desirable variety may be provided by placing your hands behind your back, by putting one hand in your pocket. The thing to remember is that *constant* change or fidgeting

261

is annoying to those who are looking at you, while relaxed hands are never noticed.

Practice in front of a mirror until you are sure that your posture is easy, confident, relaxed—but not slovenly! (See also "Objectionable Mannerisms," in this lesson.)

Platform Manners. A talk is successful only when it is given by a person who is courteous and polished. In order that we may create such an impression, let us study these few hints on platform manners.

1. While sitting on the platform waiting your turn to speak, give full attention to any preceding speaker or speakers. Never carry on a conversation with anyone who is seated with you. Do not scan the audience for relatives or friends to whom you can wave or at whom you can smile.

2. Remember to thank the person who introduces you and call him by name. Say, "Thank you, Mr. James."

3. You may elect not to use a salutation, and that is perfectly all right. If you do use a salutation, however, be sure that you do not slight anyone. For instance, if you are speaking at a school assembly, you will properly say, "Mr. (your principal), faculty members, and student body."

4. Signify in some courteous way that your talk is finished. You may pause for a moment and then smile and nod at the audience. You may choose to thank the audience for the opportunity of talking to them.

Rapport. When the feeling between the speaker and the audience is that of mutual liking and cordiality, *rapport* has been established. The successful talker is the person who knows and uses the techniques that create this invisible bond. Consider the following devices.

1. *Walking to Place.* You make your very first impression when you walk to the spot where you will talk. Walk fast enough to give the effect of confidence, but do not swagger. Walk slowly enough to show that you are at ease, but not so slowly as to seem to be putting off an ordeal.

2. *Breathing and Carrying Power.* As you walk to your place, take a few deep breaths. Before you start to speak, draw a breath

and hold it. This will preclude the possibility of having your first words emerge as frightened squeaks. Use your knowledge of proper breathing to help you to speak so that everyone in the room can hear you. Always remember that an audience will not strain to hear a speaker; if he forces them to do so, rapport will be lost. Review the lessons on tone and diction.

3. *Platform Courtesy.* Remember to acknowledge an introduction courteously. Remember to recognize, in words, the persons in charge of the occasion. Give courteous attention to any other speakers on the program. While awaiting your turn to talk, do not sprawl in your chair.

4. *Manner.* You probably will be nervous. That is a good omen, for nervousness is a sign of intelligence. Just control yourself to the extent that you do not *appear* worried or cross. Look pleasant and friendly, as though pleased to have the privilege of talking to that particular group. Your manner throughout should be sincere, natural, and modest.

5. *Conversational Tone.* Adopt the warm speaking tone you would use were you talking with your friends, for this is a *talk* you are giving. It is not an oration. Talk *to* your hearers, not *at* them. It is important that you look at the audience. You probably will see nothing but a blur of faces, but let your eyes rest on different sections of this blur. Rapport cannot be obtained by the talker who looks at the floor, at the ceiling, out of the window, or keeps his eyes glued on a point behind the audience.

Suit your vocabulary to your hearers. Do not use words that are probably unfamiliar to them. On the other hand, do not "talk down" to them by choosing only those words that are in the vocabulary of a child. Try to make each of your hearers feel that you are talking to him personally.

6. *Timing.* The art of regulating the tempo in speaking, so as to heighten the effectiveness of certain moments, is known as *timing*. Audiences are slow of comprehension. It is much more difficult to assimilate facts that are heard than facts that are read. Decide which phases of your talk you wish the audience to carry away with them. Emphasize these phases by saying them at a slower rate and by repeating them in different words. You will find that rate is governed by the length of time you hold individual tones and by the length of pauses between words and phrases.

Timing should be varied. Accelerate to indicate excitement, anger, enthusiasm, joy. Decelerate to convey thoughtfulness, solemnity, grandeur. Practice until you think you have achieved a good basic rate. Keep in mind that nervousness causes an increase in timing. Allow for this, particularly at the beginning of your talk. Remember, too, that the larger the audience or the hall, the more necessary it is that you speak slowly.

7. *The "You" Attitude.* All talks are a form of selling. You already know that the salesman must offer his arguments in such a way that the customer feels that for his own satisfaction he should purchase. The same principle holds true in a talk. The speech material must be within the experience and interests of the audience and should be presented to the hearers from their own vantage point.

A special caution is needed here—do not scold the audience or say anything that will make them want to fight back. Suppose you are a sales manager addressing a meeting of salesmen. Should you say, "*You* must sell more pencils in the next three months," a defensive attitude is created. Now, should you say, "*We* must sell more pencils in the next three months," a co-operative, action-impelling feeling is generated.

8. *Objectionable Mannerisms.* Movement of any kind attracts and too often distracts the attention of an audience. Such habits as toying with objects, clearing the throat frequently, using *uh* and *anda* become so annoying that the hearers lose the thread of the discourse.

Gestures should be used in moderation. Use only those that you would ordinarily need in conversation. Of course, if you are the sort of person who "can't talk when his hands are tied," then perhaps the last sentence would not apply. Overuse of gestures will not be necessary for the person who has a command of English and who knows about timing and body control.

9. *Poise.* The speaker who does not show embarrassment, who does not seem to be disconcerted, has poise. Audiences are entirely unpredictable. You may say something that is meant to be funny, and it may pass without a chuckle. Again, you may say something that is not meant to be funny and have it greeted with a burst of laughter. Laugh with them and wait for the noise to die down. Do not attempt, ever, to go on talking while the audience is laughing. When you have waited a reasonable time, you can show by a body

shift or by a lifting of the head that you are about to resume. The movement will give them the signal.

In the case of an unforeseen interruption, the person with a ready and reliable wit may make a joke of the mishap. In any event, you will be safe if you smile and wait quietly. Someone will always come to your rescue.

Assignment 1. Prepare a talk on any combination of topics given in this lesson. Draw freely on your own experience or on the experiences of others.

Assignment 2. In the light of the material given in this lesson and without mentioning names, list some of the speaking mannerisms of your classmates. Be sure to include the desirable as well as the undesirable mannerisms. Be prepared to give a talk on these data.

Assignment 3. Select two or three of your friends whom you consider good conversationalists. Prepare a short talk in which you will analyze the factors that make these people interesting talkers.

LESSON 54

Speech Clinic

The time has come for you to put into practice the speech principles that you have studied. The other members of the class will act as diagnosticians and prescribers for whoever gives a talk. The function of the group is to work co-operatively and objectively for the good of the speaker and for its own good.

Assignments. Unless otherwise instructed by the teacher, you may choose the assignment you wish to work out. If you are convinced of the importance of being a good talker and feel that you need the practice, you may wish to give more than one talk. Do so, by all means, if time permits.

Outline. It would be well for the speaker to make enough carbon copies of the outline of his talk so that every two members of the class may share one copy. There must be an outline for every talk.

Check List. A check list follows for the convenience of your classmates who are acting as speech consultants. For the first few times, you may think this list cumbersome to use. As you become more familiar with it, you will find that only a few moments are needed to check off the items. Possibly the speaker may collect the check lists and, at his leisure, study the criticisms.

Check List

I. Tone
    A. Pitch
        Too high . . . .
        Medium . . . .
        Too low . . . .

        Monotonous . . . .
        Varied . . . .
    B. Quality
        Harsh . . . .
        Hoarse . . . .

Check List—Continued

Nasal ....

Pleasant ....

C. Energy

Breathing ....

Carrying power

Loud enough ....

Too loud ....

Not loud enough ....

Uneven ....

II. Diction

A. Pronunciation

Words mispronounced ..

....

....

....

B. Enunciation

Clear

Precise

Slovenly

Instances of faulty enun-

ciation

....

....

C. Grammar

Violated rules ....

Colloquialisms ....

Vulgarisms ....

III. Choice of subject

A. Good ......

B. Poor ....

IV. Outline

A. Logical order ....

B. Too meager ....

C. Too long ....

D. Followed outline ......

E. Did not follow outline ..

V. Personal preparation

A. Clothing

Poorly selected ....

Well selected ....

B. Grooming

....

....

VI. Posture

A. Sitting

Good ....

Poor ....

B. Walking

Good ....

Poor ....

C. Standing

Tense ....

Easy ....

Feet ....

Hands ....

Careless ....

Chin up ....

Chin down ....

Sways from side to side .

Shifts to indicate change

in thought ....

VII. Delivery

A. Courtesy

Good ....

Poor ....

B. Manner

Friendly ....

Confident ....

Unpleasant ....

Superior ....

Nervous ....

C. Conversational tone

Talked *at* ....

Talked *to* ....

Looked at audience ....

Did not look at audi-

ence ....

Stared fixedly ....

Suitable vocabulary ....

Check List—Continued

VIII. Timing
    A. Too fast ....
    B. Too slow ....
    C. Monotonous ....
    D. Varied ....
IX. The "you" attitude
    A. Good ......
    B. Poor ....

X. Objectionable mannerisms
    ....
    ....
    ....
    ....
XI. Poise
    A. Good ....
    B. Lack of assurance ......
    C. Too much assurance ...

Assignment 1. Prepare an outline and a talk on a topic of your own choice. The time limit for the talk is three minutes.

Assignment 2. Select a topic that one of the class presented for Assignment 1 and prepare the remarks to use in introducing the person who delivered the talk.

Assignment 3. As part of a program to inform the public about the needs of education in your community, you have been asked to talk to the Rotary Club of your city on the subject "Why We Need a New High School." Prepare the outline and the talk.

Assignment 4. You have had five years of service with the Cullinane Insurance Company. During those years you have worked in the Payroll Department. The firm is ultraconservative and does not take kindly to innovations. The calculator you have been using is an old, manually operated machine. You are convinced that you could do more and better work if your employers would purchase a new calculator for your use. Mr. Cullinane has agreed to let you have ten minutes of his time. Prepare your talk.

Assignment 5. In no more than five minutes, give an illustrated talk. You may bring to class some materials connected with a hobby; or you may teach the class some operation with which you are familiar, such as typing a stencil.

Assignment 6. You are attending the twenty-fifth reunion of this class. Prepare an after-dinner talk.

Assignment 7. Be ready to give a talk designed to show how a knowledge of speech principles would be advantageous to one of the following:

A banker
A file clerk
An office manager
A telephone operator
A junior clerk
A department-store clerk
A clerk in a complaint department
A calculator operator

The manager of a credit bureau
A shipping clerk
A receptionist
A stenographer
A secretary
A bookkeeper
A salesman

Assignment 8. Prepare a talk that will be a report on some current event, a book you have read, a moving picture you have seen, a radio program, a field trip, or a like topic of your choice.

Assignment 9. Below are given some broad, general topics. Your job is to select a phase of one of these and make of it an interesting talk.

Encyclopedias
Business Dress
Dogs in Wartime
The Automat
Improvement in Grammar
Salesmanship
Courtesy in Business
The Atom Bomb

Office Routine
Education in South America
Amusements for Teen-agers
Negotiable Instruments
The Mechanics of Radio
Collections in Business
Filing
The Telephone Directory

PART V

Effective Writing

The employee who proves her ability to write clearly and effectively soon receives writing assignments from her executive.

LESSON 55

The Word, the Sentence, the Paragraph

Facility in the use of language is gained through a series of steps: First come the separate letters of the alphabet; then the combination of letters into words, and of words into sentences, in accordance with the rules of grammar; finally comes the stage when the significance of a whole sentence or paragraph is grasped at a glance.

The Word. A command of English means primarily a command of words. It was with this premise in mind that vocabulary study was made an important part of this textbook. "The right word in the right place" very well expresses the over-all aim.

You should now be aware of the fact that different words express different meanings and different shades of meaning, that some expressions are illiterate or in poor taste, and that some words—while correct—are overworked and colorless.

Your nice letter of July 30 has been received.

Is *nice* the only word you can think of to characterize the letter? Can it not be an interesting letter, a gracious letter, a splendid letter, a welcome letter, a courteous letter, a very fine letter, a cordial letter, a surprising letter, an exciting letter, or a thoughtful letter?

Business Vocabulary. You are on the road to becoming a specialist in business, and you should know the meaning of business terms. You would have very little confidence in a physician who did not know the meaning of a medical term, and your employer will have as little confidence in you if you are unacquainted with the vocabulary of business.

273

If you think you are weak in this respect, review the terms and abbreviations in any modern business textbook.

Special Vocabulary. Each business and industry has words and expressions peculiar to that business and industry. The alert employee learns the special vocabulary as quickly as he can. Information can be obtained from the files and from pamphlets and catalogues. Borrow some of these pamphlets, and take them home with you. Keep a notebook in which you list the terms and definitions. If you are a stenographer, practice the shorthand outlines for any unfamiliar words. The ability to "talk the language" will promote self-confidence.

Caution 1: Regardless of how extensive your vocabulary may be, do not seize on every occasion to display your familiarity with words. Be neither flowery nor effusive. Make a practice of saying very simply only what you need to say in order to make your meaning perfectly clear.

Caution 2: It may be that your employer is old-fashioned and that he uses trite or obsolete statements. Be assured that any correction or criticism from you will probably be most unwelcome. Be tactful. Remember: *He pays your salary.*

Assignment 1. The Allen Manufacturing Company employs you to answer correspondence. Describe briefly the probable contents of the letters to which, in reply, you refer as: inspiring, helpful, very unusual, impressive, very satisfactory.

Example: Very cheerful. The letter probably came from a salesman who reported that he was feeling well and had obtained many orders. Because business was so good, he would be out of town much longer than he expected. He asked for more expense money.

The Sentence. According to form, sentences are of three kinds: simple, compound, or complex.

A *simple* sentence contains only one independent clause—only one subject and one predicate. Either the subject or the predicate, or both, may be compound; but that does not alter the form of the sentence.

> We shall ship your order today.
> In what city is the main office of your firm? [Inverted order.]
> The main *office* and the *factory* are in Chicago. [Compound subject.]

Our receptionist *walks* and *talks* like a well-trained person. [Compound predicate.]

Ann and *Marie rubbed* and *scrubbed* all the duplicating machines. [Compound subject and compound predicate.]

A *compound* sentence contains two or more independent clauses, each of which makes a complete statement; as:

We received your order today, and we plan to make shipment tomorrow.

I must work or I shall starve.

I may work hard, but I seem to accomplish little.

Review Lesson 32 for the punctuation of compound sentences.

A *complex* sentence contains one independent clause and one or more dependent clauses. The independent clause expresses the main idea, and the dependent clause defines or describes the idea contained in the independent clause.

The error *that I pointed out to you* has not been corrected.

The error, *which is a minor one*, has not been corrected.

Review Lesson 33 for punctuation of complex sentences.

Assignment 2. Copy and classify as to form the sentences that follow. Underline each subject and supply any missing punctuation.

1. Our radio advertising campaign is very successful.

2. I cannot tell you how much I enjoy myself when your program is on the air.

3. The commercial is psychologically sound and the entertainment appeals to all age groups.

4. If you would like to see the broadcast ask Mr. Simons for tickets.

5. The leading lady who was a school friend of mine has a beautiful voice.

6. Grace sings for a living; I type for mine.

7. She and I have been very good friends for many years.

8. I like Grace very much but I do not approve of her extravagant habits.

9. She dresses and acts like a millionaire.

10. Grace is wasteful and I am thrifty.

11. She and I know our faults and make allowances for them.

12. The program that I mentioned will be on the air Tuesday evening.

The Paragraph. A *paragraph* is a sentence or a group of sentences that relate to a central thought. Should there be more than one paragraph on the central thought, each paragraph should treat of one phase of the thought.

Topic Sentence. A *topic sentence* is a sentence that states the main idea of a paragraph. This sentence may be placed at the beginning of the paragraph, which is the usual place; at the end of the paragraph; in the body of the paragraph; both at the beginning and at the end. Every paragraph should contain a topic sentence. In the following paragraph, the first sentence is the topic sentence.

Preparations are nearly complete for the intensive direct-mail campaign on our Foamy Soap Flakes. The sample packets have been delivered from our factory. The three-color circulars have been printed. Envelopes are addressed. Radio scripts are being edited. When the national advertising begins to appear on March 1, we will send out the first 10,000 mailings.

Continuity. Paragraphs must be connected, must have logical relationship. One way to secure this relationship is to use transitional words and phrases, such as *in like manner, for this reason, so, consequently, on the other hand.*

Length. There is no arbitrary rule for the length of paragraphs. It is well to remember that, when a thought ceases to relate to the topic sentence, it is time to begin a new paragraph.

In general, business letters should not contain paragraphs that are too long or too short. A full-page letter broken into only two paragraphs is unattractive in appearance and has a bad psychological effect on a busy man. On the other hand, business letters containing a long series of paragraphs of two or three lines also create a poor impression.

Assignment 3. Rewrite the following assignment. Express yourself simply, clearly, and briefly.

Yesterday, after I finished my dinner dishes, I sat down to read the papers. I never could understand why there are so many more dishes on Sunday than on any other day. I saw your advertisement of that *darling* little dress. I mean the one that was numbered 872. How in the world can you make any profit by selling a dress of that material at $16.98?

I want a dress like that, but it took me a long time to make up my mind about the color. I think I should like it in green; but if you cannot give me my size in green, I should like gray.

The size I usually get is 16½, but this dress does not come in half sizes; so I think I shall order a size 18.

I am adding an extra 10 cents for the postage. By the way, I *do* hope you will honor my personal check.

Now, I am having a tea next week, and I want the dress to wear then. It would be *so* kind of you to get the dress to me before then.

Assignment 4. Now that you know the meaning of the topic sentence, write a paragraph explaining how you can use this knowledge in preparing your homework.

LESSON 56

Qualities of Style

Almost every student makes the error of assuming that he does not need to study or to consider carefully anything that has previously been brought to his attention. Therefore, when you read here that there are four principles to which all good writing must conform:

Unity	Emphasis
Coherence	Euphony

you will probably say to yourself, "I know that." But—do you? Could you explain satisfactorily the meaning of any one of the four principles? Do you know when you are violating these principles?

Your written work will have:

Unity—if you have one idea and adhere to it.

Coherence—if there is no confusion with regard to your exact meaning.

Emphasis—if you stress that which needs to be stressed.

Euphony—if the effect of your writing is pleasing to the ear.

Unity

Unity is defined by Webster, "continuity without deviation or change; . . . the reference of the elements of a literary . . . composition to a main idea." Therefore, each sentence should contain only one main thought; each paragraph should contain only one main thought; each composition or letter should contain only one main thought.

In order to obtain unity, you must:

1. Exclude All Irrelevant Matter. Before you can write a sentence that contains only one idea, you must think in terms of main ideas. Your thoughts must be stripped of all that will not contribute directly to the message you wish to convey. The principle of *unity* would be violated if a sentence were to include anything that had little or no connection with the main thought. Consider the following sentences:

> I am not surprised that your firm has gone bankrupt, the location of the store is so poor.
> The receptionist ushered us into the private office, and we learned afterward that she was graduated from our school.
> June is a very attractive girl, and she likes her new position.
> Henry is an office boy; he makes a good worker for that firm.

Obviously, each of these sentences has two separate ideas instead of the one that is demanded by the principle of unity. Since there are two separate ideas, there should be two separate sentences.

Avoid cramming a sentence with too many loosely related thoughts. Overlong sentences irritate the reader.

> Shipment of your order, because of a disastrous fire in our No. 16 warehouse, will be delayed until December 15.

The person who receives this letter would be primarily interested in information about his order. Consciously or unconsciously, he would be annoyed at having to read so many words before the desired information could be obtained. A better effect could be achieved by wording the message, "We shall be unable to ship your order before December 15. Our stock is greatly depleted because of a disastrous fire in our No. 16 warehouse."

2. Include All Relevant Matter. Many writers, striving for what they consider businesslike brevity, produce sentences that are incorrect as well as meaningless. A sentence that contains too little is just as poor as one that contains too much. Consider:

> Your order of January 21 received.
> Have been very busy for the past week.
> Thanking you for your order.
> Mr. Garrison's office is on this floor. *Two doors down.*
> I was on time this morning. *But I shall be late tomorrow.*

> We sent you the bill this morning. *Having been instructed to do so by Mr. Stillman.*

Be sure that each sentence you write is complete with regard to meaning and that it contains a subject and a predicate.

3. Co-ordinate and Subordinate the Material Properly. Most sentences contain more than one clause. Such sentences must be written in such a way that there can be no mistake with regard to the points that the writer considers important and those that he considers contributing. Co-ordinate clauses are of equal importance. A subordinate clause contributes to the meaning of a main clause. It is said that children co-ordinate about 85 per cent of their statements, while adults co-ordinate about 50 per cent of theirs. It would follow that improper or feeble subordination is a sign of the mentally undeveloped. For a full discussion of co-ordinate and subordinate conjunctions see Lesson 28.

Consider this example:

> George refused to obey the order, and he lost his position.

The second idea is actually a result of the first; therefore, the proper subordination would make the sentence read:

> Because George refused to obey the order, he lost his position.

Suppose the idea of time were important. The sentence would then read:

> When George refused to obey the order, he lost his position.

The co-ordinate conjunction *and* is often called on to perform more than its share of work.

> I typed that letter for Mr. Brooks, *and* he found errors in it, *and* I had to type it again, *and* I decided to be more careful in the future.

Here are four main ideas strung along in one sentence. Unity requires that there be but one main idea in any sentence. Notice the improvement here.

> I typed that letter for Mr. Brooks. As he found many errors in it, I had to type it again. I decided to be more careful in the future.

A Frequent Dictator Fault. The well-trained stenographer has an excellent English background and can recognize and correct errors made by the dictator. Many executives when dictating are so concerned with thinking about the message that they hook up different thoughts into one sentence. Such a sentence is called a "run-on sentence," for it runs on and on.

Suppose that you are a stenographer and that your shorthand notes read:

We have your letter of April 30, which contains an order for one dozen 81 by 99 percale sheets, which we have already mailed to you.

This is an example of the "which" run-on sentence. There are two thoughts here: acknowledgment of the order and disposition of the order. You, as a good stenographer, would transcribe:

We have your letter of April 30, containing an order for one dozen 81 by 99 percale sheets. This order has already been filled and mailed to you.

Caution: If any deviation from the exact dictation will cause friction between you and your supervisor, transcribe his dictation word for word. Before you can feel free to revise, you must be in position to know that the dictator approves of your doing so.

4. Maintain the Point of View. The point of view will not be maintained if there is any kind of avoidable shift.

Usually, the point of view changes when the passive voice is used in one clause of the sentence and the active voice is used in another clause; as:

Since the error was made by Donald, he should make the correction.

A shift in voice results in a shift of subject. If the clauses are both made active, the reader's attention will not be divided by the two points of view. The sentence will then be:

Since Donald made the error, he should make the correction.

Use of connectives to join unlike constructions will cause a change in the point of view. Conjunctions were fully discussed in Lesson 28; so a repetition here is not necessary. The following examples will serve to illustrate the point.

Right: Henry will succeed, but Albert will fail. [*But* for contrast.]
Wrong: Henry will succeed, and Albert will fail.
Right: Talking is sometimes more effective than writing. [*Talking* and *writing* are like constructions.]
Wrong: Talking is sometimes more effective than to write.
Right: In my leisure time, I like to read and to play golf. [*And* connects like constructions.]
Wrong: In my leisure time, I like reading and to play golf.

A shift in the person of a pronoun will change the point of view; as:

I should like to know the name of a restaurant where you can get a good meal.

Why should *I* be interested in a restaurant where *you* can get a good meal? "*I* should like to know the name of a restaurant where *I* can get a good meal" is correct.

Assignment 1.   Rewrite any of the following sentences that do not have unity. After each correction place the number of the topic (see pages 279-281) that gives the principle involved.

Example: The union won its point. Though the opposition was strong.
Rewritten: Though the opposition was strong, the union won its point.
(2)

1. A secretary must be alert, or they will lose their reputation for efficiency.
2. The stenographer uses a fountain pen, and she has used one ever since she began the study of shorthand, and she thinks that a pen is more satisfactory than a pencil.
3. To buy is planned taking; selling is planned giving.
4. Mr. York's train was late, and he arrived at the office after ten o'clock.
5. When he entered the office, Mr. York told us his train was late.
6. Because the machine was used by Mary, she should clean it.
7. Byron sold the last tie at noon. Although the sale did not begin until eleven o'clock.
8. The check stub should be written, then you write the check.

9. Paul operated the new bookkeeping machine this morning, and he would have preferred to do the work by hand.

10. Our new clerk can file, take dictation, typewrite, and she can operate a calculator.

Assignment 2. Write five original compound sentences that show unity. Remember that the ideas must be closely related and of equal value.

Assignment 3. By subordinating ideas, change the five compound sentences written in Assignment 2 into complex sentences.

LESSON 57

Coherence

A sentence, a paragraph, a letter, or a composition has *coherence* if all the ideas contained are logically arranged. The finished letter or composition will lack *coherence* if the total effect is that of disorderliness. No two minds are alike; therefore, the writer must so word his thoughts that there can be no question as to the intended meaning. Violation of the principle of coherence results in word combinations that are confusing or, in many cases, downright ridiculous.

The basis of all composition is the sentence. Coherence in a sentence may be obtained by the following means:

1. Correct Arrangement. Words, phrases, and clauses should be arranged so that there is no possible doubt about what they modify. Modifiers should be placed close to the words they modify.

a. Word Modifiers. Adjectives and adverbs are frequently misplaced. Here are some adjectives out of position:

SALE

Summer girls' slacks

Flannel boys' trousers

As written, the slacks are for summer girls; the trousers are for flannel boys. Place the adjectives where they belong, and you have "girls' summer slacks" and "boys' flannel trousers."

And here are some adverbs that are out of position:

> It almost seems impossible to sell this stock.
> Do you ever expect to hear from him?

Do you think that *almost seems* expresses your meaning? The adverb *almost* is incorrectly placed. The sentence should read:

> It seems almost impossible to sell this stock.

In the second sentence, the question does not pertain to ever expecting but ever hearing. The correct position of *ever* is therefore before *hear*.

Do you expect ever to hear from him?

b. Phrases.

I sat watching the dirigible fly by in my office.
The typist ran after the office boy in the red dress.
She slipped and hurt herself in the outer office.

These sentences lose their comic flavor when the phrases are placed with the words they modify.

I sat in my office watching the dirigible fly by.
The typist in the red dress ran after the office boy.
She slipped in the outer office and hurt herself.

c. Clauses.

The personnel director selected an applicant for the position who knew shorthand.
The stenographer flourished the ruler over her head that was made of plastic.
Our lunch was delivered to us wrapped in cellophane, which we ate greedily.

By arranging each sentence so that the clause immediately follows its antecedent, coherence is obtained and the confusion is removed.

The personnel director selected for the position an applicant who knew shorthand.
The stenographer flourished over her head the ruler that was made of plastic.
Our cellophane-wrapped lunch, which we ate greedily, was delivered to us.

2. Dangling Modifiers. Sometimes modifiers are attached to no word in a sentence; sometimes they are attached to the wrong word. Such modifiers are said to dangle. They may be either participial, gerund, or infinitive phrases.

a. Dangling Participial Phrases.

> Miss Haynes saw the salesman glancing up from her desk.
> Having returned from vacation, the entire office force welcomed him.

In the first sentence, the meaning is that Miss Haynes glanced up, not the salesman. In the second sentence, the meaning is not that the office force had returned from vacation. The remedy for these poor constructions is to place the participial phrase as near the word it modifies as possible or, if the word is lacking, to supply it; thus:

> Glancing up from her typewriter, Miss Haynes saw the salesman.
> Having returned from his vacation, he was welcomed by the entire office force.

b. Dangling Gerund Phrases.

> In stepping from the elevator, my ankle was turned.

This sentence is incorrect because the gerund, *stepping*, is made to modify *ankle*. It was *I* who stepped; thus:

> In stepping from the elevator, I turned my ankle.

c. Dangling Infinitive Phrases.

> To pass the examination, ten books were read by John.

The infinitive *to pass* dangles. The meaning is not that *books* pass the examination, but *John*. Therefore:

> To pass the examination, John read ten books.

3. Split Infinitives. When a word is inserted between *to* and the verb form, the infinitive is said to be split; as, *to promptly act, to immediately leave, to fully prepare.* While some well-known authors and some journalists stoutly defend the use of the split infinitive, it would be well for the beginning writer to keep the infinitive intact.

> *Good:* We were told to clean the type thoroughly.
> *Poor:* We were told to thoroughly clean the type.

4. Pronouns without Antecedents or with Uncertain Antecedents. An antecedent is a noun to which a pronoun refers. This antecedent should be definite and determinable—a specific word. The pronoun must not refer to a phrase or to an entire clause. The pronouns *it* and *they* should not be used in the indefinite sense.

Miss Hakes told Miss Byrnes that her notebook was mislaid.

If you cannot determine whose notebook was mislaid, the antecedent is not definite. The sentence recast in the form of a direct quotation would make the reference clear.

Miss Hakes said to Miss Byrnes, "Your notebook was mislaid."

Again:

If you are a good bookkeeper, please teach it to me.

The antecedent of *it* is indefinite. Note the correction:

If you are a good bookkeeper, please teach me to do that work.

Or:

They wear plain, tailored clothes in our office.

This is a carelessly written sentence. There is no definite antecedent for *they*. Rewritten:

The girls who work in our office wear plain, tailored clothes.

Or:

My suggestion was accepted by the purchasing agent, which pleased me very much.

Here is an example of a pronoun used incorrectly to refer to an entire clause.

Good: That my suggestion was accepted by the purchasing agent pleased me very much.
Better: I was pleased that my suggestion was accepted by the purchasing agent.

Assignment 1. Copy the following sentences and make whatever corrections are necessary. Be able to discuss each correction you make.

1. I asked Lillian, when Miss Spencer came, to bring in her notebook.

2. While walking through the office, many callers were seen.

3. At the age of eighteen, my parents announced that I was to attend business college.

4. Elsie found a mouse uncovering her typewriter.

5. Edward is always pleasant, which makes him very popular.

6. Entering the office, Amy saw the long line of applicants.

7. Did you see Barr & Barr's advertisement of pure men's silk hosiery?

8. I tried to help the new stenographer, but she refused it.

9. They have many strict rules in that firm.

10. We only have the repairman once a month.

11. You must promise to thoroughly and faithfully perform your duties.

12. In writing the letter, many typing errors were made by me.

Assignment 2.   Follow the directions given for Assignment 1.

1. Eugene spoke to Mr. Bancroft about the letter he had lost.

2. Mr. Ames took the pen from my desk, which he placed in his vest pocket.

3. I can see the ocean liners sailing majestically up the river through my office window.

4. When I counted the petty cash, I found that I had only $2.87.

5. Jane hardly thought she would be able to type the letters before noon.

6. Remember to carefully check your work.

7. Only black ladies' dresses are sold on the third floor.

8. In my book of instructions it says that we are to use open punctuation.

9. Being a beginner, the noise in the office distracted him.

10. To obtain a better position, hard work will be needed.

11. A copyholder is on my typewriter that is fastened with clamps.

12. In the early years of this century, they did not have fast typists.

LESSON **58**

Emphasis

The salesman who calls at your office is able to make his points because he has at his command all the stress-giving facilities that go with speech—inflection, power, facial expression.

In business, every letter that is written is directly or indirectly a sales letter. The writer, to obtain emphasis, must utilize the following techniques.

1. Proportion. The principle of proportion, when applied to writing, means that more space should be given to important than to unimportant ideas. The writer should first be clear in his own mind as to the relative importance of the different messages he wishes to convey. If the primary purpose of the letter should be that of selling a secondhand bookkeeping machine, the principle of proportion would be violated if the letter space were filled with an enumeration of other secondhand equipment that is for sale. It might be good business to mention the other articles, but they should occupy an incidental position.

2. Position. The emphatic position is at the beginning or at the end, or at both the beginning and the end, of a sentence, a paragraph, a letter, or a composition. For the letter or the composition, the first sentence should present the main idea in an attention-compelling manner. The last sentence should repeat the main idea in such a way that action is stimulated or the point gracefully and conclusively made. For emphatic position with regard to the sentence, consider the following:

> Our new duplicator will save you both time and money, we are
> sure.
> It is our policy to give all our customers free service for one year.

> We owe our success to customers like you.
> The successful businessman is honorable, wide-awake, industrious.

These sentences, as written, are of the wishy-washy variety. A change in the position of some of the words will promote emphasis.

> Our new duplicator, we are sure, will save you both time and money.

The unimportant words, *we are sure,* are placed in the middle of the sentence. The important words are now at the beginning and at the end. The other three sentences, similarly, may be improved by rearranging the words; thus:

> *Free service for one year* to all our customers *is our policy.*
> To customers like you, we owe our success.
> The successful businessman is *industrious, wide-awake, honorable.*

The last sentence illustrates emphasis by climax. There is a logical, thought-out position of words here. The businessman, to be successful, must first be industrious, then wide-awake, and—most important of all—honorable.

3. Voice. The active voice is more emphatic than the passive voice. This principle is particularly true in business letters. Note the difference between

> Last year our machines were sold to every business firm in St. Louis.

and

> Every business firm in St. Louis bought our machines last year.

4. Use of the Periodic Sentence. The periodic sentence is one in which the meaning is not completely stated until the end of the sentence is reached; as:

> A new plastic material believed suitable for the manufacture of household furnishings of a lasting character has been developed by Plastic Products.
> The radio commentator, who had neglected to study his script and who was pressed for time, made a most ludicrous mistake.

5. Use of the Balanced Sentence. If the two clauses of a compound sentence are alike in construction, they constitute what is called a "balanced" or a "parallel" sentence. This structure is particularly effective in presenting contrasting ideas, but it should be used with moderation.

> In social gatherings, to rush is impolite; in business, to procrastinate is fatal.
> To assure means to make certain; to insure means to guarantee.
> Production is increasing; unemployment is decreasing.

6. Repetition. The intentional repetition of words, phrases, or sentence structure may occasionally be used very effectively to gain emphasis; as:

> *Healthtone* will add *years* to your *life*, and *Healthtone* will add *life* to your *years*.
> A *glance* was sufficient to show that she was a poor typist, and I had more than a *glance* at her work.

7. Use of Specific Words. The writer who has an extensive vocabulary, who is not reduced to the use of worn-out terms, who is able to depict in words the exact impression he wishes to convey, is the successful writer. Definite, picture-making words add emphasis. Note the sentence,

> We received your grand letter this morning.

Grand used in this sense is feeble. The letter might have been interesting, exciting, surprising, clever, sparkling, courteous, helpful, absorbing, friendly, amazing, humorous.

Now note the different mental impressions resulting from the wording of the following sentences:

> June arrived at the office at 9:30 this morning. [Dull.]
> June *sauntered* into the office at 9:30 this morning.
> June *dashed* into the office, or June *puffed* into the office, or June *sidled*, or *danced*, or *stalked*, or *scuttled*.

Assignments. You are the advertising manager for the XYZ Publishing Company. You are faced with the problem of writing a letter that will convincingly present to business teachers the features of *Business English*. With these facts in mind, prepare the assignments that follow.

Assignment 1. Write two sentences using the passive voice; then rewrite the sentences, using the active voice. Write two sentences illustrating emphasis by climax.

Assignment 2. Write two sentences showing emphasis by placing the most important idea at the beginning; write two periodic sentences; write two balanced sentences.

Assignment 3. Write a short paragraph showing emphasis by repetition. Write two sentences using general words; then rewrite them using specific words. Underline the picture-making words.

LESSON **59**

Euphony

Say the word *euphony* aloud. Listen to it. Do you find the sound
pleasant, smooth, musical? That is what *euphony* means. It has to
do with the way a word or a series of words sounds. Consider the
definition by Webster: "A harmonious succession of words having a
pleasing sound."

It is true that a sentence, a letter, or a composition must have a
central thought, must be clear in meaning, must be emphatic; and
it is also true that the general effect produced must be pleasing to
the ear. Start now to cultivate the ability to *hear* what you read and
write.

Euphony is destroyed by careless—

1. Repetition of Words. Since the English language is so rich in
synonyms, there is no necessity for a noticeable repetition of words.
If the writer's own vocabulary is not sufficient to suggest words to
replace the words he desires to eliminate, he should refer to the
dictionary or a good book of synonyms. The repetition of such
monosyllables as *the, at, and, of, to,* and *with* is, of course, not objectionable. Listen to:

> It is best for the customer to realize that the best firms adhere
> strictly to the old adage, "Honesty is the best policy."
> A nice thing about working in an office is that office workers have
> nice surroundings.
> The applicant applied for the position, but he found that there
> were several other applicants before him.

2. Repetition of Like Sounds. Watch lest you use words that,
although they may be different in spelling or meaning, have the
same sound. The effect upon the reader of such unnecessary repeti-

tion can range from boring to maddening. Read the following sentences and listen to them.

> When you steer your weary feet here to our restaurant, you have a mere thirty yards to cover.
> The painter at the Hawaiian hotel asked the porters to lay the leis on the quaint old table.
> We cannot understand how a businessman of his high standing can take such an antisocial stand in this matter.

3. Use of Too Many Harsh Sounds. There are in our language many unpleasant-sounding consonant sounds; as, *j, dj, ks, qu, nk, sh, s.* Listen to: *gesture, knowledge, satchel, tragic, illegible, church, cabbage, virtue, anxious, pretext, quake, bushel.* A too lavish use of *s* and *sh* sounds is aptly illustrated by the tongue-twister, "She sells seashells by the seashore." Give ear to the following sentences:

> Be assured that there will be no change in our existing policy with regard to future orders, charges, and exchanges.
> The chart shows the ship at anchor in the channel with the conquering challengers.

4. Use of Too Many Words of One Syllable. Sentences that are composed of one-syllable words are dreary and monotonous. Overuse of these words reveals the writer as the possessor of a meager vocabulary.

> We need a bright clerk who can help us with our books. I think you will suit us. Please call at our store this week so that we may talk with you to see if you can do the kind of work we want done. We hope you will not ask for more pay than we can give you.

5. Use of Too Many Short Sentences. A letter made up in most part of short sentences will sound like an automobile engine on a cold morning—go and stop, go and stop. Such a letter is displeasing not only to the ear but also to the eye. As you read the following paragraph, listen and look at the same time.

> We received your letter. It came in this morning. It was most welcome. All the salesman read it. They liked your suggestions. Your letters are always friendly. We enjoy hearing from you.

A Frequent Dictator Fault. We have already discussed one dictator fault, the run-on sentence. Stenographers will be on the alert to correct another fault—the dictating of short, choppy sentences. Suppose that your notes read:

> We received your order. It came this morning. It was most welcome.
> We have the towels you want. They will go out today. We are having a sale on towels. You will get the towels at sale price.
> Thank you very much.

If your supervisor has confidence in your knowledge of English, you will probably dare to transcribe:

> Your welcome order was received this morning.
> The towels will go out today and will be billed to you at sale price.
> Thank you very much.

6. Repetition of Identical Sentence Structure. The inexperienced writer often constructs only two kinds of sentences—the simple, and the compound with its clauses connected by *and*. This practice causes his paragraph or letter to sound like a first-grade reader. Just as the repetition of words and sounds is unnecessary because of the many synonyms there are in the English language, so monotony of sentence structure is unwarranted because of the many possible kinds of sentences. One should become skilled in forming long, short, simple, compound, complex, balanced, and periodic sentences, as well as all the overlapping combinations of the group. Notice the monotonous effect of these sentences.

> We received your letter this morning, and it was most welcome. All the salesman read it, and they liked your suggestions. Your letters are always friendly, and we enjoy hearing from you.

Assignment 1. Rewrite the paragraph given above. You are at liberty to change the wording or to expand the ideas. The result must be euphonious.

Assignment 2. Be prepared to tell wherein the following sentences violate the principle of euphony.

1. When our checks fail to come in on the date due, we must go to the bank to get more cash.
2. That is a firm that offers to the office force all that they ask for.

3. Only a patient person should choose watch repairing as a profession.

4. My employer ordered me to order the stenographers to leave their desks in good order.

5. When I finish this fringe, I intend to hint for an increase in income.

6. You must come to see us when you are free to do so, and we shall have a good time.

7. The Asiatic issue was an injudicious choice of subject.

8. One must realize that one succeeds primarily through one's own efforts.

9. The stock clerk gingerly crushed the package of crackers into the dingy box.

10. It is my delight to see a bright office boy who might climb to the heights of success.

Assignment 3.   Rewrite the preceding sentences.

Assignment 4.   From a newspaper, magazine, or book select a paragraph that you think is effective because of its euphony. List the kinds of sentences used.

PART VI

Business Letter Writing

The letter of application written by this young woman has won favorable attention. A personal interview was the result.

LESSON **60**

The Business Letter

Past, Present, and Future

Every day hundreds of thousands of business letters are written in the United States. These letters represent many types, each letter designed to do a special job for the businessman. Some letters are written to obtain information; some are written to give information; others attempt to sell a product or a service; others are written to collect overdue accounts; and still others are written to make new friends and to build good will for the business.

Because goods and services in America are exchanged freely throughout the country, the business executive must depend upon the written word to communicate with his customers and business associates. This is the job of the business letter. The business letter is the ambassador of business, the substitute for a personal visit.

Because letter writing is so important in business, there are many opportunities for those who can write effective letters. Letter writing can even be a career in itself—there are thousands of business employees whose only job is to write letters—or it can be a valuable aid in the upward march toward any executive goal.

The history of business letter writing is very interesting. It is also very important, because the style of letters used hundreds of years ago still influences our present-day correspondence habits to a great extent. Let us consider business letter writing in its three stages—past, present, and future.

The Past

Business correspondence, as we know it, had its beginning in England hundreds of years ago. A brief discussion of the times and of the people of those times will help us to understand the writing style used in the first business letters.

The Times.   Picture, if you can, a country made up of vast farms, on each of which there would be a large manor house and a straggling community of small, unsanitary cottages. The only city of note was London, a city no bigger than thousands of our present-day American towns. There were no stores, no factories, no business at all as we today think of it. Roads were paths; transportation was supplied by horses and coaches.

In the late 1700's, life in England began to undergo a change. This period marks the beginning of trade and industry and therefore marks the beginning of business correspondence. The change, called the "Industrial Revolution," was the result of the invention of various machines that made possible the manufacture of goods on a large scale.

Wars on the mainland of Europe provided a great market for manufactured goods and for produce. Spurred on by the prospect of enormous profits, the landowners raised large numbers of sheep for the wool that could be made into cloth and also raised food to be sold to feed the soldiers on the Continent.

Men were no longer able to carry on business by word of mouth; so the writing of letters became very important.

The People.   In that long-ago period, people were divided neatly into two classes—masters and servants. The masters were the "top" people, the ones who had the money and owned the land. The servants were the "bottom" people, the ones without money who served the masters. A person who was born into either class stayed there for life.

Since a person's station in life was determined at birth and no variation was possible, the relationship between the two classes was clearly defined. The master demanded as his right—and got—instant, obedient, humble service. The servant had no thought other than to give exactly the service demanded.

Business Letters.   The first business letters were probably those exchanged between master and servant. Large estates were often managed by servants called "bailiffs"; and, should the master be away from home, some correspondence was necessary between him and his bailiff. At this time there was some trade between England and other then-known countries. Letters about business were exchanged between the owner of a vessel and his servant, the captain of the ship.

The tone of the letter written by the master was abrupt, cold, imperious. The tone of the servant's letter was so humble as to be almost cringing. The master need write only, "Sell wool to Goodman Winthrop, of Salem, at tuppence the pound." The servant larded his letters with such expressions as *please advise, esteemed favor, beg to inform.* Such a closing as "Trusting this meets with your approval, I remain, Your obedient (or humble) servant" was a proper closing for that time.

Business-Correspondence Education. The Industrial Revolution was the first major economic boom, and to it can be credited the start of business-correspondence training. Up to that time, very few people could read and write; but rapidly expanding business created a demand for employees who could write business letters.

When the writing of business letters became a subject to be studied, a textbook was required to help the teacher and the pupils. The enterprising authors of the first textbooks needed model letters to illustrate their teaching, and the only available letters about business were the communications mentioned before—those exchanged between master and servant. Very sensibly, then, the authors used these letters as patterns for students to follow. For that period in history, they were excellent illustrations, because all human relations were governed by position—master or servant.

As the years went by and new correspondence books were written, the teaching part of the books changed; but there was a tendency to use, with only slight modifications, the same model letters. Let us keep this last fact in mind, for it will help us better to understand the business correspondence of

The Present

When we speak of the correspondence of the present and the future, we mean the business letters written by United States businessmen. Since the present and the future are influenced by the past, the brief overview of the origin and early development of business and business correspondence in England was necessary in order to give us understanding for this and the next section, for our first textbooks on business correspondence were those written by English authors.

The Times. The Industrial Revolution did not take place in America until after the War Between the States. Until that time, sufficient power to manufacture goods was supplied by the many rivers. After that time, however, there was an upsurge of immigration; and literally hordes of people poured into our land.

More people created the need for more goods, and water power was found to be inadequate. Too, we began to use power-driven machinery to enable us to engage in large-scale manufacture. Thus we started on the way to becoming the world power we are today.

The business scene of today shows a steady and continuing growth in commerce of all kinds. This fact is important to students of business correspondence, for business cannot be conducted without written communications. Therefore, business growth means an increase in the demand for the specially trained correspondents who can write those communications.

The People. The people in the United States are probably the most democratic on earth. This democratic freedom, to which we are so accustomed, has influenced our method of conducting business and, consequently, our letter writing. Under the American system of free enterprise the consumer (buyer) is "king" and his wants and needs are of primary importance to the businessman. The informal relationship that has developed between the businessman and the consumer has brought about a freedom of expression that is uniquely American. The trend in the business letter writing of today is toward a friendlier, more realistic writing style. The American businessman has come to realize that friends and customers are won more easily by friendly letters.

Business Letters. Many of the business letters of today, however, lag far behind the times. It is indeed odd that businessmen who pride themselves on the latest equipment, on the most modern stock, on up-to-date methods of doing business, should write letters that are antique in wording and tone.

What is it that makes these letters sound like those written in the horse-and-buggy days? First of all, some writers think that being businesslike implies being cold, formal, curt. When discussing their business letters, they boast, "I say what I have to say and then stop." They have one point, and that is that business letters should be concise; but conciseness need not mean coldness.

An old-fashioned flavor is given to the letters that contain old-fashioned wording. Such phrases as *beg to advise, hand you herewith, your favor of the 16th ult.,* are so out of tune with our times that they give the impression of bygone business days and business methods.

The master-servant attitude that is revealed in the actions of some of our people is reflected in the letters they write. For instance, the purchaser thinks of himself as the master and therefore writes a letter like this:

> Returning order No. 4523. Every article in shipment was defective. Expect a credit memorandum for $876.14 by return mail.

On the other hand, the seller thinks of himself as the servant, with the result that his letters are humble in tone. He might write a letter asking a delinquent customer to come to his office, and he would believe that he must word it something like:

> I should be very grateful if you would kindly call at my office sometime next week to discuss this question of payment.

Business-Correspondence Education. Every teacher of business correspondence and every correspondence textbook today presents very clearly the case for writing the kind of letters that will supplement the businessman's aim to increase profits. The result is that throughout the country, progressive businessmen are recognizing the fact that modern business can be promoted by modern letters.

We are making progress; but for the fruition of our efforts, we shall have to look to the letters of

The Future

The good business letter writers of today are the pioneers of the business correspondence of the future. Let us pretend that we know one of these men and have had an opportunity to study his letters. When we have analyzed our information, we shall know the qualities that will be inherent in the business correspondence of tomorrow.

Qualities of the Letters of the Future. We find that our selected pioneer, Mr. Lane, is:

Courteous. Mr. Lane's unfailing personal courtesy is mirrored in his letters. We can therefore deduce that business letters of the future will be uniformly polite.

Considerate. Our pioneer has the faculty of being able to see the other person's side of the question. His letters show that he writes from the reader's point of view rather than from his own. The correspondence of tomorrow, then, will contain more "you" tone and less "I" tone.

Firm. While Mr. Lane is kind and understanding, he is not a "softy." At no time in his letters did he write anything that would jeopardize the best interests of his company. We were amazed to see how he could refuse a request or demand some action without arousing resentment. We now know that the letters of the future will be so cleverly worded that desired action will result from them without causing ill feeling.

Democratic. We know that our pioneer is a warm, friendly person; and we are pleased to find that his letters are cordial and gracious without overstepping the bounds of good taste. Letters written to service people are just as polished and refined as those written to customers. Letters to customers show no trace of lowliness. We learn that the superior letters of tomorrow will show an eagerness to please and to be of service, but not at the expense of loss of self-respect.

Progressive. Mr. Lane is an enthusiastic student of latest developments and trends in business. He is among the first to recognize the possibilities of using business letters as contributions to the profit-making aim of business. Our study of his letters shows us that, while his main purpose in writing is to convey a clear, complete, concise message, he never loses an opportunity to:

    1. Make sales
    2. Reduce overhead
    3. Build good will

Summary

No person can envision the future without some knowledge of the present and the past. The student of business correspondence, therefore, must know something about letters that were written yesterday and that are being written today. He must be able to understand that the letters of any given period in history reflect the attitudes and beliefs of that period. He must realize that he is preparing to be the business correspondent of the future; and, as such, he must learn to compose letters that will do more than carry messages. He must be so expert that his written communications are a potent force in increasing profits by making sales, reducing overhead, and building good will.

Assignment 1. List ten words or phrases that you think stamp a letter as belonging to the correspondence of yesterday—old-fashioned letters. Suggest modern substitutes for the words or phrases.

Assignment 2. Obtain a file folder and start a collection of actual business letters. One such letter is required for the next class meeting. Be prepared to read the letter aloud in class and to give your criticisms of it.

Should you be wondering where you will get the letters for your file, here are some suggestions:

1. Use business letters received by you, your parents, or your friends.

2. Copy illustrations given in reference books.

3. Go to an office in your community and ask whether you may have copies of letters received (not sent) by that company. Be sure to say that the name of the sending firm is to be omitted. We are interested in correspondence in general, not in criticizing the letters written by any particular company.

Assignment 3. From personal experience or from observation, select some incident that proves that the master-servant idea exists today. Prepare a written outline of your account of the happening and hand it in.

Your teacher may allow you class time to make an oral report to the class.

LESSON **61**

Why We Write Business Letters

To Convey a Message

A business letter is written because somebody has something to say. Businessmen write letters for a number of different reasons— to give instructions, to answer questions, to place orders, to request or grant adjustments, to acknowledge courtesies, to collect money. Whatever the purpose may be, we can be certain that, if it were not necessary to send a message, there would be no letter. No message— no letter!

Social letters, on the other hand, are frequently written simply because "We owe Bill a letter"; and then words are used to recount a series of personal happenings. The unsuccessful business correspondent is the man who writes his business letters in the same fashion that he writes his personal letters to Bill. This businessman does not realize that the writing of business letters requires special skill and training.

The first step on the road leading to the writing of letters that get the best results will be the studying of the four basic "musts" of business correspondence: *clearness, completeness, conciseness,* and *courtesy.*

Clearness

How do you feel when you receive a message that you do not understand? Confused—and maybe a little angry? Well, that is the way a businessman feels when he receives a letter whose message is not clear.

As preparation for writing an unclouded communication, we must first of all be crystal clear in our own minds as to exactly what we want to say. Remember that muddled thinking produces a muddled message.

Just as soon as we know what we want to say, we must think of the receiver of the letter. Will he understand our clear thoughts? His chances of so doing will be increased if we express ourselves in the simplest possible words. What do you think of this paragraph?

You are indubitably correct in your epistle of the fifth when you speak of the ubiquitousness of taxes. However, in this mundane world of ours, they are a symbol of modernism.

With considerably less strain on both writer and reader the paragraph could be written:

Right you are—taxes are always with us. However, since most of us think in terms of money, they are but a sign of the times.

Enemies of Clearness. The writers of business letters frequently cloud the meaning of those letters by using run-on sentences or by failing to use coherence.

1. *Run-on Sentences.* A run-on sentence does just what its name implies—runs on and on. Consider this example:

In case we do not have the style you prefer available, we should be very glad to special order it for you; but this would take from one to three weeks for delivery but would, we are sure, please you much better than sending you goods that might not be satisfactory, and that would be against our store policy.

The writer of the foregoing sentence may have been clear as to what he wanted to say; but he ignored one of the principles of unity, the principle that each sentence should contain only one main thought. The message could be rewritten as follows:

Should the style you prefer be out of stock, we shall be very glad to special order it for you. This would mean a delivery delay of one to three weeks. You may be sure that, in accordance with our policy, every effort will be made to see to it that you get exactly what you order.

2. *Coherence.* A sentence, a paragraph, or a letter is coherent when there is orderly arrangement of thoughts and when all references are clear. The illustrations that follow show how ridiculous or confusing we are when we violate coherence.

Arrangement Fault. Faulty arrangement occurs when modifiers are not placed with the words they modify; as,

Stepping out of the elevator, the door closed on my foot.

With this arrangement, the door stepped out of the elevator. Of course, we know that the writer meant, "As I stepped out of the elevator, the door closed on my foot."

Please duplicate order No. 1567 for yellow ladies' scarves.

As written, these scarves could be worn only by women afflicted with jaundice. Written correctly, the sentence would be, "Please duplicate order No. 1567 for ladies' yellow scarves."

Reference Fault. Suppose that we receive a letter from one of our salesmen, in which he writes:

On Monday I called on Thorp, Turner, and Bunker. He has ordered 12 cases of whole-kernel corn.

Now, just who ordered the corn? Whom does he mean by *he?* This is what we mean by a reference fault.

Completeness

Completeness is really one of the essentials of clearness; for, if an important detail is omitted, the letter is not clear. The incomplete letter is a wasted letter, because another letter must be written to obtain the missing information.

Just suppose that the same salesman who wrote the letter ordering the corn sends another letter placing an order for 100 cases of 2½-sized cans of peaches. We carry two grades of peaches, but the letter does not specify which grade the customer ordered. The salesman's letter is incomplete, and we must write or telephone him before we can fill the order.

Large mail-order houses are the principal victims of incomplete letters. That is why they give so freely of their printed order forms, which contain such columns as the following:

Catalogue Number	Quantity	Name of Item	Color	Size	Price for each yard, pair, etc.	Total Price

Even then, there is no certainty that the order will be complete. The customer might neglect to fill in one of the columns.

Thus we may conclude that the chief enemy of completeness is carelessness. The untrained business letter writer frequently dashes off his letter without first planning it. Perhaps at the start of this training in writing business letters, a written outline would be of help. If we will jot down the points we want to make, there will be less danger of our writing an incomplete letter.

Conciseness

A letter that is concise is a letter that covers the entire subject in the fewest possible words. Many people think that *concise* means *brief*, but brevity is only a part of conciseness. To be concise, a letter must be complete *and* brief, but not so brief as to be discourteous Let us look at the following letter:

Gentlemen:
Please send me a pair of the boots advertised in last Sunday's paper.

Here we certainly have brevity; but could we fill the order?

On the other hand, there are some writers who compose a business letter much in the same way that they would write a social letter. These people bore the reader with details that have no bearing on the subject; and, in addition, they waste the time of the reader. In business, time is money.

Reread Assignment 3, Part V, in the lesson on "The Word, the Sentence, the Paragraph." To find out exactly what the woman who wrote this letter wanted to order, the reader had to wade through at least seventy-five words that meant nothing to him. Quite definitely, the letter was not concise.

Our problem with regard to conciseness can be solved by observing the following principle: Say everything that has to be said, but say it simply and quickly.

Courtesy

Why is it that a person who is normally polite will sometimes be impolite when he is not talking face to face with another person? Could it be cowardice? thoughtlessness? lack of good breeding? lack of emotional control?

A true lady or gentleman is courteous at all times, for courtesy is a habit; and habits work for us without any conscious direction on our part. This true lady or gentleman is, therefore, just as polite in business relationships as in social relationships; and the results are just as effective in business as they are in society. If courtesy is not yet a habit with us, perhaps we can make it so by remembering that discourtesy will lose business for us.

Here are some suggestions that will insure the writing of courteous letters.

1. *Always write the kind of letter that would give us a warm glow if we were to receive it.* This is nothing but the application of the Golden Rule, which is just as good a rule of conduct today as it was centuries ago.

2. *Remember our manners.* "Please" and "Thank you" take very little extra time.

3. *Pretend that we are talking face-to-face with the receiver of the letter.* We shall be surprised to see how our writing manners will perk up.

4. *Never answer a letter when we are angry.* If we find ourselves in the mood to "tell that fellow a thing or two," let us wait until we cool off before we write our reply.

Summary

We can sum up the principles of this lesson by setting forth two basic requirements for the writing of good business letters.

1. *Get our thoughts in order* before *we write.* The writer of the letter should have a plan for each letter. Then, when he does the actual writing, he knows *what* he wants to say and *how* he wants to say it.

2. *Check the letter* after *it is written.* Once the letter is written, the writer should pretend that he is the receiver of the letter. He will read carefully and ask himself:

   a. Is it clear?
   b. Is it complete?
   c. Is it concise?
   d. Is it courteous?

Assignment 1. Study the following letter and write a critical analysis of it. Select individual sentences that you think violate the principles of clearness, completeness, conciseness, or courtesy.

Dear Mr. LeClair:

Your letter of January 3 states that there is a belt missing from our next-to-last shipment of woolen dresses.

We are always very careful in the checking of our goods; and, in fact, we make it a rule to check every shipment twice. In this way, we are able to feel that we are making complete shipments and we are thus able to keep complaints to a minimum. That is why, in your case, we think that the person who unpacked the shipment might be the fellow who made the mistake. It may be the fault of your checker or of ours, but he should be instructed to be more careful.

You may expect the belt in a few days.

Very truly yours,

Assignment 2. Rewrite the letter, correcting the faults you have observed.

Assignment 3. The members of your class have been invited to visit the offices of the Bradley Tool Company, a manufacturing concern in your city.

a. Outline a letter to that company, showing appreciation of the invitation, stating the date and time of the visit, giving the number of students who will be in the party, and making some suggestions as to what you would particularly like to see.

b. Write the letter.

Assignment 4. If your teacher is in favor of extra-credit work, he may encourage you to work this assignment for that extra credit.

From your file of sample letters, select one that you think violates one or more of the principles taught in this lesson. Prepare a critical analysis of the letter.

Still more credit may be given if you rewrite the letter.

LESSON **62**

Why We Write Business Letters

To Build Good Will

What Is Good Will? Good will is something that has cash value and is listed on the balance sheet as an asset. Good will can therefore be sold—*but nobody can see it or touch it.* Then, what is it? Possibly the nearest we can come to a definition is to say that good will is whatever a business has that causes people to trade, and like to trade, with that house.

Perhaps you have seen an actual instance of two stores selling identical merchandise and established at opposite corners of the same block. Maybe you have observed that customers stream into one store and trickle into the other. Now, if both stores were to be put up for sale and even if the inventories amounted to the same sum, the busy store would bring more money. The good-will value of the busy store would be greater.

Good Will and Business Letters. Many of the people to whom we write never enter our place of business, never see us, never talk to us. Their impressions and their feeling toward us are formed entirely by means of the letters they receive from us.

Possibly some of our correspondents have met us and have been favorably impressed. A curt or a tactless letter to one of these correspondents could destroy all the good will we were able to build through personal dealings.

We can, therefore, say that every letter we write is a selling letter; for every letter can be worded in such a way that the receiver will have confidence in us, will feel friendly toward us, and will want to trade with us.

312

A study of the general principles of good-will building should result in the writing of letters that increase business volume and profits.

General Principles of Good-Will Building

In order to build good will by way of the business letter, we should know that good will results from:

1. A good product
2. Ethical conduct
3. Superior service
4. Warm, courteous communications
5. Prompt replies to correspondence

We can put this in equation form; thus:

A good product + ethical conduct + superior service + warm, courteous communications + prompt replies to correspondence = GOOD WILL

A Good Product. In letters, we work not only to sell whatever we manufacture or retail but also to sell our firm as a good house with which to do business. We must, then, believe with all our hearts that the merchandise we have for sale is superior and that the company for which we work is also superior. If we do believe this, our letters will reflect our sincerity. If we do not believe it, we should leave the company and apply for a job elsewhere. We cannot convince others unless we ourselves are first convinced; and we cannot write business-getting letters unless we have faith.

Suppose that a customer wrote that there was a defect in one of the bolts of cloth we had shipped to them. What do you think of the following reply?

Gentlemen:

Your complaint about the defect in the bolt of blue chambray shipped to you on June 19 is but one of many that we have received.

We are very sorry that this damaged material slipped by us, but mistakes will happen. We wish to assure you that we manufacture just as good cloth as any other firm in the field.

Please return the damaged cloth, and we will give you credit for it or will ship you a bolt of good material.

Very truly yours,

The letter seems to stress the fact that this company manufactures cloth of poor quality. Note the use of "complaint," "defect," "damaged material," "damaged cloth."

The following reply makes an effort to retain confidence in the manufacturer and his product and to build good will.

Gentlemen:

We are very sorry that the bolt of blue chambray shipped to you on June 19 did not meet our standard of perfection. How that particular bolt of cloth passed our checkers is a mystery.

As a result of your letter, we have devised a method of inspecting finished goods that should prevent such an incident in the future. Thank you for helping us to maintain our reputation for manufacturing quality goods.

If you will return the chambray, we will give you credit for it or will send you another bolt.

Very sincerely yours,

Ethical Conduct.   Ethical conduct means fair, honest, upright dealing in all situations and with all people. A reputation for the best in moral standards will be enjoyed by any firm that always keeps its word, that never takes advantage of any other firm or person, and that pays all bills promptly. A sense of the importance of a "good name" will be with us whenever we write a business letter.

We can illustrate this principle by writing two letters that represent alternate answers to a vendor who wants to know why $3.87 was deducted from our check of June 4.

Gentlemen:

The deduction of $3.87 from our check of June 4 was for transportation charges that were to be paid by you.

Very truly yours,

This letter is cold, abrupt, and incomplete. The vendor will want to know by what authority the deduction was made; and, if more than one shipment happened to be made during that month, he will want to know which one was to have been prepaid. He will certainly be irked by the necessity of writing another letter asking for full information.

The letter was in reply to a question about money, and we know that we must be very careful about any misunderstanding when money is involved. Therefore, we can see that the writer of the letter did nothing to cultivate good will.

The following reply contains more words, but it is clear; and it has the "good-will touch."

Gentlemen:

We have your letter of June 16, calling attention to our deduction of $3.87 on your May 31 statement.

This sum represents transportation charges for the May 15 shipment. According to Mr. E. B. Mason's letter of May 2, these charges were to be paid by you.

Should there still be any question, please feel free to write us. We are always glad to co-operate.

Sincerely yours,

Whenever possible, the correspondent will stress the fact that his firm keeps promises. The utmost tact must be used when writing to a customer who feels that he has been treated unfairly. Many retail stores go to the extreme of satisfying the customer even when they know that he is taking advantage of them and when the process of adjusting the difficulty will cost the store a considerable sum of money. Thus you can see how highly retailers value their reputation for ethical conduct.

The decision with regard to any action to be taken probably will rest with the supervisor, but the writing of the letter will be our job. That letter will be honest and sincere and, at the same time, tactful. When the customer finishes reading, he will be convinced that he is doing business with an honorable firm.

Superior Service. When a person receives good service, he is flattered; but when he receives poor service, he is dissatisfied. Dissatisfaction is the chief enemy of good will. Most firms make top service a company policy, for they know that the best in service *all the time* keeps old customers and makes old customers out of new ones. If at all possible, our business letters will be used to stress the fact that ours is a service-minded company. We want to establish a reputation for service.

One of the secrets of building a reputation for "super" service is *action*. Should an order be received, fill it immediately. Should a request be received, do something about it right away. Should a complaint be received, attend to it without delay. Our letters will use words that will show the customer or the vendor that we are giving him personal attention.

Suppose that we are a manufacturing concern and that a customer writes that ten of the castings we shipped him were defective. This man's firm is located less than a hundred miles from us, and our idea of service-plus is to instruct one of our truck drivers to take ten replacement castings to him immediately and to pick up those that are faulty. Notice that we do not ship them by freight, but that we send them by truck. The customer, consequently, will get the castings on the very day that we received his letter.

Then we write a letter designed to emphasize the service we offer. We do this deliberately, for we know that a letter will make the incident stand out in the customer's mind. We write:

Gentlemen:

We have just received your letter notifying us that the castings shipped on October 5 are not usable.

One of our trucks, carrying ten replacement castings, has already left our factory and is now on the way to you.

Thank you for giving us an opportunity to make good on this order.

Cordially yours,

The customer would undoubtedly be impressed by getting service within twenty-four hours, but the pressure of his work might make him forget. The next day, when he receives our letter and the wording of that letter fixes the happening in his mind, he will probably think or say—and *remember*—"That's real service!"

Warm, Courteous Communications. The spoken word may be soon forgotten, but the written word creates a lasting impression. Letter writers must learn to put words together in such a way that they will create a lasting, favorable impression.

Some businessmen believe that the ideal letter is one that contains absolutely no unnecessary words. Such a letter might be clear, complete, and concise; but it will not be warm and courteous—and it is warmth and courtesy that build good will! We may use a few more words than do the businessmen referred to, but we shall make our customers our friends.

To illustrate this point, pretend that we are the vendor mentioned in the section on ethical conduct. When we found out that our employee, E. B. Mason, agreed to prepay the May 15 shipment, we were furious. You see, we have a company policy that states that all shipping charges are to be paid by the customer. Nevertheless, we must support Mason; so we are obliged to write and say that the misunderstanding has been cleared up. The letter follows.

Gentlemen:
Understand fully about deduction of $3.87 on May 31 statement. Credited that sum to your account.
Thanks.

Yours truly,

Gracious and warm, would you say?

The trained letter writer would realize that, since the deduction must be accepted, he might just as well seize the opportunity to write a letter that will promote good will. He might write:

Gentlemen:
Thank you very much for your letter of June 17, explaining the deduction of $3.87 from our May 31 statement. Your account now shows no balance due.

We are sorry that we did not record the fact that the May 15 shipment was to be sent prepaid. You may rest assured that we will make every effort to prevent the recurrence of any failure to note special terms.

Very sincerely yours,

Prompt Replies to Correspondence. Failure to reply to a business letter is as truly insulting as to snub somebody on the street. Profits are not made by insulting the customers; so immediate replies will be made to all letters that require an answer.

Delay in replying is also rude and, by the same token, poor business. The longer the correspondent has to wait for a reply, the more will he think that we consider him of little importance. Delay tears down the good will that we are supposed to be building in the writing of letters.

Sometimes we are unable to answer promptly; if so, we should be very careful to let the correspondent know that the delay was unavoidable. For instance, suppose that we have been out of town on a business trip; and, on our return, the first thing we do is to tackle the correspondence that has piled up during our absence. Probably we would use for an opening paragraph something like:

I have just returned to the office after a four-day trip, and the first act of my business day is to answer correspondence, among which is your letter of July 8.

Thus we explain the delay and inject the personal note.

Summary. Business good will is the friendly feeling of respect that exists between buyer and seller. A firm makes or loses money in accordance with its ability to obtain and retain good will. The writer of a business letter has an excellent chance to make money for his company if his letters show that:

1. He believes that the product of the firm is one of the best, if not *the* best, in the world.

2. He believes that his firm stands for all that is honest, dependable, upright.

3. He believes that his firm provides service that is "super."

4. He believes that his letters must be warm, gracious, and courteous and that his customers are his friends.

5. He believes that the height of correspondence discourtesy is to fail to answer or to delay answering any letter that calls for a reply.

This writer knows that *every phase of good will can be promoted by the skillful writing of business letters.*

Assignment 1. Rewrite the sample letter given in the section on a good product in such a way that you will show that you believe in your company and in your product.

Assignment 2. During an emergency, you have been substituting for another employee and have not been in your office for a week. Now you are back and are faced with the task of answering the letters that came in during your absence. Write a paragraph that will explain the delay and will promote good will.

Assignment 3. A customer writes that one of our salespersons sold her a coat for $69.95, but that on her bill the item was listed at $79.95. Your supervisor has checked and found that what she reports is true. He tells you to write and tell her that the correct price is $69.95. Write the letter.

Assignment 4. From the sample letters in your file, select one that you think is a good-will builder. Quote the sentences that demonstrate the principles studied in this lesson. Be prepared to read to the class the letter and your quotations. If time permits, you might lead a class discussion on the merits of the letter you selected.

Why We Write Business Letters

To Build Good Will (Continued)

We have just studied the general principles of good-will building, and now comes the time to apply that knowledge to the writing of letters to the three different classes of people with whom we wish to establish and maintain good will. The general principles will hold true in the writing of all letters, but we must know when and how to adapt them in order to sustain and promote:

1. Customer good will
2. Vendor good will
3. Co-worker good will

Customer Good Will

Customers will buy from us year after year if we give them prompt, courteous, personal service when we supply them with satisfactory goods at a fair price.

Since dissatisfaction is the main cause of loss of good will, our letters will be used, whenever possible, to *prevent* dissatisfaction. This means that, when writing to a customer, we are going to check and recheck before we make any written promises, before we quote prices, before we offer any services. Perhaps we can file away in our memories this little catch phrase: *customer—prevent dissatisfaction.*

Consider this problem situation in which we might use the writing of a letter to prevent customer dissatisfaction.

Problem Situation. We are a large department store, and our over-the-counter business is good. Management has decided to put on a drive to increase our mail-order business and has directed that all letters to mail-order customers be carefully composed.

We have an order for a Sprite nightgown, pink, size 14, from a new customer, Mrs. Hastings, who asks that we rush shipment. The Lingerie Department reports that this make of gown in the pink shade has been sold out and that we must wait two weeks before the reorder comes in. What are we to do? If Mrs. Hastings has to wait two weeks for a rush order, she certainly will be dissatisfied. Our personal shopper, Mary Gail, suggests that we send her a gown made up in the new Dawn shade, which lists at 25 cents more than the standard colors.

Our supervisor says to us, "Write Mrs. Hastings and tell her that we are sending her a gown in Dawn at no extra charge." Very simple for him, but what about us? There is a distinct possibility that the customer may be displeased because she did not get exactly what she ordered. Knowledge of the delicacy of the situation helps in writing the following letter:

Dear Mrs. Hastings:
Immediately upon receipt of your order for a Sprite nightgown, pink, size 14, we checked with our Lingerie Department, only to find that this gown in the pink shade is temporarily out of stock.

We consulted with our personal shopper, Mary Gail, and it is at her suggestion that we are sending you today a Sprite gown in the new Dawn color. Although the Dawn model retails at a slightly higher price, we are billing you for $7.98, the price of the standard colors.

We do hope you like the choice we have made for you.
Cordially yours,

What is it that we hope will be the result of writing this letter? We hope that Mrs. Hastings will feel that she received immediate and personal attention. We hope that she will realize that she got a bargain, something very few women can resist. We hope that she will be so impressed that she will tell all her friends about our treatment of her, for we know that the best kind of advertising for a retail store is word-of-mouth advertising.

In line with the aim of forestalling displeasure, perhaps we should send the letter with the package. If Mrs. Hastings reads the letter before she looks at the merchandise, there is a good chance that she will have a positive attitude toward the substitution.

Vendor Good Will

A vendor is a person or a firm from whom we buy. Sometimes vendors are called "resources." A most interesting fact is that, while most businessmen are very conscious of the necessity of maintaining customer good will, very few seem to be aware that vendor good will is just as important.

Maybe this is a hang-over from the first business letters, the master-to-bailiff letters. The average businessman's feeling is that the vendor exists for the purpose of supplying goods for which he is paid; therefore the vendor is a servant. Why waste any courtesy on him?

Modern, progressive business people know that vendors are important people in this country of free enterprise and that letters to vendors should be warm, cordial, and courteous. The smart business-man realizes what vendors can do for him.

What Can Vendors Do? Consider some of the benefits that can be derived from promoting vendor good will. The resource who respects us and likes to do business with us will be likely to:

1. Make prompt delivery of goods and materials we need.

2. Exert himself to get merchandise for us that we find difficult to obtain.

3. Give us an opportunity to be among the first to purchase any newly manufactured goods.

4. Offer us, whenever possible, special terms or discounts.

5. Bestow favors, such as minor replacements, at no charge.

6. Afford us an opportunity to buy goods and materials at reduced prices. Savings that are effected in this way can be passed along to customers and will be a means of promoting customer good will.

We must exert ourselves to build vendor good will. Our letters, then, will show that we are people who keep our word; that we pay our bills promptly; that we are fair, reasonable, and prompt about returning merchandise that we did not order or that we cannot use; that we are uniformly courteous and friendly. We shall insure a smooth, steady supply of goods, without which we could not do business.

Illustration. A vendor has written that, in order to reduce his inventory, he is offering a special price on worm gears. Suppose that we need the gears and that we place an order for them. When we write the order letter, we would be very smart to use the last paragraph to express our appreciation of the chance to purchase at the reduced price; something like,

We very much appreciate the opportunity of buying these gears at your special price.

Now suppose that we are overstocked with gears, that we cannot handle any more. Do you know what the average businessman would do in a situation like this? He would read the vendor's offer and then would put it aside and forget it.

We, however, would look ahead a little and see that there might be a time when we should be very happy to have a chance to buy at less than the usual price. We would build for the future and would take a little time to write:

Gentlemen:
We have your letter of May 16, giving us a special price on worm gears.
We wish that we could take advantage of the offer, but we ourselves are overstocked right now.
Please continue to think of us whenever you have any good buys.
Cordially yours,

Here we are using our knowledge of human behavior, the knowledge that people prefer to do favors for those who are appreciative and who *show* their appreciation. Thus, by means of the business letter, the correspondent builds vendor good will.

Co-Worker Good Will

Teamwork is stressed and built by football coaches the country over. Social organizations stand or fall according to the amount of co-operation there is among members. The armed services talk about *esprit de corps,* which is but the common spirit of a group. Loyal, willing, enthusiastic "togetherness" produces the best results wherever two or more people are engaged in a common enterprise.

If cordial, friendly relationships exist among employees in the same business, the business will prosper. We have previously discussed the advantages of promoting good will between us and outsiders, and here we point out the desirability of building good will among ourselves. Everyone knows that a happy worker is a productive worker; so let us see what we can do by way of the written word to make for a happy business life, for promotion of co-worker good will.

Interoffice Correspondence. Sometimes notes are exchanged between members of the same organization. These memorandums may be written to other employees in the same building, or they may be written to branch offices located in other cities.

An interoffice memorandum will be clear, complete, concise, and, at the same time, courteous. The language will be informal, for we are writing to members of our business family; but the fact that they are family does not give us license to be rude. Cold, impolite memorandums will interfere with good teamwork.

Illustration. After our supervisor finishes reading his mail, he says to us, "Humph! Three complaints about not getting merchandise on time. Write a memo to Huntley (our head shipping clerk) and tell him about them. Tell him to get on the ball and keep that stuff moving." Following instructions without thinking, we write:

MEMORANDUM

Date . . . .

To: E. C. Huntley
From: S. D. Williams
Subject: Shipping Delay

Received three complaints in this morning's mail about slow delivery. Get on the ball and keep that stuff moving.

Just stop a moment and think of the effect on Huntley. Then read this memorandum:

Today's mail contained three complaints about slow delivery.
Your fine record with the company leads me to believe that the delay in shipping must have been caused by some emergency. Is there anything I can do to help you prevent any more such complaints?

Which of these two do you think will cause Huntley to "get on the ball and keep that stuff moving"?

Summary. The general principles of good-will building are applied to three areas:

1. Building customer good will
2. Building vendor good will
3. Building co-worker good will

When writing letters to customers, we concentrate on preventing dissatisfaction. In our correspondence with vendors, we keep in mind that we want and need their friendship. All interoffice memorandums are simple and clear; and above all they are as courteous and tactful as any letters sent to customers or vendors.

Every written communication must be planned, thought of, and checked in the light of its good-will value.

Assignment 1. Write a letter to our branch office in Chicago, telling the manager that:

1. His sales for October were 5 per cent below those of last year.
2. His sales for November were 8 per cent below those of last year.
3. We want him to account for the falling off of sales.

Assignment 2. Write a letter to a customer, Bryan Manufacturing Company, saying that his order No. 4687 for steel springs cannot be filled until three weeks from the date of your letter. The reason is that your order for steel was delayed three weeks.

Assignment 3. Write a letter to a vendor, Tully's Toggery, and ask him "what was the big idea of sending us the No. 6728 shipment of men's suits with unlined jackets instead of the lined jackets we ordered." Tell him we are returning the shipment; and, if he can't fill our orders as we specify, we're going to give our business to some other resource.

Assignment 4. You work for the plant manager of your concern. He has discovered that some of the men are consistently late to work, but that their time cards record that they are on time. Obviously, their friends are ringing in their cards for them. He wants you to write a bulletin that will be posted on all the time clocks in the factory. You are to state the facts and warn that any person who rings in a card other than his own will be discharged. Write the bulletin—and make it tough!

Assignment 5. We received a letter from a vendor, asking that we be prompt in returning merchandise that we cannot use. We waited four weeks before returning the last lot, and our delay caused the vendor to lose the sale of the goods. Write him an apology.

Assignment 6. We operate a gift shop. Mrs. Cullinane, one of our best customers, selected a bridal gift for Miss Elsa Houston. She asked us to gift wrap it and send it to Miss Houston. Now, it so happened that Mrs. Cullinane was at Miss Houston's house when the gift arrived; and, when the package was opened, Mrs. Cullinane was much embarrassed to see the bill tucked in with the gift. The clerk who does our gift wrapping must have been on a mental vacation; for, instead of sending the slip to the accounting department, he sent it with the gift.

Mrs. Cullinane has sent us a scorching letter, and your job is to write a reply to that letter. This assignment is a test of your ability to write a letter that will build customer good will.

LESSON 64

Overhead and the Business Letter

Overhead is the cost of doing business and includes all costs other than the purchase price of goods sold. Some examples of overhead are such items as salaries, supplies, rent, equipment, light. The owner of a business or, in the case of a large industry, top management is very much concerned with the problem of keeping down overhead costs; but the average employee does not realize that excessive overhead may keep the businessman from making even a fair profit.

The citizens of the United States are a wasteful people—wasteful of natural resources, of time, of food, of money. They also have a tendency to be less careful of the other fellow's property than they are of their own. For these reasons, the reducing of overhead has become the businessman's ever-present problem. He would, therefore, value highly the employee who is alert to the opportunities for preventing waste.

Salesmen make money for the company by selling goods. Correspondents make money for their firm by thrifty and wise use and care of supplies and equipment. The old adage that a penny saved is a penny earned points out to us letter writers the way in which we can increase profits.

Letter Cost. The Better Letters Institute survey, conducted under the personal supervision of Hiram N. Rasely, executive vice-president of Burdett College, Boston,[1] reported that the cost to the businessman for each dictated letter averaged 75 cents. This study was made in 1950; so, considering the way prices have risen, we would

[1] Report on a survey conducted by the Better Letters Institute, "Business Letters Cost Too Much, According to Recent Survey," *The Business Education World,* January, 1950, p. 239.

be justified in assuming that, by this time, the cost per letter is much more than 75 cents.

The 1950 letter cost is for a dictated letter, but the letters we write would be figured at a price very little below that of a dictated letter. This sum represents not only big expense but also unnecessary expense, for it is possible to reduce it. The purpose of this lesson is to teach us how to prevent needless overhead costs.

Outlining the Business Letter. If a letter is not clear or complete, a second letter will have to be written to explain that which is not clear or complete. We may say, then, that the cost of such a letter must be figured at more than the rate determined by any survey. If a letter is not concise, the excess words cause a waste of time, both for the writer and for the reader. Time is money!

Sometimes, when checking a letter after it is written, the writer finds that he wants to make a change or an addition and must, therefore, discard that letter and write another. Whenever a letter is rewritten, the cost of the letter increases.

Our written communications will have a better chance of being clear, complete, and concise and of being correct at the first writing if we acquire the habit of outlining them. At first, we must take a little time in order to do a complete and thorough job; but, as we gain practice in outlining, the time consumed will grow less and less. Eventually we shall reach the point where a few jotted notes will be sufficient to enable us to write excellent letters and memorandums.

An example of the outline for a letter quoting the wholesale price on portable radios is:

1. Acknowledge receipt of inquiry.
2. Quote $15.95 each in lots of 50 for Belltone portable.
3. Explain that batteries are not included with radios.
4. Quote price on batteries—65 cents each in lots of 50.
5. Promise delivery within five days, to speed order.

The accomplished writer who always outlines letters would need only brief notations; as:

1. Acknowledge inquiry
2. Belltone, $15.95 each in lots of 50, no batteries
3. Batteries 65 cents each in lots of 50
4. Delivery within five days

The letter written from the outline follows.

Gentlemen:

We were pleased to receive your inquiry about the wholesale price of our BELLTONE portable radio.

This model sells for $15.95 each in lots of 50, without batteries. Our price for batteries is 65 cents each in lots of 50.

You will not have to wait long for the receipt of your order, for our policy is to make delivery within five days. May we give you this fast service for our fine radio?

Sincerely yours,

Supplies and Overhead. Care and proper use of supplies will allow us to get the most use out of those supplies. Correspondents are frequently wasteful in the use of supplies. Perhaps we should start to think of all waste in terms of unnecessary overhead.

Orderliness. Keeping all supplies in special places provided for them is probably the first step in conservation. Much time is wasted by the office worker who habitually questions himself thus, "Now where did I put that box of carbons?" The person whose task it is to write business communications will find that a systematic method of carefully storing supplies will result in elimination of waste and confusion.

Stationery. Office letterheads are usually printed on good bond paper. Letterheads are expensive and should be used with care and good judgment. Since letters are important in that they are the window dressing for the employing company, do not go to the extreme of sending out communications on dog-eared or dirty paper. The saving thus effected would be more than offset by a loss of prestige. On the other hand, be sufficiently conservation-conscious not to use a fresh letterhead for scrap paper.

Very thin paper, called "onionskin," is ordinarily used for carbon copies. It is advisable to keep this paper under cover, for it blows about easily and snatching crumples the paper and makes it unusable.

Carbon paper is an important item of office expense; and, if waste in this area is to be prevented, we must know something about its proper use. Always handle carbon paper carefully. Careless handling will wrinkle or crease the paper and will render it unusable. Keeping carbon paper neatly in a folder when not in use will save wear and tear. When returning the paper to the folder, place each sheet face, or shiny, side down.

A good practice is to turn the carbon sheet around from top to bottom after each typing. Failure to do this will result in a concentration of wear in one place; much of the sheet, consequently, will be thrown away unused.

When a job requires several copies of more than one page, change the order of the carbons after typing each page. This will insure even wear on all the sheets used. The finished piece of work will look better, for the last carbon copy should be as clear as the first.

Equipment and Overhead. Equipment of all kinds should be kept clean and in good working order. The piece of equipment that most concerns writers of letters is the typewriter; so the proper care and use of that machine is important.

A typewriter should be thoroughly cleaned once a day. If stencils are typed on the machine, it should be cleaned after each stencil is typed. We are studying this text in order to be able to write the best in business letters, but no letter is good if it is written on a machine that has dirty type.

The typewriter ribbon ought to move freely; otherwise, holes will be worn in the ribbon. Then there will be a choice of discarding it and boosting overhead or of continuing to use it, with a resultant detraction from the appearance of our letters.

When erasing, we shall do as we have been taught by the typewriting teacher, move the carriage to one side so that the eraser crumbs will fall to the desk instead of into the type basket. Careless erasing will clog the openings between type bars, will slow the action of the machine, will cause "piling" of keys, and will necessitate a visit from the repairman. Each call he makes adds to overhead costs.

Fatigue and Overhead. The tired worker cannot operate so well or so fast as the fresh employee can. Decreased production means increased overhead. Many people do not realize that weariness may be caused by some little difficulty that can be overcome very easily. If exhaustion creeps in after a few hours of work, an effort should be made to discover the reason for it.

Could there be unnecessary eyestrain? Is the copy too far away or too near? Are we facing the light? Should we move our desk out of that dark corner? Do we need glasses? Is the bulb in the desk light wearing out? If we tire easily or quickly, it may be that our fatigue is caused by eyestrain.

Maybe we are bodily tired, aching all over. Are we sitting too close to the typewriter or too far away? Is the machine at the right height? How about our typing position? Of course we remember how our typing teacher used to emphasize position of our feet and hands. We also remember that, when the teacher was looking at us, we would assume the correct position; but, when he was working with some other pupil, we would again curl our toes around the legs of the chair. Now we know that the teacher worked so hard because he knew that the typist whose position was correct could work longer hours without being tired to the point of decreased efficiency. Correct any bad position habits, for poor posture may be what slows production.

Then, too, we may be mentally tired. In all businesses there comes a time when the pressure of work reaches a peak. Some of us allow ourselves to think and worry about *all* the tasks that have to be done, and we are worn out before we start. Very obviously, we can do only one job at a time; therefore we should think of and concentrate on and do only one job at a time. Perhaps we should arrange the duties in the order of priority, listing first the things that should be done first. As far as possible, we should devote our entire attention to the work at hand; and, when we finish one piece of work, concentrate on the next. We owe it to ourselves and to our employer to conserve and to use our energies to the best advantage.

After studying this lesson on overhead, possibly we may be thinking that the points made are minor and unimportant. If so, keep this in mind: One little instance of waste is merely a drop in the bucket, but one little instance by each person each day in a large organization can turn the drop into a raging torrent.

Summary.   Writers of business communications will be conscious of the need for helping employers keep down the costs of doing business. They will outline all letters so that unnecessary expense will not be incurred in the rewriting of communications. They will prevent waste and confusion by keeping all supplies in their appointed places, by proper use and care of supplies and equipment. They will also prevent waste of their own power and energy by discovering and eliminating whatever causes avoidable fatigue.

All employees who take time to think know that they have a personal stake in the reduction of overhead. They know that, when they cut down expense, they increase profits. The more money the company makes, the higher salaries will that firm be able to pay. The office worker's own financial success or failure depends on whether his organization makes or loses money. No employee can afford to be wasteful of company time or materials, for each employee is the company!

Assignment 1. Outline a letter to your teacher, explaining the meaning of the term "overhead."

Assignment 2. Write the letter outlined in Assignment 1.

Assignment 3. You have observed some instances of unnecessary overhead in your school, caused by pupils who are careless or who are not conscious of overhead cost. Prepare an outline for a letter to be written to your principal, telling him of your observations. You will, of course, mention no names.

Assignment 4. Write the letter outlined in the previous assignment.

Assignment 5. Outline a letter to your typing teacher, thanking him for his efforts to prepare you to type with a minimum of fatigue.

Assignment 6. Write the letter outlined in Assignment 5.

Assignment 7. Outline a letter to your father, telling him what you have learned by studying this lesson.

Assignment 8. Write the letter outlined in Assignment 7.

Assignment 9. Outline and write a letter to your teacher, telling what you think you personally can do to reduce overhead in your school life.

LESSON **65**

The Words We Use

Words are the tools of our trade, and with these tools we fashion the letters we write. As master craftsmen, we must have the right tools for each job we do; and we must be sure that the tools are the best in quality and of the latest design.

Our previous vocabulary study has prepared us for the selection of correct words. This vocabulary study has taught us to distinguish properly between words whose meanings are frequently confused. We already know that the best written language is simple, clear, and meaningful.

The purpose in studying this lesson is to learn to avoid the words and phrases that stamp a letter writer as being dull, out of date, or deficient in the principles of good salesmanship.

Master-Bailiff Words and Phrases. Why many business correspondents should continue to use expressions that were in style hundreds of years ago is a complete mystery. Just look at this: "Your esteemed favor of the 16th is at hand." What an outmoded way of saying, "We have received your letter of May 16"! Yet, antique expressions are still in use by the very businessmen who are so enthusiastic about modernizing their plants, stock, and equipment.

Study the following list of outdated words and phrases, for it is important that we know what *not* to use. Twentieth-century letters should have the flavor of the twentieth century.

Master-Bailiff	*Twentieth Century*
Acknowledge receipt of	We received
Advise	Say, tell, inform, let us know
And oblige	Do not use this.
As per, per	As, according to

332

Master-Bailiff	*Twentieth Century*
At an early date	Soon, or give specific date
At hand	Has been received
At that time	Then
At this time, at the present time, at the present writing	Now, at present
Attached hereto	Attached
Beg	Do not use. We are not beggars.
Contents carefully noted	Do not use.
Due to the fact that	As, because, since
Duly	Do not use. It is superfluous.
Enclosed please find	Enclosed is
Even date	Give specific date.
Esteemed	Too flowery
Favor	Letter
Hand you herewith	Enclosed
Have before me	Do not use.
Herewith	Do not use, except in legal work.
In re	Regarding, concerning
In the event that	In case, or if
In this matter	Do not use.
Instant (Inst.)	Give exact date.
Kindly	Please
Our check in the amount of	Our check for
Party	Person, except in legal work
Proximo	Give exact date.
Recent date	Give exact date.
Same	It, they, them, or whatever is meant
State	Say, tell
Take pleasure	Pleased, are happy, are glad
Thank you in advance	Do not use. It is a discourteous expression.
The writer	I, me
Trust	Hope, know, believe
Ultimo	Give exact date.
Under date of	On
Under separate cover	By freight, or whatever the means of sending
Up to this writing	Previously
Valued (letter or order)	Do not use.
Via	By way of

Master-Bailiff	*Twentieth Century*
We wish to thank you	Thank you
Would ask, remind, say, suggest	Go ahead and say it without warning.
Yours received and contents noted	Unnecessary. The letter must have been received and read if it is being answered.

Overworked Words and Phrases.   When a writer has been performing his duties day after day and year after year, he sometimes loses his enthusiasm, his freshness of spirit. His letters become dull and monotonous. He uses the same small stock of words over and over. When this point is reached, the writer is in a rut; and his chance for success stays right in the rut with him.

The following list calls our attention to some of the overworked expressions and gives us suggestions for substitutions. Let's keep out of the rut!

Overworked	*Suggested Substitutions*
Along the lines of	Like
Asset	Advantage, gain, possession, resource
At all times	Always
By means of	By
Deal	Agreement, arrangement, transaction
Factor	Event, occurrence, part
Field	Branch, department, domain, point, question, range, realm, region, scene, scope, sphere, subject, theme
Fix	Adjust, arrange, attach, bind, mend, confirm, define, establish, limit, place, prepare, repair
Inasmuch as	Since
In the near future	Soon, or state the exact time.
Line	Business, merchandise, goods, stock
Matter	Situation, question, subject, point
Nice	Pleasant, agreeable
Our Mr. Smith	Our representative, Mr. Smith
Previous to, prior to	Before

Overworked	Suggested Substitutions
Proposition	Proposal, undertaking, offer, plan, affair, recommendation, idea
Reaction	Opinion, attitude, impression
Recent communication	Letter of (give appropriate date)
Run	Manage, direct, operate

Unnecessary Repetitions. Careless, unnecessary, and incorrect repetitions in speech have led to their use in writing business letters. We are going to eliminate all unnecessary words from our vocabulary. We know that excess words increase overhead; and we know that any careless repetition will convict us of lack of polish. Study very carefully the following list.

Use	Avoid
About	*At* about
Above	*Up* above
Accept	Accept *of*
Alike	*Both* alike
Beginner	*New* beginner
Check	Check *into*
Co-operate	Co-operate *together*
Connect	Connect *up*
Continue	Continue *on* or *to remain*
Converted	Converted *over*
Depreciate	Depreciate *in value*
During	During *the course of*
Etc.	*And* etc.
Experience	*Past* experience
Completion	*Final* completion
Follows	Follows *after*
Gratis	*Free* gratis
Identical	*Same* identical
Indorse	Indorse *on the back*
Inside	Inside *of* (If referring to time, use *within*.)
Lose	Lose *out*
May	May *perhaps*
Monopoly	*Complete* monopoly
Near	Near *to*
Otherwise	*As* otherwise
Outside	Outside *of*

Use	*Avoid*
Over	Over *with*
Practice	*Customary* practice
Rarely	Rarely *ever*
Refer	Refer *back*
Remember	Remember *of*
Repeat	Repeat *again*
Seldom	Seldom *ever*
Together	Both *together*

Negative Words. Letters should be so carefully written that they will contain no word that will reflect adversely on the employer or on the goods sold.

As an illustration, suppose that we write letters for a retail store. One of our customers has written to say that she is dissatisfied with a purchase she made. The reply we send to her contains the following sentence, "We have instructed our driver to pick up the unsatisfactory goods." What have we done? By the use of one word, "unsatisfactory," we have planted in that woman's mind the idea that we carry merchandise that is not up to standard.

Now we change the sentence from negative to positive by writing, "We have instructed our driver to pick up the dress you wish to return."

That we may always accentuate the positive, we must avoid the use of the following negative words:

Blunder	Damage	Error	Mistake	Unfavorable
Claim	Defective	Failure	Neglected	Unfortunately
Complaint	Delay	Inability	Poor	Unsatisfactory
Conflicts	Displeasure	Inadequate	Regret	
Criticism	Dissatisfied	Inferior	Trouble	

Summary. For the truly polished letter writer, the ability to select and use correct words is not the whole story. The modern, finished writer will eliminate from his vocabulary all words that smack of the dead past. His letters will sparkle, for he will refuse to use the same words again and again. He will give evidence of a fine vocabulary by refraining from the use of any unnecessary words. Finally, he will be one of the best salesmen in the company, for he will always present his organization in a favorable light by avoiding the use of negative words.

THE WORDS WE USE

Assignment 1. The first two assignments are a test of how well you have learned to distinguish between or among words that are often confused or used incorrectly.

On a separate sheet of paper, write your choice of the correct word for each of the following sentences.

1. Excessive heat or cold will (affect, effect) production.

2. That typist is not (apt, likely, liable) to be promoted unless she learns to concentrate.

3. You (can, may) see Mr. Holland on Monday at ten o'clock.

4. The sailing of the ship was delayed several hours because its (complement, compliment) of officers and men was not complete.

5. You can whisper (in, into) the microphone and still be heard.

6. Treat your customers just (like, as) you want to be treated.

7. Sandra could be found anywhere in the building except (at, to) her desk.

8. The quality of this grade of cotton is not (as good as, so good as) it used to be.

9. (Leave, let) me type that last page for you.

10. These continued interruptions (aggravate, irritate, exasperate) me to the point of desperation.

11. No (fewer, less) than ten absences were reported this week.

12. Our supervisor divided the work (among, between) us three typists.

13. Thousands of refugees have (emigrated, immigrated) from the Balkan countries.

14. Conscientious workers seldom (loose, lose) their positions.

15. The (principal, principle) (s) that are most desirable in daily living are those that are valued most highly in business.

16. Our office manager will (accept, except) no excuse for tardiness.

17. Maria was (all ready, already) for work at 7:45 this morning.

18. Dorothy received a bonus when her idea was (adapt, adopt) (ed) by the company.

19. Prices today are (all together, altogether) too high.

20. Your banker's (advice, advise) is excellent.

21. (Most, Almost) all the figures are now compiled.

22. Those (kind, kinds) of mistakes are totally unnecessary.

23. Who else is to go (beside, besides) Henry and me?

24. After two years you will be (eligible, legible) to take another examination.

25. At the unveiling, the hero was (formally, formerly) presented with a medal.

Assignment 2. Follow the directions given for Assignment 1.

1. I shall take my vacation (some time, sometime) after June 1.

2. You will find the stylus (in back of, behind) the small box.

3. A good supervisor must have special (ability, capacity) in working with people.

4. The (affect, effect) of the bonus plan was shown in increased production.

5. The bus (most, almost) always runs on schedule.

6. By noon the big job was (all ready, already) finished.

7. (All right, Alright), I'll come right away.

8. There are ten file clerks (all together, altogether).

9. Please put the box any (place, where).

10. Send half the order on May 1 and the (balance, remainder, rest) on May 15.

11. The work of the manager was hampered by (continual, continuous) interruptions.

12. All the (personal, personnel) received Christmas gifts.

13. There is a (loose, lose) screw in my line spacer.

14. Mr. Mason (may be, maybe) our next president.

15. Are there typewriters (anywhere, anywheres) on this floor of the building?

16. All the girls helped (each other, one another).

17. Evelyn has not (quiet, quite) finished filing the letters.

18. In the basement of our building there is a (stationary, stationery) pump.

19. Don't you wish you could type (like, as) Barbara?

20. We haven't seen that salesman for (some time, sometime).

21. Lillian keeps a dictionary on (both, each) side(s) of her typewriter.

22. Please (bring, take) this message to the main office.

23. Wholehearted (co-operation, corporation) contributes much to pleasant working hours.

24. She said that (may be, maybe) she would come in today.

25. An office seems so (quiet, quite) after business hours.

Assignment 3. Revise the following sentences by modernizing the wording.

1. Due to a recent change in accounting procedures, you will receive your bill on the tenth of the month instead of on the first.
2. We trust that you will agree with us.
3. Please advise as to what disposition you wish to make of order No. 684.
4. We are replacing the broken gasket and will rush same to you.
5. The goods were shipped as per your order of June 5.
6. Thanks for your esteemed favor of April 2.
7. Attached hereto is our check for $49.95.
8. Please mark your reply for the attention of the writer.
9. We are sending you under separate cover a sample box of our greeting cards.
10. We are enclosing our check in the amount of $35.
11. Please reply by return mail and oblige.
12. We wrote you under date of December 21.
13. Your letter of the 16th ult. has been received.
14. Please send us your check at an early date.
15. Your letter of August 17 is at hand.
16. We beg to inform you that your order will be shipped on Friday of this week.
17. In re your letter of even date, the discount on order No. 482 will be allowed.
18. Kindly refer this letter to Mr. Bunker.
19. Your valued order of May 6 is being shipped today.
20. We wish to thank you for your order No. 2345.

Assignment 4. Revise the following sentences, substituting syn nyms for all overworked words.

1. We were glad to get your nice letter of March 7.
2. The new furniture store is run by Mr. Foley.
3. What is your reaction to this plan?
4. We will write you later about the matter.
5. The Emporium has a good line of children's clothing.
6. Inasmuch as the sheets were soiled, we are returning them.
7. We should like to close this deal within a week.
8. Time is an important factor in this particular case.

9. We wish you would make us a definite proposition.
10. Our Mr. Eppler will call on you next Monday.
11. Your personal, warm friendliness is an asset to your company.
12. We hope to hear from you in the near future.
13. Please send a mechanic to fix the machine.
14. He does very good work in the field of public relations.
15. Prior to the receipt of your letter, we were uncertain about delivery date.
16. We serve our credit customers faster by means of Charga-Plates.
17. We are glad to make fair adjustments at all times.
18. Your recent communication explains satisfactorily your delay in sending the check.
19. Our Accounting Department operates along the lines of Bryan's.
20. Your nice letter of congratulation was received today.

Assignment 5. On a separate sheet of paper, list the unnecessary words in the following sentences.

1. My employer rarely ever travels by air.
2. I certainly do not remember of telling her to file the letter under "state of."
3. Please bring with you notebook, pen, eraser, and etc.
4. Before it can be cashed, every check must be indorsed on the back.
5. Sue may perhaps come to work tomorrow.
6. Clean your typewriter each day, as otherwise you will not get the best use from it.
7. Janet stood inside of the doorway to shield herself from the rain.
8. The rush was over with before five o'clock.
9. I shall not repeat the instructions again.
10. Past experience has taught us that we must collect bills promptly.
11. Today we all had coffee free gratis.
12. Before the holiday, we shall close at about three o'clock.
13. Those two new typewriters are both alike.
14. We have asked Mr. Stone to check into the problem.
15. Before we do government work, our machinery must be converted over.
16. The bus stop is very near to our office.
17. The stock clerk stores the pencils up above the paper.

18. June wore to work the same identical dress.
19. I want you to continue on with the specifications.
20. We should try to help all new beginners.

Assignment 6. Revise the following sentences so that the impression given will be positive rather than negative.

1. We were surprised to learn that you found order No. 467 unsatisfactory.
2. We will replace the chair that you claim was broken in transit.
3. We are sorry that you were dissatisfied with the suit we sent you.
4. Your error of 10 cents in the check of May 26 can be corrected by sending us that amount in stamps.
5. Your criticisms of April 6 are just ones.
6. We have received your complaint of December 26.
7. Unfortunately, shipment of your order will be delayed until next week.
8. We neglected to prepay your order No. 682.
9. It is too bad that the drill press was defective.
10. We are sure that you will understand our inability to pay before next Tuesday.
11. We hope that the substitution will not cause you any displeasure.
12. We are sorry that the dresses on your order No. 856 were of inferior grade.
13. Your failure to send us your check of the 15th has forced us to carry your account beyond the time limit set in our contract.
14. The terms quoted in your letter of June 25 are unfavorable to us.
15. Delay in paying bills is poor business policy.
16. Your reasons for refusing shipment are inadequate.
17. You may return the damaged goods.
18. Your understanding of the terms quoted for order No. 842 conflicts with ours.
19. We hope that the delay in shipment did not cause you any trouble.
20. Please make all complaints to our Adjustment Department.

Assignment 7. From your file of sample letters, select one letter that is poorly worded. Rewrite the letter, applying the knowledge you have gained from studying this lesson. Give your teacher both the original and the revision.

LESSON **66**

Business Letter Format

The word *format* is borrowed from publishers of books, magazines, and newspapers. They use it to mean size, shape, and make-up of their publications; and, when we say "business letter format," we are talking about the mechanical setup of business letters. The message is our major consideration, but the message will be more effective if it is correctly and attractively framed.

The Parts of a Business Letter. Our study of format will start with the learning of correct usage as applied to the parts of a business letter. Look carefully at the illustration on the facing page.

The parts of the letter have been marked, and the key to the numbers is:

1. The heading
2. The date line
3. The inside address
4. The attention line
5. The salutation
6. The subject line
7. The body of the letter
8. The complimentary closing
9-10. The signature lines
11. Identification initials
12. Enclosure reference

Parts 1, 2, 3, 5, 7, 8, 9, 10, and 11 must be included in *every* letter. Parts 4, 6, and 12 are used whenever needed.

1. The Heading. The heading consists of the name of the firm or the individual proprietor and the street, city, and state address.

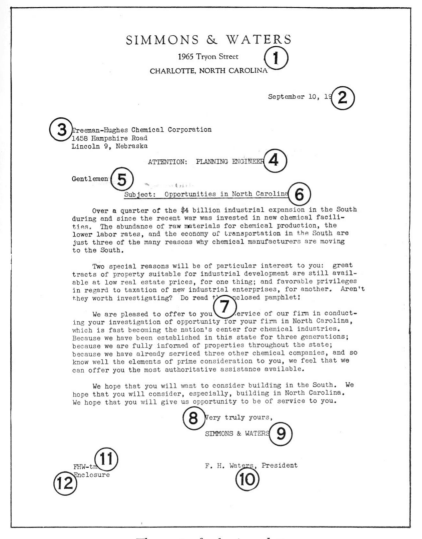

The parts of a business letter.

These are the essentials for a printed letterhead, although there may be additional printed data.

Office people become so accustomed to using printed letterheads that they sometimes forget to type the heading when they write personal-business letters on blank paper. A personnel manager for a well-known industry once remarked, "I received a splendid letter of application today. I'd certainly hire that girl if only I knew her address."

For a typed heading, use one of the following forms:

>   1645 Madison Avenue
>   Middletown, Ohio
>   (Date)

>   CHAPMAN SECRETARIAL SCHOOL
>   45 Midtown Avenue
>   Boise, Idaho

2. The Date Line. The date line contains the month, the day of the month, and the year. Do not abbreviate the month or the year. We have a choice of centering the date, of typing it flush with the right margin, of starting it at the center point of the page, or, in extreme block-style letters, of starting it at the left margin.

Always be sure that letters are dated correctly. In some cases, such as a contract bid, the date may be extremely important.

3. The Inside Address. The inside address consists of the name and address of the person or the firm to whom the letter is written and should correspond in essentials to the envelope address. Avoid the use of any abbreviations, and be very careful about the spelling of names. The misspelling of a name annoys the owner of that name, and annoying customers or vendors is no way to promote good will. If we have any doubt as to spelling, let us check and get it right!

The inside address is written after the date and is placed at the left margin, except in friendly or very formal letters. Then it is written below the signature at the left margin.

Titles in Inside Addresses. For reasons of courtesy, with every name we use a title; such as: *Mr., Miss,* or *Mrs.* If the addressee holds some special title, like *Doctor, Professor,* or *Honorable,* we use that title. These are called courtesy titles. While we may use a courtesy title and an official title for the same person, we never use two courtesy titles. We should be incorrect in writing "Dr. John Hunt, LL.D.," because both *Dr.* and *LL.D.* are abbreviations of doctors' degrees. When using both a courtesy and an official title, we have a choice with regard to the placement of the official title; as:

Mr. John Ames, President
Ames Manufacturing Company
468 Fifth Avenue
Provo, Utah

Miss Margaret Cunningham
Head of Business Department   (Title on separate line for better
Fitch High School   balance)
Groton, Connecticut

City and State. Always spell out the names of cities and usually those of states. If we have any question about abbreviations, let us consult a reference manual.

4. The Attention Line. An attention line is used when it is important that the letter reach quickly the person who is best qualified to take care of the subject of the letter.

In a block-style letter, the attention line is typed at the left margin, two lines below the inside address. In an indented-style letter, the line may be centered on the same line as the salutation or may be typed two lines below the inside address and indented five spaces.

5. The Salutation. The salutation always starts at the left margin and, in business letters, is followed by a colon. In social correspondence, a comma may follow the salutation.

Let us remember:

a. That we abbreviate only *Mr., Mrs.,* and *Messrs.*

b. That we capitalize *dear* only when it is the *first* word of the salutation.

c. That we choose the salutation that is suitable and correct for the firm and person to whom we write.

The correct salutation for a firm composed of men or of men and women is *Gentlemen. Dear Sirs* is out of date. For a firm or organization composed entirely of women, use *Mesdames.* Salutations for individuals, in the order of formal to informal, are:

Sir: Madam:
My dear Sir: My dear Madam:
My dear Mr. Thorp: My dear Mrs. Thorp:
Dear Mr. Thorp: Dear Mrs. Thorp:

Consult the Reference Section of this book for forms of address for official correspondence.

Important. The salutation always agrees with the first line of the inside address. Study the following illustrations.

The Stillman Velvet Company
Boston 4
Massachusetts

Attention: Mr. Robert Stillman

Gentlemen: (to agree with *The Stillman Velvet Company*)

If the salutation "Dear Mr. Stillman" is desired, set up the letter like this:

Mr. Robert Stillman
c/o The Stillman Velvet Company
Boston 4, Massachusetts

Dear Mr. Stillman:

6. The Subject Line. Although not all firms use a subject line, it has the advantage of enabling the reader at a glance to know what the letter is about. The subject line is also an aid in filing and in finding a filed letter. The style and the position of the line are usually decided by office preference. It may be typed two lines below the salutation (at the margin, indented five spaces, or centered) or centered on a line with the salutation.

Internal Revenue Department
1426 Pearl Street
Hartford 2, Connecticut

Gentlemen:

           Subject: Case No. 167

                or

Gentlemen: *Case No. 167*

7. The Body of the Letter. The body of the letter contains the message. The writing of the message will be treated later, but appearance is the point to be emphasized here. Be careful to have:

    a. Generous margins of white space, so that the letter looks like a picture in a frame.

    b. Short paragraphs.

 c. As even a right-hand margin as possible.

 d. Neat typing, no strikeovers, no noticeable erasures.

8. The Complimentary Closing. The complimentary closing is the leave-taking line of the letter and should be in keeping with the message contained in the letter. Only the first word of the complimentary closing is capitalized. The most used forms, ranging from formal to informal, are:

Very truly yours,	Sincerely yours,
Yours very truly,	Very cordially yours,
Very sincerely yours,	Yours very cordially,
Yours very sincerely,	Yours cordially,
Yours sincerely,	Cordially yours,

Note that the closing "Yours truly" is not included in the list. This closing went out with high-buttoned shoes. Note also that the word *yours* appears in all illustrations. We are permitted to omit *yours* only when we are on extremely friendly terms with the person to whom we write.

If we are writing to superior authority and wish to use one of the *respectfully* closings—Very respectfully yours, Yours very respectfully, Yours respectfully, Respectfully yours—we must not make the error of using *respectively* for *respectfully*.

9–10. The Signature Lines. All letters must have a pen-written signature. Should the signature be that of a woman and *Mrs.* is not written before her name, the assumption is that she is a *Miss*.

Secretaries often sign mail for their employers. The following style is then used:

Barbara Richards
Secretary to Mr. Carlin

If the signer is not actually the secretary, the form should be:

Barbara Richards
For Mr. Carlin

The following is an illustration of the most commonly used form for signature lines.

This is the last line of the body of the letter.

> (*Two lines*)
>
>   Very cordially yours,
>
> (*Two lines*)
>
>   CULVER REALTY COMPANY
>
> (*Four lines*)
>
>   John J. Culver   (*Typed signature*)
>   President   (*Official title is optional*)

11. Identification Initials. Identification initials are always placed at the left margin. They may be typed on a line with the last signature line or two lines below the last signature line.

In a dictated letter in which two sets of initials are used, the dictator's initials are written first. Sometimes, when the dictator signs the letter, only the stenographer's initials appear. When the writer of the letter is also the typist, he places his own initials in the identification space.

12. Enclosure Reference. Should a letter contain an enclosure, indicate that fact by using an enclosure reference typed one or two lines below the identification initials. Once more, the style is that of the preference of a particular office. Here are some suggested enclosure reference forms:

Enc.

Encl.

Enclosure

Encls.

Enc. 2

Enc. (2)

3 Enc.—Original draft of report
      Retyped copy
      Carbon of retyped copy

Enclosures
      Check
      Statement

Open and Close Punctuation. When open punctuation is used, omit commas and periods at the ends of all lines other than those in the body of the letter. Naturally, when the last word in a line is an abbreviation, use a period for that abbreviation. Close punctuation requires commas or periods at the ends of lines.

The modern trend seems to be to use open punctuation, with the exception of the colon after the salutation and the comma after the complimentary closing.

Letterheads. The standard size of business letter paper is 8½ by 11, but this does not mean that all letters are typed on 8½-by-11 paper. The setting up of a letter on any other size of paper will present no difficulty if we remember that there are 10 pica spaces to the horizontal inch, 12 elite spaces to the horizontal inch, and 6 lines to the vertical inch.

For instance, measurement shows that the letterhead we are to use is the Baronial size, 5½ by 8½. If our typewriter is equipped with pica type, we know that there are 55 spaces across the paper. For a 1-inch margin, we set our stops at 10 and 45. If we have elite type, there are 66 horizontal spaces; and our stops will be set at 12 and 54. Regardless of the size of type, there are 51 lines on the paper. All that is necessary to produce an attractive letter on any size of paper is a ruler and a knowledge of the number of spaces and lines to the inch.

The Second Page. Sometimes letters cannot be completed on the first page, and we must use a second page. For all pages after the initial letterhead:

1. Type an identification line containing the name of the addressee, the date of letter, and the page number.

Mrs. L. A. Brooks, December 4, 19—		-2-
Mrs. L. A. Brooks	-2-	December 4, 19—
Mrs. L. A. Brooks—2		December 4, 19—

2. Use a blank sheet of paper of the same quality as the printed letterhead.

3. Type at least three lines of the body of the letter.

4. Begin typing four lines below the identification line.

Envelope Address. The information contained in the envelope address should correspond to that of the inside address. Since the postal authorities prefer that the name of the state be typed on a line by itself, do this whenever possible. Here are some points to remember about envelope addresses.

1. Avoid two-line addresses.

2. Double space three- and four-line addresses; single space addresses containing more than four lines.

3. The attention line may be typed in the lower left-hand corner or may appear as the second line of the envelope address.

4. If the envelope does not contain a printed return address, be sure to type it in the upper left-hand corner.

5. The address may be centered slightly below the center of the envelope, or it may be started about three spaces to the right of center. No part of the address should be typed in the upper half of the envelope space.

Summary. A neat, correct, attractively arranged letter sets the stage for respectful consideration of the message contained in that letter. Study of this lesson is preparation for correct and modern practice with regard to:

1. The parts of a business letter.
2. Open and close punctuation.
3. Setup of letters on paper other than 8½-by-11 size.
4. Second-page procedure.
5. Addressing of envelopes.

Assignment 1. You are writing a friendly, personal-business letter to Edward B. Hunt—47 Houston Street in Paris, Texas—on April 1 of the current year.

a. Type the lines through the salutation line.
b. Type the first line on the second page.
c. Show how you would sign the letter.
d. What, if any, identification initials would you use?
e. Cut paper to envelope size, and type an envelope address for your letter.

Assignment 2. Name the eleven parts of the business letter. Place a star beside the parts that must be included in every business letter.

Assignment 3. List the correct items among the following and hand in your list:

a. Mr. John J. Cronin, Ph.D.
b. Dr. Thomas Lawton, M.D.
c. Dr. Thomas Lawton, President
d. Peter E. Bessette, Manager
e. Mrs. M. R. Hobson, Secretary
f. Miss Mary E. Ahern, Editor
g. Honorable Simon Tibbitts, Esq.
h. Phyllis Wood, Treasurer
i. Professor Eugene Stewart, Dean
j. Dr. T. Allen Crowe, Superintendent

Assignment 4. Name one outdated salutation and one outdated complimentary closing.

Assignment 5. Your supervisor tells you to write a letter to the Ferrie Manufacturing Company, 1237 Broadway, New York 18, New York. He wants you to mark the letter to the attention of E. R. Hobart; and he insists on the salutation, "Dear Ed." How are you going to set up the letter?

Assignment 6. In your own words, state the rule for the correct salutation to use in a letter containing an attention line.

Assignment 7. Perhaps you have noticed that there is a wide choice with regard to such items as placement of the subject line, style of identification initials, enclosure references. These details are usually decided by office preference. As a new employee, how can you find out the style preferred in your office?

Assignment 8. Suppose that the letter you are typing will go over to a second page and you have available only printed letterheads. What will you do?

Assignment 9. The letterheads used in your department measure $6\frac{1}{2}$ by $9\frac{1}{2}$ inches. Your supervisor wants you to have a 1-inch margin for all letters. Where will you set your stops for pica type? for elite type? How many lines are there on the letterhead?

Assignment 10. On a separate sheet of paper, rewrite any of the following salutations and complimentary closings that you consider incorrect or poor form in a business letter.

My Dear Mr. Brown:	Y'rs truly,
Dear Prof. Pampel:	Very Cordially yours,
Dear Mr. E. S. Law:	Sincerely,
My dear Mrs. Palmer:	Yours Very Sincerely,
Gentleman:	Yours very truly,

Assignment 11. Write the salutation and the complimentary closing for each of the following:

a. A letter to the local postmaster, asking him to trace a package.

b. A letter to a good customer, Martin Roll, asking him to be your guest at a banquet.

c. A letter to a vendor firm, explaining that your check arrived late because of a washout on the railroad line.

d. A letter to a firm composed exclusively of women, offering space in your store for a demonstration of its product.

e. A letter to a woman customer, answering her complaint about poor service rendered her by one of our salespersons.

Assignment 12. Correct the following:

a. Fallon Velvet Company
1267 State Street
New London, Ohio

Dear Mr. Fallon

b. James Drugstore
462 Main Street
Norwich, Connecticut

Attention: Mrs. F. S. Mull

Dear Mrs. Mull:

c. Mrs. Todd Cochran
423 Water Street
Stamford, Nebraska.

Dear Mrs. Cochran:

d. Cottrell Line and Twine Company
56 Pearl St.
Ames, Iowa

Gentlemen:

e. John H. McCaffery
263 Falmouth Avenue
Quincy 48, Massachusetts

Dear Mr. McCaffery:

f. Barrie Lumber Company
358 Elm Street
New Haven 16, Connecticut

Gentlemen:

Attention: Mr. A. B. Brown

g. Dear Sir:

. . . .

               Cordially yours,

h. Occum Casements
14 Central Avenue
Mason, Nevada

Subject: Picture Windows

Gentlemen:

i. Mr. F. X. Falvey
355 High Street
Charlotte, 6 North Carolina

Dear Mr. Falvey:

j. Pacific Insurance Company
Bartlett Building
Tacoma 6, Washington

Gentlemen,

k. Mr. Pelton Snyder
666 Mill Street
Media, Illinois

Dear Mr. Pelton:

l. Dear Mr. Griffin:

. . . .

            Very truly yours,

Assignment 13. Cut ten pieces of paper to envelope size, and type envelope addresses for the ten full addresses given in Assignment 12.

Assignment 14. Outline and write a letter to your teacher, telling him how your knowledge of business letter layout has been increased through your study of this lesson.

LESSON **67**

Styles in Business Letters

Within the limits of our pocketbooks, we all choose our clothes with a view to selecting what is fashionable, suitable, and becoming. We are very conscious of the value of dress in creating an impression. A boy who was presenting himself for a personal interview would wear his best suit and necktie. A girl certainly would not apply for an office job while clad in dungarees or any other leisure-time garb.

When the successful applicant begins work, he may find that his firm has dress regulations that govern the style and color of his business clothes. Many large department stores issue such dress regulations, for they know the importance of using style and color in all areas of their business.

Now just as there is suitability in clothing, so is there appropriateness in the letter form that we choose to use; and so may we clothe our letters in a style that will produce a desired effect.

Business letter styles fall into three broad classes: indented, extreme-block, and semiblock styles. These different forms, together with the necessary fashion accessories, will be our subjects for study in this lesson.

Indented Style. For an indented-style letter, the placement of the date line, the complimentary closing, and the signature lines is decided by personal or office preference.

In the inside address, the second line is indented five spaces; and each following line is indented an additional five spaces. All paragraphs are indented five spaces. Study the illustration on page 355.

In addition to knowing what indented style is, the letter writer must know when to use it, when it would be effective. The following reasoning presents the case for the use of this style of letter.

The indented style is the oldest letter form. Many people connect age with soundness, dependability, integrity. The indented form, then, would be suitable for any establishment that handles other people's money. The banker, the investment broker, the insurance company, all could use this style to further the impression of trustworthiness that is so necessary for their kinds of business transactions.

April 11, 19—

Mr. Clark A. Appleton
  823 Island Road
    Elgin
      Nevada
Dear Mr. Appleton:
  Your request for information with regard to a mortgage on your house has been referred to me.
  I am not clear about the value of your house, the security you are prepared to give, or the amount you wish to borrow. Perhaps we should get together and talk over your problem.
  Just drop in on any business day and ask for me. I should be very happy to explain the many services we offer.
Cordially yours,

Extreme-Block Style. In a letter that is set up in extreme-block style, each line starts at the left margin. The advantage of using this form is that the typist does not have to use the tabular key. The disadvantage is that to some people the finished product may appear one-sided, unbalanced. This form would be incorrect for a double-spaced letter. Indent for paragraphs when typing a double-spaced letter.

The extreme-block style is the most advanced style and would probably be used by a firm that wished to give the impression of being ahead of the times, not merely abreast of the times; such as an advertising agency, a sales-promotion agency, a business that specializes in directing community drives. See first letter on page 356.

A firm that has for its main objective the saving of time might choose for its letter style the form supported by the National Office Management Association (NOMA). This letter is extreme block in style and:

1. Omits the salutation and the complimentary closing.

2. Sets up in capital letters the subject and the typed signature lines.

3. Indents five spaces for listings, except when numbers or letters precede the items. When numbers or letters are used, the listings are blocked. No periods are typed after such numbers or letters.

June 1, 19—

Mr. Robert J. Leary
935 Hamilton Drive
Ames, Iowa

Dear Mr. Leary:

We are enclosing our contract form in duplicate to cover your purchase of a Clearsite television set.

If the terms outlined in the contract are satisfactory, please sign and return both copies to us, together with your deposit of $75.

Thank you for giving us this opportunity to help you provide many hours of enjoyment for your family.

Sincerely yours,

CLEARSITE TELEVISION

E. R. Trumbull
Credit Manager

ERT:c
Enclosure

July 8, 19—

Mr. John L. Sullivan
Personnel Director
Wisconsin Dairy Company
Madison 12, Wisconsin

REFERENCE FOR MR. A. R. LOWE

Mr. Lowe was employed by us as assistant controller from May 6, 1949, to June 8, 1953. We found him:

1 An excellent accountant.

2 An industrious, dependable, efficient worker.

3 An employee whose relationships with his fellow workers were completely satisfactory.

Mr. Lowe resigned voluntarily because he wished to work in a city where he would have an opportunity to attend evening classes, thereby furthering his education.

We are happy to recommend him to you.

JAMES W. ELLIS—PERSONNEL DIRECTOR

Semiblock Style. There are many letter styles that are a combination of the indented and the extreme-block forms. There is no business standard by which one can point to any letter style and say that it is incorrect. Letter make-up is entirely a matter of personal taste and preference. Four of the possible combinations are given below.

Semiblock Style 1. The writer of a business letter might like the indented form, but might think it a trifle old-fashioned for his business. He would probably use a form in which the address is blocked and the paragraphs indented five spaces. The placement of the date and the closing lines is variable. They may be centered or typed flush with the right margin.

May 21, 19—

Mr. W. B. Astor
Hotel Hibiscus
Miami Beach 6, Florida

Dear Mr. Astor:

In accordance with your request of May 16, we are sending you duplicate statements for February, March, and April.

We do not understand why your instructions were not followed by our Billing Department, but we will make every effort to see that such a situation does not occur in the future.

Please accept our apologies for this oversight and be assured that there will be no reflection on your excellent credit standing.

Sincerely yours,
TURMAN HABERDASHERY

R. C. Emmett

Semiblock Style 2. Another business letter writer might like the appearance of the block style, except for the fact that the extreme-block form looks out of balance. Perhaps he would choose to block all lines except the date and closing lines.

May 5, 19—

Mr. James Connors
346 Royal Avenue
Windsor, Illinois

Dear Mr. Connors:

Thank you for your letter of May 2, in which you enclosed a check for $125 to be credited to your account.

Your arrangement for payment of the balance is perfectly satisfactory, and we have marked our records to August 1 for payment in full.

We are always happy to co-operate with a good friend of TATE, CLOTHIERS.

Cordially yours,

Semiblock Style 3. Then there is the letter writer whose desire for self-expression or whose type of business might demand a letter form that would be quite out of the ordinary. He might elect to use the hanging-indented style. In this letter make-up, the inside address and the first line of each paragraph are blocked; but each succeeding paragraph line is indented five spaces.

April 5, 19—

Mrs. H. A. Williams
46 Country Drive
Rye, New York

Dear Mrs. Williams:

Our interior decorator, David Robinson, tells us that you are planning to have your house redecorated.

You might be interested to know that we are equipped to handle any changes you would like to make. Our large staff of expert consultants would be at your service. Not only are we prepared to furnish materials at prices that compare favorably with those of any other firm, but we will also supervise any and all installations.

Mr. Robinson will make an appointment to see you again next week and will bring with him color schemes and samples of materials. We should like very much to help you.

Cordially yours,

Semiblock Style 4. For the letter writer who likes balance and who is interested in saving typing time, the following form is good.

In this style, block at the left margin all lines except the date and closing lines, which are blocked at the center point. Only one tabular stop must be set for this form.

March 17, 19—

Bardston, Inc.
721 Madison Avenue
New York 16, N. Y.

Gentlemen:

Thank you for your letter of March 14 and for your February 2 duplicate invoice for $277.61.

Our records show that this bill was paid by us on February 15. Our check was for $265.59, which represents the net price.

We hope that this information will enable you to correct the balance on our account.

Sincerely yours,
DEAN FURNITURE COMPANY

Howard Ives
Chief Accountant

HI JC

Style Accessories. In our dress we know that the basic garments are important, but we also know that we are dependent upon other little touches and colors to heighten or to create certain effects.

The chosen letter style might be called the basic garment for the letters. Now let us learn about such accessories as stationery, letter head design, and typewriter ribbons. This knowledge is necessary, for without it we may make an error in good taste or we may fail to use to the greatest extent some aids to the writing of impressive-looking letters.

Stationery. The use of cheap stationery for letterheads is very poor business economy. The receiver of a letter that is written on cheap paper will quite logically think of the sending firm as a cheap company. Thus prestige is threatened.

White bond paper is used by most business organizations. Would you like to be able to tell whether or not you are using bond paper? Take a sheet of business paper and hold it to the light. If it is good paper, there will be a watermark in it, a sort of shadow printing that will give the name of the manufacturer and the word "bond." Paper that is marked "rag content" is good paper.

Although white paper is preferred for business usage, very pale colors are considered good form. Should colored paper be used, be sure to have matching envelopes.

Carbon copies for the files are typed on inexpensive paper that is firm enough to give a good carbon impression. If the letterheads are of inferior quality, possibly we should find out the cost of the carbon-copy paper. Perhaps cheaper copy paper could be used and the saving applied toward the purchase of better-quality letterheads.

Letterhead Design. The design of a letterhead is the expression of the artistic taste of the person or persons responsible for its selection. In a space of not more than $2\frac{1}{2}$ inches should appear the letterhead information, set up in a style that is suitable to the company and to the nature of its business.

The designing of a letterhead is indeed a problem. What information is to appear? What style of printing is to be used? Shall we have a picture of our plant? What size and weight of type should be selected? Do we prefer black or colored printing? What is right for *us?*

Some firms seem to think that they should crowd as much information as possible into the letterhead space. The effect they create is similar to that produced by overcrowded show windows—such a jumble that nothing stands out.

Generally speaking, the effective letterhead is one that gives the impression of artistic simplicity.

Typewriter Ribbons. Our letters will be those whose print is clear and black. When a ribbon is worn to the point where the impression is even a little dim, discard it and replace it with a new one. In most schools, ribbons are used for many weeks after the time when they should have been wastebasket fillers. There is a distinct possibility that we might be so accustomed to faint print that on the job we may fail to change ribbons at the proper time.

Ribbons are available in colors other than black. Most of us are familiar with those that are half red and half black, but some of us do not know that we can obtain other colors—purple, green, brown, blue. Why should we have this knowledge? Well, suppose that we are working for a concern that builds boats. Their letterhead is printed in green. Perhaps we could carry out the color scheme by using a green ribbon.

Caution: Remember always that our style accessories should be used for the purpose of *adding to* the effectiveness of our letters. We should not, then, be so carried away with the idea of accessories that we overdo it by being so startling that we obscure the message.

Summary. The really accomplished business letter writer selects for his letters the style that reflects the light in which he wants his firm to shine. This business letter artist knows that somewhere in the choice of indented, extreme-block, or semiblock forms there is one particular style that is appropriate for and becoming to him. He also knows that time and thought expended on choosing such style accessories as stationery, letterhead design, and typewriter ribbons will produce the attractive framework that his superior writing deserves.

Assignment 1. Write an interoffice memorandum in which you discuss the hanging-indented style of letter. State the advantages and the disadvantages of using this form.

Assignment 2. Design a letterhead that you think would be suitable for use in your correspondence class.

Assignment 3. Write a letter to your teacher, using the letterhead designed for Assignment 2. In the letter, state your reasons for designing your particular letterhead.

Assignment 4. Select three different firms or industries in your community. Choose the letter style that you think would be suitable for each of these companies.

Assignment 5. Your correspondence class is a business organization known as "Correspondence, Inc." Write a letter to Correspondence, Inc., giving your reasons for the style selections you made in Assignment 4.

Assignment 6. You are writing letters for a very successful cosmetics company, and you have been asked to make recommendations with regard to letterhead design, letter style, and letter accessories. Write your recommendations in the form of an interoffice memorandum.

Assignment 7. From your folder of sample letters, select at least five different letterhead designs. Be prepared to display these to the class and to discuss the appropriateness of the letterheads and of the letter styles.

LESSON 68

Paragraphing the Business Letter

The paragraphing of a business letter is a little different from the paragraphing of a theme or of a composition. Composition students are taught that each paragraph develops a single topic of the subject of the composition. The result is that many times the paragraphs are very long.

A business letter, on the other hand, usually deals with only one topic; but this topic can be split into parts and a paragraph assigned to each part. The splitting is not a hit-or-miss thing; there must be a definite plan. Knowledge of paragraphing must be applied to make the message clear, concise, and complete.

In addition, the correspondent must be conscious of the importance of the appearance of his letters. That is why he will probably use single spacing and have paragraphs that are short enough to give the open look that pleases the eye and makes for easy reading.

Paragraph Plan. An over-all idea of the paragraph plan of a business letter could be obtained by likening it to a business call. The plan for a personal visit would be:

1. Greeting.
2. Statement of the business of the call.
3. Words of leave-taking.

The average business letter will follow the same plan, in that it will include:

1. An opening paragraph.
2. Paragraph or paragraphs containing the message.
3. A closing paragraph, containing words of leave-taking.

The following letter applies this plan.

362

Gentlemen:

Thank you for your duplicate credit A-666 for $8.23.

We shall be unable to apply this credit properly unless you tell us our debit or repair number that covered the return.

We should appreciate your sending us this information soon, for we want your account to show the correct balance.

While the average business letter will fall under the three-paragraph plan, we must not assume that *all* letters should contain exactly three paragraphs. Some communications require a great deal of explanatory wording; and the message would have to be broken into two, three, or more paragraphs. Then we would have a letter made up of several paragraphs.

Sometimes the end of the second paragraph rounds out the letter, making a closing paragraph unnecessary. So we might have a two-paragraph letter; as:

Dear Miss Mattson:

Your letter of March 15, with regard to the repair of your watch, has been referred to me for investigation and reply.

Your particular case is of such importance that I feel that it cannot be handled properly by means of written communications. Could you find time to come in to see me? I am sure that we can arrive at a mutually agreeable solution to your problem.

Very sincerely yours,

Business letters, then, may contain from two to as many paragraphs as are needed to accomplish the object in writing the letter. Our one hard-and-fast rule will be that the one-paragraph letter shall be avoided. The appearance and the reading difficulty of such a communication would destroy the effect of the most cleverly worded message.

Maybe the letter is very short, and the writer sees it as a one-paragraph letter; as:

Gentlemen:

Thank you for your letter of March 2. Please ship at once the remainder of our order No. 2268 at the new price.

Sincerely yours,

Even here, we could make a separate paragraph of each sentence.

Thank you for your letter of March 2.

Please ship at once the remainder of our order No. 2268 at the new price.

Paragraph Length. How long should paragraphs be and why? That seems to be the question here.

Avoid long paragraphs; and, in order to know what is long, let us say that the average paragraph is one of about six lines. When we are writing a paragraph and have typed four or five lines, we should be on the alert for some slight shift in thought that will give us an opportunity to start another paragraph.

Business people are busy people who do not have time to waste. Long paragraphs are difficult to read; and, when a businessman looks at an uninterrupted mass of typing, he feels that the reading of the letter will be a chore. We run the risk of his giving the letter the "once over lightly" treatment. In such a case, *we* have wasted *our* time and energy in constructing a skillfully worded message.

On the other hand, be careful not to go to the extreme of over-paragraphing. A letter that is composed of many very short paragraphs gives the impression of jerkiness and wears the reader down. This kind of letter lacks the smoothness and polish of the communications we are trained to write. Just read the following letter.

Dear Mrs. Ickes:

We are sorry to hear that the teapot you ordered arrived damaged.

Fortunately, we were able to duplicate it immediately; and it should arrive soon.

It will not be necessary to return the other one to us.

If we can be helpful to you in any way, please do not hesitate to let us know.

Cordially yours,

As you read, did you get a feeling of "bumpiness"? We can remove the jolts by regrouping the sentences and by getting rid of those "its."

We are sorry to hear that the teapot you ordered arrived damaged. Fortunately, we were able to duplicate this merchandise immediately; and a perfect teapot will be delivered to you within a few days. Please do not bother to return the other one to us.

If ever we can be helpful to you in any way, do not hesitate to let us know.

An occasional short paragraph does, however, have value. Possibly there are one or two sentences that we consider the high light of the letter. We can bring out our point by making a single paragraph of the one sentence.

Opening Paragraph. The opening paragraph is usually short, frequently consisting of only one sentence, and is written for the purpose of serving as an introduction to the letter message. Even though this paragraph may be short, it is one of the most important paragraphs of our letter—second only in importance to the closing one. Why? Because our opening words will dispose the mind of the reader to accept or reject the ideas we present in the following paragraphs.

The first sentence will direct attention to the subject of the letter, will be written positively and courteously; will not make use of hackneyed words and phrases; and will refer, if necessary, to the date of the letter that was received.

We are going to study some sample opening paragraphs, but letters are of such a variety that it would be impossible to give examples that would cover all letters. Remember that our opening paragraph will be geared to the reader and to the subject of that particular letter.

Many correspondents who write excellent intervening paragraphs fall into the lazy habit of using only one or two stock opening sentences; as:

Thank you for your letter of May 6.
We have your letter of May 6.

There are some writers who do not approve of the opening paragraph as such, but believe that the first sentence should deal directly with the action that is to be taken or the information that has been requested. Among the sample openings given here, you will note some that follow this practice.

Sample Opening Paragraphs

Thank you for— *or* Thank you very much for—
your inquiry (order, letter, check) of the 18th
writing us about the . . . we sent you on April 7
reminding us about the . . . .

the care you have taken in answering our request for information regarding . . . .

We are pleased—

to learn from your letter of August 1 that you are interested in . . . .
to answer your inquiry of July 8
to send you the . . . ordered in your letter of May 2

Your interesting (gracious, stimulating, thoughtful, warm) letter of March 17 was most welcome.

We take real pleasure in answering your letter of the 8th.

You will be glad to know that the . . . about which you wrote us on June 4 is . . . .

You were most thoughtful to call our attention to the . . . .
We are always pleased to be called on to help . . . .
We shall be glad indeed to arrange . . . .
Your letter of May 2 gave us food for thought.
We value highly the suggestions you made in your letter of the 6th.

Closing Paragraph. The closing paragraph is the means by which the letter writer stimulates action or brings the letter visit to a courteous, gracious conclusion. Some correspondents find the writing of the final paragraph the most difficult part of their job, for they just cannot think of a graceful or action-promoting exit line.

The closing paragraph is important for the reason that the last impression is usually the lasting impression. A letter may be very well written except for the fact that the last paragraph is weak, empty, insignificant, or wishy-washy. Such a closing can kill a letter as effectively as carbon monoxide can kill a man.

In the days of long ago before letter writing became the art that it is today, every letter ended with a participial conclusion; as:

Thanking you for your kind favor, I am,
Hoping to hear from you soon, I remain,
Trusting that you will approve our action, I am,

The letter writers of the twentieth century will never use an *ing* word to start a closing paragraph, for this type of closing is weak as well as old-fashioned.

Because some writers become bored with their task, they frequently overuse a certain final paragraph. The closing is sometimes discourteous, although they do not realize it. "Thank you in advance" is rude. "Thank you for your co-operation," when the reader has as yet had no opportunity to co-operate, is also a little highhanded. We thank people when they have done something to merit the thanks. To thank them before they have had a chance to grant the request gives the idea that we think ourselves so important that there is no question about their doing whatever we want them to do. Let us use "Thank you" in a closing paragraph only when the reader has previously done something for which thanks are indicated.

The construction of a good closing paragraph depends entirely on the subject of that particular letter and on the impression we wish to leave with the reader. The examples listed here, or adaptations of them, may help in writing the kind of closing that will be the most polished for a given letter. They are to be regarded merely as suggestions.

Sample Closing Paragraphs

Any information that you may care to send us will be held in strict confidence and will be used only in aiding us to supply your needs in merchandise.

If we do not hear from you within ten days, we shall be obliged to place this account in the hands of our attorney for collection.

Please ship by parcel post.

Fill out the enclosed card and drop it in a letter box; a sample will be mailed you without charge.

May I call at the office and talk this problem over with you?

Your order, written on the back of this letter, will receive our immediate and personal attention.

May we have your decision by June 3?

We are always pleased to have you call on us for a contribution to your cause.

We are enclosing a business reply envelope for your convenience.

Please come in to see us soon.

We deeply appreciate your efforts in our behalf.

We are very glad to be of service to you.

Please feel free to call on us at any time.

If we can be of further assistance, do not hesitate to let us know.

We have always enjoyed doing business with your firm.

We sincerely regret our inability to make the adjustment.

We shall appreciate anything that you can do to speed delivery.

Intervening Paragraphs. Between the opening and the closing paragraphs is the space reserved for the message, the business of the call-by-mail. This is where we put to use the principles we have studied previously; such as using the four C's to the best advantage; outlining so that we have a logical order for the presentation of the subject; planning the length and content of paragraphs.

Some consideration should be given to the use of connecting or linking words to keep the paragraphs short and still have an unbroken line of thought. Without a knowledge of the use of connectives to slide from one paragraph to the next, letters may be abrupt and awkward. Some of these links are:

in the first place	next	on the other hand
furthermore	however	in this way
at any rate	naturally	consequently
equally important	nevertheless	moreover
for instance	of course	on the contrary

Should we have several definite points to present, the most effective and attractive-looking setup might be achieved by numbering the points and setting them up as separate paragraphs, or by using subtitles for the paragraphs, or by combining the two methods as illustrated in the following letter.

Dear Mr. Grossman:

We have had the pleasure of servicing your cars on many occasions. Now that winter is approaching, let us remind you that, to get the greatest satisfaction out of your driving, your car should be checked carefully to see that all the following features are functioning properly:

1. *Motor.* Change your motor oil every 1,000 miles. Change to lighter winter oil now. When the carburetor and the ignition system are in good condition, proper use of the choke will make starting easy and will save your battery.

2. *Rear Axle and Transmission.* Heavy grease will not sufficiently lubricate the bearings. The old grease in the transmission and the differential should be flushed out and new light grease put in.

3. *Cooling System.* The radiator should be thoroughly cleaned by flushing before alcohol or other antifreezing mixture is put in. Many anti-

freezing compounds are unsatisfactory. An automatic radiator shutter, or winter front, is a desirable accessory even though antifreezing fluids are used. It saves gas and keeps the motor heated to the proper degree for most efficient operation.

4. *Brakes.* Brakes should be equalized. On slippery and wet days, skidding is more likely to occur when the adjustment is uneven.

We are making special prices for winter conditioning during the month of October. May we serve you?

Cordially yours,

Now consider one more point that will aid in writing business letters that get results. In order to prevent monotony, be careful not to start every paragraph with "we" or "I." This is a habit that can grow on us without our knowing it.

Summary. The good modern letter writer uses his knowledge of paragraphing to make his letter attractive in appearance, easy to read, and expressive in content. Before he starts to write his letters, he will have a plan for his paragraphs; he will know the disadvantage of using long paragraphs; he will avoid too many short paragraphs, but he will know when to use a short paragraph effectively; he will be aware of the best techniques to be applied to the writing of opening, closing, and intervening paragraphs.

Assignment 1. Mr. E. B. Benton purchased a nylon shirt from us for $8.98. The first time this shirt was laundered, the stitching on the collar ripped. He has written to us to ask what we are going to do about it. We are going to give him his choice of a cash refund or a new shirt. Write the salutation, the opening and closing paragraphs, and the complimentary closing for our letter.

Assignment 2. Write the intervening paragraph or paragraphs for Assignment 1.

Assignment 3. In the form of an interoffice memorandum, revise and write a brief criticism of each of the following opening sentences:

1. This is to acknowledge receipt of your letter of May 9th.

2. Thank you for your recent inquiry.

3. We were sorry to learn from your letter that you were disappointed in the performance of the record player you purchased from us.

4. Not having heard from you in reply to our letter, we assume that your order for curtain rods has been taken care of. Therefore, we are closing our records concerning it.

5. It will be satisfactory to us to have you duplicate changes for the hassock on our order No. 7678.

Assignment 4. In the form of an interoffice memorandum, revise and write a brief criticism of each of the following closing sentences:

1. Hoping that this letter finds you in the best of health, I remain,
2. Thank you in advance for attending promptly to our request.
3. Please advise.
4. We trust that our decision meets with your kind approval.
5. We know that the above explanation will be of value in this matter.

Assignment 5. Write a letter to a very good customer, telling him about our forthcoming sale of overcoats.

Assignment 6. Write a letter to a firm with which we have never before done business, asking that a salesman be sent to call on us.

Assignment 7. Write a letter to your local postmaster (whom you do not know personally), asking him to trace a package that you mailed from his office.

Assignment 8. From your folder of actual business letters, select one letter for revision. Hand in the original as well as the revision.

Assignment 9. Write a letter to a vendor, telling him:

1. That you have received your order No. 8462
2. That the colors of the merchandise were not the ones you specified
3. That you are returning the entire shipment

LESSON 69

Letter Tone

Since many customers and vendors never see the letter writer or his place of business, they form their opinions entirely by the effect produced by letters. The tone of each letter, therefore, is very important; for it is the tone that will determine whether or not the business relationships will be harmonious. If the correspondent were talking to the readers of his letters, he would have the advantage of using facial expressions and voice inflections to stress his points and make his meaning clear. In a written communication, only the words on paper are the means by which he can sell himself and his employer as honest, gracious people—wonderful people with whom to do business!

Able handling of letter tone will increase the regard in which a firm is held, but that is not the only reason for mastering this lesson. Choice of words and the way they are put together can induce the reader to take some action that the writer very much wants him to take. Mastery of this skill will keep an employer smiling, because business will be good.

To become proficient in the art of letter writing, the correspondent must make a special study of business-promoting, action-promoting, and business-destroying letter tone.

Business-Promoting Letter Tone

The writers of business-getting letters know the qualities that produce favorable impressions, and they apply this knowledge to the writing of all business communications.

The most important of these qualities are discussed and illustrated on the following pages.

Courtesy. Consciously or unconsciously, everybody is impressed by and pleased with courteous treatment. This fact is recognized by businessmen everywhere, for millions of dollars are spent annually on just the word *please*.

If we stop for a few moments and think of some of our experiences, we may be able to remember some one person for whom we were delighted to do favors. An analysis of our eagerness to help him would reveal that he always showed his appreciation, and it was the *expression* of his gratitude that made us want to do more and more for him. Keep our experiences in mind when we write letters, and we shall soon find ourselves unfailing in the use of "thank you" for a favor done and "please" for a favor requested.

We must not think, however, that good manners are dependent solely on "please" and "thank you." True courtesy is a spirit of graciousness that breathes through all our letters. An air of warmth will exude from letters that contain such expressions as:

    You were most thoughtful to . . . .
    We can always rely on you for . . . .
    We are indeed happy to . . . .
    We were gratified to learn that . . . .
    We should very much appreciate . . . .

There is one lesson in good breeding that will advance any person in social as well as business life. So many people, when faced with the necessity of doing something that they do not wish to do, show their resentment by being sulky. This practice is a little on the stupid side; for, since they *must* do whatever it is, they might just as well be gracious about it. This is the way to "win friends and influence people."

As an illustration, suppose that we receive an order given with the provision that we allow a special discount of 5 per cent. Since our salesman offered the customer this particular favor, we must grant it, although we make no profit on the sale. We are going to write that customer a letter and tell him that such a thing is not going to happen again!

Dear Sir:
    Your letter of July 8 asking for a special discount of 5 per cent on your order No. 8423 was received today.

Although we do not make a practice of allowing such special discounts, we are granting it for this one order.

Please do not make any more such requests, for we have decided that we will not give future special discounts.

Very truly yours,

If you were the customer and had made the request, how would you feel upon reading this letter? Notice the coldness of both the salutation and the complimentary closing. What do you think of the following revision?

Dear Mr. Taylor:

We are very glad to allow you a special 5 per cent discount on your order No. 8423.

You will be interested to know that your request was the subject of a sales conference called for the purpose of determining policy with regard to special discounts. The decision was that, because we operate on such a narrow margin of profit, we can in the future give only the discounts listed in our catalogue.

We are looking forward to filling many more orders for you.

Sincerely yours,

Friendliness. Businessmen of the past were frequently of the type that we would now describe as "stuffed shirts." They wrote letters that were cold, formal, or even high and mighty. That was the fashion for their day, but it is not our way of increasing profits. We build volume of business by writing letters that are friendly in character.

In order to write a friendly letter, we must *feel* friendly toward other people. Until a man has proved himself unworthy, we must assume that he is our good neighbor; and our writing will reflect the warmth of our feeling for him. We simply cannot write a friendly letter if we believe that everybody else is just waiting for a chance to take advantage of us.

We can write letters of a friendly nature if we use such expressions as:

We understand your problem and . . . .
Your request pleases us greatly, for . . . .
Letters like yours are always welcome.
Please feel free to call on us whenever . . . .
You can depend on us to . . . .

We need not be wordy to be friendly. Consider this last paragraph:

An immediate delivery would be appreciated.

Six words were used to say something that leaves the reader cold. We could use nine words to warm the statement without dimming the urgency.

We know that, as usual, you will ship immediately.

Right here seems to be a good place for a word to the wise. Unless you are personally acquainted with your reader, you will be careful not to let your friendliness extend to the "chummy" stage. The tone we are working for is the dignified, warm tone; and we must not be so friendly that we grate on the reader's sensibilities.

Helpfulness.   The pace of our life today is so swift that we sometimes do not take the time that is necessary to extend a helping hand. We are the losers, for we do not obtain the deep satisfaction that comes from aiding others.

We lose businesswise, too. A correspondent who receives a letter that saves him time and trouble will have a glow in his heart for the writer of that letter. We cannot lose by seizing every possible opportunity to help someone else. If we have any information that will be helpful to a man, let us give it to him. A helpful letter is an impressive letter.

For instance, suppose that we receive an order for goods that we do not manufacture. We know, however, that American Products of Boston does make the article. Let us look up the address of American and write the following letter:

Gentlemen:

Your order No. 7463 for pinking shears was received today.

Since we do not manufacture shears, we are unable to fill the order. We looked up the nearest manufacturer of this article, however, and found it to be American Products, 727 Codman Street, Boston 8, Massachusetts.

We are sending you our catalogue and hope that we may be able to fill some future orders for you.

Cordially yours,

In this letter we were not only helpful, but we were also on the alert to build business. Do you like the closing paragraph?

Positiveness. A positive tone is obtained by stating the message in such a way that the movement of the words is onward and upward. In Lesson 65, "The Words We Use," we had a section on negative words. Our tone will be positive if we refrain from using the words given in that section. But, for a better knowledge of the subject, we should look at some that are positive in implication; such as:

advancement	cordial	genuine	satisfaction
agreeable	eager	gratify	success
attractive	earnest	happy	trustworthy
cheerful	easy	liberal	value
comfortable	enjoy	pleasure	victory
compensation	fortunate	profit	welcome
confident	generosity	progress	willingness

If we must disappoint the reader, let us write so that the effect of disappointment is softened. If we search hard enough, we can always find some feature of a situation that will be favorable to the reader. One way to insure a positive tone is to mention the favorable news before the unfavorable. Here is a letter that starts out with the unfavorable aspect:

Dear Miss Lee:

We have your application for employment as a stenographer in our company. We are sorry, however, that there are no openings at present in that department, even for a young lady with your thorough training.

We are placing your application on file in case an opening should occur in the future.

Very cordially yours,

See how in the following letter the unfavorable aspect is subordinated.

Dear Miss Lee:

Thank you for submitting your application for employment as a stenographer in our company. We like your qualifications and are happy to place your name on file, as we often have openings in that department.

Although we have no position open now, you can be sure that when we do we shall want to interview you.

Very cordially yours,

Frank Admission of Mistakes.   Do you like the person who always has a glib excuse for every slip he makes, who never admits that he is wrong? Do you sense that he is "covering up"? Do you respect him? Of course you know people like that, and of course you do not like or respect them.

In business letters, admit mistakes. Many times we can hold an irate customer by some such wording as "The mistake was ours, and we are taking steps to rectify it immediately," or "We will do our utmost to prevent the recurrence of . . . ." In any situation where we are entirely at fault, an attempt to evade the issue will result in arousing anger and resentment, with consequent loss of business.

At the same time that we freely admit that we are wrong, let us hasten to tell our correspondent that we are going to do something about it—*right away*. The fact that a mistake was made will then be subordinated to the fact that we think Mr. Correspondent a very important person.

If we consistently follow the practice of accepting blame when blame is due, our readers will believe us when we say that we are not at fault.

Action-Promoting Letter Tone

Once there was a woman whose three children wanted to learn to drive a car. Since the driving fever struck them during summer vacation, there was no rest from their entreaties. Now this woman was a businesswoman, and she understood the principles underlying the obtaining of desirable action. So she agreed to spend as many minutes on driving lessons as the youngsters spent on housework. Never before was a house kept so clean so joyously!

What was the point of telling this story? The object was to present the idea that back of every action is a reason that has to do with the promotion of personal satisfaction.

Many letters are written for the purpose of getting the reader to do something; so, we should put our words together in a fashion that will prompt him to act the way we want him to act. Perhaps we should know that pride causes some people to act, reasons of health or happiness will motivate others, but financial gain is the spur that works with every businessman.

Producing an action-promoting tone will be easy for the writer who puts himself in the reader's place. As he writes, he will pretend that, as the reader, he is asking, "What do *I* get out of this? What will it do for *me?*" Very shortly, he will find that he uses the pronoun *you* more often than *I* or *we*. He puts the reader's interest first. He shows how the action will work to the advantage of the reader. Consider the following examples.

Suppose that a customer is tardy with a payment, and we write:

Please send us your check for $16.89, so that we may balance our books.

Is there anything here that would move the reader to sit right down, write the check, and mail it to us? Indeed not, for the customer cares not a hoot if the writer's books remain unbalanced forever. Maybe there would be a better chance of collecting if we appealed to his pride.

Your check for $16.89 will balance your account and maintain your good credit standing.

Suppose that we hear that a man is going to install a new oil burner, and we want to sell him our Airflo. We write:

We have found from experience that our Airflo is not only a great time-saver but a money saver as well.

The tone of this sentence is a "we" tone, and the words do not bring out the self-interest of the reader. The message could be rewritten to show what the prospect will get for himself if he buys our product.

You will be delighted to find how much the Airflo will save you not only in time but in MONEY.

Here is another example.

Our Albi Six performs most acceptably in any climate, consumes little oil, runs twenty miles to the gallon of gas, and is equipped with long-wearing parts.

The sentence can be rewritten, giving the same information, but wording it so that the reader will picture the happiness that will be provided not only for himself but also for his family.

You and your family will spend many sunny, happy days in the Albi Six at little expense; for this sturdy car performs well in any climate, consumes little oil, runs twenty miles on each gallon of gas, and is equipped with long-wearing parts.

Summary. The tone of a letter is a manner of written expression used to create a desired impression or reaction. Letter tone is of great importance, for written communications are often the only means by which correspondents can become acquainted. Readers will be most co-operative when letters are courteous, friendly, helpful, positive, and honest. If letters are written for the purpose of stimulating action, best results can be obtained by wording the message from the reader's point of view, by appealing to his self-interest, by showing how the action will redound to the advantage of the reader.

Assignment 1. Select some person of your acquaintance who has the qualities that you think are necessary for the successful carrying on of business. Without mentioning this person's real name, write for him a letter recommending him for an executive position. State his good qualities and tell why you think these fit him for the job.

Assignment 2. The qualities that make your Assignment 1 acquaintance a good executive are the qualities that are the foundations of good letter tone. Write an interoffice memorandum stating your reasons for believing that his letters will build good business relationships. We are assuming that he has the ability to express himself well.

Assignment 3. Study the sample closing paragraphs in Lesson 68, and list them in the order of most to least friendly.

Assignment 4. In the form of an interoffice memorandum, list five examples of business courtesy that you have observed. As an example, you might remember that a telephone operator always says "Thank you."

Assignment 5. Rewrite the following sentences, emphasizing a positive element in each.

1. We cannot understand your dissatisfaction with the explanation we gave you in our letter of the 10th regarding the guarantee on our watches.

2. We shall be obliged to return to stock the merchandise we have been holding for you unless we receive your check for the balance due us.

3. It will be some time before our Repair Department can take time to repair small items such as yours.

4. We are sorry that the canned peaches were not good.

5. We hope you will not be disappointed in our inability to send you the order before the 15th.

6. Unfortunately, the shirts you ordered are out of stock.

7. Your criticism of our method of handling deliveries has been received.

8. We are sorry that our action has caused you trouble and distress.

9. You neglected to state size and color for the dresses on your order No. 856.

10. We have your complaint regarding our last shipment.

Assignment 6. Rewrite the following sentences, emphasizing the reader's interest.

1. It is our opinion that our goods will be money-makers for you.

2. Will you do us the favor of sending this information right away?

3. We wish to announce that for the month of May we are offering a 10 per cent discount on all dining room furniture.

4. We believe very firmly that you can sell our merchandise at a good profit.

5. We are going to tell you that our "Everlasting" sox have been best sellers for years.

6. We think that you can cut your price on china and still make a fair profit.

7. We take pleasure in informing you that we are going to give you an opportunity to preview the fall fashions.

8. We think our winterizing plan will suit you as well as that of any other garage operator.

9. Why don't you let us send you a sample of our mayonnaise?

10. We suggest that we send our sales representative, Mr. Edward Dunbar, to call on you.

Assignment 7. From the sample letters in your folder, select two that you consider helpful letters. From these letters, quote the sentences or paragraphs that contain the helpful notes.

LESSON 70

Letter Tone (Continued)

Like the farmer who knows the difference between weeds and vegetables and who roots out the weeds, the letter writer must know and refrain from using whatever wording would destroy the effect he is trying to create. There are many pitfalls in the path of the writer, represented by words and wording that arouse irritation or even anger. We shall discuss these danger spots, so that upon rereading our letters we can be sure that we have avoided them.

Business-Destroying Letter Tone

Tactlessness. Every person is born with a little core that represents him as an individual. Any threat to the importance of that innermost being will cause resentment, and profitable business cannot be carried on with an offended customer or resource. If we want to stimulate desirable action, we must be careful to write in such a way that the reader feels that we consider him important and that we have confidence in his integrity.

We must, then, consider each letter as a particular problem in tact; and application of the Golden Rule would probably be our best guide. Let us reread each letter we write and ask ourselves, "How would *I* feel if I were the reader?" Never will we write anything that could be construed as a criticism of the reader personally, of the goods he sells, or of the way he conducts his business.

You failed to keep your promise to deliver our order No. 645 on June 4.

This is a tactless opening sentence, for we have told the reader that he is not an honorable man. A little thought would have changed the wording to:

380

Our order No. 645 did not arrive on June 4, but we know there must be some good reason for nondelivery.

Suppose that we bought a lot of curtains at a reduced price, and they were totally unsatisfactory. A sentence in an intervening paragraph in our letter to the manufacturer read:

Your bargain curtains turned out to be duds, and you unloaded them at the right time.

The manufacturer sold the curtains in good faith, and ours was the first complaint he received. Do you think he will, with good grace, hasten to make an adjustment? Will he have an anger bias toward every subsequent letter we write? He will! But we would not have written such a sentence. We would have put it this way:

The No. 678 curtains ordered on April 2 did not turn out so well as expected. They . . . .

Then there is the letter written about a pressing matter, and we want immediate action. As a closing paragraph, we write:

Please give this request your prompt attention.

What have we done? We have used "bossy" wording, and we have implied that the reader sleeps on the job. See how the mental attitude of the reader would differ if we worded the sentence:

We know that you will give our request your usual prompt attention.

Vagueness.   We have discussed clearness, completeness, and conciseness from the point of view of reducing overhead. If a message is not clear or complete, extra letters must be written to obtain the missing information; and letters cost money.

Now let us think about the effect on the emotions of a reader when the letter he receives is vague. Yes, his temper will be tried; and he will always regard us as unbusinesslike people. This would be a pity, for we try so hard to build the prestige of our firm.

Every letter we write should be explicit, so that the reader has all the information he needs. Let us state specifically all dates, names, order numbers, and prices that are required for full identification.

Such an expression as "your letter of recent date" is poor on two counts—it is old-fashioned; it is also vague. "Your letter of June 9" is definite.

"Our last order" might mean rummaging through the files before the reader can find the order we mean. The time thus wasted will contribute nothing to the good will between his firm and ours. "Our March 3 order No. 489" might save time and good will.

"The price on our order No. 672 is a little higher than that quoted us yesterday by Byrnes" might also necessitate a trip to the files, but "The price of $5.96 for boys' gabardine jackets on our order No. 672" makes everything perfectly clear.

"I expect to be in New York on Monday and will call on you sometime during the week" is vague enough for anyone. "I expect to be in New York on Monday and will call your secretary to make an appointment to see you sometime during the week" would relieve the correspondent of the feeling of momentarily expecting us to pop in.

"I met one of your salesmen at the Housewares Show, and he told me" could cause a considerable waste of time trying to find out which salesman talked to the man who wrote the letter. "I met your salesman, Mr. Edward R. Main, at the . . . ." would prevent irritation that could be directed toward us.

Breeziness. There are some people who are naturally breezy in manner and speech, and the offhand liveliness is part of their charm. This same airiness in the tone of a business letter could be offensive. Keep in mind the fact that the reader gains all his impressions from what he sees on paper; and, if he does not know the high-spirited writer personally, he may think him "fresh."

"Thanks for your letter of October 15" might be a natural opening sentence for you, but the effect of blitheness might strike the wrong note with the reader. "Thank you" is less free and easy.

"Sincerely" could be a good closing when writing to a friend, but "Sincerely yours" would be better taste for the closing of the ordinary business letter.

"Toss your worries out the window and let us collect your bad bills" is a spritely sentence, but it may be too brisk for the man who is really worried about collections. "Your worries will be reduced the minute you place your slow-paying accounts in our hands" will give the same idea in a more dignified manner.

High-flown Language. What happens if we do not keep our language simple, clear, and direct? The reader will be annoyed; and, if he understands the meaning of those long, unusual words, he will consider us "show-offs." If the reader's vocabulary is poor, he will be made to feel stupid, uneducated. Any way we look at it, long, unusual words will lose business for us.

"The complexities and subtleties of this onerous obligation will be apparent to any institution not eleemosynary in character" is a very puzzling way of saying "The difficulties of performing this heavy task can be seen by the members of any firm that is in business to make money."

Just imagine being confronted with "This man is a cunctator" when the meaning is "This man always puts off all action"!

Monotony. Any person who performs the same task day after day is in danger of falling into a rut, of grinding out the work by using the same pattern for all the jobs. The letter writer who uses the same words and phrases in all his letters soon loses joy in his work, for, in addition to boring his readers, he bores himself.

We all know the importance of having at our command different words that can be used to express one idea—that is, synonyms. Now, let us apply the knowledge to the writing of business letters.

Gentlemen:

It was good to get your letter of July 9. We are blessed with a good many friends in the trade, but your firm is probably among our best.

We shall immediately reduce our price on imported gloves, and it is a good thing for us that you notified us that they will soon be a drug on the market.

Many thanks for the tip and good luck to you always!

Cordially yours,

As you read, were you conscious of the overuse of the word *good*? Notice how the repetition of this one word detracted from what was otherwise a warm, friendly communication. Let us read all our letters with a critical eye for repetitious wording.

Many people have difficulty in thinking of word substitutions, and even those who are possessed of a fine vocabulary will occasionally meet a stumbling block. To help us in our time of need, we should have within easy reach a book of synonyms or a thesaurus. The next time you are in the library, ask to see a thesaurus and learn how to use it. Remember, though, that the synonym you choose should be simple, so that you will not fall into the error of using the "high-flown" language discussed in the previous section.

Flattery.   Sincere praise is one thing and flowery compliments are another. When a businessman receives a letter that is excessive in praise, he wonders what the writer has up his sleeve. Flattery accomplishes nothing except a lessening of respect and esteem.

A letter from a vendor containing this sentence, "Your firm has such a superior reputation that we are highly honored to be associated with you in a business way," would lead the average hardheaded businessman to suspect that the vendor was getting ready to try to sell some old stock.

Sarcasm.   A sarcastic remark offends the little "you" that lives deep within every person. Oddly enough, a statement that was considered sarcastic might have been meant to be laughable. That is why we must be careful not to be humorous except with business friends who are also personal friends.

The man who wrote the following sentences might have thought that they would make the reader smile. But read them and hear how they sound.

You must have had these goods since before the war—Revolutionary War, of course.

When we asked for delivery by March 15, we meant this year, not next.

The trained letter writer who constructs his letters from the point of view of the reader would never have written these sentences. He would know that the effect on the vendor would be that of indignant displeasure, a very poor basis on which to build good will.

The writer who is deliberately sarcastic is probably an angry man, but anger in business is a luxury that we cannot afford. When we receive a letter that causes us to say to ourselves, "Why, that . . . . , I'll write him a letter that he'll remember for a long time," we have two courses open to us:

1. We can mark the letter "to be answered tomorrow" and put it away. By tomorrow we shall have cooled off enough to write our usual polished letter.

2. We can sit right down, write him a scorcher, and then *tear it up.*

Let us make a rule for ourselves never to answer a letter when our emotions are out of control.

Kowtowing. At all costs we must avoid writing a letter that gives the impression of kneeling on the ground begging for something. Unnecessarily humble wording is inconsistent with our proud American heritage. If we sell a good product at a fair price and if we have business integrity, we need not lower ourselves before any man. We are a free people, and we do not expect to give or to take servile treatment.

So much has been said and written about the quality of graciousness in the business letter that some writers carry their tone so far that graciousness becomes actual lowliness. Consider the following examples and revisions:

Gracious: Thank you for your continued confidence in the Brooks Manufacturing Company.

Kowtowing: It is with much appreciation that we express our thanks for your very valued patronage.

Gracious: We shall be most grateful if you will return the statement containing the special notation.
Or
Please return the statement containing the special notation.

Kowtowing: We shall be most grateful if you will kindly return the statement containing the special notation.

In the last example, the use of the unnecessarily humble word "kindly" gave the sentence a fawning tone.

Flat Notes. A singer who flats some of his notes ruins his performance. The writer of a business letter should be aware of two particular letter notes which, if flatted, will ruin his letter performance. They are:

Name Errors. To any man the sweetest music in the world is the sound of his own name, and he gets pleasure out of hearing and looking at his own name. We can just imagine how he feels when his name is misspelled or an incorrect middle initial is used. The first line that meets his eye as he looks at the letter is the name line in the inside address; and, if his name is not correctly written, he will be ruffled before he starts to read the message.

If a man's name is Duggan, let us not write it *Dugan.* If Mr. Clarke spells his name with a final *e,* let us be sure that we write it so. If the old-fashioned Edith changes to *Edythe,* let us humor her by writing it the new way. If our correspondent is Paul M. Barnes, let us not write to Paul W. Barnes.

Check any name about which there could possibly be a question. To save checking time, many writers insist on having on their desks all letters that must be answered.

Delay in Answering Letters. Have you ever had the experience of having an appointment with a man for two o'clock and being made to wait forty-five minutes before you could see him? As the minutes after two o'clock rolled by, your resentment and irritation mounted. Why? Because you were made to feel that you were not very important, and the little "you" that lives in you was hurt. Too, as you sat there twiddling your thumbs, you were thinking of the work you could have done in those forty-five minutes.

This is exactly the situation that is created when a correspondent does not receive a reply to his letter within a reasonable time. His personal importance is minimized, and he will always remember that he was made to feel insignificant. But, more than that, possibly his business suffered in the meantime. Maybe he needed some information in order to make a sale, and the delay in receiving the information caused him to lose the sale. Bad business, isn't it?

This particular flat note will be avoided if we make it a rule to answer all correspondence promptly.

Summary. Knowing what *not* to do is just as important as knowing what to do. As far as letter tone is concerned, best results can be obtained by avoiding any wording that would cause the reader to feel cool toward us. We shall, then, proofread all letters to be sure that we are not guilty of tactlessness, vagueness, breeziness, high-flown language, monotony, flattery, sarcasm, kowtowing. We can avoid all these and still destroy good letter tone if we misspell names or if we fail to answer promptly every letter we receive.

Assignment 1. Find synonyms for the following words. The synonyms should be simple words that would be suitable for use in business letters.

abandon	acknowledge	animate
above-mentioned	acquiesce	announce
accelerate	adjacent	apparel
accentuate	alternative	arduous

awful	caution	compunction
baffle	chary	concur
brink	colleague	construct
candid	compensate	covenant
		debar

Assignment 2. Follow the same procedure as for Assignment 1.

declare	inconceivable	orifice
delectation	inter	overwhelming
dilatory	languid	paramount
expedient	laudatory	penurious
fallacy	manifestation	perceive
futile	marvelous	recapitulate
impartial	numerous	relinquish
impetuous	obvious	skepticism
		spurious

Assignment 3. Write a letter to your teacher telling what you have learned through your study of this lesson.

Assignment 4. The following letter was written to you by a cleaning firm in another city. You investigated and found that nobody in your organization made any derogatory remarks about the cleaning job done on Suzanne's coat. You did send the coat to another cleaner, however, and the garment was cleaned to the complete satisfaction of the customer. Reply to the letter, being sure to avoid business-destroying tone.

Dear Mr. Student:

Miss Suzanne Brooks, of your city, brought a coat to me to be cleaned. I was unable to do a good job because the material was shoddy.

Miss Brooks talked with the salesman who sold her the coat, and he told her to bring the garment to him. He said that he would take it to a good cleaner. He also said that some firms were noted for their sloppy work. Now, he meant us; and I want you to shut his mouth.

Nobody could take the dirt out of a coat made of such cheap goods.

Yours truly,

Assignment 5. Study the sample letters in your folder, and select from them five sentences or paragraphs that are written in a business-destroying tone.

Assignment 6. Revise the sentences or paragraphs selected in Assignment 5.

Assignment 7. Ask your teacher for ten of the sentences or paragraphs handed in for Assignments 5 and 6. Try to improve the revisions made by your classmates.

LESSON 71

Everyday Letters

By everyday letters we mean the letters that make up the bulk of our correspondence, the letters that we write frequently day in and day out; such as, letters of acknowledgment, order letters, letters of inquiry, of transmittal, of remittance, of confirmation, request letters, and letters of cancellation. These letters present the correspondent with the same business-building opportunities that customers afford a salesperson.

The average business letter writer does not see the connection between everyday letters and a customer at the door, and that is why he remains an average correspondent. He becomes bored by the necessity of writing the "same old letters," and his work becomes flat and mechanical. Then he complains because someone else gets the promotion that he thinks he should get!

Every person in a business organization is charged with the responsibility of making sales, of reducing overhead, and of building good will. Writers of business letters have many opportunities for carrying out their responsibilities. We have been taught to put ourselves in the other person's place and to give prompt, courteous, business-building service via mail. We must know and use the words and actions that bring in the business, and we must know and avoid the words and actions that drive business away.

We are studying this text for the purpose of learning the letter-writing trade. Let us, therefore, consider these everyday letters as a challenge to our ability to use the tools of our trade, and let us consider them as a ready-made means of making sales and gaining good will.

389

Letters of Acknowledgment

Any letter that is written as a reply is an acknowledgment letter. If you can imagine the number of replies that are written during the business day, you will have some idea of the value of being able to put into practice the principles of business science that make big business really big.

One of the principles is that we must never do anything that will make another person feel unimportant. Now, if we fail to answer a letter, we very plainly tell the correspondent that he is totally unimportant to us; and, if we delay answering his letter, we tell him that he is far back in our regard. In either case, we have hurt his feelings; and we cannot expect to get any business he may have to give us.

For this reason, in many offices the rule is to acknowledge all letters within twenty-four hours. If by "acknowledge" is meant a personally written letter, this rule may be a trifle shortsighted and may result in unnecessary overhead. There are instances where a printed form may be used. For instance, in acknowledging receipt of manuscripts, a publishing house might use the following form:

> Your manuscript has been received and is now being reviewed. Thank you for submitting it.

Hotels might reduce overhead by using a printed postal card for the making of reservations, as:

> A .... room ..... bath has been reserved for you for ......
> ....
> We will do everything in our power to promote your pleasure and comfort during your stay with us.

While there may be some few cases where, in the interests of economy, a printed form can be used without loss of business, most acknowledgments should be personal letters. Let us study some of the different kinds of acknowledgments.

Order Acknowledgments. For routine acknowledgment of orders from customers with whom our business relations are established, we might use a printed form. We *must*, however, write a personal acknowledgment whenever we receive an unusually large order from an old customer; whenever we receive an order from a new customer; or whenever we cannot immediately and completely fill an order.

The following letter illustrates an acknowledgment of an unusually large order from an old customer. Our object in writing him is to build still more good will.

Dear Mr. Burnett:

Thank you very much for your order No. 3681 for twelve plastic sheet machines.

These machines are being shipped today by freight, and they should arrive well before the December 1 delivery date specified by you.

Doing business with your firm is always a real pleasure.

Cordially yours,

Next, let us look at a letter that acknowledges an order from a new customer. We are writing this letter to build good will and to bring in *more* orders.

Gentlemen:

Your order No. 4621 for six Monarch Spinners is being shipped to you today by freight. In accordance with your request, we are opening an account for you.

We are happy to welcome you into our large family of satisfied customers; and we are placing at your disposal all our services, including the advice of our staff of engineers and consultants. Please do not hesitate to call on us whenever you think we can be of help.

Cordially yours,

Suppose that we receive an order from a customer, old or new, and we find that there will be a delay in filling the order. For goodwill purposes, a letter explaining the delay is indicated; as:

Gentlemen:

Thank you for your order No. 723 for twenty-four No. 31 occasional chairs.

We are able to fill this order except for the six floral-chintz style There has been such a demand for chairs with this type of covering that they are temporarily out of stock. A new supply will be ready by next week.

You will receive eighteen No. 31 chairs within three days, and the remaining six will arrive one week later We are sure that the value, beauty, and sales appeal of the new lot of floral coverings will make your wait well worth while.

Cordially yours,

Now, suppose that we receive an order for goods that we do not manufacture any longer. Remembering that we are in business to sell merchandise, we must write an acknowledgment that could double as a sales letter; like:

Dear Mr. Steers:

Thank you for your order No. 843 for 10,000 No. 6 steel cotter pins.

We have discontinued manufacturing the No. 6 steel pins and are now making No. 9 brass pins. The change from steel to brass is the result of research and experimentation that proved that the brass pins wear at least twice as long as those made of steel, although the increase in price is only $20 a thousand.

Just as soon as we receive your order for the No. 9 brass cotter pins, we will make our usual prompt delivery.

Cordially yours,

Remittance Acknowledgments. Some firms acknowledge remittances by returning invoices marked paid. This practice is quick and economical, but it represents lost opportunities for the building of sales. The cost of writing a letter of acknowledgment, if the writer were an expert, would be completely blotted out by the profits from increased sales.

A customer who pays his bill may be regarded as a satisfied customer and therefore should be considered a potential for future sales. Read the following letter and see how a remittance acknowledgment can be used as an instrument for making additional sales.

Gentlemen:

Thank you for your check for $596.23. Your account is now paid in full.

We are indeed glad to know that the paper towels are proving so satisfactory and are selling so well. You will be interested to hear that we are manufacturing wall dispensers for our towels, dispensers that combine usefulness with beauty and that are available in six different colors. You will readily see that the dispensers are a natural tie-in with the sale of the towels.

For further information and for your convenience in ordering, we are enclosing the dispenser literature.

Cordially yours,

Inquiry Acknowledgments. In our country, millions of dollars are spent annually for advertising, the object being to create interest in and desire for some particular product. Advertising starts to pay off the moment the first question is asked.

All this brings us directly to the study of writing inquiry acknowledgments; for, whenever we receive an inquiry, that first question has been asked. Therefore, without spending a cent, we are in a position that is reached by others only after dollars have been expended.

Many different kinds of inquiries will be received. Some will be about goods that we sell, some about brands that we do not carry, and some will be about subjects that have nothing to do with current sales possibilities. In every single case, however, we shall regard an inquiry letter as a challenge, an opportunity. We shall give each acknowledgment special attention; for, even if there is no opportunity to sell, we can write the kind of friendly, gracious letter that will cause our correspondent to think of us when he does want to buy.

Suppose that we work for a department store and that we receive a letter asking whether we carry Thirsty towels in the 24-by-46 size. The customer is interested in that brand of towel in that size; so she must be "ripe" for a sale. We do stock the goods; therefore let us write the kind of letter that will sell them.

Dear Mrs. Cary:

Yes, we do carry Thirsty towels in the 24-by-46 size. You may have a color choice of medium blue, sunburst, rose, medium green, flamingo, or peach.

These beautiful, thick, fluffy towels are priced at $1.49 each, or two for $2.75. You will save $1.02 by purchasing in lots of six, for we make a special price of *six for $7.92.*

Don't bother to write us an order letter. Just jot down on the back of this letter the number you want and the color you choose. Enclose your check, and the towels will be sent to you in the first delivery truck that is routed your way.

Cordially yours,

The next letter we open asks about the Speedy washer. This make of machine is carried by Allen-Brent, a competitor. The washing machine we sell is the Pushbutton washer. What shall we do about this inquiry? Failure to answer would lose us an opportunity to build good will and might lose a chance to make a sale. An ungracious acknowledgment would be worse than none at all. Let us put our training to work and write:

Dear Mrs. Manning:

We are unable to answer your questions about the Speedy washer, for we sell the Pushbutton machine. We inquired, however, and found that the Speedy is carried by Allen-Brent, of this city. We hope that this information will be helpful to you.

If you are shopping around for a washing machine, we should like very much to have you come in to see our Pushbutton. We think its price and performance make it the best washer buy on the market.

Sincerely yours,

Then, to put the extra lick of polish on this job, we shall enclose our advertising literature for the Pushbutton.

Now we open a letter written by a man who called on us last week. He wants to know who installed the new lighting fixtures in our office.

We would write immediately and give him this information solely because we are the kind of people who want to help others. But even the sort of person who has none of the milk of human kindness would be smart enough to do the same thing, although his motive might be only that of building good will. Nobody could possibly lose by writing something like this:

Dear Mr. Boswell:

We are very glad to answer your inquiry about the lighting fixtures recently installed in our office.

The work was done by the Sherwood Electrical Company, 214 Tenth Street, of this city, whom we are very happy to recommend.

An improved model of fixture has been developed since ours was installed, and we suggest that you get information on the latest product before you make your selection.

If we can be of further help, please do not hesitate to write again.

Sincerely yours,

Request Acknowledgments. The best way to acknowledge a request is generally thought to be the *immediate furnishing* of that service. A letter of acknowledgment would be necessary, however, when there will be a delay in getting the service to the customer; as:

Gentlemen:

We are sure that the turret lathe you purchased from us recently needs only a slight adjustment in order to correct the difficulty reported by you on May 6.

The setter-up who services your territory has been ill for a few days and is expected to return to work on Thursday.

His first assignment will be a visit to your factory.

Sincerely yours,

Whether or not to write a request acknowledgment is a problem that depends for its solution on the purpose behind the writing of the letter. For instance, if we work for a large, established mail-order house and receive a request for a catalogue, we would probably merely send the catalogue and would not write an acknowledgment letter.

If, however, we work for a concern that is interested in building up a mail-order business, we might consider an acknowledgment letter an important step in the build-up process. The letter cost would thus be swallowed up by the sales and advertising value.

Let us look at such a letter.

Dear Mrs. Quinn:

The catalogue you requested is being mailed today.

We are so proud of the values and prices of the beds, springs, and mattresses illustrated on pages 625-675 that we cannot refrain from calling them to your attention. Never before have we been able to pass on such savings to our customers!

May this catalogue be the means of laying the foundation for long and profitable business relations between you and us.

Very sincerely yours,

Remember: Every reply is an acknowledgment, and every acknowledgment is a challenge to the letter writer's ability to produce results in the form of increase in profits.

We write letters for King Bros., a firm that manufactures men's clothing. Write acknowledgment letters covering the following situations:

Assignment 1. A check for $875 has been received from the haberdashers, Manning & Brooks, in full payment for a shipment of men's summer suits.

Assignment 2. Order No. 723 for shop coats from Taylor's Toggery cannot be filled completely because the dozen ordered in medium tan twill have been sold out. We call the shop foreman and find that the tan twill coats are now being made up and will be ready for sale in five days' time.

Assignment 3. Henson Clothiers wants to know whether we manufacture rayon lounging robes. We do.

Assignment 4. Sheffield & Company writes to ask the price of nylon shirts. The letter just stated "nylon," but we manufacture nylon crepe and nylon tricot shirts. The crepe shirts wholesale for $75 a dozen and the tricot for $78 a dozen.

Assignment 5. The dry-cleaning firm of Burns & Lee is considering installing new pressing machines, and we receive a letter asking what make and model presser we use. We are equipped with the Foss electrically operated, heavy-duty, steam pressers; and we find them very satisfactory.

Assignment 6. Today we received from our old friend Dana & Sons order No. 815 for fifty gabardine topcoats. This is the largest order this firm has ever given us.

Assignment 7. We offer all our customers free consultation service with regard to the effective display of our goods. This is Monday, and we have a letter from Jay F. Anderson requesting the service. Mr. Allen, our display consultant, is booked until Saturday and will not be able to get to Mr. Anderson until next Monday.

Assignment 8. You are the supervisor of a corps of twelve letter writers For a few weeks now, you have noticed that the replies written by your fellow workers have been dull and afflicted with a deadly sameness. Evidently they are beginning to get into a rut, and part of your job is to prevent such a happening. Prepare a memorandum to be distributed to these correspondents, impressing upon them the importance of their letters in the total business scene. To strengthen your case for the writing of business-getting replies, you may draw on any points made in this lesson.

LESSON **72**

Everyday Letters (Continued)

Order Letters

A printed form called a "purchase order" is used by many firms when ordering goods. Each form is numbered. When writing about an order, the correspondent always states the order number. This practice speeds action by making identification quick and easy.

If we order goods by filling in a form, we must be very sure that we are clear, concise, complete, and accurate. Careless performance of even a supposedly easy task can result in increased overhead. Look at the following illustration of a purchase order.

PURCHASE ORDER

Name and Address
of
Ordering Firm   No. . . . .

                      Date

Name and Address
of Vendor

Please enter our order for the following:
325—Straight Plush Loom Knives 3-11/32″ by 1-1/2″ by .021
   No. 15/1.35   Quality I—No slot

                By . . . .

Dept. Supply
Gf:kb

The order blanks furnished by large mail-order houses are in reality purchase orders. These firms go to the expense of printing and distributing forms for the purpose of trying to get clear, complete, and accurate orders; but carelessness and inaccuracy are so

397

common that many letters requesting additional information still
have to be written.

We may never work for a firm that orders merchandise by purchase order. We may not have available a catalogue order blank.
For these reasons and also for personal-use reasons, we should know
how to write a correct order letter.

Possibly we should know that, if we make a mistake in our order
and if the vendor accepts the order, we are legally bound to pay for
the goods, even though we cannot use them. Of course, such a situation is unlikely to occur; for a vendor would lose good will by forc-
ing the customer to accept and pay for goods ordered by mistake.
But it could happen!

Check List for Order Letters. To insure speedy delivery and to
keep letter-writing overhead costs to a minimum, let us study and
apply the following check list for all written orders.

Catalogue Number. If the goods we order are listed in a catalogue, the number of that item will be the first unit we type.

Quantity. Let us double check the quantity. Even very careful
people have been known to transpose numbers—writing *1265* for
1256.

Name and Description of Article. Should we fail here to be absolutely explicit, we must not be surprised to find that there is a
mix-up in the order. Suppose that we are ordering bolts, which are
made of different materials and have heads of different shapes. If we
specify "hex-head steel bolts," we leave no doubt in the vendor's
mind as to exactly what we want shipped.

Color. This point will not apply in some orders; but, if there is a
color choice, we must be sure to state it.

Size. If we want to receive the correct size, we must order the
correct size.

Price and Provision for Payment. When typing the price of the
goods, do not write the sum in words and in figures. In the day of
handwritten letters, this practice was used because it was necessary
to have the price written both ways in case one or the other was illegible. A typed figure cannot be misread; so the numbers written
in words are unnecessary.

Unless credit has already been established, a statement of provision for payment must be made. For instance, the order may be accompanied by a check or instructions may be given to send it C.O.D.

Directions for Shipping. Many large firms have on their staff an expert whose business it is to know the best and cheapest way to ship goods. If we are ordering from a vendor who employs such an expert, shipping directions are unnecessary. If we are not certain that the vendor has a shipping specialist, we shall state how we want the goods sent—parcel post, freight, railway express, truck transportation line.

Setup of Order Letters. Letter writers who are also typists know that they can set up letters in such a way that readability is promoted and mistakes are prevented. When setting up an order letter, be sure to place each order item on a separate line, as in the following illustration.

221 State Street
Milton, Illinois
May 23, 19—

Ward Bent Company
826 Missouri Avenue
Chicago 22, Illinois

Gentlemen:
    Please send me by parcel post the following articles selected from your summer-sale catalogue:

6y92	1	Duffel Bag gray	18 by 30	$6.99
6y98	1	Linen Golf Bag		9.95
6y31	1	O'Neil Reel	cap. 100 yds.	
			18-lb. test	4.79
		Total		$21.73
		Postage		.63
				$22.36

I am enclosing a check for $22.36.

Very truly yours,

Inquiry Letters

A letter of inquiry will result in a prompt and satisfactory answer only when it is correctly written. Therefore, even so simple a task as asking for information requires know-how on the part of the writer. The inquiry letters that boost overhead expense are the ones that cause the reader to exclaim, "What in the world is he driving at!"

Asking for information will be a one-letter job if we know and use the following points that apply to the writing of inquiry letters.

1. Write to the person who is in position to answer the particular inquiry. We may not know the name of that person, but we should know the official title of the man who would have the information we want. For instance, if we were asking a question about personnel, we would write to the Personnel Director. Of course, our letters will be much more effective if we write to our prospective informant by name.

2. Be clear in your own mind as to exactly what you want to know. Once *you* are clear, be sure that you write in such a way that the *reader* immediately grasps your meaning.

3. Give your reason for making the inquiry. Make this part of the letter as concise as possible without being so abrupt as to appear discourteous.

4. Be courteous. Probably the note of courtesy can be sounded in the final paragraph. Do not, however, fall into the error of "Thank you in advance" or, worse still, "Thanking you in advance."

5. Do not cause unnecessary work for the reader by asking for information that you could have obtained from reference books. This is no way to build good will.

6. Enclose a stamped, self-addressed envelope if the reply is to be a personal favor, as in the illustration that follows. Should the letter deal with routine business, you will not enclose the envelope.

Dear Mr. Crane:

We are considering the installation of fluorescent lighting in our offices and should like to get in touch with a reputable electrical firm that specializes in that type of work.

When I visited your offices, I was particularly impressed with the lighting job that was recently done for you. Will you give us the name of the company that did the work?

We shall very much appreciate any help you can give us. Please use the enclosed self-addressed envelope for your reply.

Cordially yours,

Transmittal Letters

A transmittal letter is often referred to as a "covering letter." It is a letter that accompanies, and often explains or commends, an enclosure. We shall make it an invariable practice to send such a letter with every valuable document—mortgage, deed, will, stock, bond, specifications, contract, manuscript—that is sent by mail or messenger. The carbon copy that we keep in our files thus becomes a permanent record of the transaction.

The transmittal, or covering, letter is always brief; and the chief requirement is that it clearly identify the document. Although there is little or no opportunity to warm this type of letter with words, we can increase prestige by accurate and neat typing and by attractive letter setup. Here is such a letter:

Dear Mr. Green:
    With this letter I am returning your insurance policy No. 837353.
    I have read the policy carefully and have made several notes to discuss different points with you when we meet on the 25th of this month.
                       Cordially yours,

In some offices, printed forms with blank spaces are used in place of individually typed transmittal letters. If we use such forms, we shall type in the proper spaces only the information required; and we shall be sure to make a carbon for the files.

Whenever we send valuable documents by mail, we shall register them and request a return receipt.

Remittance Letters

Whenever we write a letter and enclose in that letter a remittance, we shall be sure to state: the amount of the remittance; the form in which it is sent—personal or company check, money order, cashier's or certified check, bank draft; the way in which the money is to be applied—part or full payment of account or of order No. . . . . .

A gracious closing sentence in a remittance letter can be used to promote vendor good will. Read critically the following illustration.

Gentlemen:

I am enclosing a check for $696.21 in payment of my order No. 428.

The towels are very satisfactory and are selling well, so well that you may expect another order soon.

Sincerely yours,

Confirmation Letters

A confirmation letter should be written immediately after concluding a telephone call, a personal conference, or after sending a wire. The purpose is to prevent mistakes or misunderstandings and to furnish a written record for the files. Failure to "cover" a conversation or a wire by letter may prove costly. Here is a sample:

Gentlemen:

In confirmation of our telephone conversation on June 5, I am writing to tell you that my understanding with regard to the ovenware to fit our stock of No. 49 Kool kitchen ranges is:

1. You will deliver to us 28 sets of brown ovenware.
2. They will be sent on a no-charge basis.
3. You will mark the shipment for the attention of our Department 38.

Thank you for your continued splendid co-operation.

Sincerely yours,

Request Letters

Many different kinds of request letters are written daily, among them requests for services, for reservations, for appointments. The key to the writing of a good request letter is the same key that applies to all the other everyday letters—they must be so clear, concise, complete, and accurate that only one letter needs to be written.

We have learned previously that we avoid a one-paragraph letter; but the very nature of some request letters sometimes makes necessary the writing of very brief letters, even one-paragraph letters.

Let us study a few examples of request letters.

Request for Free Services.   Perhaps we write to ask for a catalogue, a letter like:

Gentlemen:

We should appreciate your sending us your latest parts catalogue, which will be of assistance to us in our Purchasing Department.

Very truly yours,

Or it might be that we write to ask for the services of a typewriter repairman, a service to which we are entitled because the machines are new and carry a guarantee of one year.

Gentlemen:
Please send a typewriter repairman to our office.
Two of our machines are out of order, and the loss of their use is causing us great inconvenience.
Very truly yours,

Request for Reservation. When we write for a reservation—hotel, plane, train—we shall be sure that we give all necessary details.

When making hotel reservations, we shall state whether we want a double, twin-bed, or single room, with or without bath, price range, day and hour of arrival, and the day and hour we plan to leave. If an immediate reply is desired and if we ask for a confirmation by wire, we know that the wire will come collect.

Plane or train reservations will state the points of departure and destination; one-way or round trip; day, date, and hour of departure and return. If the train reservation is to include a berth, we shall specify the kind of sleeping accommodations we want. We can prevent unnecessary overhead by being so clear and complete that a second letter will not have to be written.

Let us suppose that in early May we learn that we must take a business trip to Chicago. Let us make the hotel reservation.

Gentlemen:
Please reserve for me a single, medium-priced room with bath for Wednesday and Thursday, June 15 and 16.
I expect to arrive before 9 p.m. on Wednesday, June 15, and to leave before 3 p.m. on Friday, June 17.
Very truly yours,

If we plan to fly, we must make a plane reservation.

Gentlemen:
Please make the following reservations for me:
Round trip between New York and Chicago
Leave New York on Wednesday, June 15, at 2:45 p.m.
Leave Chicago on Friday, June 17, at 2 p.m.
Very truly yours,

Suppose that we prefer to travel by train. We could visit the passenger station and make personal reservations, or we could write:

Gentlemen:
Please make the following reservations for me:
New York to Chicago and return
Roomette accommodations both ways
Leave New York Tuesday, June 14, at 6 p.m. on the Wolverine
Leave Chicago Friday, June 17, at 3 p.m. on the Badger.
Very truly yours,

Travel Services.   Of course, we could save ourselves the trouble and letter expense of reservations by making use of any one of the travel services that operate all over the country. Their services are free; and, if we furnish them with the details, they will make all reservations for us.

This does not mean that we do not need to know how to make reservations by letter. Nobody can foresee the demands that will be made on him in the future, and inability to write a reservation letter may cause a business letter writer to lose prestige.

Request for Appointment.   If we live in the same city as a man with whom we wish to make an appointment, we would probably do the business by telephone. If the person we wish to see lives in another city and if we have enough advance notice of the time we shall be in that place, we would probably make an appointment by letter.

Our appointment letter will be brief, but not to the point of failing to be explicit about the time, the date, and the place. The reason for making the appointment should be stated, as in the following letter, unless there has been previous correspondence and the subject of the call is understood.

Dear Mr. Fisher:
Would it be convenient for you to see me at your office on Thursday afternoon, July 8, at three o'clock?
I expect to be in Boston on that day, and I should like to get your advice about annuities.
Very sincerely yours,

Cancellation Letters

If we must make a cancellation and if time permits, we shall write a cancellation letter. Otherwise, we shall telephone or wire. We shall be clear about the subject of the letter, and we shall always state courteously the reason for the cancellation.

Failure to cancel, as in the case of an appointment, would stamp us as uncouth and would lose us good will. A curt letter, without a convincing reason, would be very little better when considered from the point of view of good will.

Here is an illustration of an appointment cancellation.

Dear Mr. Fisher:

I shall be unable to keep my appointment with you for Thursday, July 8, at 3 p.m.

My trip to Boston has been delayed one week because a sales conference has been called for the week of July 5. As you probably know, I am sales manager for our Atlantic territory.

May I have an appointment for the same time on July 15?

Very sincerely yours,

Sometimes we find it necessary to cancel all or part of an order. Such cancellation is really asking a favor, for the vendor could rightfully refuse. Without being humble, let us word our order cancellations with the purpose of promoting vendor good will; as:

Gentlemen:

Please cancel the 25 end tables on our order No. 4893, dated yesterday, May 26.

Our warehouse manager submitted his inventory this morning, and we found that our supply of end tables is sufficient for about a month.

Perhaps we should consider this cancellation merely a delayed order; for, when we are ready to purchase more end tables, your firm will certainly get the order.

Sincerely yours,

Summary

The expert business correspondent makes every letter he writes a sales letter. He has many, many chances to sell when he writes everyday letters; for these are the letters that are most frequently written. They are therefore his treasure chest of sales opportunities. His intelligence in recognizing the value of everyday letters, his enthusiasm, and his knowledge of what makes people "tick" are the reasons for his becoming the expert that he is.

Assignment 1. If you were afforded an opportunity to learn how to write only one of the letter types discussed in this lesson, which one would you choose? In the form of an interoffice memorandum, state your choice and your reasons for making the choice.

Assignment 2. Write a letter to the *Saturday Evening Post,* asking the charge for a full-page advertisement. It might be interesting to choose the best letter written by a class member and mail it. The reply would give some idea of advertising costs and would also be a sample of an inquiry acknowledgment.

Assignment 3. Write a letter to Barnes & Barnes, enclosing a check for $962.43. You are paying in full for your last order for Jimson swim suits. The entire order was sold in four days.

Assignment 4. Clip from a newspaper an advertisement for some article of wearing apparel. Write a letter ordering the goods advertised.

Assignment 5. You work for a firm of stockbrokers. Edward James, of 54 Elm Street, New London, Connecticut, has purchased from your company twenty-five shares of Rockford common stock. Write the transmittal letter that will be sent with the stock.

Assignment 6. Consult a mail-order catalogue and make out an order for five items. Use the printed form.

Assignment 7. Write a letter making an appointment to see John J. Weber, of Thornhild, Brokers, 823 Fortune Street, Utopia, Texas. You want to talk with him about investment possibilities.

Assignment 8. You are unable to keep the appointment made in Assignment 7. Write the cancellation letter.

Assignment 9. You talked over the telephone with Ray W. Ross, of Smart Apparel, located in a neighboring city. You accepted his offer to send you 50 ladies' cashmere sweaters and to allow you to pay for them after they were sold. Write the confirmation letter.

Assignment 10. Make an appointment to see a business executive in your city or town. When you keep the appointment, tell him what you have learned from your study of this lesson and ask his opinion of the value of everyday letters.

Without mentioning the name of the executive, prepare an interoffice memorandum that will contain the information you received. Perhaps you might like to read the memorandum to the class and lead a discussion of the contents.

LESSON **73**

Letters of Refusal

The little word *no* can cause more ill will than any other word in the English language.

This undisputed fact has great significance for us, the writers of business letters. We know that modern business grows in direct proportion to the amount of *good* will built up by business and industry. We believe that the letters we write are powerful contributions to the promotion of good will. Yet there are times when we must write letters of refusal, the *no* letters that might injure good business relationships.

Our problem, then, is to learn how to say no without actually saying it. We must word our refusals so graciously, tactfully, and wisely that our correspondents will continue to think well of us and to feel friendly toward us.

Perhaps we can become polished writers of refusal letters by studying first the general principles underlying the exactly right wording and tone of these letters and then applying them in different refusal situations. The general principles to be observed are:

1. Accentuate the positive
2. Give logical reasons for refusals
3. Keep open the lines of communication
4. Avoid kowtowing

General Principles

1. Accentuate the Positive. We shall be particularly watchful lest negative words slip into our refusal letters; such words as error, failure, displeasure, dissatisfied, neglected, poor, trouble, unfortunately, unfavorable, unsatisfactory.

407

We shall put together the words that we do use in such a fashion that a positive, rather than a negative, effect is produced. Let us give careful attention to the wording of the first paragraph, for it is here that the tone is established.

The following illustrations show how a negative tone can be changed to positive.

Negative: We deeply regret that we cannot contribute . . . .
Positive: We wish it were possible for us to contribute . . . .

Negative: Unfortunately, we are not able to . . . .
Positive: We should like very much to . . . , but . . . .

2. Give Logical Reasons for Refusals. Possibly a very common and homely illustration can be used to illustrate the application of this principle.

Suppose that you asked your father whether you might use the family car on Monday night; and he said simply, but maybe explosively, "No!" How would you feel? Well, you probably would not mutter and grumble in his presence, but you would do plenty of it as soon as you were away from him.

Now suppose that he said, "I'm sorry, Son, but your mother and I are using it to go to the entertainment in Midfield." See what a difference these words would make! You would be disappointed, but you would not be resentful. In business, it is resentment that destroys good will.

Every refusal, then, should be accompanied by a logical, convincing reason. Of course, the most convincing reason is usually the true, not the invented, reason. Consider the following illustrations.

. . . , but we are already operating on such a narrow margin of profit that a further reduction in price would be financially unsound.

. . . , but company policy forces us to limit our donations to causes that are purely charitable in nature.

. . . , but we are bound by agreement with Downes not to give this information.

3. Keep Open the Lines of Communication. We may be positive in tone, we may prevent irritation by giving a good reason for our refusal; but, unless we leave the way open for future business transactions, our refusal letter falls short of the perfection we seek.

A refusal letter states that we will not or cannot do something that is asked of us. In order to keep open the lines of communication, let us try very hard to think of something that we can do, either now or later. Let us be so gracious that we leave with our correspondent a lasting impression that will move him to place with us his dollars-and-cents business.

Suppose that we are refusing to donate to the Ladies' Aid Society. A sample open-communication sentence might be:

However, we shall be happy to post your bazaar announcement on our office bulletin board.

Or, when refusing to give space in our store for a kitchen-range demonstration, we might be able to write:

We should be more than pleased to talk to your demonstrator, Miss Dennehey, sometime in August. We may be able to arrange for a demonstration during one of the fall months.

4. Avoid Kowtowing. A discussion of this principle is necessary because many writers are so sold on the first three principles that their letters positively grovel. Uncalled-for humility is as out of date as celluloid collars are and accomplishes nothing but the loss of respect.

The main danger point is the last paragraph of the refusal letter. Here is where the writer often tries to influence good will by getting down and crawling. Look at the following horrible examples.

We trust that there will be no hard feelings between us.
We should be grateful if you would kindly accept our regrets.
We hope that we have not incurred your displeasure.

Sickening, aren't they?

Refusal Situations

Order Refusals. Much as it may hurt, there are times when we must refuse orders. The customer may want a special discount, may quote a price that we cannot meet, may owe us so much money that we cannot extend him any more credit. Maybe we are wholesalers and receive a retail order. If we are forced to refuse an order, we must write the kind of refusal letter that will not allow a customer to slip through our fingers.

Let us pretend that we are wholesale furniture manufacturers and have received a retail order for a sectional sofa. We cannot fill the order directly, but we can indirectly by writing:

Dear Mrs. Culbert:

We are delighted to know that you wish to purchase one of our Dunbar sectional sofas, but we do business only on a wholesale basis.

We recommend that you visit the Home Furnishings Store in your community, where you can see this sofa in a variety of beautiful coverings. You will then be able to choose the exact hue that harmonizes best with the color scheme of your living room. Careful, personal selection of the Dunbar is wise because it is lifetime furniture.

Your letter has been forwarded to Mr. Himes, of the Home Furnishings Store, and you will undoubtedly hear from him soon.

Very cordially yours,

Let us see what we can do with a really "tough one," a letter refusing an order because the customer already owes us too much money.

Dear Mr. Evans:

Thank you for your order No. 426.

Nothing would please us better than to ship the order to you today, but we have a company rule to the effect that no orders can be filled for customers who have not kept their accounts open for at least three months. Your place in this category is undoubtedly due to an oversight.

But we can and will be happy to send you the order on a C.O.D. basis. Just jot down, "Send C.O.D." and mail the request to us. The goods will be on the way as soon as it is humanly possible for us to get them off.

Very cordially yours,

Donation Refusals. Every businessman and every business firm is considered fair game when it comes to asking for donations. Business is solicited by everyone, from the business staff of the high school paper to the Ways and Means Committees of all community groups. Requests may be for money contributions, for advertisements in papers and programs, or for articles of merchandise to be taken from stock.

In the interests of good-will building, businessmen are glad to make contributions to worthy causes; and they do donate generously. However, when the giving of these free-will offerings reaches the point that they threaten profits, refusals become necessary. This type of refusal is very difficult to write, for the writer is saying *no* not only to the solicitor, but also to the entire organization that he represents. Therefore, the danger of creating ill will is more widespread than appears at first glance.

What do you think of the following illustration?

Dear Mr. Platt:

Thank you for thinking of us in connection with the forthcoming reunion of Shannock School Class of 1941.

Because of the many requests received from members of various worthy organizations, a donation policy has been set up by our firm. All contributions are taken care of by a yearly, substantial money donation to the Community Chest; and we are not allowed to make other contributions of any kind.

We wish we could make an exception in your case, for we count many of your classmates among our best friends. You can readily see, however, that even one exception would destroy the effectiveness of the policy.

We extend to the Class of 1941 our very best wishes for a happy reunion.

Very cordially yours,

Since there is no opportunity here by letter to keep open the lines of communication, perhaps we could apply the principle by sending a congratulatory telegram to be read on the night of the banquet.

Invitation Refusals. Many invitations are received by business firms or by individual members of the company—so many that refusals are frequently necessary. Refusal to attend a Housewares Show might have to be written because another commitment has been made. An invitation to exhibit at a show might be refused because analysis reveals that the exhibition would be a losing financial undertaking.

Complete coverage of all invitation refusal situations would be impossible here; but we probably can write good letters if we remember always to express appreciation for the invitation, to give the reason for refusal, and to remember to keep open the lines of communication.

As an illustration, let us suppose that we have been asked to be the guest speaker at a Chamber of Commerce banquet. We are so busy that we just cannot accept the invitation; so we refuse; as:

Dear Mr. Miller:

You have indeed paid me a great compliment by inviting me to be the guest speaker at your February 4 banquet.

It just so happens that I am already committed to act as general chairman for the American Association of Manufacturers convention to be held in St. Louis on February 2, 3, and 4. I have tried to get someone else to take over my duties on February 4, to allow me time to get to your banquet, but I have met with no success. I want you to know that I cannot accept your invitation because of sheer physical impossibility.

Please keep me in mind when the next invitation time rolls around.

Cordially yours,

Information Refusal. While there may be some people who, for selfish reasons, refuse to give information to others, business people feel that the exchange of information promotes the growth of business. The forward-looking businessman is more than willing to give what information he can, for sometime he may be placed in the position of seeking information. This is but an application of the Golden Rule.

There are occasions, however, when the giving of information would be a breach of ethics or would be financially unwise; and then a refusal letter must be written.

Suppose that we receive a letter asking for samples of the collection letters we write. Now, James R. Roberts is our correspondence consultant and is the author of a textbook on business correspondence. We paid him a large sum to adapt his collection-letter material to our needs. We have made a written agreement with Mr. Roberts whereby we are restrained from giving any information about the letters he has set up for us. To our correspondent, then, we must write a letter refusing to give him the information he requests; as:

Dear Mr. Haines:

We should like very much to send you samples of the collection letters we write, but we are restrained from doing so by a written agreement.

Mr. James R. Roberts, 287 Broad Street, of this city, is our correspondence consultant; and he has written forms to cover the various types of letters we write. Our contract with him specifies that we are to refrain from giving any information about these forms.

However, Mr. Roberts is the author of an excellent business-correspondence text, *Business-Promoting Letters;* and you might be able to get from his book the information you seek. The publishers are:

Caxton Book Company, Inc.
230 East 42d Street
New York 16, New York

Although we are unable to give you any information this time, please do not hesitate in the future to ask us for assistance. We are always glad to help.

Cordially yours,

Purchase Refusals. Some businessmen might think that the careful construction of a refusal letter to a vendor would be a waste of time. Others might think it a waste of money to reply at all. They reason this way: They do not intend to take advantage of the offer, and they can tell the vendor so by not answering his letter.

Successful businessmen in top-management positions would not agree with this thinking. You see, they attained their high positions by hard work and by applying the principles of sound business— make sales, reduce overhead, build good will. For good-will reasons they would write the vendor the same kind of well-bred letter that they would write to anyone else.

For illustrative purposes, let us suppose that we receive a letter from a vendor offering us a very good price on closet accessories— garment bags, shoe racks, suit hangers. We are in the process of reorganizing the department where such items are sold, and we are not going to make any purchases until the reorganization is complete. Therefore, we must refuse to purchase. We write:

Gentlemen:

Thank you for your fine offer of January 21.

Our Department 38, where closet accessories are sold, is now in the process of reorganization. We feel that we must defer all purchases for this department until the reorganization has been completed. You will understand that only then can we buy intelligently.

We sincerely appreciate your thinking of us, and we hope that you will continue to remember us whenever you give special price reductions to the trade.

Sincerely yours,

Summary

No writer of business letters can consider himself an expert unless he can write the kind of refusal letters that will win or retain the friendship of his correspondents.

Refusal letters written by experts are positive and self-respecting in wording and tone. They present sound and convincing reasons for the refusals. Courtesy and good business sense demand that somewhere in each letter will be a suggestion that will lead to continuing business relationships. Yes, it takes a real expert to write first-rate refusal letters.

Assignment 1. You have received notice from an insurance company that the insurance policy on your office building is being renewed. You have decided to insure with another company, a company that has offered you the same coverage at a saving of $125 a year. Write the letter refusing to renew the policy.

Assignment 2. For six months you have been trying to collect an account amounting to $846.23 from Foley & Griffin, of Summit, Utah. You receive a letter from them offering to settle for 95 cents on the dollar. Write a letter refusing their offer.

Assignment 3. The president of your local Board of Trade has notified you that you have been appointed to serve on the business research committee for next year. You feel that you cannot spare the time to do the work, although you know full well how important it is. Besides, your work takes you out of the city frequently, with little or no advance notice. Show your teacher what a smooth refusal letter you can write.

Assignment 4. Miss June Hart, of Hansen Stores, 826 Fifth Avenue, New York 12, New York, has written to offer to buy from you a shipment of nylon pajamas in pastel shades at $120 a dozen. Your best price for these goods is $144 a dozen; so you cannot fill the order. Write the refusal letter.

Assignment 5. An old customer, Hakes & Company, is getting ready for an anniversary sale. They want to feature your Deepsleep mattress, and they write to ask for a special discount of 5 per cent on 125 mattresses. This you simply cannot do; for, if you start giving special discounts, you will soon have to give so many that you will be bankrupt. Write and tell them so.

Assignment 6. The Lions Club of your community is planning to have a carnival to raise money to send underprivileged children to camp. They write to ask for a donation of merchandise. Write a refusal letter, but try to think of something that you *can* do.

Assignment 7. You work for a company that publishes textbooks. You have received an invitation to exhibit at a regional teachers' meeting. The expense involved would be too great for the returns to be expected from the few teachers who would be present at such a meeting. What kind of refusal letter would you write?

Assignment 8. In the form of an interoffice memorandum, list three good reasons that could be given for refusing to advertise in your school annual.

Assignment 9. In the form of an interoffice memorandum, list four sentences or sets of sentences that could be used in any letter for the purpose of keeping open the lines of communication.

Assignment 10. Which of the above assignments appealed most to you? Ask your teacher whether you may have the letters written by your classmates in fulfillment of that assignment. Prepare a written analysis of these letters, quoting the wording that you think is good or bad.

Perhaps you may be given time to present your findings to the class and lead a following discussion.

LESSON **74**

Credit and Collection Letters

Before we spend our time studying how to write credit and collection letters, let us see whether it is worth our while to bother with them. What is credit? It is buying now and paying later. Stop right here and think of the many commodities that you know are bought and sold on time payments. After you have thought for a few minutes, you will not be at all surprised to learn that more than 75 per cent of all the business in the United States is done on a credit basis.

Because of results in the form of increased volume of sales and increased amount of money in circulation, credit buying has had a rapid growth. Whether continuing growth is safe or whether it is a bubble that will burst depends upon the character of the American people. Remembering that there is no profit unless goods are paid for, perhaps we can say that credit business will be safe just as long as the customers can and will meet the time payments promptly and honestly. Let us see how the system works.

Maybe you have noticed on an invoice figures like these—2/10/n/30. They mean that the businessman will get a 2 per cent discount if he pays his bill within ten days; but if he does not take the discount, the amount owed must be paid within thirty days. A case like this represents a credit transaction, for payment is not made immediately.

The advantage to the businessman of being able to wait thirty days before paying is that he has an opportunity to sell the goods and make his profit before meeting the obligation. In the meantime, he has had the use of the payment money for other things, such as repairs, maintenance, expansion. This accounts for the increased circulation of money.

Whenever possible, smart businessmen take advantage of the 2 per cent discount and pay their bills within ten days. By so doing, they are able to make an extra profit.

To retail customers, the advantage of time payments is that they can enjoy the use of merchandise while they are paying for it. Many perfectly honest people do not have the ability to save money until they have a sufficient amount for a big purchase. They will, however, meet regular monthly payments spread over a period of time. They are willing to pay the carrying charges (interest) for the opportunity to buy "on time."

Large department stores eagerly offer charge-account privileges. They know that the average person who has a charge account will buy more than the person who pays cash. Human nature is such that we are more likely to purchase on the spur of the moment if we do not have to dig into our pocketbooks for the coins and folding money. The charge-account customer must be of strong character to look at an article he very much wants and be able to say to himself, "I'll have to pay for it eventually, and I really cannot afford it. I won't buy it." Strong characters are in the minority; so the fact remains that the extension of credit increases the volume of sales.

After all this, we realize that almost any correspondence position we take will involve the writing of letters that have to do with credit and collection. Let us learn how to write the very best letters.

Credit Letters

Establishing Credit. Businessmen do not grant credit privileges in a hit-or-miss fashion. They want to be reasonably sure that they will get paid for the goods they sell; therefore, each prospective charge-account customer is investigated carefully before credit is extended to him. What is it that businessmen want to know about the prospect and how do they get the information?

In a way, the extension of credit is a gamble; and, in order to lessen the risk, something must be known about the kind of person the credit applicant is. He must be ready, willing, and able to pay his bills. He must, then, possess the three Credit C's—character, capital, capacity.

Character is the most important of the three, for a person of proved good character is one who pays his bills willingly and promptly. The amount of *capital* a credit applicant has will represent his ability to pay, because his capital is the total of his ready money and his assets in excess of his liabilities. Capital is the amount that he has available for the paying of his bills. By *capacity* we mean his business ability. If the applicant is a sound businessman, he will continue to be able to pay his bills. He will always be ready to pay.

Now that we know what a credit manager looks for when he is considering the extension of credit, let us see how he gets his information. The applicant must furnish at least three names for reference. Sometimes he must present copies of his most recent profit and loss statements. Information about business concerns can often be obtained from mercantile agencies whose business it is to supply such information. When investigating a personal application, information about the position the person holds and the salary he makes is important. Inquiries about character, capital, and capacity will answer the three questions the credit manager asks: *Will* the applicant pay? *Can* he pay now? *Can* he continue to pay?

Credit will not be granted to anyone until a most careful investigation is made.

Granting Credit. The writing of letters that grant credit is a pleasant task because the correspondent is paving the way for the fulfillment of one of his purposes—to make sales. The letters, therefore, should reflect that pleasure. They should be so warm and welcoming that the customer will feel that he wants very much to take advantage of his credit privilege. Here is an illustration of a letter to a business firm.

Gentlemen:

We are very glad to open an account for you, and your order No. 624 is being shipped today on open account. The terms are 2/10/n/30.

We are delighted to number you among our accounts receivable friends, and we hope that your first order may be the beginning of long and prosperous business relations between us.

Cordially yours,

If we were a retail store and were writing a letter granting charge-account privileges, we might word our letter something like this:

Dear Mrs. Fielding:

We are mailing you today an account plate for you to use when purchasing at Bolton's. Please feel free to come in and use it often.

Any purchase you make will be gift-wrapped without charge if you so desire. Our delivery truck goes to your community on Wednesday and Friday; so, when you shop with us, you need not carry bulky packages. We have an exchange department that is interested first of all in seeing to it that you are perfectly satisfied with every purchase you make. All special services are at your command.

We want you to know that we will exert every effort to make your visits to our store pleasant and profitable.

Cordially yours,

Refusing Credit. When investigation shows that the credit applicant is a poor risk, the correspondent must write a letter refusing him credit. All such letters must be worded very tactfully because we are in business to make sales and to build good will. If we are clever, we shall be able to retain the customer on a cash basis.

In our study of *Letters of Refusal* we learned that a reason for refusal should be given. In writing credit-refusal letters, we shall give our reason if it is one that will not offend; such as applicant is under legal age; insufficient number of references were given.

If we learn that the applicant does not pay his obligations, our letter will not contain any reason for refusal. We simply cannot write anything like this:

We must refuse your application for credit. Our investigation showed that you do not pay your bills; and we are in business to make money, not lose it.

We can, however, write a smooth letter like:

Gentlemen:
We should like very much to fill your order No. 452, but we think it inadvisable to open an account for you at this time.
You really should have the merchandise, for it heads our list of best sellers. May we send order No. 452 on a cash or C.O.D. basis?

Very sincerely yours,

If this customer places a cash order, we should clear the check before shipping the goods. If his credit is poor, he might be capable of sending us a bad check.

Then there is the letter that refuses further credit. The credit manager knows how much capital his charge-account customers have, and he also knows how much money the customers make. It is his business to know when any one of his clientele is ordering more goods than he will be able to pay for. Should such a situation occur, he will protect the customer as well as his company by writing:

Dear Mr. Stockton:

Thank you for your order for a living-room suite.

We should like very much to send you the furniture, but we are unable to do so right now. We have a company rule that states that charge-account balances must not exceed $500, and filling your order would break that rule.

Please believe that we are very well satisfied with the way you have met your obligations. You are one of our best customers; and, as soon as your account is within handling range, we shall be delighted to send you the living-room suite.

Cordially yours,

Giving Credit References. When we receive a request for credit information, that request will probably be in the form of a printed questionnaire. If we can give a favorable report, we shall simply fill in the proper spaces on the form. If we are unable to give the applicant a good reference, we must be very careful not to say anything that could make us the defendants in a libel suit.

We should not ignore a request for credit information, even though we cannot recommend the applicant. We might prefer not to fill in the form, but we could write a letter saying:

Gentlemen:

We have your request for credit information about James G. Preston.

Much as we should like to help you, we do not feel that we have had sufficient business experience with Mr. Preston to warrant giving a reference.

Very sincerely yours,

Other Kinds of Credit Letters. Correspondents in a thriving credit department write many letters other than those granting and refusing credit.

The progressive credit supervisor is on the alert to build his credit business. He may know of some cash customers who would make good charge customers, and he might give us the assignment of writing letters that would convince those customers of the advantages of charge accounts. In which case, we would write:

Dear Mrs. Byrne:

You are cordially invited to join the ranks of Benson's charge customers.

You will enjoy the convenience of being able to shop without carrying large sums of money. Merchandise that you really need now can be purchased now, and you will not have to wait for the pleasure of using it. You will be impressed with the ease with which you can exchange goods and obtain adjustments of all kinds. You will be delighted with the personal attention that will be given you.

We are looking forward to receiving your application for membership in our charge-account brotherhood.

Cordially yours,

Important as it is to obtain new accounts, more important still is the retaining of old accounts. For this reason, the credit supervisor keeps accurate records; and he knows when an account is falling off and when a customer has stopped using his charge account. In either case, a personal letter has great value in reactivating or building up the purchasing habit.

To stimulate more purchases on the part of the customer whose account is getting smaller all the time, possibly a letter calling attention to some item of stock might build up the account. Maybe the customer has gardening as a hobby, which fact we know because he has purchased from us some gardening implements. To him we might write:

Dear Mr. Reid:

As a special service to you, we should like to tell you about the new shipment of garden tools received today.

Never before have we had such a fine assortment at such reasonable prices. The man possessed of a "green thumb" can find in this shipment anything he needs to make his work easier and more productive. And he will not have to wreck his budget in order to buy it!

We think you will enjoy coming in to see the very latest in garden implements. If you do not have time to pay us a visit, just order whatever you need. We will give you our usual personal attention.

Cordially yours,

We might be given the assignment of writing to find out why a customer has stopped buying from us. Such a letter would be sound business practice. Many times customers become offended by something that could be rectified very easily; but, instead of making a complaint, they simply take their trade elsewhere. We can increase sales by finding the reason for not ordering and by making an adjustment of some kind. A letter can often be the means of resuming business relations, a letter like this:

Dear Mr. Dolan:

We should consider it a real favor if you would take time to tell us why your charge account remains inactive.

Pride in our reputation for prompt, efficient, courteous, satisfactory service is so great that we are eager to prevent anything that would threaten that reputation.

Do you know of any failure on our part? If so, you would be performing a neighborly act by giving us this information.

Sincerely yours,

Collection Letters

No matter how careful a credit investigation may be, sometimes credit is extended to people who are not willing to pay promptly, if at all. We must, therefore, know how to write collection letters that will bring in the money. There is no profit in sales unless cash is received for the goods sold.

When a customer owes us, we are losing the use of money that is due us. But more than that, very probably we are losing that customer's current business. By some quirk of human nature, a customer who owes a bill to one firm will trade with and pay cash to another company until he has cleared his account. Do you see how we can increase sales by writing the kind of collection letters that induce the customers to pay promptly?

Collection letters are thought of as a series of letters, increasing in harshness of tone. Many firms have a timetable for the writing of these letters. The first letter must be written so many days after the account is due. If no reply is received, a certain number of days will elapse; and then the next letter is written. And so it goes.

For study purposes, we shall make our collection letters a series of four, as follows:

Collection Letter 1. The first letter is a reminder that the bill was not paid on time. We must assume that nonpayment was an oversight; and, in some cases, this might be true. We cannot risk offending a customer who is willing to pay his bills promptly, but who happened to overlook this particular one. So we write:

Dear Mr. Porter:

Our attention has just been called to the fact that we have not received your check for $147.85, due on the statement mailed to you on May 1.

You are such a busy man that we know how easy it would be for you to overlook our statement. We are writing this letter simply as a reminder.

Cordially yours,

Collection Letter 2.   If the check does not come in, the question arises as to how long a time should elapse before the second letter is sent. The timing of collection letters should be left to the judgment of the supervisor.

The second letter will be a helpful letter, still assuming that the customer is willing to pay. Our primary aim is to get the money; so we may make a suggestion for method of payment; as:

Dear Mr. Porter:

On May 25 we sent you a reminder of the fact that we had not received your check for $147.85, due on May 1.

In view of your excellent reputation, we think that your delay in remitting may be caused by some temporary financial difficulty. If so, would you like to make arrangements to pay this sum in monthly installments?

We shall be happy to come to some agreement with you, for we want to help you retain your good credit standing.

Sincerely yours,

Collection Letter 3.   If we receive no reply to our first two letters, we must strongly suspect that the customer does not intend to pay. Now we are justified in being firm and in being insistent about payment. We must put the pressure on our fictional Mr. Porter by setting a time limit for payment; as:

Dear Mr. Porter:

We have sent you two letters reminding you that your check for $147.85, due on May 1, has not been received.

We are sure that you will not risk your business reputation by delaying payment beyond the time that it will take to put the check in the enclosed envelope and mail it to us.

We expect to balance your account by June 18 at the very latest.

Yours very truly,

Collection Letter 4.   This is the last letter in the series and is the one reserved for making a threat. However, unless the threat will be carried out, it should not be made. Maybe we could call this the "last straw" letter. We club Mr. Porter over the head with:

Dear Sir:

Despite three reminder letters written to you, we have not received your check for $147.85, due on May 1. You can readily understand that we must now assume that failure to pay is deliberate.

Unless we receive full payment by July 3, we shall be forced to turn your account over to our attorney (Legal Department, Collection Agency) for collection.

Please do not make it necessary for us to take this disagreeable step.

Very truly yours,

Analysis. Did you notice how the complimentary closing changed to fit the letter tone? Look at the salutation for the last letter. Note that the amount due was specifically stated in each letter. Were you conscious of the appeal to the pride of the delinquent customer? Could you feel, as well as see, the increasing severity of the wording?

Do not jump to the conclusion that the writing of Letter 4 means no more orders from Mr. Porter. If he is the sort of person who has the audacity to try to get goods without paying for them, he will have the boldness to try it again once his bill is paid. Let us watch out for him and put his future purchases on a cash or C.O.D. basis.

Summary. Because more than 75 per cent of all business is done on a credit basis, the business correspondent must be an expert in the writing of credit and collection letters. As far as credit is concerned, he must know:

1. How credit is established.
2. How to write letters granting credit.
3. How to write letters refusing credit.
4. How to give credit information.
5. How to write collection letters.
6. How to write the many other letters that fit into the credit picture.

In addition to being able to write letters that will build up and retain credit business, he must be able to write the kind of collection letters that will bring in the money and make charge-account business profitable. Mastery of the techniques of writing superior credit and collection letters will place the correspondent very near the top in his profession.

Student: In the following assignments, you are to supply suitable addresses.

Assignment 1. Robert E. McCaffery has given your name as a credit reference. He has been a customer of yours for ten years and has always paid his bills promptly. Write the reply to the request for credit information.

Assignment 2. Mrs. E. F. Jeffrey has applied to your store for charge-account privileges. You have investigated her references and found that she is just the kind of customer you want. Write and tell her so.

Assignment 3. Jensen Manufacturing Company has sent you two orders accompanied with checks. You have made some discreet inquiries and have learned that the firm is a good credit risk. You would like to add them to your accounts receivable list. Write and invite them to open an account with you.

Assignment 4. Boling Products has written asking to open an account with your firm. You have investigated and found that their credit rating is poor. Write a letter refusing them credit.

Assignment 5. George T. Dumont has given your name as a credit reference. He has always paid you, but never on time. While you still keep him on your books, you consider him "slow pay." Write the reply to the request for reference.

Assignment 6. You write letters for a department store. Mrs. Thomas F. Lawson has been a very good customer, but for the last three months she has purchased very little. Write a letter designed to build up her account.

Assignment 7. Write John B. Kent a letter asking why he has not used his charge-account privilege recently.

Assignments 8, 9, 10, 11. In Assignment 3, you wrote Jensen Manufacturing Company offering them credit privileges. They accepted, and their references were good. But there must have been a slip somewhere, for they have not paid the $629.41 due on the first charge order they gave you. Write them the four collection letters.

Assignment 12. You want to buy a television set. Although you do not have the ready money, you do have the required amount in the form of government bonds. The problem that faces you is whether to buy on credit or to sell your bonds and pay cash. Figure the amount of interest you are getting on your bonds and then find out how much the carrying charges would be. Subtract and see how much more the carrying charges are. Report the figures to the class.

Now, think of the length of time it took you to get together the money to buy the bonds. If you cash them, you will have to work a long time before you can build up this capital again. So you decide to buy on credit. Write a letter asking to purchase on a deferred-payment plan.

LESSON **75**

Claim and Adjustment Letters

Have you been perfectly satisfied with everything in your life so far? Of course not, and nobody else has, either. An entirely un-ruffled existence is impossible for human beings.

Just as impossible is it to carry on a business without making or receiving claims caused by dissatisfaction, however efficient the business may be. Since many claims are made and received by mail, the business letter writer has to know how to write the letters that make claims and the letters that adjust claims. Composing these letters is a very delicate job; and the correspondent must have special training in order to save money, keep customers, and continue to build good will. The purpose of this lesson is to provide that special training.

Claim letters are those that we write when *we* are dissatisfied. They used to be called "complaints," but that word now is in such disfavor that every effort is made to avoid using it. Confidentially, though, claim letters are complaint letters.

Adjustment letters are the letters we write in reply to a claim that has been received. The correspondent who can write superior adjustment letters will be invaluable to his company, for he will be able to turn a dissatisfied customer into a satisfied customer. A satis-fied customer represents continued sales, but a dissatisfied customer stands for nothing but lost business.

Let us learn how to write peerless claim and adjustment letters.

Claim Letters

When we write a claim letter, we shall be particular to express ourselves clearly, completely, and concisely. If we cannot present our claim well, the adjuster will be unable to do his work until more letters have been exchanged. This word of warning is needed here because few people have the ability to present facts clearly.

Let us learn how to state our case and how to ask for an adjustment. Only a good-will claim letter will result in a prompt and cheerful adjustment. Whenever we are dissatisfied with merchandise, bills, or service, we shall write a letter that can be easily understood and that is polished in tone and careful in wording.

Tone.   Never will we write a claim letter when we are angry. Anger, to some degree, is always present when we are dissatisfied; and a claim letter is an expression of dissatisfaction. We do not, however, need to write an ungracious or rude letter. A very natural impulse is to write a scorcher that plainly shows how we feel. An opening paragraph like this:

You ought to be proud of that bunch of junk you sent us on our order No. 465

would probably relieve our feelings, but it would be contrary to acceptable business conduct. We are too courteous and too well trained to descend to sarcasm.

Most of our claim letters will be written to vendors. Look back at Lesson 63 and reread the section that tells what vendors can do for us. Remember that they are not going to do anything extra for us if we write them caustic letters.

Wording.   The positive, friendly, courteous tone that we seek is achieved by using gracious, positive words and wording. Obviously, we must avoid the negative. That is why *complaint* becomes *suggestion* or *claim* or why *criticism* becomes an *analysis of the situation.*

We demand; we must insist; you will have to; unless you do thus and so, we will have to; you must—all are illustrations of the wrong way to ask for an adjustment. If you were the adjuster and received a letter containing any one of those arrogant demands for settlement, how fast would you move to satisfy the customer? You would be much more likely to exert yourself if the wording were: *we feel that we are justified, I know that you will agree, you have always co-operated so well in the past that, your reputation for good service is so well known that. . . .*

Merchandise Claim. Probably most of our claim letters will be about merchandise—wrong items, size, color, weight; damaged condition; failure to wear well. Vendors realize that, if the merchandise they sell to us is not exactly right, our customers will make claims on us. In turn, we expect the vendor to "cover" us on all adjustments. We shall find that the great majority of vendors will adjust claims fairly.

The following illustration is that of a letter that claims an adjustment as a matter of course. Note the positive, gracious tone.

Gentlemen:

We have today returned on our debit memorandum No. S3928 two men's brown corduroy sport coats. One coat has a hole on the left shoulder; the other has a misweave on the right shoulder.

Our buyers have often remarked on the fact that few imperfect pieces of goods pass your inspectors; so we know that this is an unusual happening. Please credit the coats to our account.

Sincerely yours,

Not quite so easy to write would be a letter concerning goods that did not wear well. Suppose that we did receive such merchandise and suppose that we have already adjusted four claims made on us. We want the vendor to make the same adjustment with us. We write:

Gentlemen:

We have sold all the merchandise on our order No. 4734, and our customers are now telling us that the shirts lose body and become sleazy after the first laundering. Four claims already have been made; so it looks as though we shall have to settle for the entire shipment.

These first four claimants were well satisfied with a 25 per cent refund, amounting to $1 for each shirt. We, too, are going to be satisfied by receiving from you the amount refunded on all shirts in the order.

We made this settlement knowing full well that you would cover any loss connected with the sale of any of your merchandise.

Cordially yours,

Suppose that the manufacturer ignored the letter. This would happen rarely, but we must know that a second letter will be firmer in tone; as:

Gentlemen:

For lack of a reply to our letter of May 26, this is a second letter telling you about our order No. 4734.

The shirts did not stand up after the first laundering, and we have been giving a 25 per cent refund on each item, which amounts to $1 for each shirt. We wrote and asked you to cover us, dollar for dollar, on all adjustments.

We know that you will agree that the fair thing to do is to let us know immediately that you will prevent us from losing money on any merchandise you sell to us. We should dislike very much to have an incident like this disrupt our pleasant business relations.

Sincerely yours,

Money Claim. Some of our claim letters will be written about money matters. There might be an error in the total of our account. Maybe an agreed-upon discount is not allowed. Sometimes we may be charged for freight that should have been prepaid. Once in a while a mistake about terms of shipment will occur. Whenever we make a money claim, let us double check to be sure that all figures are correct.

The following letter illustrates a money claim.

Gentlemen:

Thank you for your statement of May 31. May we call your attention to a lack of agreement between the total of your statement and the total in our accounts payable?

We find that you do not credit us with the 25 cents deducted in our May 7 remittance for $35.21 net. You will probably recall that the 25 cents was for parcel-post insurance; but, since our orders carry a printed notation stating that parcel-post shipments should be made uninsured, we deducted that amount when we sent you our check.

We should very much appreciate receiving a corrected statement soon.

Sincerely yours,

Service Claim. Our claim letters about service subjects might be caused by: shipping delay, nonarrival of goods, shipping directions not followed, receipt of rude communications. The point to remember here is that service failure causes inconvenience, and inconvenience causes dissatisfaction and disappointment. Therefore, when we write these letters, we shall be watchful lest some trace of irritation creep into them. There is no slightest hint of anger in the following:

Gentlemen:

The dungarees on our order No. 7862 were purchased on March 30, to be completed April 15.

In the two weeks since April 15, we have had many calls for dungarees; and every day we wait means that we are losing business.

Because sales by us result in orders for you, we know that you will rush the merchandise the day you receive this letter.

Sincerely yours,

Adjustment Letters

The purpose of an adjustment letter is to satisfy the customer and to keep his business. Many correspondents dislike to write this type of letter because of the unpleasantness connected with it, but such letter writers are not very farseeing. If a customer is dissatisfied and does not make a claim, we may be sure that he will stop trading with us. Therefore, a claim letter gives us an opportunity to keep the customer; and claim letters should be welcomed. An adjustment letter is a sales letter; it sells satisfaction.

The adjustment letter will grant or refuse a claim or will make a partial settlement. Many firms have a set policy with regard to adjusting claims, and correspondents for these companies need only to follow the rules. A letter writer in his first position or starting to work for a different firm would be wise to let his supervisor make adjustment decisions.

Writers of the best adjustment letters are masters of tone and wording. They are so accomplished that they frequently become supervisors, and then they make decisions with regard to settlement of claims. Should we reach that important and responsible position, we must know that the first step in an adjustment is getting the facts and fixing the blame. Only then can we make an intelligent and a fair settlement. We should know that adjustments fall into four classes: when the seller is at fault; when the customer is at fault; when fault is divided between seller and customer; when a third party is at fault, such as a transportation company.

Tone and Wording. The wording of adjustment letters is of supreme importance. Our primary aim is to keep the customer; so masterpiece adjustment letters will retain business by granting warmly or by refusing so graciously that the customer loses his feeling of being wronged. A partial adjustment is usually satisfactory if the customer feels that he is getting a little the better of the bargain.

The elements of specialized wording for adjustment letters are: fast action, sympathy, fairness, elimination of negative wording.

Fast Action. The longer a customer remains dissatisfied, the stronger grows his feeling of grievance; and the fewer grow our chances for making a happy adjustment. The wording should show that we consider the customer and his claim important enough for immediate action. We might open the letter with:

The minute I finished reading your letter of June 23, I investigated and found that . . . .

Do you see the psychology behind such an opening? The customer is made to feel that he carries much weight with us, and the words put him in a receptive frame of mind. If the claim is granted, he will feel that we are wonderful people to deal with. If the claim is refused, the opening words pave the way for the refusal.

The fast-action note can be sounded anywhere in the letter; for example, some expressions like:

We lost no time in making inquiries about your . . . .

The replacement items are being shipped to you today, for we want you to have the goods just as soon as it is possible to get them to you.

Fast action means decisive action. We shall not spread the adjustment over several letters but will grant, refuse, or partially adjust in the first letter we write. A vague answer opens the way for an exchange of letters, and the customer will be annoyed and disgusted at having to dillydally before he knows where he stands.

If time will be needed in order to get the facts about a claim, a letter should be written giving the customer this information. The letter will contain a sentence like this:

We are right now investigating the nonarrival of your order No. 286, and we expect to write you fully within two days.

Sympathy. Nothing so mollifies an angry person as does an expression of sympathy. The customer who makes a claim is irritated to some degree and is probably ready to do battle. When he receives a letter that views his claim from his own point of view, he is completely disarmed. Sympathy does not mean abject self-blame, such as: our stupid mistake; the terrible blunder we made; our almost-unpardonable failure. Examples of positive sympathy are:

We know just how you feel about . . . .
You are so right about . . . .
Indeed we can understand that . . . .
Your point is well taken.
We ourselves have been in the same situation and . . . .

Fairness.   The sense of fairness of the people of the United States is well developed. We consider fair treatment our inalienable right, and even the suggestion of injustice leads to ill feeling. This is why a company policy with regard to adjustments is advisable, for similar claims should be settled in the same way. Granting an adjustment to one customer and refusing another customer when the cases are alike is very bad business.

We are unfair when we use wording like: *you claim; you say that; you assert; we cannot undertand,* or *we are at a loss to understand; you neglected; your failure to.* These expressions intimate that the customer is trying to bamboozle us, which is most unjust.

Elimination of Negative Wording.   The words we put together should be cheerful and positive. This effect can be achieved by refraining from the use of words that are actually negative or that give a negative impression. A study of the following illustrations will help us to use smooth, positive wording.

Positive: Thank you for your helpful letter of June 3.
Negative: We have received your complaint of June 3.

Positive: We are so glad that you called our attention to the late arrival of your order No. 4286.
Negative: We are sorry to hear of the unfortunate delay in the delivery of your order No. 4286.

Positive: Thank you for the friendly suggestion made in your letter of July 8.
Negative: Your July 8 criticism has been received.

Positive: We will check even more carefully than usual all your future orders.
Negative: Please accept our apologies for sending you unsatisfactory goods.

Positive: Our driver brought your parcel back to the store because the house number was omitted from the address.
Negative: Because of your failure to give us your house number, our driver had to bring back the parcel, thus delaying delivery for three days.

Strong: You will be glad to know that we are taking measures to insure prompt shipment of your future orders.

Weak: A delay of this kind will never happen again. (Weak because it is unbelievable)

Strong: We are sincerely happy to be of assistance; so please feel free to write us whenever we can be of help.

Weak: If this is not satisfactory, please let us know. (Raises a doubt in customer's mind)

Strong: We investigated immediately and found that . . . .

Weak: Our records show that . . . . (Meaningless and overworked)

Four Classes of Adjustments. We are studying business correspondence for the purpose of becoming so good at our work that we have a chance to advance to the position of supervisor. In that event, we shall have to make adjustment decisions; so let us learn how to make fair and business-retaining settlements. When we have the facts before us, we know who is at fault in each individual claim; and that knowledge is the basis for making the adjustment.

Seller at Fault. Whenever we are at fault, we must grant the claim; so let us not be grudging about it. Let us be gracious, for an ungracious letter would arouse just as much indignant displeasure as a refusal letter would. We cannot afford to write any letter other than the kind illustrated below.

Dear Mr. Doyle:

Thank you for reporting to us the incorrect spelling of your name on the soap you ordered.

You will be glad to know that a new order is being made up for you. On Tuesday, our driver will pick up the soap you wish to return and will deliver the substitute order within a week.

We will try very hard to see to it that you will not have to write another such letter.

Cordially yours,

Customer at Fault. Here is where we must put to use all our training. If the customer made a claim, he must have felt that he was justified or that he had a good chance of getting a satisfactory settlement. A "super" reply will be needed in order to make him feel that a refusal is fair.

We have all heard the slogan, "The customer is always right"; but a business would lose money by following through on the principle.

Obviously, the customer cannot be right all the time; so refusal letters are written in every adjustment department.

Suppose that a customer writes to tell us that he is returning goods for credit, and our investigation shows that he is trying to unload old stock. Do we "tell him off"? Indeed not! We write:

Gentlemen:

Thank you for the suggestion made in your letter of August 4.

We should like very much to give you credit for the twenty-four hassocks you returned to us, but we find that we have discontinued making this number and that our last shipment of hassocks was made to you six months ago. You can readily see that there is no hope of our disposing of the goods on a wholesale basis.

Would it be possible for you to cut your loss by running the hassocks as a Saturday lead special? Their sale at cost price should bring customers into your store.

We very much appreciate your giving us an opportunity to explain why it is necessary that we return the shipment to you.

Sincerely yours,

Sometimes we grant a claim when we know the customer to be at fault. The adjustment may cost so little that we prefer to make it and charge it to good will. In a case of this kind, we follow the rules for granting settlement—cheerful, gracious wording.

Suppose that we received the claim letter illustrated in this lesson under Money Claim. We find that the order referred to was not written on their printed form and that we were justified in shipping insured and charging for it. But for 25 cents would we run the risk of causing displeasure? We could buy good will cheaply by:

Gentlemen:

Thank you for calling our attention to the 25 cent insurance charge on our statement of May 31.

This amount has been deducted from your account; and complying with your request, we are enclosing a statement showing the deduction.

In the future we will be most careful not to insure your parcel-post shipments.

Cordially yours,

Divided Fault. Sometimes an assembling of the facts with regard to a claim shows that both the seller and the customer are at fault. Adjustment of a claim of this kind would involve cheerful acknowledgment of our fault and tactful mention of the fault of the customer. Some sort of give-and-take settlement should be proposed.

For illustrative purposes let us suppose that we sold Mrs. Jayne a fur jacket. She sent it back to us, together with a letter telling us how poorly it has worn. We find that its bedraggled appearance is due to the fact that she did not store the garment during the summer months. Investigating further, we find that we failed to send Mrs. Jayne our booklet on the care of fur coats. The fault is therefore divided, and we would probably adjust by writing:

Dear Mrs. Jayne:

You did just right in sending us your black kidskin jacket for examination.

Our fur expert has looked the coat over carefully, and he reports that the fine hairs are matted, which could have been caused by not storing the coat during the warm weather. There are no worn skins. He also tells us that our new cleaning and glazing process will make the coat just like new.

We should like very much to restore your jacket to its original condition; and we are prepared to do so at a cost of $15, a reduction of $10 on our price for this service. In addition, we will store your coat without charge for the coming summer.

These two offers are made because we think that we are partly to blame for the appearance of the coat. We find that we did not send you our booklet on the care of furs. Had we done so, you probably would not have had to return the garment for attention.

Just as soon as we receive authorization from you, we will proceed to make your jacket a coat that you will be proud to wear.

Cordially yours,

Third Party at Fault. Receipt of damaged goods or delay in receiving shipment may be the fault of the transportation company. Some sellers refer the customer to the carrier and ask the customer to press for settlement. This is a poor way to adjust a claim because the customer has to perform an extra task, thereby increasing dissatisfaction.

Usually there is a contract between seller and transportation company stating that the carrier is liable for all damage to goods while they are in his hands. Prompt, cheerful, and full adjustment can be made with the customer for damaged goods; and a claim can be

Assignment 11. Select five adjustment letters from your folder of sample letters or from illustrations in correspondence textbooks. In the form of an interoffice memorandum, analyze the letters. Quote any wording that you think is good and any wording that you think is poor.

LESSON **76**

Sales Letters

Every letter we write is a sales letter, for every letter sells merchandise, services, good will. While our slogan could well be "Every Letter a Sales Letter," we shall find, when we get on the job, that we shall be asked to write letters designed to sell some one particular product or service. These are the letters that we call *sales letters*.

We need to know and to be able to use the distinctive skills involved in writing sales letters because they can bring in orders as effectively as salesmen's visits—and at much less cost.

We might obtain a position with a firm that maintains a close and productive alliance between their correspondence and sales departments. Then our sales letters would increase volume by supplementing the work of the salesmen. A letter written before the salesman makes his call would pave the way for him. A letter written after the call might be just the "clincher" that would be needed to get the customer to send in his order.

To become really proficient in the writing of sales letters, we must study:

1. The relation between sales and human behavior.
2. The general principles applicable to sales letters.
3. The letter plan designed especially for sales letters.

Sales and Human Behavior

Purchases are made when the customer *needs* something or *wants* something. In the case of a need, no selling effort is required. If you break the handle of your toothbrush, you are going to buy another; and nobody has to convince you that you must do it immediately. Real selling is involved when the customer does not need, does not want, or does not realize that he wants. The money-making sales letter creates a want or increases a dimly felt desire. Perhaps we could say that the successful sales letter turns a want into a need.

Of course, now we want to know how we can induce the customer to feel that he cannot get along without our product. Well, we must in some way show him that he would be happier if he owned what we have to sell. This is the secret; for every person in the world, whether he knows it or not, seeks happiness. The promotion of happiness, however, means different things to different people. That is why we are going to study the varied emotions and desires to which we can appeal when writing our sales letters; as:

Pride. Pride takes different forms—pride in self, in possessions, in family. Maybe an appeal to pride would make a sales letter productive. For instance, if we are selling men's wearing apparel, a sentence like this would appeal to self-pride: "SUCCESS is written all over the man who wears one of our suits." If we are selling a wax finish for automobiles, we might appeal to pride in possessions by writing: "Your car will shine like new." Should we be selling an electric toaster, we could bring in the family by writing: "Even the children will enjoy using the Brownquik toaster."

Thrift. Not everyone is thrifty, but for some reason everyone likes to think that he is economical. That is why store sales are so successful. Shoppers will buy articles for which they have absolutely no use and will justify themselves with: "I just couldn't afford to pass it up at that price." In a sales letter, the thrift appeal might be just the push that is needed to edge the customer to the buying point. We might be selling outside paint and somewhere in the letter we write: "Our outside paint carries a five-year guarantee. To you this means five years without paint-upkeep bills."

Comfort. In the sales of many products an appeal can be made to the desire for comfort or for the saving of labor. Look at furniture, mattress, furnace, soap powder, and various household appliance advertisements. See how they use the increase-in-comfort approach.

To illustrate, let us pretend that we are selling power lawn mowers. Now the average man comes home tired and hot after his day's work. If he has a lawn, the grass must be cut; and, if he uses a hand cutter, you can imagine how he must dread that summer job. In our sales letter, we capitalize on the desire for comfort by writing something like this: "Just start the motor and let it do the work. Your part in the operation will consist of gentle exercise in the fresh air."

Pleasure. "All work and no play" is not the rule for most of us, and that is as it should be. The well-balanced life includes provision for pleasure. It may be that the product we sell can make life more enjoyable. If so, let us stress this fact.

If we are selling television sets, we might use the pleasure appeal to bring action. We could write: "See the news as it happens. Enjoy good musicals, plays, sporting events—right in your own living room!"

Fear. The motive for purchasing some goods or services might be fear. "Scare" selling methods are used by fur-storage operators, by the sellers of mothproofing agents, by fire and accident insurance companies. If our merchandise or service will prevent partial or total loss, we shall probably sell by appealing to the customer's fear of loss.

For instance, an accident insurance policy might be sold by using this question in the opening paragraph: "Who pays the bills when you are out of work?"

Appetite. The need for food is one of the basic human drives, and food products are sold by strengthening that drive. This is done by using such vivid descriptive words that the customer can almost taste the product. Food, then, is sold by making a "mouth-watering" appeal. The deep-freeze operator selling packaged steaks refers to them as "thick, juicy steaks." The manufacturer of bottled sauce sells "tangy, zestful sauce." The makers of pie-crust mix sell "pie crust that melts in your mouth."

Security. Another need that we humans have is the need for security, protection. We shall keep this in mind; and, when we are composing a sales letter, let us see whether ownership of our goods will increase security. Do we sell locks of any kind? Lightning rods? Safes or strongboxes? Annuities? If so, let us point out the security value.

Suppose we sell strongboxes. For our main selling point we could use: "Your valuable papers will be safe when you own one of our fireproof strongboxes, equipped with a combination lock."

Health. As an indication of the pulling power of health as a sales appeal, think of the thousands of advertisements that use this spur. Think of all the soaps, detergents, shampoos, toothpastes that maintain health through cleanliness. Read or listen to cigarette advertisements and see how the manufacturers try to show that there will be no damage to health for the users of their brands. Notice how many cold, headache, cough remedies are manufactured. We are more health conscious than any other nation in the world.

Could we use interest in health to make a sale? Suppose that we sell children's shoes. Knowing that the right kind of shoes will promote foot health and knowing that ours are the right kind, we could write: "Strong, healthy growing feet belong to children who wear BUCKSKIN shoes."

General Principles

The writer of a good sales letter must have training that will make for effective selling by teaching him the skills he can apply and the pitfalls that he must avoid. We refer to this kind of training as the general principles that apply particularly to sales letters, and they are:

Know Your Product. The sales-letter specialist must be enthusiastic about the goods he sells. "First sell yourself; then sell others" is an old adage, but it is so true that it is worth quoting here. The enthusiasm that empowers a correspondent to generate eagerness to buy comes from a thorough knowledge of the item he sells. The writer must study the merchandise, must know what it will do for the buyer. If he does not really feel that the customer would be happier if he bought our product, the correspondent will be totally unable to write a sales letter that will be successful.

Know Your Competitors' Products. A study of our own sales item is not enough. We must study the like products that are manufactured by other companies. We can never hope to meet competition unless we know what the competition is. Once we have found the good points in the other fellow's specialty, we shall know wherein ours is different or better. This knowledge will help us write better sales letters.

Know Your Customers.   While all customers are interested in the price of goods, some want *quality* and price and others want *quantity* and price. We have studied our product; so we should know to what type of customer our sales item would appeal. If we are selling an article of name-brand furniture, we shall play up the quality of that merchandise with the full knowledge that prospective buyers will be those whose income is fairly good. On the other hand, if we are selling neckties at a package rate—six for $4.98—we shall gear our letter to appeal to buyers whose income is not so high and who want a great deal for their money.

Results of a customer survey show that a sales letter that arrives on a Tuesday brings the best results. We can only speculate on the reason for this. Possibly Monday is poor because the customer is recovering from the week end. Later days of the week are probably taken up by the many demands of his work, and a sales letter would get little attention.

Let us study an illustration of a sales letter written to appeal to customers who want quantity at a price.

A DIFFERENT TIE FOR EVERY DAY OF THE WEEK can be yours for less than 80 cents a tie.

Plain colors, stripes, plaids, prints, in beautiful materials—ties to suit all tastes. Do you need a conservative tie to go with that striped suit? Do you want a startling tie to perk up that dark, plain suit? We offer you a varied selection at below-budget price.

Examine the enclosed samples, select any seven of them, and send the samples with your order. Think of it! You can own *seven different ties* for only $5.50.

Delay in placing your order might mean losing the opportunity of a lifetime. We expect a fast sellout, for we are making this special offer to men who know value when they see it.

SUPERIOR TIE COMPANY

Please check the following form, enclose samples, and send to us—TODAY!
C.O.D. order—purchaser pays postage . . . .
Cash order—postage prepaid . . . .

Letter Setup.   A one-page sales letter is considered more effective than a two-page letter. This makes sense, for most customers will not take time to wade through a lot of words. They will probably read the first paragraph and then toss the letter into the wastebasket.

Principles of good advertising are used in sales letters, and these include the emphasizing of important sales points. By letter, we can bring out certain words or thoughts by using all caps, underscoring, exclamation points, dashes, asterisks, and color.

The use of color in the sales letter is a debatable question. A sales letter is designed to get attention, and many writers use color for that reason. There is the danger, however, of making the letter so startling in appearance that the message is lost.

We can safely say that the real sales-letter expert is so good at his job that he can achieve selling success by word manipulation.

Picture-Making Words. The sales-letter specialist has the ability to use words that make the reader see himself using the product. This expert has a command of descriptive adjectives, and he knows the importance of the "you" attitude.

When the proficient writer sells food products, he writes in such a way that the reader's mouth waters. If he is selling vacation trips, he uses words that make the reader actually see himself relaxing on the beach or pulling fish out of some quiet stream. If he sells a household appliance, such as a washing machine, he writes: "Just one flick of a button and your washday troubles are over. No worry, no timing—the LIGHTNING shuts off automatically." The words start a chain of pictures in the housewife's mind. Possibly she will see herself out chatting with a neighbor while the machine is doing the drudgery. She might see herself downtown shopping or out on the links playing golf. Whatever she sees, the picture will show the substitution of pleasure for perspiration.

Pitfalls. The beginning correspondent may be so enthusiastic about his goods that he will fall into the error of being wildly extravagant in his statements. Many seasoned writers also think that successful selling depends on such exaggerations as: *gigantic, colossal, stupendous, terrific, world-shaking.* As a matter of fact, consistent overuse of words like these will destroy sales possibilities. The intelligent customer will laugh at them.

There is very real danger in making outsized claims for our merchandise. While some latitude is given to such sales statements as "best on the market," "never before in history," a claim may be challenged and may have to be proved. Buyers are protected by law; and, if we make a false statement, we are liable for legal action. This, of course, is another reason for knowing what our product can and cannot do for the customer.

Another pitfall that will swallow the unwary is the writing of anything that can be construed as "knocking" a competitor. Yes, we have studied the products manufactured by competitors, but it was for the purpose of knowing what we were up against when trying to sell our own product. Remember that nobody ever advanced an inch by trying to push someone else down that inch. Any slurring of a competitor or his goods can result only in the loss of respect. Rather let us write something like this: "The Pushbutton is a good washer. However, we think the LIGHTNING gives more pleasure and satisfaction because it . . . ."

Follow-up Sales Letters.   Sometimes the writing of sales letters becomes a campaign. If no action results from the first letter, a second is written. As many as six, eight, or more letters may be sent. The number of follow-up letters that are to be written in a series will depend on the product, the cost, and the market. Therefore, special instructions probably will be given for each campaign.

Each follow-up letter will try to make the sale by varying the appeal. The opening paragraph of each successive letter should be so constructed that the writing of the letter seems to be a natural thing to do. For instance, suppose that we sell name plates for house doors. When writing a follow-up, we might say: "Since we wrote you on June 2 telling you about Distinction Name Plates, four more of your fellow townsmen have purchased them." On the face of it, we are telling the customer some news. Actually, we are appealing to his pride, to his desire to "keep up with the Joneses."

The correspondent who knows the principles that apply to the writing of sales letters will be able to write as many follow-up letters as are required.

Plan of Sales Letter

The plan for sales letters consists of four steps:

1. Get in touch with the reader. Make him want to read the rest of the letter.

2. Create or strengthen desire.

3. Convince the reader that it would be to his advantage to purchase.

4. Get action.

Before using the letter plan, however, we must outline our plan of action for each letter. We must decide what sales appeal or appeals we are going to use and what selling feature of the product we are going to stress. Only then are we ready to use the letter plan.

Get in Touch with the Reader. This is the function of the first paragraph. Here we must excite curiosity, or start a train of thought, or attract attention in some way. Sample openings are:

> They said it couldn't be done, but we did it! [Excite curiosity.]
> Other women find time to spend with their children, and so can you. [Start train of thought.]
> How would you like to be the best-dressed man in town—without any strain on your budget? [Attract attention.]

Create or Strengthen Desire. Now that we have written such a good first paragraph that the customer reads on, let us heighten his interest by using a sales appeal that will make him want to own our product. We use our picture-making words to show him the beauty and usefulness of the article and to make him actually see himself using it.

Just for the sake of illustration, let us suppose that we are writing to a woman about our linoleum rugs. We used the "spend time with the children" first paragraph. Now we continue with:

> Our SPOTLESS linoleum rugs can be purchased in beautiful floral patterns that will bring out the color of your rooms or in designs that resemble hardwood flooring. Cleaning will be a pleasure when you own a SPOTLESS, for a single whisk of the mop makes your house just like the name of the linoleum—spotless! And the time saved will allow you to give your children the attention they want and need.

Convince the Reader. If we have done our work well so far, the reader is already half convinced. You know how readily anybody can find reasons for buying what he wants to buy. Nevertheless, our job now is to show the customer how it will be to his advantage to own the product. The idea is to convince him that he really cannot afford not to buy it.

Continuing the letter about the linoleum rug, we shall provide Mrs. Housewife with some arguments that she can use on her husband:

All this beauty and leisure time will be yours for only $17.98 cash, or $1.60 a month for twelve months; and you get a 9-by-12 rug that will be a delight to the whole family. The SPOTLESS five-year guarantee brings the average daily cost down to less than one cent. Pretty cheap for gracious living, isn't it?

Get Action.   Now we have arrived at the last paragraph. There would be no point in our writing a fine sales letter, creating desire and convincing the reader, if nothing happened. Maybe we could get action by enclosing a return envelope. Maybe the customer is a little short of money right now and would be interested in time payments. Maybe we could use the good old "Act now before it is too late. These gadgets are going like wildfire!" method of getting action.

The action-getting paragraph for our rug might read:

You do not have to write us a letter. Just check the enclosed order blank, sign it, and mail it to us. In less than a week's time, the rug will be on your floor; and you will be sitting out in the sunshine.

Watch the construction of this last paragraph lest it backfire like the one written by the laundryman who was trying to sell his service:

Don't kill your wife. Let us do your dirty work for you.

Below is an illustration of a sales letter. We are pretending that the correspondence material you are now studying is contained in a separate text and that it is yet unpublished. We write the letter to get advance orders and to pave the way for our salesmen. We hope that, because of this letter, some teacher, principal, or superintendent will say to one of our representatives, "Tell me more about the new correspondence text that is coming out in January."

Dear Mr. Crouch:

Learning can be fun! And fun can result in better education when the subject is business correspondence and the text used is *The English of Correspondence*—publication date, January of 19—.

Students will learn more and teachers will enjoy teaching with the aid of this book because of its:

Sound Business Psychology. The student is taken behind the scenes and shown how business operates. When his study has been completed, he will know how to write excellent business letters; and he also will have received a thorough grounding in business science.

Comprehensive Coverage. Pupils will learn how to write every type of business letter. Unusual treatment is given to everyday letters, to refusal letters, to social-business letters, and to the writing of reports. The types of letters that are standards for correspondence texts are presented in an interesting and entirely new manner.

Conversational Tone. The reader, whether student or teacher, will feel that this book was written especially for and to him. He will feel as though he were entertaining a visitor in his own home. Reading is easy; learning sticks.

Many Use Situations. Each lesson contains many opportunities to practice the principles taught. The assignments are carefully thought out and approximate as closely as possible real business situations. There is no "busy work."

All this adds up to an exciting and educative learning-teaching experience.

Your order, written on the back of this letter, will insure you priority at the time of publication. Be the first with the best!

Very sincerely yours,

Summary. Sales letters are letters that concentrate on the selling of individual items of merchandise or the selling of some particular service. The sales-letter specialist becomes an expert when he has studied the relation between sales and human behavior, when he knows the principles behind the writing of fine sales letters, and when he has studied and learned how to use skillfully the sales letter plan.

Assignment 1. Study advertisements for ten different products. In the form of an interoffice memorandum, name the products and state the sales appeal or appeals used in each advertisement.

Assignment 2. Can you think of any good, psychological appeals that were not used in the ten advertisements studied for the previous assignment? You will have to be very keen to do this, for advertisements are written by highly paid specialists. Write your teacher a letter telling him of any appeals that the advertisements could have used but failed to use. If you cannot think of any, just write a letter telling your teacher exactly that.

Assignment 3. Write a letter to Mr. Joseph F. Weston, Sales Manager, Universal Department Stores, telling him what sales appeals could be used to induce *you* to buy. Pleasure would probably be the first appeal on your list.

Assignment 4. Your firm manufactures an electric refrigerator, and you are in charge of all sales letters that deal with this item. Make a study of three leading electric refrigerators now on the market. In the form of an interoffice memorandum, name the refrigerators and state the features that make strong selling points.

Assignment 5. Think of some improvement or of some new and different feature that would promote the sales of your product. Write a letter to your teacher telling him about the difference between your refrigerator and the others that you have studied.

Assignment 6. In the form of an interoffice memorandum, list the human desires to which you could appeal when writing sales letters about your refrigerator.

Assignment 7. Write a letter to your teacher stating the points you are going to use in order to convince your prospect.

Assignment 8. Outline a sales letter that you would write for the purpose of selling your refrigerator.

Assignment 9. Write the letter outlined in Assignment 8.

Assignment 10. You have received no reply to the letter written in Assignment 9. Write a follow-up letter.

Assignment 11. Analyze ten sales letters written by your classmates for Assignment 9. Report your findings in the form of an interoffice memorandum. If time permits, you might report to the class and lead a discussion of your analysis.

LESSON **77**

Application Letters

We have been studying how to write letters that will increase profits for our employer. Now let us study the letter that will mean profit or a livelihood for *us*—the letter of application.

When we write an application letter, we are composing the most important sales letter of our lives. We are trying to sell ourselves and our services. At some time in the future, the ability to write a superior letter may represent for us the difference between eating and not eating.

America is known as the land of opportunity, but it could well be called the land of lost opportunities. So many people, through lack of interest or lack of understanding, fail to prepare to take advantage of an opportunity when it presents itself.

Unfortunately, young people are the outstanding opportunity-losers, as witness the fact that very few people can write an accepta-ble letter of application. Certainly, teachers all over the country have endeavored to teach well this phase of correspondence; but the results, alas, have been poor. Probably the reason is that students are not aware that this momentous sales letter may be a key that will unlock the door to success.

Well, we understand the importance of learning how to write a good application letter; so let us start to work for ourselves.

Purpose of the Letter. The main purpose of the letter of applica-tion is to make so good an impression that the prospective employer cannot wait to interview us. In order to achieve such an effect, we must sell him the idea that we have so much to offer that he will get more than his money's worth if he hires us.

Perhaps we should understand that our letter will move the

451

employer to make an interview appointment only if it is original and well written. We should be very foolish to copy our letter from any book—even this book. We shall accomplish our purpose by learning and applying the principles taught in the following sections of this lesson.

Appearance of the Letter. You would be surprised if you knew how few application letters are actually read by the person who receives them. If a quick glance at the envelope shows incorrect placement of the address, poor typing, crooked stamp, or smudges, that letter will very probably be tossed into the wastebasket without being opened. The remaining letters will be screened in the same way, and only those that meet the appearance test will be read.

It behooves us, therefore, to be sure that our letters are written on good bond paper, that they are immaculately clean, that they are attractively set up, and that our typing is perfect.

Tone of the Letter. The tone of our application letter will depend on our judgment and on our knowledge of the firm to which we are applying.

If we write to obtain a position with a firm that we know to be conservative, we should be unwise to use a modern or very unusual approach. You see, the reader would think us pert and would believe that we would not fit into his office atmosphere. On the other hand, this same tone, when used in writing to an ultraprogressive company, might strike just the right note.

Now suppose that we know nothing about the firm. Our letter should be conservative enough to impress those who prefer established ways of doing things and original enough to appeal to those who like to keep ahead of the times. This last may be accomplished by a good, but different, letter setup.

Our choice of salutation and complimentary closing will contribute much to our letter tone. If we are writing to a company or writing in answer to a "blind" advertisement, an advertisement that gives a box number as the address, we shall use *Gentlemen*. In writing to an individual, whether to use *Dear Sir* or *Dear Mr. . . . .* is a matter for the exercising of our judgment. *Dear Sir* is conservative, *Dear Mr. . . . .* is friendly and modern.

Respectfully yours was once the standard closing for all letters of application, but now we think it a little humble. This is just as well;

for, if we do not use it, we shall not make what was the common error of writing *Respectively* for *Respectfully*. *Very truly yours* or *Yours very truly* would be formal enough, but *Very sincerely yours* would warm up the letter.

We shall be sure to sign the letter and to type the heading. Failure to do so may destroy all our efforts to develop good letter tone.

Plan of the Letter. Our letter of application must contain the information that the businessman wants, and that information must be arranged according to a logical plan. The paragraphs of the letter, therefore, should follow this order:

1. Opening paragraph
2. Education
   Optional: Extracurricular activities
3. Experience
4. References
5. Closing paragraph

Whether or not the "Optional" paragraph is to be used is something for us to decide in planning each letter. Modern businessmen are becoming increasingly aware of the value of extracurricular participation for training students in industriousness, initiative, dependability, and working and playing with people.

1. Opening Paragraph. Remember that we are writing a sales letter and that the opening paragraph must create a desire for the product—in this case, our services. In addition, the first paragraph of the application letter should contain a stated request to be considered an applicant plus a statement of the source of information about the vacancy.

The chief sources of information are classified advertisements, a person who may be known or unknown to the employer, and a general rumor of a vacancy. Occasionally, we may write a letter of application because we should like to obtain a position with that particular concern, and we wish our application to be on file.

In these opening paragraphs, the range in tone is from conservative to progressive.

Please consider me an applicant for the stenographic position advertised in yesterday's *Evening Times*.

Miss Ferris, who is head of our business department, tells me that you have an opening in your office for a junior bookkeeper. I should like to apply for this position.

If there is a vacancy in your office for an exceptionally accurate clerical worker, may I be considered an applicant?

I understand that you are looking for a stenographer who can type at the rate of 60 words a minute; who can take dictation at 120 words a minute; who can transcribe quickly, neatly, and accurately; and who has a sound English and correspondence background. I should like to apply for this position, for I feel confident that I have these qualifications.

2. Education. We should be missing a real opportunity if we used this paragraph for a dull recitation of the subjects we studied in school instead of presenting our education facts in such a way that the employer will know that we are fitted for the job. We who are trained shall stress those subjects that qualify us for the particular position for which we are applying. We shall mention any awards or honors received. We shall try to bring in naturally the information that our health is good, an important point in this day of high costs caused by absenteeism. We shall remember that the school graduates us and say "I shall be graduated" or "I was graduated." Study the following illustration:

I shall be graduated from the Millbrook School in June of this year. Records will show that I was on the honor roll and that I was absent from school only ten days while enrolled there. I completed the secretarial course requirements and received awards for typing at the rate of 60 words a minute and for taking dictation at 120 words a minute. My English and correspondence grades are well above average.

Extracurricular Activities (Optional). If we think that the employer will be interested in knowing that we are social beings, we shall list our extracurricular efforts, state the offices we held, and show why we think the activities important.

While at school, I participated in many extracurricular activities, such as the dramatic club, business club, school paper. I was editor in chief of the paper and president of the business club. These activities have added to my store of knowledge, for I learned to understand people and to work well with others. I also had an opportunity to exercise my own judgment and initiative.

3. Experience. We must never omit this paragraph, nor must we cover the subject by "I have had no experience." Surely, if you do a little thinking, you will discover that you have done *something* in your life that would be regarded as experience. Maybe the only thing you have to offer is part-time work as a stock clerk in a retail store. Well, all right! That is experience, but the employer may not consider it so unless you show him the relation between a good stock clerk and a good office worker. You might say:

> For two years I have worked part time as stock clerk for the Gorham Stores. I think that this experience will help to make me a good office clerical worker because I know how to follow directions and how to get out the most work in the least time.

4. References. One thing we shall always do is ask permission before using a name as a reference. Once we have obtained permission, we shall list the names of three persons, none of whom are relatives, who can testify about our character and working ability. The applicant for a first position might like to give the name of a teacher who can tell how well the applicant did in school and in extracurricular work. To show that we know enough to ask for reference permission, we might start this paragraph with, "I am permitted to refer you to . . . ." or "With permission, I refer you to . . . ."

The complete and correct address should be given for each reference, together with any titles the references may have. Carelessness here might lose us the job.

5. Closing Paragraph. Why are we writing our letter of application? To get a chance to talk with the employer, of course. Then, once more applying the principles of a good sales letter, we shall use the last paragraph of an application letter to stimulate action. We must write something that will make it easy for our businessman to make an interview appointment at once; as:

> I should very much appreciate the opportunity of talking with you whenever it may be convenient for you. My telephone number is WE-5228.

May I talk with you and tell you more about the services I have to offer? My telephone number is BU-3523.

My telephone number is ST-53967, and a call from your secretary will bring me to your office at any time of the day.

Now let us make it really easy for the employer to give us an interview. Let us get a postal card, address it to ourselves, and type on the back:

Mr. Jones will see Janet Keegan on . . . . at . . . . . . o'clock.

Then our last paragraph will read:

I am enclosing a self-addressed postal card that you may use to make an appointment when convenient for you.

Two Letters of Application

Address of Applicant
Date

Mr. Edward J. Ainsworth
Personnel Director
Hartem Plastics
Milford, Iowa

Dear Mr. Ainsworth:

May I be considered an applicant for the clerical position advertised in yesterday's *Daily Sun?*

I shall be graduated from Acme Business School in June; and I have taken all the subjects in the general clerical course, which includes penmanship, filing, typing, and record keeping. My school record shows above-average grades and an attendance report in which I take a great deal of pride.

To mention a few of my extracurricular activities, I was a member of the Student Council, the Business Club, and the Dramatics Club. The position of treasurer of the Business Club was the most interesting office I held. Participation in these activities is important to me, and I think to you, because I have learned much about getting along with other people, about co-operating on a job, and about standing on my own two feet.

The clerical work I have done in the school office for the past six months was the try-out period that proved to me that I would be happy in a clerical position.

With regard to my character and ability, I am permitted to refer you to:

The Reverend John F. Keaton
Christ Episcopal Church
Telephone: 9876

Miss Lillian K. Dunn
Acme Business School
Telephone: Home, 834

Mr. Jay M. Ash, Principal
Milford High School
Telephone: Home, 342
School, 465

School, 156

I should like very much to tell you more about my qualifications and about the services I think I can give you. May I have an appointment? My telephone number is 684.

Very sincerely yours,

(Signature)

Perhaps we could make our letter more attractive and easier to read by setting it up this way:

Your Telephone Number

Your Address
Date

Mr. Peter E. Bessette
Personnel Manager
Burley Manufacturing Company
Springfield, Colorado

Dear Mr. Bessette:

Your advertisement in today's *Daily Times* lists an opening for a junior bookkeeper. I should like to apply for this position, because I believe that I have the qualifications, the aptitude, and the liking for work that would suit you. My qualifications are:

Education. I was graduated last week from Modern Training School, where I majored in bookkeeping and accounting. I was able to maintain a high "B" average in all bookkeeping subjects, which may be due partly to the fact that I lost no time by being absent.

Extracurricular. You might be interested to know that I learned how to work well with other people, how to use my own judgment, and how to carry out orders by belonging to the Bookkeeping Club, the Hobby Club, and the Journalism Club at school. Since last November, I have written the school column for our town newspaper.

Experience. For the past two years, I have worked as cashier and bookkeeper for my father, who is a general contractor in this city. I was the only bookkeeper he had; so I was charged with the entire responsibility of keeping his records straight and of making reports.

References. I am permitted to refer you to: my pastor, The Reverend Mark J. Carson, 27 Elm Street, telephone—8246; a man with whom my father does business, Mr. Paul M. Stark, Plant Building, telephone—4646; and my bookkeeping teacher, Mr. Robert Hastings, Modern Training School, telephone—9175.

I should like to have an opportunity to tell you more about what services I am prepared to give you. I am enclosing a self-addressed postal card on which you can jot down the day and the time for an appointment.

Very sincerely yours,

Enclosure   (Signature)

Personal Data Sheet. Businessmen are busy men, and they appreciate anything that will make their work easier. Many of them prefer that a letter of application contain a personal data sheet. This is simply a listing of the personal qualities, the education, skills, experience, and references in tabulated form.

After studying the illustration of the data sheet, we might like to use this form for our own letters of application. We must remember that a letter always accompanies the data sheet. In the letter, we attempt to do the selling job; and we offer the sheet as statistical proof. If we decide to include a photograph, we shall paste it in the upper left-hand corner of the paper.

Here is an illustration of a letter that is sent with a data sheet.

Your Address
Date

Mr. Edward J. Martin
Personnel Manager
Brown & Fox
Paris, Ohio
Dear Mr. Martin:

I understand that there is an opening in your Mail Order Department for a clerk-typist. Please consider me an applicant for that position.

I should like very much to work in your store, and I believe that you would be well satisfied with the speed and the quality of my production. The enclosed data sheet lists my qualifications in detail.

A data sheet gives facts, but a personal interview tells a great deal more. If you will have your secretary call PA-8524, I shall be very happy to meet any appointment time that she may set.

Very sincerely yours,

(Signature)

Initials
Enclosure

Illustration of personal data sheet enclosed with preceding letter:

Elizabeth M. Crowley
627 Boulder Drive
Canton, Ohio
Telephone: 6842

Personal
Age: 18
Birthplace: Canton, Ohio
Height and weight: 5′ 6″, 115 pounds
Health: Excellent, absent from school four days in four years

Education
Graduate of Canton High School, 19—
Ranked in upper quarter of class
Attending Blank Business School evenings
"A" grades in typing, English, correspondence, record keeping, operation of duplicating machines

Extracurricular
Typist, school annual
Corresponding Secretary, Student Council
Chairman, school assemblies committee
Member, intramural basketball team

Experience
Salesperson, Christmas holidays, Benson Stores
Student secretary to two members of high school faculty

References (with permission)
The Reverend Luke Carter, Pastor, First Baptist Church
Mr. Joseph E. White, Section Manager, Benson Stores
Mr. Woodrow Douville, Teacher, Canton High School

Application Form. Many personnel directors require an applicant to fill out an application blank, even if a letter of application has been received. This requirement may simplify a filing problem. Perhaps the interviewer likes to have the form before him when he talks to the applicant, for his practiced eye can select very quickly

(Do Not Write In This Box)		
INTERVIEWED BY_____	PERSONNEL RELATIONS DEPARTMENT	DATE OF APPLICATION *May 6, 19--*
DATE EMPLOYED_____	**EMPLOYMENT APPLICATION**	SALARY DESIRED *$55*
DEPARTMENT_____		
POSITION_____	POSITION APPLIED FOR *Editorial Secretary* / *Stenographer*	
SALARY_____	First Choice Second Choice	

Please answer each question fully. All information will be considered confidential.

FULL NAME (Printed) *Barbara*   *Jean*   *Simmons*   MALE ☐ FEMALE ☒   AGE *21*
    First   Middle   Last

PRESENT ADDRESS *1318 Elm Street, Linden, New Jersey*   PHONE NO. *Jr 3-4201*
    Street   City   State

DATE OF BIRTH *June 18, 19--*   ARE YOU A CITIZEN OF THE U. S. A. YES ☒ NO ☐   FATHER'S OCCUPATION *Printer*

IF YOU HAVE SERVED IN THE U. S. ARMED SERVICES PLEASE ANSWER

BRANCH *—*   FROM *—*   TO *—*   RANK *—*

DESCRIBE ANY DUTIES PERFORMED THAT MIGHT APPLY TO CIVILIAN OCCUPATIONS

_____

Check Your Status:

	SINGLE ✓	SEPARATED ___	HOME OWNER ___	NUMBER OF DEPENDENTS *0*	
	MARRIED ___	WIDOW ___	LIVING AT HOME ✓	(DO NOT COUNT YOURSELF)	
	DIVORCED ___	WIDOWER ___	BOARD ___		
			RENT ___	SOCIAL SECURITY NO. *355-24-4896*	

STATE OF HEALTH   EXC. ☒   GOOD ☐   POOR ☐   WEIGHT *116*   HEIGHT *5'4"*   TIME LOST THROUGH ILLNESS IN LAST THREE YEARS *4 days*   NATURE OF ILLNESS *Colds*

WHO REFERRED YOU TO US? _____ PLEASE GIVE PARTICULARS_____

SPECIAL INTERESTS OUTSIDE OF BUSINESS ARE:
1. *Photography*
2. *Church activities*
3. *Reading*

HOURS PER WEEK DEVOTED TO INTERESTS:
1. *4*
2. *3*
3. *5*

PARENT OR OTHER PERSON TO BE NOTIFIED IN CASE OF ILLNESS OR EMERGENCY: NAME *Dwight E. Simmons* PHONE NO. *Jr 3-4201*
ADDRESS *1318 Elm Street, Linden, New Jersey*

EDUCATION

GRADE	NAME OF SCHOOL	LOCATION	MAJOR	COURSES TAKEN	No. Years Attended	Did You Graduate?	Year Graduated
ELEMENTARY	*Jackson School*	*Linden, N. J.*	X X X X X		*8*	*Yes*	*19--*
PREPARATORY OR HIGH	*Linden High School*	*" "*	X X X X X	*Commercial*	*4*	*Yes*	*19--*
COLLEGE	*New Jersey College for Women*	*New Brunswick, N. J.*		*English*	*2*	*No*	
OTHERS							
BUSINESS OR VOCATIONAL	*Brockton Business School*	*Elizabeth, N. J.*		*Secretarial*	*1*	*Yes*	*19--*
PRESENT							

5078

(over)

A filled-in application blank (*face*)

EMPLOYMENT RECORD
(Beginning with Last)

FORMER EMPLOYERS	YOUR POSITION AND DUTIES	DATES	SALARY RECEIVED	SUPERVISOR'S NAME	REASON FOR LEAVING
NAME Anderson Motors ADDRESS Linden, New Jersey	Secretary — general clerical work and payroll	FROM June, 19— Present	START 47.50 FINAL $50.00	John Anderson Manager — Owner TITLE	Desire better job
NAME Beekman Dept. Store ADDRESS Linden, New Jersey	Salesclerk	Summers FROM 1952 To and 1953	START $38.00 FINAL $40.00	Jane Durwood Asst. Manager TITLE	Attending School
NAME ADDRESS		FROM TO	START FINAL	TITLE	
NAME ADDRESS		FROM TO	START FINAL	TITLE	
NAME ADDRESS		FROM TO	START FINAL	TITLE	

PERSONAL REFERENCES
(Not Relatives or Former Employers)

NAME	ADDRESS	OCCUPATION	YEARS ACQUAINTED
Peter K. Rahway	1814 South Main Street	Engineer	6
Mrs. Andre Shelby	243 Franklin Avenue	YWCA Director	13

KNOWLEDGE SUMMARY

OFFICE — PLEASE GIVE SPECIFIC INFORMATION CONCERNING YOUR WORKING KNOWLEDGE OF:

CLERICAL One year — all types of clerical work in a one-girl office

BOOKKEEPING OR ACCOUNTING Three years' study in high school

TYPING YES ☑ NO ☐ SPEED: 60 w.p.m. SHORTHAND YES ☑ NO ☐ SPEED: 120 w.p.m.

OFFICE MACHINES Adding and billing

PUBLISHING — EDITORIAL High School correspondent for Linden Gazette

BUSINESS

SELLING

ILLUSTRATION

GENERAL — Other

(Do Not Fill In Space Below)

I certify that answers given in this application are correct. As a condition of employment I agree to undergo a physical examination by a physician designated by the Company.

SIGNED Barbara Jean Simmons

A filled-in application blank (*reverse*)

the important items. Then, too, a filled-out application form gives
a great deal of information about the applicant: information regarding his penmanship, accuracy, carefulness, neatness, and ability to
follow written directions. Let us keep this last point in mind whenever we write on an application form.

Our handwriting does not have to be fancy, but it must be legible.
Figures should be carefully written. Illegible penmanship may
cause delays in business, and delays cost money. If the interviewer
has difficulty in reading our writing, we shall start our interview
with at least two strikes against us.

We should not regard the filling out of an application form as
a simple task that we can skim right through. When we have
finished, let us check our work. In the section marked "Date of
Birth.....Month...Day...Year...," many people give the present
year instead of the year of their birth. That, of course, makes them
much too young to work.

Since most forms are written in ink, perhaps we should have
enough forethought to take with us our own pen. The pens provided
for public use are usually not dependable, and a scratchy or blotted
form will reflect on our neatness.

Never shall we leave blank any part of the form. If the information asked for does not apply to us, we shall draw a line in that
space. Otherwise, the interviewer may think that we were careless
and did not see some of the items.

Let us read all directions carefully and follow them exactly. An
applicant who cannot follow directions that he can read several
times certainly will not be able to follow the many oral instructions
that are given in the office. If the directions say to print, then let
us do so. We shall notice the order in which our name should be
written and write it in that order. We may have:

   Name ....
          Last   First   Middle

                          or:

   Name ....
          First   Middle   Last

The section for the employment record may not apply to us, for
we may not have been employed previously. If we do write in the

space, we shall see that the record starts with present or last employment and works backward in time.

Let us take pride in knowing that our application form is neat, legible, and absolutely correct.

Summary. An application letter will get results if the applicant has the special education and training to:

1. Write a polished sales letter, a letter that will sell himself and his services.
2. Understand the importance of the appearance of the letter and to apply his knowledge.
3. Use the right tone for each prospect.
4. Include all the information that will be important to the employer.
5. Select the letter form that best suits his personality and that will best appeal to the reader.
6. Cement the good impression made by his application letter by filling out correctly and neatly an application form.

Assignment 1. Write the opening paragraphs for an application for a stenographic position:

a. Advertised in your local paper. You are writing to "Box 363, Daily News."
b. Advertised by a firm that you know to be very modern and up to date.
c. Advertised by a very conservative firm.
d. Advertised by a close friend of your family.

Assignment 2. In outline form, list the items of information that an employer can obtain from reading a filled-out application form.

Assignment 3. Write a letter to your teacher, asking permission to use his name as a reference when applying for a position.

Assignment 4. Set up and type a personal data sheet that you could use when applying for a position.

Assignment 5. Now write the letter that will accompany the personal data sheet written in Assignment 4.

Assignment 6. Obtain an application form from some industry in your community and fill it out as you have been taught in this lesson.

Assignment 7. Decide upon the type of position you would really like to obtain and the firm for which you would really like to work. Write a letter of application to that firm for that job.

Assignment 8. Write a closing paragraph for a letter of application. Use some device that you think will promote action. This must be original.

LESSON **78**

The Employment Interview

We studied the letter of application so that we could write the kind of letter that would make a prospective employer say to himself, "Hmm. I must take a look at this fellow (or this girl)." That splendid letter may get us an opportunity to talk to the man who does the hiring; but unless we know how to conduct ourselves at the interview, our chances of getting the job are very slim.

The interview will represent what will probably be the biggest selling performance of our lives, for we are trying to sell our most precious commodity—our services. We must show the employer by our appearance, manner, and speech that he will be getting the most for his money if he hires us.

Obtaining a position may not always require the writing of a letter of application, but getting a job does always involve being interviewed. Our sale of services, then, will be outstanding only if we know what preliminary preparations are necessary, what to say and how to say it, how to conduct ourselves, what the interviewer has in mind as he questions us. This knowledge does not come to us out of the air. We must *study* interview techniques.

As we take up topic after topic in this lesson, note how the principles learned in previous lessons can be used to help us to make the impression that will cause the interviewer to say, "I knew it! When I read that letter of application, I knew this fellow was just the person we want for the job!"

Physical Preparation. The same careful grooming and selection of clothing that we discussed in Lesson 53, "The Talk—Delivery," will apply when preparing for an interview. Choose clothing that is neat, clean, appropriate, comfortable. Perhaps the boys should be

465

warned that the clothing and grooming that seem to be acceptable for school wear are entirely inappropriate for an interview.

While the interviewer is talking with you, he will be noticing such details as nails, teeth, makeup, hair. You can just imagine what he will think of you if you should be chewing gum! The trained interviewer believes that there is a direct relation between personal habits and work habits—slovenly person, slovenly work.

The importance of a full eight hours of sleep on the night preceding the interview cannot be overemphasized. The applicant who is blear-eyed from lack of sleep cannot hope to present the fresh, alert appearance that marks the good office employee.

Mental Preparation. You are going to be interviewed; you have a sales prospect. As a good salesman you must give plenty of thought to the goods you have for sale, to a study of your prospect, and to the answers you will give to questions that may be asked.

Know Your Wares. To do a good selling job, we must know all about the merchandise we have to offer—our own skills and personal qualities. Very few people really know themselves, for ordinarily they do not take time to analyze themselves. This we must do if we are to gain a knowledge of our own wares.

Let us draw up a personal balance sheet, on one side listing our assets and on the other side our liabilities. On the assets side, we shall list skills and whatever characteristics we think will make us good office employees. This is rather difficult to do, for we all fear that we may be accused of bragging. On the liabilities side, we shall list just as honestly those qualities that may prevent us from doing a top job. The liabilities side is important, for we cannot correct faults unless we know we have them. A sample personal balance sheet would look like this:

Beverly J. Brooks

PERSONAL BALANCE SHEET

Assets	*Liabilities*
Proficiency in typing and shorthand	Impatience
Filing	Distaste for checking work
Good English	Bossiness
Honors and awards	Daydreaming
Good appearance	Carelessness

Assets	Liabilities
Even disposition	Poor erasures
Pleasant manner	Inability to take criticism
Ability to get along with others	
Ability to follow directions	
Honesty	
Dependability	

Study your Prospect. Just as a person has his own tastes, preferences, way of life, so does a business concern have its own distinctive beliefs and practices. Our mental preparation for each interview will be geared to the interviewer and to the firm for which we hope to work, a principle we learned in preparing to give a talk—consider the audience.

Our problem, of course, is how to go about finding out something about that particular interviewer and his company. Usually we know someone who knows the interviewer, and by judicious questioning we might find out what kind of man he is. By listening to employees of that firm talk about their work, we can also gain a great deal of knowledge. Then we can always drop in and ask for free literature, which we shall take home and study. Only by thus making a study of the prospect can we put on the best interview performance and avoid striking false notes.

Prepare for Questioning. The average personnel manager of today is a man or woman who has studied the techniques of interviewing and who has had considerable experience in "sizing up" applicants for positions. This person is charged with the responsibility of obtaining the best employees for his firm; and his questions will be asked for the purpose of finding out all he can about the applicant's education, experience, character, and ability to get along with other people.

We are going to discuss here some of the typical interviewer questions, so that we may think about answers that are honest and that will show us in the best possible light. These exact words may not be used in questioning you, but you may consider yourself prepared mentally when you know the purpose behind each question.

"You are applying for a bookkeeping position, aren't you?" The interviewer may be looking right at your filled-out application blank and still ask this question. He is trying to find out if you really know what you want to do. You might answer, "Yes. I majored in bookkeeping, and I think I should be happy doing that kind of work." You might add, "My training also fits me for general clerical work." Under no circumstances will you give a wishy-washy answer like this, "Yes. But I will take any kind of job."

"What school subjects did you enjoy most?" Now he wants to know about your education. If you are wise, you will mention first of all those subjects that would be good preparation for the vacancy he is trying to fill. Perhaps you should have with you any awards you have won. Perhaps you should have a folder containing samples of the work you have done. Here is your opportunity not only to tell him but also to *show* him.

"Did you participate in any extracurricular activities?" If you belonged to school clubs, if you served on any committees, if you took part in any public school performances, you have learned something about working with other people; and you will probably be able to work well with other people in an office. Be ready to list the activities and to mention any offices you may have held.

"What do you do with your out-of-school time?" Your answer to this question will tell the interviewer a great deal about the real you. If unprepared for the question, you might answer, "Go to the movies, listen to the radio, look at television"; and the interviewer will probably think you a featherbrain. The well-adjusted person during his leisure time does something to improve himself, something for exercise, something just for fun. This would be a good time to mention any hobbies you have. If you work part time, say so very simply; for such work proves that you are industrious.

"What experience have you had?" Since you are applying for your first full-time job, you must make the most of any kind of work that you have done. Even if baby-sitting is all you have to offer, you can say that this experience was valuable because you learned to follow directions and to assume responsibility. If you have had absolutely no experience, capitalize on this by pointing out that you should be able to learn quickly because you have not acquired any bad habits. This question should never be answered by a flat "No!"

"Why do you want to work for this company?" The little research you did when you were studying your prospect will repay you now.

You know something about the company and how its employees are treated. Your knowledge should enable you to select an answer that will be honest and that will show that you know what the firm has to offer you.

"Would you be willing to work overtime if necessary?" Remember that you are paid for overtime. If you are willing to work after hours, then you are dependable, conscientious, not a clock watcher. If you are not willing occasionally to put in extra time, you will not make a desirable employee.

"What salary would you expect?" This question as such means nothing. Practically every industry has a set salary for beginners in all positions, and employment laws take care of minimum wages. If you should be caught unawares and state a sum that is less than the law allows, the interviewer will know that you are uninformed, that you do not read the newspapers. If you mention a salary that is much higher than the position warrants, the interviewer will think that you have an exaggerated idea of your own worth. Probably the wisest answer would be something like, "I would expect to receive whatever salary a firm of your reputation pays its beginning employees."

"Have you any questions?" The interviewer will learn much about you from the questions *you* ask. One personnel manager reported that the questions most frequently asked him by applicants were: How long a lunch hour do you give? How many weeks do you have for vacations? What are the working hours? Such questions would lead an employer to think that workers were more interested in loafing than in working. We would not need to ask any of these questions, for we would know the answers from our study of the prospect. Any questions that we do ask will have been carefully thought out, for we do not want to create a false impression.

Posture and the Interview. The way you stand, walk, and sit will mean something to the interviewer. The walk from the door to the personnel manager's desk may be likened to the walk to the front of a platform when giving a speech. You will probably be very, very nervous; so be sure not to betray this fact by a frightened-rabbit scurrying. If your courage needs bolstering, think of the assets side of your personal balance sheet. Say to yourself, "I can

do this job. I have what it takes." If you must stand for a minute
before the interview starts, remember the instructions given you
in the chapter on Effective Speech. When you sit, hold yourself erect,
but not stiffly so. A sprawling sitting position makes you look lazy.

Interview Etiquette. Everyone knows that good manners are
absolutely necessary for good personal relationships. Oddly enough,
good manners are taken for granted; but any lapse or omission is
noticed immediately. A favorite practice of one man when interviewing is to drop something on the floor just to see whether the
applicant will pick it up. He considers this a test of the applicant's
courtesy. We are going to discuss very briefly interview manners
from the point of view of the applicant.

Be on time or a few minutes early for your appointment. Not only
would tardiness be rude, but also the lack of punctuality would lead
the interviewer to think that obtaining a position with his firm is
unimportant to you. Rushing to be on time is unnecessary and leaves
you breathless. Start early enough to allow for any unforeseen
delays.

You will shake hands with the interviewer only if he offers to do
so. If he does offer his hand, grasp it firmly. The limp handshake is
indicative of a person who has no forcefulness.

Wait for an invitation before seating yourself. The interviewer is
your host for the time being, and it is his privilege to seat you
where he wants you at the time he is ready to issue the invitation.

The tact and graciousness you would exhibit when taking part in
any conversation will be applied while talking to an interviewer.
Never interrupt him, even if he is long-winded or if you think of
something you want to tell him right then. Of course you would
not contradict him or point out by words or implication that he is
wrong. You will be safe here if you put into practice the rules of
courtesy that have been drilled into you all your lives.

Your last chance to show good manners will occur at the close
of the interview. Remember to thank the interviewer for giving
you his time, just as you would thank any host when leaving his
home. In the excitement and under the tension of what may have
been an ordeal, you may forget to put this final touch of polish on
your interview performance.

Talking to the Interviewer. Now comes the opportunity to use many of the principles you have studied. Have you worked to improve your voice? How is your grammar? Diction? Do you still say "Yeah" for "Yes"? If you have really worked and have applied all that you have learned, you will have the advantage of being able to forget voice and speech and to concentrate on questions and answers.

Many interviewers comment on the fact that applicants just graduated from high school are very hard to talk to. The reason for this is that they have only one of two replies to make—"Yes," or "No." Such applicants have probably had no training for being interviewed. We who have done our mental preparation will know what the interviewer is trying to find out; and we shall answer questions fully, but simply. We shall understand the importance of carrying the conversational ball.

The applicant's manner should be friendly, but respectful. A pleasant, easy manner is much to be desired; but we must be careful not to overdo it, to the extent of being "fresh" friendly.

As we talk to the interviewer, let us look at him. He is our audience, and we have been taught that rapport cannot be established unless we look at our audience. Most of us have preconceived notions that may be right or wrong, but we think they are right. Interviewers have some notions, too. If you look everywhere except at the interviewer, be assured that he will say to himself, "This boy impresses me as being sly, shifty. Not once did he look me right in the eye."

You may have an opportunity to show your familiarity with the products manufactured by the interviewer's company. You *are* familiar with them, for you made a study of this company. Remember?

If the firm manufactures plastic articles and the interviewer mentions that fact, you might say something like, "I was interested to know that you make the squeeze bottles for Lovely Hand Lotion." If you are applying for a stenographic position, you might say that you have the literature of the company and have practiced shorthand outlines for the words used in that business. The interviewer, however, will be impressed by your alertness only if your comments are made in the natural course of the conversation.

Possibly you may make a job-getting impression because you have studied the topics that interest people. You will apply the instructions contained in Lesson 51, "The Talk—Choice of Subject." For instance, if the interviewer wants to talk about his son, who is just your age, you will know enough to encourage him. Maybe the personnel man will do most of the talking, but he will so enjoy himself that he will think *you* a brilliant conversationalist.

Closing the Interview.   When the interviewer is ready to end the conversation, he will indicate in some way that he is finished. He may gather together some papers on his desk and look as though he were thinking of doing some of his other work. He may give a closing impression by words or by the tone of his voice. However he does it, be on the watch for this moment. This is the time to stand up, thank him, and make a good exit. Do not try to prolong the interview beyond that time, for all you will accomplish is the annoyance of the man who might have selected you for the position.

Summary.   The interview is a real-life test of how well you have been trained and how well you can apply what you have learned. In addition, you must have special knowledge and training in order to succeed in getting exactly the job you want; for business is highly competitive.

The successful candidate is the person whose appearance, manner, and speech are outstanding. He prepares for each separate interview, and he knows what type of questions he may be asked and why they are asked. He is ready, therefore, with the best possible answers.

The employment interview is an important moment in the life of every job seeker, so important that it merits particular and special study.

Assignment 1.   Prepare a personal balance sheet. On one side list your assets; on the other side, your liabilities.

Assignment 2.   List your leisure-time pursuits. Then write a criticism of your activities from the point of view of an interviewer.

Assignment 3.   Decide upon a particular job for which you would like to apply, and then list the items you would take with you to show to an interviewer.

Assignment 4. Write a memorandum to your teacher, stating the work that you could mention in answer to the question, "What experience have you had?" Be sure to show the experience value of all work that you have done.

Assignment 5. Select some industry for which you would like to work. Find out all you can about this company, and report your findings in the form of a written memorandum.

Assignment 6. List the extracurricular activities in which you have engaged during your school life. Point out the values of such activities, and show how you can apply them in your future business life.

Assignment 7. You are the personnel manager for the largest industry in your community. You have an opening for a general clerical worker. In memorandum form, list the skills and personal qualities that you would be looking for when interviewing applicants for this vacancy. State how you plan to find out whether or not and to what degree an applicant possesses them.

Assignment 8. Volunteer to be interviewed by your teacher during class time. Give advance notice about the name of the firm and about the kind of job for which you are applying. Come to school dressed for the interview. Ask your classmates to take notes during your interview and to be ready to analyze your performance.

LESSON **79**

Social-Business Letters

Men and women in business today conduct their businesses in friendly fashion. They have learned that success depends to a great extent on the depth of good feeling that exists between them and their customers, vendors, associates, and even competitors. Although business people realize the importance of being affable and neighborly when they meet others face to face, they are not yet fully aware of the business letter possibilities for cementing good business connections.

Probably the reason for this is that business letters are thought of as communications relating solely to business affairs. The main reason for writing is, of course, to convey a message about business. When we work to promote warm personal relationships, however, we cannot stop in the morning at the office door and say to ourselves, "For the next eight hours I must be cold, abrupt, and attentive only to merchandise."

Thus we arrive at the thought that business involves much social interplay; and, since this is true, we must know how to write the social letters that are part of the job of a business correspondent. These are letters of: appreciation, congratulation, appointment, recommendation, introduction, resignation, invitation, announcement, sympathy.

Many executives who write excellent letters about goods and services find very difficult the composing of social-business letters. One of the privileges of any executive is the assigning to someone else of the tasks that are distasteful to him. Therefore, as junior correspondents, we can expect to be asked to write the social-business letters. Let us not be caught napping!

474

Appreciation

The well-bred person does not leave his manners at home; courtesy is as much a part of him as his eyes or his nose. This is the rule, but there is at least one exception. It is a fact that many men of refinement do not always observe the rules of polite conduct when they are working in business offices.

One of the marks of good breeding is the saying of "Thank you" for favors done or for extra services rendered, but too often the businessman does not bring his "Thank you" manners to work with him. One reason for this is the old-fashioned attitude—he considers special favors his due. "So, what! That's what they get paid for, isn't it?"

Another reason is that some executives do not know how to word "Thank you" letters, and they put off the writing until the favor done is so stale that there would be no point in writing.

Let us set up some problem situations and write letters of appreciation.

"Thank You" to Vendor. Suppose that we received an offer from a vendor to supply free literature about the costume jewelry we purchased from him. The literature is in the form of little pamphlets that can be enclosed in letters we write to customers who might be interested in jewelry. Such printed material is referred to as "stuffers." We accept the offer by writing the following letter:

Gentlemen:

Thank you very much for offering to send us stuffers for Verdi jewelry. We should be very glad to have as many copies as you would like to send us.

We think that the use of the stuffers will be a valuable aid in increasing our sale of Verdi products.

Cordially yours,

The question of when to write a special "Thank you" letter is a problem that requires the exercise of good judgment. We are always conscious of the fact that an unnecessary letter increases operating expense; but we also know that an expression of appreciation is proper as well as good business practice.

As an example of good thinking, let us suppose that we asked a vendor for rush delivery of an order. Although he had to work hard, he got the shipment to us in the shortest possible time. We might not think that a special letter of thanks should be written; but, in the next regular business letter we send him, we shall certainly include something like: "Thank you very much for the prompt delivery of our order No. 4821. You were of great help in satisfying a difficult customer."

"Thank You" to Employee.   To illustrate the far-reaching possibilities of the writing of social-business letters, let us consider an area hitherto pretty much overlooked—promotion of employee good will. The rank and file of business executives notice and comment upon only the work that is unsatisfactory. Employees of such men have no urge to go on to bigger and better deeds.

We all like to have good work recognized; and an expression of recognition spurs us on to try to better our own record. A letter of appreciation is more valuable than a spoken word of praise, for the oral commendation floats away on the breeze. The letter can be kept and reread, and every reading will give a little push to ambition.

Suppose that we have a new salesman who turned in more orders for a particular month than had ever been obtained before. Or maybe the salesman is an old employee. At any rate, the performance is outstanding and should be recognized by letter; as:

Dear Bill:

We thought you might be as pleased as we are to know that your sales for the month of May broke all records.

We consider ourselves fortunate to have a go-getter like you on our staff.

Cordially yours,

Bread-and-Butter Letters.   Bread-and-butter letters are those we write to thank someone for having entertained us. Socially, such letters are a "must"; and businesswise they are, too. If a business associate entertains us in any way, we shall remember to thank him by letter just as soon as we can. Here is a luncheon "Thank you":

Dear Mr. Suffield:

Thank you so much for the fine luncheon you gave Mrs. Sands and me at the Cookfest in New York. The food was delicious, and the company was interesting and stimulating.

We are hoping to have the privilege of entertaining you soon.

Cordially yours,

Congratulation

Whenever we receive some kind of special recognition, a promotion or an honor, that is the time that we value our friends. Friends are those people who are sincerely glad to see us advance and who tell us so. Since this is true, we can make business colleagues our friends by congratulating them on any outstanding achievement.

Suppose that an assistant editor of our local newspaper has worked so closely with us that we are on first-name terms with him. We hear that he has been promoted to managing editor; so, of course, we write him a congratulatory letter; as:

Dear John:

I have just received the news about your appointment as Managing Editor of the *Blade*, and I want you to know that I think the owners of the paper showed excellent judgment in selecting you for the promotion. You are indeed the right man for the job.

The entire staff of Bolton's wishes you every success in your new position.

Cordially yours,

Now suppose that another business associate, whom we do not know so well, has been elected president of the local Chamber of Commerce. To him we would write:

Dear Mr. Chalmers:

Please accept my sincere congratulations on your election to the presidency of the Hereford Chamber of Commerce.

I am happy indeed to know that your long and efficient service to Hereford is being recognized; and I know that your leadership will result in increased business for our city.

The businessmen of this community are proud of you!

Very sincerely yours,

Appointment

By appointment letters we mean those letters that are written to tell some one person that he has been appointed to a new position, to membership on a committee, to some honorary post.

A letter of this kind may be written to you sometime. After working for a firm as correspondent, you would be more than pleased to receive a letter like this:

Dear Peter:

We are very happy to tell you that you have been selected for the position of Business Correspondence Supervisor. Your excellent work as a correspondent proved to us that, with you in charge, our business letters will be models for all other houses to follow.

Could you come to my office Thursday at ten o'clock? You and I should talk over the details connected with your appointment before you assume your new duties on Monday of next week.

Cordially yours,

Recommendation

Letters of recommendation are of two types: general and specific. A general letter of recommendation uses for a salutation "To Whom It May Concern" and is a general and often vague statement of an applicant's character and capabilities. The person recommended keeps the letter to show to any prospective employer. The fact that such a letter is so general and the fact that the applicant knows what is in the letter make this type almost worthless.

A specific letter is written to a particular person at his request. Much more information can be given in a specific letter, for it is considered a confidential report. The statements made in a letter of recommendation must be true, or reflection is cast on the character of the writer. In cases where enthusiastic recommendations cannot be made, the writer may be able to emphasize the good qualities of the applicant and ignore the poor. As stated in another lesson, let us be careful to write nothing libelous.

Suppose that, with permission, you gave your former employer as a reference. On request, he will write a specific letter because he is writing to one particular person. If you were really good, he can say so freely. For you, he might write:

Dear Mr. Pampel:

I am very glad to tell you about Robert J. Bessette, who worked for us as a correspondent from October, 19—, to January, 19—. He left us to work for Kyte Brothers at a substantial increase in salary.

Mr. Bessette was a real loss to our organization, for his work was excellent. In addition to superiority in the writing of letters, he has the kind of personality that makes working with him a pleasure. Never, at any time, did we have any criticism of him or of his work.

We know that Mr. Bessette will do outstanding correspondence work for any firm that is fortunate enough to obtain his services. We recommend him wholeheartedly.

Very sincerely yours,

Introduction

How we fumble sometimes when we try to start a conversation with someone we do not know and what a long time it takes to get under way! But if we were introduced to that person, we could converse freely because each is first made known to the other.

If we move into a new community and if we have letters of introduction to some of the townspeople, we are able to get acquainted quickly. If we want to talk to a businessman who is a stranger, a letter of introduction would smooth the way for us. That is why letters of introduction are written in business.

An introduction letter introduces, tells the reason for the introduction, and gives information about the person introduced. If the relationship is that of warm friendship, the letter may close with an expression of personal appreciation for any special consideration that may be given to the introduced person; as: "I shall very much appreciate any courtesies extended to Mr. Farwell."

Let us not use the hackneyed opening, "This is to introduce . . . ." Instead, let us write: "May I present," "I should like to introduce," "I want you to meet."

If the letter is to be presented personally, it will be enclosed in an unsealed envelope and, with one addition, will be addressed in the usual manner. The addition consists of writing in the lower left-hand corner "Introducing Mr. James Hunt."

As an illustration, let us suppose that Donald F. Seton, a very good friend, wants to see the operation of the bottle machines used by Hartem Plastics. We know Eugene Eppler, who is plant manager for Hartem; so we offer to open the door for Seton by writing the following letter of introduction:

Dear Mr. Eppler:

I should like you to meet Donald F. Seton, Plant Engineer for Blaisdell Company, who is one of my best friends.

Mr. Seton is making a study preparatory to replacing some outdated machinery and is now working on bottle machines. When I told him about the efficiency with which your machines do the work, he expressed a desire to see them in operation. You immediately came to mind as the person best qualified to show them to him.

I know that you will enjoy a visit with Mr. Seton, for you two have much in common.

Cordially yours,

Resignation

Of course, we can always resign by going to the supervisor and saying, "I quit!" But a much better way would be to write a letter of resignation that will be delivered at least two weeks before the date of leaving.

Such a letter is really a refusal letter, for we are in effect refusing to work any longer for the company. With our training in the writing of refusal letters, we can easily adapt that training to resignation letters. We shall make a statement of resignation, give the reason, and keep open the lines of communication.

The last point is especially important. Very frequently, we leave a position because we are dissatisfied, and it would give us great satisfaction to say in writing something like: "I think I shall enjoy working for Palmer's because my new supervisor is reputed to be a very considerate gentleman. This will be a delightful change."

The making of any sarcastic or belittling statement in a resignation letter would be sheer stupidity. Nobody knows what is to occur in the future, and any ill will that is purposely created may pop up sometime to work to our disadvantage. Then, too, it could be that our work is so superior that the company would be eager to keep us and would make some adjustment in the way of a transfer with an increase in salary. Let us always be gracious; for ungraciousness never, never pays.

Study the following illustration of a letter of resignation and see how it follows the rules for a refusal letter.

Dear Mr. Sheffield:

Please accept my resignation as junior correspondent, to take effect on June 30.

I have an opportunity to do correspondence work for the Union Company at a substantial increase in salary, and I really feel that reasons of personal advancement demand that I take advantage of their offer.

As a partial return for the consideration shown me while I have been a member of your staff, I shall be glad to assist in the training of the correspondent who will take my place. I should consider it a pleasure to give any extra service that might be required in the remaining two weeks.

Very sincerely yours,

Invitation

In business, the occasions for writing invitation letters are just about as frequent as they are in social life; and the same rules apply. The invitation is extended; and the time, place, and date are stated.

Perhaps we should know that some invitations are written in the third person. These are formal invitations and are worded like this: "The Heather Company cordially invites Mr. and Mrs. John H. Brant to be guests at the annual dinner . . . ." When accepting or declining an invitation, always write the letter in the same person as the invitation was written. For instance, when declining the sample third-person invitation given above, the wording would be: "Mr. and Mrs. John H. Brant sincerely regret that they will be unable to attend the annual dinner given by The Heather Company on . . . ."

Let us look at an informal invitation extended to Mr. Brant.

Dear Mr. Brant:

We should like very much to have you and Mrs. Brant as our guests at our annual dinner to be held at the Hotel James at six o'clock on Monday, May 21.

The business association between us has been so pleasant that we feel that your presence at the dinner will add much to its success.

Cordially yours,

R.S.V.P.

The initials *R.S.V.P.* at the bottom of the letter stand for a French phrase that, freely translated, means "a reply is requested." We usually find these initials on any invitation to partake of food, and the request should never be ignored.

Announcements

Announcements are invitations with this difference: Instead of inviting individual people, they invite many people. Announcements might be written by a firm that is opening a new business, by a company that is having an open house, by an established business that is moving to a new location, by a specialty shop that is having a fashion show, or for many other occasions.

An announcement of a fashion show might read:

You are cordially invited to attend the Fashion Show to be given by the Smart Shoppe on Tuesday, March 5, at two o'clock in the afternoon.

Exciting new spring styles will be on view, with models to parade before you all the best and latest developments of the leading designers of the world. The fabrics this year are richer in hue and more practical in wearing qualities than ever before in the history of textiles.

Tea will be served at four o'clock.

THE SMART SHOPPE

Sympathy

Letters of sympathy are written when there is loss of material things or when there is loss occasioned by death.

If a business friend, or even a competitor, sustains a serious loss of goods, the writing of a letter of sympathy would be a good-neighbor act. As an illustration, let us suppose that a competitor suffered a disastrous warehouse fire. Do we sit and gloat over his misfortune? We do not, for we are really big people. We write him something like this:

Dear Mr. Mechlon:

I want you to know that I am sincerely sorry to hear that your warehouse was destroyed by fire.

I am right now in the process of repacking the merchandise on the second floor of our warehouse, and I should like to offer you half that floor space for any use to which you might like to put it.

If there is any other way in which I can help, please do not hesitate to let me know.

Sincerely yours,

Letters of condolence, written to sympathize with a person on the passing of a relative or a close friend, are extremely difficult to compose. In such situations, the writer feels so helpless; for he thinks that there is nothing that he can do to lighten the load of the grieving person. This is not so, for letters of sympathy do help and console the mourner; and for this reason they should be written.

Even the writing of a sample letter of condolence is difficult, because such a letter springs from the heart and is called for only when the emotions are deeply stirred. You should know, however, that condolences ought to be sincere, brief, and comforting; as:

Dear Mrs. Lawton:
    Please accept my deepest sympathy for you in the loss of your husband.
    Mr. Lawton was an associate of mine for many years, and his sterling character and fine principles were a shining example to me and to all others who knew him. He will be sorely missed.

Very sincerely yours,

Summary

Now, as never before, businessmen are taking recognition of the fact that successful conduct of their business depends on all the individual persons concerned. We have reached the stage where we know that it would be fatal to treat our vendors, customers, employees, and competitors as robots.

This trend toward humanizing business and industry means much to the business correspondent. Hitherto he has had a "letter-writing job," but now he must be able to fill a "business-correspondent position." The difference is that the old way of writing curt letters about strictly business affairs has become the highly complicated task of writing better business letters and also of writing the social letters that are required in business. The modern correspondent must be able to write superior letters of: appreciation, congratulation, appointment, recommendation, introduction, resignation, invitation, announcement, and sympathy.

Assignment 1. Pretend that one of your classmates has asked you to give him a letter of recommendation. Write a general letter recommending him for a clerical position.

Assignment 2. Another classmate has given your name as a reference. Write a letter to a personnel director in some industry in your community, recommending that classmate for a correspondent's position.

Assignment 3. Under the section marked "Sympathy" there is an illustration of a letter written to a competitor. Pretend that you are that competitor and write a gracious "Thank you" letter.

Assignment 4. Your firm is to receive an observation visit from Lord Pondhurst, a noted English industrialist. You are going to give a luncheon in his honor. Ten of the leading business executives in your community are going to be invited to meet Lord Pondhurst at the luncheon in your plant restaurant. These men are your very good friends. Write the letter of invitation.

Assignment 5. Now pretend that you are one of the men who received the invitation extended in Assignment 4. Write a letter saying that you will be unable to attend.

Assignment 6. At a meeting of your Board of Directors yesterday, George Carey was elected a vice-president in the place of David Dean, who has resigned his position with our company. Write Mr. Carey the appointment letter.

Assignment 7. Now you are David Dean, who is resigning as vice-president in order to become a partner in the firm of Barstow and Company. Write your letter of resignation.

Assignment 8. As a business friend, write George Carey a letter congratulating him on his appointment as vice-president.

Assignment 9. Write a letter introducing one friend, Ronald James, to another friend, Stephen Clay. Mr. James is an architect, and he has heard that Mr. Clay has been appointed chairman of the building committee for a new school in his community. Mr. James asks you to write the letter so that he will have the entering wedge necessary to see Mr. Clay and to show him plans for school buildings.

Assignment 10. Your company is going to hold an open house for employees and for the general public. Write the announcement letter that will go to employees. Tell them of the coming event and invite them and their families to attend.

Assignment 11. Reread this lesson with the purpose of determining the general principles that can be applied to the writing of social-business letters. In the form of an interoffice memorandum, state the principles that you think would embody complete coverage of the subject.

LESSON **80**

Form Letters

Form letters are letters that contain the same wording and that are sent to a number of persons or firms. Reduction of overhead is the prime mover behind the writing of form letters, for they cost roughly two-thirds that of original letters.

Cutting letter costs by the use of form letters is profitable only when the results are as good as those achieved by the more expensive individual letters. In order to compose form letters that will make sales and build good will as well as reduce overhead, we correspondents must have at our command many special knowledges and skills.

Ability to construct moneysaving and business-getting form letters will be the reward of the correspondent who is familiar with the different phases of the subject embodied in the following outline:

1. Recognition of the need for writing form letters.
2. Knowledge of the kinds of form letters:
   a. Duplicated.
   b. Pattern.
3. Ability to key and to use keys for duplicated and pattern letters.
4. Use of techniques applicable to form-letter content.

Recognition of Need for Writing Form Letters

The alert correspondent will be on the lookout for letters that in the past have required similar answers; and, if he expects many such future letters, he will construct a form letter to cover the situation.

A correspondent who is alert will also recognize the instances where form letters may be used profitably. For example, overhead could be reduced by writing form letters in the following circum-

485

stances: to tell customers about a new service that is being offered; to express appreciation for the trade of good charge customers; to stimulate purchases by customers whose charge accounts are not being used; to forestall claims.

To show how a form letter can be used to forestall claims, let us assume that we are in the mothproofing business. Every article that we treat is guaranteed to be mothproof for five years, and each customer receives a certificate of guarantee. We find that we are about three weeks behind in the issuance of certificates because several of our typists have been ill and unable to work.

If we do not send our customers letters telling them why they have not received their guarantees, we shall be flooded with letters from them. Any letter written after the complaint, no matter how well worded it may be, will never erase from the customer's mind the impression that we gave him poor service. So, just as soon as we know that there will be a delay in sending the certificates, we duplicate and send to our customers the following letter:

Dear Customer:

Your certificate of guarantee for the Nomoth service we performed should reach you in about three weeks.

Our usual practice is to send the guarantee within two days after delivery of the mothproofed article, but illness among our typists prevents us this once from carrying on the practice.

We want you to know that you have not been forgotten.

Very sincerely yours,

Duplicated Form Letters

Duplicated form letters are those that are set up and run off in quantity by the use of any one of the various duplicating machines. The machine used for the duplicating process is an important factor in our study of form letters.

When we receive a letter that is written especially to us, we read it with close attention. When we receive a letter that is obviously a form letter, we may not read it at all; or we may just skim the contents. The first requirement for an effective form letter, then, is that it *look* like a personal letter.

We do not have space here for a discussion of all the different kinds of duplicators; so let us select four types for study.

Liquid Duplicators. A liquid duplicator, by means of a liquid, reproduces the material typed on a master copy. You probably have such a machine right in your own school.

This method of quantity production is excellent for institutional use, and the well-trained typist can do a very satisfactory job at relatively little cost. We might use a liquid duplicator for general announcements or for any other form communications that are not too personal in nature.

Stencil Duplicators. We are coming more and more to use the term "mimeograph" when we refer to any machine that duplicates a stencil previously cut on a typewriter.

The effectiveness of a mimeographed form letter depends greatly upon expert typing of the stencil, skillful operation of the machine, and cleverness in matching the ribbon for fill-ins. Many form letters have a space left for the typing of the inside address. When the shade of the ribbon used for typing is too different from the shade of the mimeograph inking, the personal touch is lost.

For communications of an impersonal nature, such as general announcements to the trade, mimeographed letters would be inexpensive and would get good results.

Multigraph. The Multigraph is a machine equipped with typewriter type; but the type must be set by the operator, much as type is set for printing. Not only does this machine use regular typewriter type, but a typewriter ribbon is used to make the imprint. The clever typist who can match the ribbon for all fill-ins will produce a letter that closely resembles an original letter.

The Multigraph could be used advantageously for order letters and for letters or postal cards acknowledging orders and remittances. For instance, the skilled operator would do a good fill-in job on a postal card such as:

> Your order for   has been received,
> and delivery will be made   .

Automatic Typewriter. The automatic typewriter is a typewriter that is controlled by a mechanism much like that of a player piano. If the inside address or a fill-in is necessary, the operator can turn off the motor and can type by hand the address or fill-in. The motor then will be turned on and will automatically complete the letter.

This type of duplicator is perhaps the most effective for the correspondent who specializes in form letters that are personal and cordial in tone. Assuming proper operation, the finished product looks like and is a typewritten letter.

Pattern Form Letters

A pattern form letter is a prepared letter that can be used by a typist as a guide when typing a business letter. In many businesses there are certain types of letters that must be written frequently. A pattern letter for each type could be constructed, and a typist could do the work of a correspondent by following the pattern and filling in the blank spaces.

For example, in a really large business there is always a necessity for writing vendors about delayed delivery of orders. A pattern letter like this might be set up:

Gentlemen:

Our order No. (. . . .) has not yet been received.

The merchandise can be used to the best advantage only if we can have delivery by (. . . . .) at the very latest.

We know that we can depend on you to ship the order as soon as you receive this reminder.

Very sincerely yours,

Any time that a letter about delay in delivery needs to be written, a typist can be instructed to type from the pattern, supplying the inside address, the order number, and the specified date of delivery.

Advantages. A pattern form letter saves time and money and, in addition, carries the personal touch lacking in most duplicated forms.

Time and money are saved when the person who ordinarily would have to compose a letter can instruct a typist to reply by using a pattern letter. Suppose that we receive from the Accounting Department a list of ten names of customers who need to be reminded that their bills have not been paid. Certainly we could reduce overhead by handing the names to a typist and saying, "Please send these customers the first collection letter."

Duplicated form letters save time and money in the same way that pattern letters do; but pattern letters, because they are individually typed, have more personal-touch value than most duplicated forms.

Let us see whether we can illustrate this outstanding advantage of a pattern letter.

Suppose that you, as correspondent, were asked to compose a form to be duplicated and sent to purchasers of "hold" merchandise stacked in the warehouse. The warehouse manager has complained that valuable storage space is being taken up by goods ordered to be held until called for or until delivery was authorized. He wants to move this merchandise, and your job is to help him by writing a form letter like:

Dear Customer:

Since the period for holding the merchandise you purchased from us has expired, we should appreciate receiving shipping instructions from you as soon as possible.

A self-addressed stamped envelope is enclosed for your convenience, and you may use the reverse side of this letter for your instructions.

We are eager to be of service to you.

Sincerely yours,

Ten days later, the warehouse manager came in to tell your supervisor that the response to the duplicated form was poor. You were called into conference and asked for suggestions. Knowing the appeal of an individually typed letter, you offered to compose a pattern letter in an endeavor to move the merchandise. You wrote:

Dear Mrs. . . . .

We are very much concerned because you are losing the use of the (name of article) that is being held for you in our warehouse. The many duties of your busy life have probably prevented your notifying us about the disposal of your purchase.

To promote speedy enjoyment of your (. . . . . .), we have typed at the bottom of this letter a form that you can check and return to us in the enclosed self-addressed stamped envelope.

Cordially yours,

Send merchandise on next regular delivery . . . .
Will call for merchandise within a week . . . .
Return my purchase to stock, with forfeiture of initial payment . . . .

Don't you think that the pattern letter would bring better results than the duplicated form?

Disadvantages. One disadvantage of using pattern letters is that too much dependence may be placed on typists who, after all, are not expected to have correspondence training. Unless the typist is educated beyond the typing job requirement, the error risk is great. A typing mistake in wording, price, order number, or date could cost more than the saving afforded by the use of pattern letters.

Another disadvantage is that pattern letters may be written so often that they lose their value because they bore the customers. As correspondents, we should know that revisions of pattern letters should be made at least once a year; and revisions, of course, are part of our job.

Keying Form Letters

As time goes on and more and more form letters are composed, the need arises for some method for filing and for finding filed forms. Possibly we could key our letters by marking them with the letters of the alphabet, the first letter "A," the second "B," and so on. Keying saves time, for when we see that an incoming letter can be answered by using a form, we can place the key letter over the inside address and give the letter to a typist to be answered. The typist will take the pile of letters that require form-letter replies and, by using the key, will be able to send the correct form to each addressee.

Large business firms may key form letters by departments. Thus, the typist who sees "Adj. C" above the inside address knows that the reply will be the "C" letter in the "Adjustment" file. "Col. F" would be the "F" letter in the "Collection" file.

Keying form letters also saves time by making combinations possible. For instance, "1-b, 2-g, 3-h" over the inside address would mean that the first paragraph is to be copied from Letter B, the second paragraph from Letter G, and the third from Letter H. Such combinations are especially valuable when the keying is for pattern letters.

The preliminary training of a correspondent sometimes consists of a tour of duty as a typist who sends out the various form letters. If we start our careers this way, let us first of all be sure that we understand the system of keying used. Then let us study the forms and get the "feel" of our company. We can learn a great deal from examining form letters, can build background knowledge about company policies, about merchandise, and about the tone of the letters.

Tone is important, for the tone of the letters will reflect the tone of the company.

Form-Letter Content

We know that a form letter is good to the degree to which it *looks* like a personal letter, and this knowledge represents the first half of form-letter training. Now we must complete our education by learning how to write form letters that *sound* like personal letters.

A form letter cannot be composed on the spur of the moment, because we cannot dash off any letter that will go to hundreds of readers. Much careful thinking and planning must be done *before* we write the letter, and careful checking is necessary *after* it is written.

Forethought. We might be able to write some of our business letters without outlining them beforehand, but an outline or notes of some kind are an absolutely necessary preliminary to the writing of form letters.

We must consider our audience, the people who will read our letter. Perhaps, if we visualize the type of reader and if we pretend that we are writing to one person of that type, our letters will not have the coldness that destroys tone in many form letters. Our first note will probably have to do with the type of reader.

The "you" attitude in form letters is extremely important. We shall jot down notes that will help us to show what the subject matter of the letter can do for the reader.

As we make our notes, let us be careful not to use any words or expressions that are frigid and formal. Even here, we shall write easily and naturally.

The opening paragraph deserves special consideration, for our first words determine whether or not the rest of the letter will be read. The place to work out a really good opening paragraph is in our notes. To illustrate the opening-wedge possibilities of the first paragraph, let us look at the one used by a manufacturer who was overstocked with small-machine tools:

The Fulton Manufacturing Company is pleased to offer its customers a reduction of 2 per cent on all small-machine tools.

This is a dignified, gracious opening; but contrast its effectiveness with:

How would you like to save 2 per cent on the purchase of all small-machine tools?

Here the correspondent captures interest by simply and directly piercing the businessman's vulnerable spot—his pocketbook!

An illustration would probably help us to tie together our "fore-thought" instruction. Notice how forethought was used in the following situation.

Suppose that we work for a department store that is trying to build its mail-order business. We have received the assignment of composing a form letter announcing a new service that is being offered, the service of a personal shopper.

From the many pages of notes we have made, we finally have the following outline, from which we are going to write the letter.

What kind of people purchase by mail?
    Those who are too busy to shop in stores.
    Those who dislike to shop.
    Those who live too far away to make store visits.
    Our mail-order customers mostly women—but why wouldn't service appeal to men? Last paragraph: "Perhaps the men in your family would also like to know about the convenience of our Personal Shopper service. Won't you tell them about it?"

What would customer gain by using service?
    Personal attention to each order.
    Merchandise selection made by person of taste and training.
    Special services—accessories, choosing gifts and wrapping and sending them.

Tone—sincere desire to be of help to customer
Convincer—something for nothing offered as a timesaver
    There is no charge for this service. Just write and tell June Barnes what you want and state the price you are prepared to pay. She will select and send you exactly the article that you yourself would have chosen after hours of shopping.

First paragraph:
    Your orders will receive individual, careful, personal attention if you address your letters to June Barnes, our Personal Shopper.

The result of our forethought will be a form letter something like this:

Your orders will receive individual, careful, personal attention if you address your letters to June Barnes, our Personal Shopper.

We have engaged Miss Barnes to look after you personally because your mail-order business is very important to us. She will comb the stock to get any article you order. She will select accessories of all kinds. If you desire, she will choose a gift and have it wrapped and sent. She is completely at your service, and she will enjoy shopping for you.

There is no charge for this personal attention. Just write and tell June Barnes what you want and state the price you are prepared to pay. She will select and send you exactly the article that you yourself would have chosen after hours of shopping.

Perhaps the men in your family would also like to know about the convenience of our Personal Shopper service. Won't you tell them about it?

Cordially yours,

Afterthought. When our form letter has been written, we must check it carefully before it is duplicated. The letter will go, not to one, but maybe to hundreds, of customers. One error in wording will mean hundreds of errors, with the resultant necessity of writing hundreds of other letters.

A price error might mean a money loss. Suppose that we write to one man for the purpose of selling him a raincoat. We type the price as $14.95, and it should be $15.95. That error will cost the company $1. Now suppose that we made the same error in a form that was sent to a thousand customers. The letter was so well written that all recipients ordered raincoats. Now the loss amounts to $1,000—*and our job.*

As we check our letter, we shall be watchful for questions that might arise in the minds of our readers. We shall be aware of the fact that this one letter will be read by many different people, with their own quirks and with their individual ideas of interpretation. Our test question with regard to our own composition is: Have I covered every point in such a way that no misunderstanding will occur?

A good form letter will not exceed one page in length, and that one page will not be packed to the edges with long paragraphs. Our training in written expression will enable us to make our letters concise and forceful.

If, however, we frequently find ourselves at the danger point of having to type a second page, we might consider the advisability of using an elite-type typewriter so that we can get more words in less space. Maybe, after we have been working for a few months, we might suggest that the next replacement typewriter be elite, rather than pica, type. There is no extra charge for an elite-type machine, provided that size of type is specified at the time of purchase.

Illustrations

The Sharon Manufacturing Company, maker of fine furniture, has just put on the market a coffee table that can double as a table for the dispensing of refreshments. There are leaves at the sides, with hollowed-out places for dishes. When not needed, the leaves slide under the table. The Sharon coffee table is being advertised extensively in all the leading magazines, and the manufacturer expects that many inquiries will be received.

A situation such as this will necessitate the preparation of three form letters, two by the manufacturer and one by the retailer.

Manufacturer to Inquirer.   It may be that the manufacturer already has a duplicated form designed to answer all inquiries; as:

Thank you for your inquiry about our fine home equipment.

Furniture that is as useful and beautiful as the item we advertised should be seen to be appreciated. We are therefore referring you to our outlet for your area, the dealer whose name appears at the bottom of this letter.

On your next shopping trip, stop in at the store and ask to see the furniture of which we are so justly proud.

Sincerely yours,

Dealer:

Let us discuss this form letter. Since it is constructed to cover all inquiries, the form would save time and money. But, when we think of all the money that was spent on advertising, the wholesale coverage looks like penny pinching. Note that there is nothing in the form that would maintain or heighten the interest aroused by the advertisement.

Perhaps we could promote sales and make more money if we inserted between the first and second paragraphs some wording like this:

You would be delighted to own the Sharon. Used as a coffee table, the quality and design make it a piece of furniture that would adorn any home. With the leaves extended and holding dishes heaped with tempting food, you will be able to serve your guests with a minimum of fuss and bother. The Sharon serves the twofold purpose of adding to the beauty of your surroundings and of furthering your reputation for gracious hospitality.

Possibly a still better idea would be to set up a letter that would be used to answer specific inquiries about the coffee table; as:

We are happy to hear that you are interested in knowing more about the new Sharon coffee table.

(Second paragraph a copy of the sample given above)

You really should see and examine the beautiful and useful Sharon; and this opportunity will be yours if you will visit our representative for your area, the dealer whose name appears at the bottom of this letter.

On your next shopping trip, stop in at the store and ask to see the table that will make entertaining pure joy.

Very cordially yours,

Dealer:

Manufacturer to Retailer. The manufacturer will send to his outlet the names and addresses of all people who have written letters of inquiry. These names will furnish the retailer with leads, for a person who is interested enough to write for more information is a prospective customer.

There is no question here of whether or not the recipient of the letter will pay attention to it, for a lead is the breath of life to the retailer. All that is necessary in this instance is to have a duplicated form that will give the essential information; as:

(Space for inside address)
INQUIRY ABOUT: Sharon coffee table
RECEIVED FROM: Mrs. A. E. Petersen
           2967 Second Avenue, N.
           Seattle 4, Washington

Retailer to Prospect. The retailer will write to the prospect a letter planned for the express purpose of motivating the customer to come in and look at the table—and buy! In order to keep old customers and to gain new customers, the retailer must write communications that are friendly, neighborly; and, for that reason, his letters must give a person-to-person impression. Therefore, the best duplicating method he could use for his letter to the prospect would be the automatic typewriter.

Lacking an automatic typewriter, the retail correspondent's best course of action would be to compose a pattern for furniture leads; as:

Dear Mrs. . . . .

The manufacturers of (the Sharon coffee table) have notified us that you are interested in knowing more about their product.

Since we are the representatives in the Seattle area for (Sharon furniture), we cordially invite you to visit our store, examine the (coffee table), and talk with us about it.

We are looking forward to seeing you soon.

Cordially yours,

Summary

The business correspondent who has had specialized form-letter training will: (1) Know when a form letter is indicated. (2) Know when a duplicated form could be used advantageously. (3) Know when a pattern form would be more effective than a duplicated form. (4) Know how to key form letters and how to use a key. (5) Know and be able to use the wording techniques that will make form letters a positive force in the reduction of operating expense and in the promotion of sales.

Assignment 1.   Select a form letter from your folder of sample letters. Write an analysis of the letter from the point of view of *looking* like a personal letter.

Assignment 2.   Write an analysis of the same letter from the point of view of *sounding* like a personal letter.

Assignment 3.   The sales manager has given you a list of 125 customers whose accounts are inactive. Prepare a form letter written for the purpose of reviving the accounts.

Assignment 4.   Since you work for a firm that has a large credit clientele, you write many letters granting credit privileges. Compose a form letter to cover the granting of credit.

Assignment 5. Your supervisor has requested you to give an opinion about writing a form letter to all customers, asking them to report any failures in service or merchandise. Think this question through carefully and then, in the form of an interoffice memorandum, state your opinion and give your reasons.

Assignment 6. You work for a large firm that has on its payroll a recreation director. His business is to provide the employees with opportunities for participation in different social gatherings and sports; such as bowling, golfing, swimming, baseball, card playing. He wants to send each new employee a welcoming letter that will extend an invitation to use the recreational facilities. You are to prepare a form letter for him.

Assignment 7. Your Infants Wear Department manager has sent in a request for the preparation of a form letter to be sent to mothers of new babies. Write a congratulatory letter that has the hidden purpose of inducing the mother to outfit her baby at your store.

Assignment 8. You work for a fur-storage firm where storage policies are issued for each garment accepted. Business has been so brisk that you are getting behind in the typing of the policies. Prepare a form letter that will prevent customer complaints about nonreceipt of the storage policies.

Assignment 9. In Assignments 3, 4, 6, 7, 8, you were asked to compose form letters. Would you duplicate these forms or would you prepare patterns? Decide this question for each of the assignments, and report your decisions and reasons in writing.

Assignment 10. Survey your community offices to find the types of duplicating machines that are in use. Make a written report to your teacher and an oral report to the class.

If your teacher approves, you might make arrangements for your class to visit an office where the operation of at least one of these machines could be observed.

LESSON 81

Wire Communications

Up to this point in our correspondence study, we have been learning how to write letters that are clear, complete, concise, courteous, gracious. We have learned how to write letters that would make sales, build good will, and reduce overhead. In this lesson, we have an entirely different type of education to acquire—learning how to compose wire communications that will get the best results at the least possible cost.

Wires, rather than letters, are sent when there is need for haste or when there is need for producing a distinctive impression.

Some illustrations of wires sent because the business is urgent would be wiring to order goods that are needed right away; obtain credit information; encourage purchase of additional items, to be added to orders already received; inform salesmen of changes in prices, of overstocks, of names of new prospects; send money that is needed immediately.

Wires that may be sent for the purpose of gaining special attention are those for encouraging salesmen; acknowledging a customer's first order; announcing special prices; requesting replies to unanswered letters; collecting delinquent accounts.

Our main consideration in the composing of wires is reduction of overhead. Our communications must be clear and complete; otherwise additional wires will have to be sent. Wires must be concise, because charges are based on the number of words; and each unnecessary or useless word represents needless expense.

We may be able to compose wires that are clear, complete, and concise; but, unless we are familiar with the kinds and economical uses of the different services available, we may still be the cause of excessive operating expense.

498

Let us learn how to write and how to send moneysaving wire communications.

Telegrams

Telegrams were chosen for our first study topic because they are the wire communications that we shall probably send most frequently and because we can apply the knowledge gained here to the writing of other wire communications.

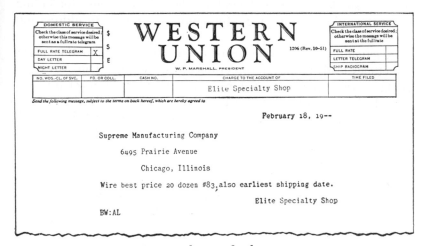

A properly typed telegram

Types of Telegrams. In the upper left-hand corner of the message form is a space in which we can place a check mark to indicate what class of service is desired. These classes are:

Full-Rate Telegram. This is the fastest service offered, and delivery takes place as soon as the wire is received. The minimum charge is for fifteen words.

Day Letter (DL). A day letter may be filed at any time and will be delivered on that same day, but it will be sent *after* all the full-rate telegrams filed before it. The minimum charge is for fifty words.

Before deciding to use the day-letter class of service, we probably should see whether the message can be compressed into few enough words so that a full-rate telegram would be cheaper as well as quicker.

Night Letter (*NL*). A night letter can be filed at any time (up to 2 a.m.) for delivery the following morning. The minimum charge is for fifty words.

No-Charge Items. We are so conscious of the need for saving money when we write our wires that, unless we know what items are transmitted free, we may unnecessarily endanger clearness, completeness, and prompt delivery. The no-charge items are:

Address and Signature. No charge is made for a single address or for a single signature. Therefore, there is no excuse for failing to give complete, identifying information with regard to address and signature.

Punctuation Marks. The misuse or omission of punctuation marks sometimes leads to misinterpretation of the message. Our wires will contain correct punctuation, for we know that there is no charge for: period, comma, question mark, colon, semicolon, hyphen, dash, parentheses, apostrophe. If punctuation marks are spelled out, such as *comma* or *stop* (to indicate a period), they will be charged as words.

Hold for Arrival and *Time for Delivery.* If we wish our telegram held for the arrival of the addressee or if we wish to specify a time for the delivery of the wire, there will be no charge made for these instructions. The directions should be typed on a line with the name of the addressee; as:

Ray B. Bliss, Hold for Arrival Statler Hotel New York, N. Y.	Ray B. Bliss, Deliver 5 p.m. Statler Hotel New York, N. Y.

Care of and *Attention Lines.* A care of or an attention line will be transmitted without charge provided it is written as the second line in the address; as:

Arthur J. Payne c/o Reservations Clerk Statler Hotel New York, N. Y.	Southwestern Corporation Attention Carl F. Larsen 4557 Elm Avenue Hudson, New York

Paragraphing. If we wish the message transmitted in paragraphs, we type, at the top of the message, the words "Send in paragraphs."

There is no charge for this service, but the message will not be paragraphed unless directions are so given.

Recall of Telegrams. We may cancel a telegram and will not have to pay for it if the telegraph company receives the cancellation instruction before the wire is sent.

Chargeable Items. We must learn how the wire companies count and charge for the message portion of the communication, for our composition of wires will depend to a great extent on our knowledge of word-counting procedures. Items for which charge is made are:

Words. The rule for counting words in the body of a wire is: Any word that is given as one word in the dictionary is counted and charged for as one word in a wire.

Hyphenated Words. There is no charge for hyphens themselves; but, if a hyphenated word is sent in a message, there will be a charge for each word in the combination. If we write about "sound-proof glass," we know that the charge will be for three words. If we write "soundproof glass," the charge will be for two words.

Proper Names. Proper names are counted and charged for according to the number of words they contain. *United States* is two words, *de la Grange* is three words, but *Vanderbilt* is one word

Abbreviations. If an abbreviation representing more than one word is written "solid" or without spacing after periods, it will be counted as one word. If it is written with spacing after the periods, each separate letter will be counted as one word; as:

fob or f.o.b.	one word
f. o. b.	three words
FEPC or F.E.P.C.	one word
F. E. P. C.	four words

Initials. The rule for the counting of initials is the same as that for abbreviations; as:

JHM or J.H.M. Blaine	one word for initials
J. H. M. Blaine	three words
SE or S.E. Sheffield	one word for initials
S. E. Sheffield	two words

Coined Words. There are some five-letter words that are made up for use in wires, and the telegraph companies recognize their usage and count them as one word each. Some examples are:

retel—regarding your telegram
relet—regarding your letter
antel—answer by telegram
anfon—answer by telephone
anlet—answer by letter

Figures and Special Signs. Figures and special signs are counted at the rate of one word for every five characters or fewer. The period, decimal point, comma, colon, hyphen, and apostrophe used with a figure group are considered punctuation and are not counted. Thus *$1,000* would be counted as one word, as would *$18.23.*

$, %, /, #, &, ' for *feet*, " for *inches*, and X for *by* are counted as one character each. If we are wiring about a five-figure order number and if we place the number sign with it (#24679), we shall be charged for two words. If we omit the number sign, we shall be charged for one word. If we write a mixed fraction like 32 1/2, we have five chargeable characters counting as one word. If we write the number as 32½, we shall be charged for two words.

Report Delivery. If a report of delivery is desired, we shall type "Report delivery" beside the inside address. These two words will be charged. If the telegram is being sent to a delinquent customer, we shall be very glad to pay for the two words in order to obtain evidence of the delivery of the wire.

Repeat Back. In the case of a very important telegram, such as a wire submitting a bid on a contract, it might be advisable to have the message repeated for the purpose of verification. The words "Repeat back" will be typed above the message and will be charged as two words.

Typing Procedures. Because we ourselves may type wire communications or because we may supervise such typing, we ought to know the correct typing procedures for all wires we send.

First the typist checks the class of service desired and fills in the printed column headings. He will state whether the wire is paid for, is to be charged to his company's account, or is to be sent collect. The time of day should be typed in the proper column, for the time element might be very important in the case of any dispute with regard to a business transaction. The date is the first item in the message portion of the wire.

Telegrams should be double spaced and should be typed like any other message, using upper-case characters only when necessary. The wires that come to us from the telegraph company will be typed in all capital letters because their machines do not have lower-case characters. Our typewriters do, however, and we may be able to prevent errors by typing our wires according to standard typing practices.

All business wires should contain identification initials. Should there be a question, the knowledge of who sent what wire might be of the utmost importance.

Day or night letters may require the use of a second page. All wire second pages will be typed on plain paper, not on wire forms.

We shall make at least one carbon copy of each wire and shall file that copy. This is a "must," for telegrams are admissible as evidence in a court of law. Some firms require two carbons, one to be mailed to the addressee for confirmation and one to be kept in the files. The beginning correspondent should probably ask for wire-carbon instructions.

Time Differences. The time differences in our country may influence both our message and the class of service we would use in sending the message. We all know that, when it is four o'clock in New York, it is three o'clock in the Chicago area, two o'clock in the mountain states, and one o'clock on the Pacific coast. Let us see how we can save money by taking time differences into consideration.

Suppose that we work in a Chicago office and at four-thirty we find that we must send a wire to New York. We know that the New York time is five-thirty; so a full-rate telegram would not be delivered until the next morning. An air-mail special-delivery letter would in this instance serve the same purpose as a full-rate telegram. But maybe there are two or three other messages that we would like to send to that New York firm. If so, we could send a night letter that would contain all messages and that would be delivered early the next morning.

If the wire were to be sent to Los Angeles, we would know that there was plenty of time for a full-rate telegram to be delivered, because four-thirty in Chicago is two-thirty in Los Angeles.

Composing the Message. The able composer of wires has the ability to pack into the fewest possible words a clear and complete message. Intent as he is on keeping the number of words to a minimum, he knows that sacrificing clearness and completeness to conciseness is false economy. If he needs the sixteenth word in a full-rate telegram in order to be sure that the message will not be misunderstood, he will use that sixteenth word.

Let us look at some telegrams and revisions and see whether we can learn by example how to compose wires that will be effective and economical.

Suppose that we need to wire for a hotel reservation. We could compose the following message:

Would appreciate your reserving for me a single room with bath, medium priced, for the night of Wednesday, August 17. Would arrive before 9 p.m. Please confirm.

This full-rate message contains twenty-seven words, a total of twelve words more than the fifteen on which the minimum charge is based. The extra words were not needed, and they represent money thrown away.

We can condense the message into fifteen words that will be clear and complete. *Would appreciate your reserving for me a* can be expressed by using the single word *reserve. The night of Wednesday* can be omitted without obscuring the message. All hotels have and use calendars. The *would* in *would arrive before 9 p.m.* could be omitted, as could the *please* in *please confirm.* Here is the revised wire, containing fifteen words:

Reserve single room with bath, medium priced, for August 17. Arrive before 9 p.m. Confirm.

Look at the following rather chatty rush-delivery telegram.

Ship immediately green topper, size 16, on our order No. 48263. Customer leaving for Florida Monday and wants to take topper with her.

Twenty-three words were used to say what could be said in eight words:

Rush green topper, size 16, on order 48263.

Since we have seven words yet to use, we might emphasize the urgency of our request by adding "Must have topper by this week Friday."

Telegrams are often of assistance in collecting bad debts. The "Hurry, hurry!" air that surrounds a wire sometimes gets results that are not achieved by means of letters. Let us write a telegram that is a last-ditch effort to collect from a customer who has ignored all our collection letters. We could write:

Unless your account is paid in full by September 15, our attorney will start legal procedures.

We have used sixteen words in this telegram, but we could have held it to fifteen by writing *is fully paid* instead of *is paid in full*.

Very often only a slight revision is necessary in order to fit the message into the minimum-rate number of words. In the following telegram, we could substitute *antel* for *Please reply*.

Have you shipped order numbers 174296, 164598, and 167776? Check shipment. Please reply.

We would also have a total of fifteen words if we omitted the *and* in the series of order numbers.

At eleven-thirty on the first morning of our week-long sale of household linens, we find that there has been an unprecedented sale of towels. We must wire for more stock; and, because of the number of words needed, we have a choice between a day or a night letter. We decide to send a day letter, for we know that the manufacturer will get the wire today and will have time enough to ship the goods today. A night letter would be cheaper, but this class of service would delay shipment for one day. We compose the following day letter and mark it SEND IN PARAGRAPHS:

Towel stock getting low. Rush following replacements on our order No. 25345:
Bath size—ten dozen plain white, ten dozen coral, fifteen dozen mint, twenty dozen multicolored, ten dozen yellow.
Hand size—white, colored borders—ten dozen blue, ten dozen hunter, ten dozen red, fifteen dozen cherry.
Complete sets—five dozen chartreuse, five dozen wine, five dozen flamingo, ten dozen sunshine.

We used sixty-one words, twenty-one of which were unnecessary. Look at the following revision and see how we achieve conciseness without sacrificing clearness and completeness.

Rush replacements our order 25345:
Bath size—240 multicolored, 180 mint, 120 each in white, coral, yellow.
Hand size—white, colored borders—180 cherry, 120 each in blue, hunter, red.
Complete sets—120 sunshine, 60 each in chartreuse, wine, flamingo.

The revision leaves us a margin of ten words. We might like to use some of them for an added spur; such as: "Stock must be replenished by tomorrow." Or maybe we would write something like: "Your usual prompt service much needed."

To gain competency in the composing of wires, we probably should first write the wire message with clearness and completeness in mind. Then we should revise the message for the purpose of making it concise.

Telephoning Messages.   In small businesses, wires are telephoned to the telegraph company. If that is the custom in our company, we shall write the message and read it over the telephone. The one thing that we must be careful about is to be sure that the operator understands us, and for this reason it may be necessary for us to key the spelling of some of our words. For instance, we might dictate the name "Byrnes" and would key the spelling: *B* as in Boston; *y* as in young; *r* as in Robert; *n* as in New York; *e* as in Edward; *s* as in sugar.

Telegraphic Money Orders.   Where money must be sent with speed and safety, it can be transmitted by telegraphic money order. The charges are based on the amount of money sent plus the distance involved. An overnight money-order service is available and will cost less than the faster day order.

International Telegraphic Services

Opportunities for fast communication with other countries are also at our disposal. If we work for a company that frequently exchanges messages with foreign countries, that company will have on file a manual of directions to guide the correspondent in writing international messages. The purpose of this section, therefore, is to provide general background knowledge that should be possessed by all of us who write communications.

Cablegrams. Cablegrams are messages sent to other countries by means of cables laid under the oceans. Our general information with regard to cablegrams consists of:

Classes of Service. A cablegram, like a telegram, has different classes of service; and the speed of the class determines the cost. For instance, a full-rate cablegram, with a minimum charge for five words, is the fastest service. Deferred cables are cheaper than the full-rate class because they are sent after all full-rate cablegrams are transmitted. A cable night letter is still cheaper, for it is an overnight service. The night letter minimum charge is for twenty-two words.

Word Count. Every word in a cablegram, including address and signature, is counted and charged. Punctuation marks are counted as one word each.

Use of Codes. Code words (secret language) may be used in a cablegram. The advantage of using a code is that one word may represent a complete thought; as: *brox* might mean *send us a repeat of our last order.*

Recognized standard codes are always accepted; but, if a private code is to be used, a check should be made with the telegraph company. Some countries will not accept an incoming message written in a private code.

Since addresses are counted and charged for, code addresses are frequently used. For instance, Waller, Baker, and Broom might be coded as Walbabro. All code addresses must be registered with the telegraph company, and a small charge is made for the registration.

Shore-Ship Messages. Communications to and from ships in all parts of the world may be sent. There is only one class of service for shore-ship messages, and the cablegram word count applies.

International Money Orders. When money must be sent speedily to a foreign country, we can send it by international money order. We deposit the cash with the telegraph company, which will charge us a small percentage of the amount sent plus full-rate charge for each word of the money order. Naturally, if there is an accompanying message, that message is also charged.

Summary

Any person who accepts a position as a business correspondent must expect that his correspondence duties will involve the writing of wire communications. In order to fulfill his obligation to reduce overhead, the professionally competent correspondent must know what kinds of classes of wire services are available; must know how words are counted and charged; must know typing procedures; and above all, must be able to compose wires that state the messages clearly, completely, and concisely.

Assignment 1. A new customer has sent you an unusually large order, and his check accompanied the order. Send him an acknowledgment wire.

Assignment 2. In the form of an interoffice memorandum, state the class of service you would use in each of the following problems:

1. At 9 a.m. you send a message to one of your salesmen, telling him of twenty price changes that go into effect today.
2. Your supervisor comes to you in a great rush and tells you to cancel order No. 3256.
3. You work in an office in Seattle, and at 2 p.m. you want to send a wire to a New York manufacturer. Your message will cancel eight items on one order and will add seven items to another order.

Assignment 3. Revise the following full-rate telegram. Use as many words as you need in order to make the message clear and complete. Try very hard, however, to condense it into fifteen words.

An emergency has arisen here in the office, and I shall not be able to meet you on Monday. Would Wednesday at the same time be convenient for you?

Assignment 4. You received today an order for twenty junior-miss suits at $72. You have a new line of matching coats, also priced at $72 each. Compose a wire designed to obtain an order for twenty coats to match the suits already ordered. After you have written and revised the wire, decide what class of service you will use and state the class at the top of your message.

Assignment 5. You work for a newspaper that has several foreign correspondents. From your reporter in Iran you received word of an uprising there. Wire him to submit a fifty-word digest of the latest developments. How would you send the wire?

Assignment 6. John H. Williams, of your city, has applied to you for credit. Compose a telegram to a credit agency asking for credit information about Mr. Williams.

Assignment 7. One of your salesmen has sent you a wire telling you that he must have $75 immediately. Wire him the money, and write the message that goes with it.

Assignment 8. You have received an irate letter from a very good customer, telling you that you sent him the wrong style of bridge lamps. Wire him that you are shipping immediately the style he ordered. Ask him to return the first shipment.

Assignment 9. Joesph F. Hardwick applied to your firm for an accountant's position. You wrote him a letter telling him that the job was his. A week has elapsed, and no answer has been received. You cannot hold the position open much longer; so send him a wire.

Assignment 10. Your best friend is in Bermuda on vacation. You find unexpectedly that you are able to spend a few days with him. Cable him that you are going to join him and ask him to meet you.

Take the message you have written to your local telegraph company offices and find out how much the charge would be. Tell the person who waits on you that this is a school assignment, and see how very helpful he will be.

In an oral report to your classmates, read the message you composed, state the cost of the cablegram, and tell them what you learned on your visit.

Business Reports

Fifty or seventy-five years ago, most businesses were so small that one man could, and frequently did, supervise and direct all operations of his firm. When the president or the manager of the company wanted information, he would go to the person who could supply it and ask a question such as: "Jim, how's that new stitching machine working?" Information acquired this way could be remembered, for business moved at such a slow pace that the memory load was not too heavy.

Can you imagine a present-day executive trying to remember all the information that is necessary for the conduct of modern successful business? Such a memory feat would be absolutely impossible, and it would also be needless. The businessman of today has in his files written reports about all phases of his business. Whenever he needs information of any kind, he asks the best-qualified person to present the facts in the form of a written report. Despite the fact that the paper work is now so voluminous, not too many business people know how to write a good report.

We, the business correspondents of today and tomorrow, will be called on often to write reports and to help others in the writing of their reports. For our own use, then, and for the purpose of gaining the respect that is always accorded a person who knows his business, let us study the types of reports we may be asked to write; the kind of preliminary planning that we must do; the methods of assembling, organizing, and presenting our facts; the effective typing setup that will make our reports attractive to the eye and easy to read.

Types of Reports

A report is an impartial presentation of facts. The wording should be simple, clear, complete, concise; and the facts should be accurate.

Let us begin our study of report writing by learning about the three types of reports that may be included in some of our future business correspondence assignments.

Routine Reports. Routine, or periodic, reports are those that are submitted at regular intervals and that are considered part of the job; such as daily, weekly, monthly, annual reports from people in all areas of operation—salesmen, time clerks, payroll clerks, heads of departments, even the president of the company.

Routine reports are written for the purpose of furnishing the facts and figures that management must have in order to determine how well or how poorly the business is doing. The tone is straight reporting of the necessary information.

Requested Special Reports. Whenever there is need for information other than that which is furnished by routine reports, somebody is assigned the task of gathering the facts and writing a report. For instance, if a new machine has been in use for a month, management will want to know how it is working and what its effect is on production and laborsaving. The shop foreman probably will be asked to write the report; or the correspondent might write it, using data given him by the foreman.

Sometimes a written report is requested because help is needed in solving a problem. Suppose that the sales reports for girls' apparel in the 7-14 age range show that this department lags behind all the others. The merchandise manager will want to know why the situation exists and what can be done to increase business. He might ask two or three people to investigate and report. From a study of the reports, he may find a solution to the problem.

You have already written several requested special reports. Whenever you worked an assignment, the directions for which read, "In the form of an interoffice memorandum, state your choice and the reasons for making the choice," you wrote this type of report.

Unsolicited Reports. The interested, enthusiastic employee becomes a thinking part of the organization for which he works. This means that he is alert to find opportunities to save money for his firm, because he knows that his own personal fortunes rise and fall with those of the company. Therefore, if he has any ideas that will contribute toward profit making, he will offer such ideas to the person who has the authority to carry them out.

If he makes his suggestion orally, it may be lost. The supervisor may be inattentive; or, under the pressure of work, he may forget. Much more attention would be paid to a written communication; therefore a really good idea should be presented in the form of a written report.

To illustrate, let us suppose that we work in an office where the letterheads used are of poor quality. This we know to be poor economy; but, if we want to induce management to purchase good stationery, we shall have to prove that the change is needed and that it can be effected at little or no cost.

Observation reveals that the carbon-copy paper we use is of better-than-average quality. We make a study of the price of paper; and, if we find that the cost of bond letterheads would be offset by the purchase of cheaper carbon-copy paper, we are ready to write a worth-while report.

Preliminary Planning

Before we work on report-writing procedures, we must be mentally clear about some points that have an important bearing on the power of any report we write. The interoffice memorandum form furnishes us with a ready-made outline for our preliminary planning; as:

Memorandum to.   Our first thought will be given to the person or persons who will read our report. We must consider our audience, for our choice of language and our presentation of facts must be geared to the reader.

Suppose that we were asked by the personnel manager to report on office absenteeism for the month of May. We would study the records and write a report that would list the absences. We would not waste this man's time by listing reasons for absence, by including any personal history of employees, or by pointing out that there was an unusually large number of absences during May. We know who our reader is and what he wants to know; so we give him exactly the information requested and give it in the most direct way.

Memorandum from.   After due thought has been given to the reader of the report, we must consider ourselves as the writer. Our position with the company, the type of report, and our length of service will determine the tone of the writing. If we hold an executive position and if we are writing a requested report, we would probably be qualified to make "recommendations." As a junior correspondent writing an unsolicited report, we would make "suggestions."

We would be very unwise to submit any unsolicited report until we have been with the company long enough to be sure that our ideas will be welcome, that our facts are accurate, and that our suggestions are of sufficient worth to take up the reading time of the supervisor.

Subject. We must always state the subject of our communication so that it is clear and complete. A report gets off to a bad start if the reader has to glance through it before he knows what it is all about.

Let us assume that we have been asked to report on a time-and-motion study conducted for our company. For our subject we might use "Time-and-Motion Study." This heading would be very poor, because it does not tell the whole story. We might better choose to use more words in order to be explicit; as, "Report of Results of Time-and-Motion Study Conducted from May 1, 19—, to August 1, 19—."

Composition of the subject line before writing the report helps the writer to organize facts that are related directly to the subject.

Date. We shall date every report and shall be careful to include the year of the date. A report becomes part of the permanent records of a company, and an undated report confuses the records.

Report Writing

The writing of a routine report is a very simple matter, for many times the job consists of simply filling in a form. Requested special reports and unsolicited reports are the ones that require the specific training that we are going to get in this part of our lesson.

A good report can be written only with the help of an outline. This makes sense when we think of all the facts we need to assemble, check, analyze. We may have to spend hours of study in order to get the information we need; and as we study, we make our notes. When we have the notes arranged in orderly manner, we know *what* we are going to write. There remains only the problem of *how* we are going to word the report.

The broad general outline of a report is the same as that for a speech: *introduction, body, conclusion.*

Introduction. Rather obviously, we cannot plunge into a report without some kind of introduction. We must have at least one sentence that will lead the mind of the reader to the subject matter we want to present. Then, too, since reports are sometimes kept on file for years, the introduction may supply some needed information.

Consider this illustration of an introductory sentence, "At the request of Mr. Alexander, I have investigated the time-and-motion study conducted from May 1, 19—, to August 1, 19—, by representatives of Engineers, Inc."

At the time the report is submitted, this sentence prepares for what is to follow. Three years later, someone may want to know who ordered the investigation or when the time-and-motion study was made or who conducted it. The introductory sentence will tell the inquirer what he wants to know.

Sometimes a letter of transmittal accompanies a report. Since the letter will contain whatever information would be included in an introduction, the report itself need not contain any introduction.

Body of the Report. The body of a report is concerned with the presentation of assembled facts; so we shall divide our study into two parts: assembling facts and presenting facts.

Assembling Facts. We must be sure of the accuracy of the data that we present as facts. If we need to check ten times before we can be certain that the figures and statements are correct, then let us check ten times. The results will be worth all our labor. There is absolutely no excuse for an inaccuracy in a written report, and any carelessness on our part may haunt us for as long as we work for the company.

The method we use to get the facts is our first consideration. Depending on the subject of our report, we may have to consult trade journals or reference books of various kinds. We may have to talk with people who have the information we need. We may have to make a survey by sending questionnaires. We may have to study our own records. The first topic in our outline for the body of the report, then, will be something like: "How can I get the information?"

For instance, suppose that we were asked to find out why the stenographer who works in the linen-department office is so slow in getting out her letters. Under the first topic outline, we would jot down: Visit linen-department office and observe; talk with stenographer; talk with supervisor.

Once we have gathered the facts and have checked them very carefully, we are ready to analyze them. Our purpose now is to screen all our information so that we cross out all facts that do not have a direct bearing on the report subject. Thus we shall have left only pertinent facts. If we neglect the analyzing process, we shall be in danger of writing the kind of long, rambling report that is so often written by the untrained reporter. For our outline topic, we could have: "What are the important facts?"

Let us see what notes we made after visiting the linen-department office.

1. Office too small—not enough floor space for two people to work—merchandise strewn everywhere.

2. Stenographer has to perform many clerical duties.

3. No filing cabinet—file folders placed wherever room for them can be found.

4. Stenographer interrupted continually by floor salespeople.

5. Supervisor impatient, demanding, inconsiderate. Gives his dictation fifteen minutes before closing time.

6. Poor lighting—one window—not enough light fixtures.

7. Typewriter table too low and chair uncomfortable.

8. Supervisor's request for additional clerical help refused.

9. Wall paint dingy and dirty.

Now we are ready to screen the notes. Let us cross out No. 2, because the stenographer has time to do needed clerical work. We shall cross out No. 4, because the interruptions go with the job. In No. 5, the important point is the time of day selected for dictation. Everything else will be disregarded. We think No. 8 and No. 9 have little or no bearing; so we shall cross them out.

The last step in the assembling procedure is the grouping of our facts. We must determine which facts are most important and must present these facts first, arranging with them any supporting facts. Possibly for some reports we may have to marshal our facts in the order of time. We could have for our topic outline: "In what order shall I present my facts?"

The notes we have taken and screened for the report on the linen-department stenographer would probably be grouped:

1. Crowded quarters:

Insufficient floor space slows work.

Lack of storage space for merchandise creates confusion—confusion slows production.

2. Inadequate equipment:

No file cabinet—folders placed wherever space can be found—time wasted looking for filed material.

Table used for typewriter—wrong height, causing fatigue—no place to keep stationery and supplies.

Stenographer's chair uncomfortable—causes fatigue—fatigue slows production.

3. Dictation given late in the day:

Dictation customarily given fifteen minutes before closing time means that letters cannot be transcribed until next day.

4. Poor lighting:

One window—not enough light fixtures—resultant eyestrain retards production.

To summarize, we could say that the outline for the study part of our report work would include three operations:

1. Assembling the facts
2. Analyzing the facts
3. Organizing the facts

Presenting the Facts. With the finished outline right at our elbow, we are ready to write the first draft of our report. We may have to rewrite several times before we get a report that satisfies us, but we must make a start by putting something down on paper.

The actual writing of the report should be easier for us than for other people because we are trained in written expression. We know how to use correct language, how to make our wording clear and complete; and we know the value of being concise. When we present the facts, we put to use all the correspondence training we have received.

Let us write the first draft of the report about the linen-department stenographer:

Crowded Quarters. Space restrictions in the linen-department office retard production. Time is lost when two workers cannot move without bumping into each other. Time is also lost when looking for merchandise and various other articles that, because of lack of room, are piled in hit-or-miss fashion.

Inadequate Equipment. There is no file cabinet in the office and no room for one. File folders are placed wherever space for them can be found. In this office, consulting the files takes too much time.

A typewriter table, instead of a desk, is provided for the stenographer. The table is below standard height and causes operator fatigue. There is no space for the storing of stationery and supplies.

The chair used by the stenographer is uncomfortable and unsuited to her work, causing fatigue that slows production.

Dictation Time. Dictation is usually given just before the closing time and is not transcribed until the following day. Mailing of letters so dictated and so transcribed is always delayed for one day.

Insufficient Lighting. The one window in the office does not provide sufficient light; consequently, artificial lighting must be used. The office is not equipped with enough lighting fixtures to prevent the eyestrain that causes fatigue. Fatigue slows production.

Conclusion. A report up to this point tells why the report was written and what the facts are. Maybe this is all that is required, and a conclusion would not be necessary. Then again, if there is no conclusion, the report may have an "up-in-the-air" effect. The kind of ending, if any, can be decided only by the person who is writing the report.

Should the reporter be asked to investigate and give an opinion, he might start his last paragraph, "Therefore, it would seem advisable to. . . ." Maybe the writer is a consultant; and, if so, he would write, "I therefore recommend that. . . ." Possibly the writer was asked to investigate for the purpose of solving a problem, in which case he would round out his work with a paragraph starting, "Our best course for the future seems to be. . . ."

If we write a report that we feel needs some sort of conclusion and we are doubtful as to the correct wording for us to use, we can always summarize. Many readers would very much appreciate having the facts boiled down to a few words. We could word the beginning of our paragraph thus: "A summary of the points brought out in the investigation is:" Then, we would list the points of the summary.

For the conclusion of the illustrative report we have been using in this part of the lesson, we could write:

My investigation shows that production in the linen-department office might be increased by:

1. Providing more working space, which would make possible the saving of much time that is now lost.

2. Reducing fatigue by providing adequate lighting and suitable job equipment.

3. Changing dictation time to the earlier hours of the working day, thus insuring that letters will be mailed on the day they are dictated.

Typing Setup

Expert typing and setting up of a report will increase the forcefulness of the communication by helping the reader to read rapidly and to absorb quickly the main points.

All reports should be double spaced. If there is more than one page, we shall be sure to identify and number each succeeding page. When the typing is completed, we shall staple the pages or secure them with a paper clip.

Unless we receive directions to the contrary, we shall place our date at the right margin, about 1 inch from the top of the paper. The date so placed makes for quick finding of a filed report. The name of the reporter is placed at the left margin on a line with the date, and the subject is centered three lines below; as:

Name of Writer   Date
SUBJECT OF REPORT

Whenever possible, we shall use topical headings—a word or group of words containing the gist of the paragraph. Look at the first-draft report under "Presenting the Facts." You can see that a heading is a strong force in bringing out a point.

We might be able to promote easier reading by setting up material in tabulated form. For instance, suppose that we were asked to find out how many hours a certain six men worked during the week of June 4. We could set up a paragraph thus:

During the week ending June 4, John Ames worked 24 hours; Joseph Ferrie, 36 hours; James Beran, 40 hours; George Foley, 38 hours; Fred Buckler, 35 hours; and Peter Mackay, 32 hours.

Now look at the following setup and see how much clearer it is:

During the week ending June 4:

Ames, John	worked	24 hours
Beran, James	worked	40 hours
Buckler, Fred	worked	35 hours
Ferrie, Joseph	worked	36 hours
Foley, George	worked	38 hours
Mackay, Peter	worked	32 hours

Note that, in addition to tabulating our information, we arranged the names in alphabetic order.

We should be sure to type at least one carbon copy of every report we write. We must not wait to observe this rule until the time comes that we are told that the single copy we typed has been lost. Having to write the report again would be learning the hard way.

If at any time we write an unsolicited report offering an idea or a suggestion, we should type an extra carbon and place it in a personal folder. If our suggestion is adopted, we shall make a notation on our carbon copy—"Adopted July 2, 19—." Our reason for making a carbon for our own file is to keep a record of the contributions we have made to our company.

Illustrations

Routine Report. A typical routine report is shown on page 520.

Requested Special Report. The illustration that follows is a report written by one of the persons asked to find out what could be done to increase sales in Department 37—the department where girls' apparel, sizes 7-14, is sold. As you study the report, prepare to discuss it from the point of view of the report-writing techniques you have learned.

Name   Date

IDEAS FOR PROMOTING SALES IN DEPARTMENT 37

Mr. Lane has requested that I study the below-average sales condition existing in Department 37, with the purpose of offering suggestions that will increase sales. The procedures used, the findings, and the suggestions are as follows:

Source of Information. The only people who really know why they do

Inter-Office Memorandum

TO	Mr. Blackwell, Sales Manager	FROM	R. J. Keene, Advertising Manager
LOCATION	Room 604, 3d Floor	LOCATION	Room 312, 8th Floor
SUBJECT	Monthly Advertising Report	DATE	April 3, 19--

Following is the monthly summary of the advertising expenditures for March:

1. Magazine Advertising

	Space	Cost
Modern Business	½ page.	$375.00
Office Supervision	1 page	200.00
Today's Manager	¼ page	90.00
Equipment Dealer	¼ page	35.00
Total Magazine Advertising		$700.00

2. Circular Advertising

	Quantity	Unit	Cost
Circular B (Mfg. List)	3,000	.113	$ 340.00
Circular X (Office Mgr. List)	2,800	.099	278.00
NBI Letter (General List)	6,000	.079	472.00
Total Circular Advertising			$1,090.00

Total spent during March	$1,790.00
(February:	$1,782.00)

Of special interest is the new printing rate on the NBI Letter. Although the rates for Circular B and Circular X have increased slightly over last month, we were able to lower the unit rate on the NBI Letter from .098 to .079 because of the new size and format.

Mr. Kingston, of Premier Printing, is now getting new cost estimates on Circulars B and X based on our revised design of these pieces. We are hopeful that we can bring our total costs down to $1,600 and still have more effective circulars.

R. J. Keene

A typical routine report

not buy are the customers. I therefore went to the Bureau of Vital Statistics and copied the names and addresses of mothers of girls born 7-14 years ago.

Method of Obtaining Information. A form letter containing a questionnaire was sent to each mother on the list. A copy of the form is attached.

Analysis of Information. Of the 1,114 questionnaires sent, 426 were returned, representing a 38 per cent response. Analysis of the returned questionnaires showed that:

> 128 mothers of girls in the 7-10 age range reported that they are unable to buy at our store because we do not carry enough "chubby" sizes.
>
> 119 reported that the stock is too expensive.
>
> 81 reported that the "Foreteen" clothes we offer for sale are too mature in style for the marked sizes.
>
> 74 mothers of girls in the 10-14 age range reported that the styles of our dresses are too dressy, frilly.
>
> 24 reported that the salespersons in the department do not give satisfactory service.

Conclusion. On the basis of the information received and analyzed, I offer the following suggestions for increasing sales in Department 37:

1. That more "chubby" sizes in the 7-10 range be purchased.
2. That inexpensive dresses be stocked.
3. That the "Foreteen" line be discontinued.
4. That dresses in the 10-14 range be selected with a view to emphasizing plain lines.
5. That additional training be given the salespersons in the department.

Unsolicited Report. You have been working for the company about six months, and during that time you have noticed that the typists in your office frequently have to make twelve copies of assignments. Some typists duplicate the work and others use carbons, typing the material three times. You have a suggestion that would make possible the production of twelve copies in a single typing. You present your suggestion in the following report:

Name   Date

SUGGESTIONS FOR INCREASING TYPING PRODUCTION

In the interests of increasing typing production, I should like to present the following facts and suggestions:

Facts. In our office, twelve copies of typing assignments frequently have to be made. The present practices for making the copies are:

1. *Duplicating,* involving two operations—typing and duplicating.

2. *Using carbon paper,* involving three operations. In order to get clear carbons, the material has to be typed three times.

Suggestions. Twelve copies of assignments can be made at a single typing if:

1. *A special hard platen were purchased.* The typewriter companies manufacture a special hard platen for use in making multiple carbon copies. The cost of the platen is $12.50.

Because the platens in the typewriters we use are removable and because our typists could share the use of a special platen, it might be possible to speed production of twelve-copy jobs by the purchase of one special platen.

2. *Lightweight carbon paper were supplied.* The carbon paper we use is of standard weight. The use of lightweight carbon paper makes possible the typing of more and better copies.

3. *Thin copy paper were furnished.* The paper we use for carbon copies is regular typing paper. Use of thin copy paper, such as onionskin, would be of help in typing a number of carbon copies.

Summary. Typing production in our office could be increased by purchasing and using:

1. A special hard platen
2. Lightweight carbon paper
3. Thin copy paper

Summary

Men and women today in top-management positions must have at their command a wide variety of knowledge and information. They must know what has been done in the past, how the different phases of operation are progressing, and what ideas are valuable for the future growth of their businesses. Their extensive knowledge is gained from the many, many reports written by the various members of their organizations.

The one person in business who is expected to know the techniques of report writing and to know how to use those techniques is the business correspondent. Therefore, the correspondent must be able to write good reports; and he will be able to do so with less drudgery and more strength than the untrained person if his report-writing education includes:

Knowledge of the different types of reports that may be required.

Familiarity with the kind of preliminary planning he must do.

Training in assembling, analyzing, organizing, and presenting convincingly all necessary facts.

Methods of setting up the typing in ways that will contribute to the force of his written statements.

Assignment 1.   Bring to class a copy of a routine report. Possibly your teacher will allow a few minutes for a discussion of the kinds and uses of this type of report.

Assignment 2.   You have been assigned a study of the correspondence part of this text for the purpose of determining which lesson has the most value. Write the heading and the introduction for the report you will make. Make a copy for use in Assignment 4.

Assignment 3.   Write the body of the report requested in the preceding assignment. Make a copy for use in Assignment 4.

Assignment 4.   Write the concluding paragraph for your report. Hand in the complete report, adding the final paragraph to the parts written in Assignments 2 and 3.

Assignment 5.   In the section headed *Presenting the Facts*, there is a first draft of a report on the production lag in the linen-department office of a store. Revise and rewrite this first draft.

Assignment 6.   Which make of typewriter do you prefer to use? Write a report telling what advantages you think your choice has over the other makes of machines.

Assignment 7.   You write letters for the credit department of a mail-order concern. There are thirty-two customers, good customers, who have not charged any merchandise for three months or longer. You think that letters to these customers might cause them to use their charge accounts. Prepare a report to your immediate superior presenting this idea.

Assignment 8.   Select some school condition or situation that needs improvement. Write a report to your principal, stating the facts of the situation and offering suggestions for improvement.

Assignment 9.   Write a report on the activities of some school club or organization of which you are or have been a member. State the facts concerning the purpose of the organization and how the purpose is achieved. Tell what participation in the activity has meant to you personally.

Assignment 10. Select ten letters from your folder of sample letters and analyze them from the point of view of overworked, negative, and out-of-date wording. Submit your findings in the form of a report.

Forms of Address for Official Correspondence

Certain established forms of address are used in correspondence with government officials, diplomatic representatives, military and naval personnel, church dignitaries, and other persons prominent in public life. It is not possible to include here all the forms for such persons, but the following forms are approved for *business* correspondence with the officials most often addressed.

Government Officials—Federal, State, and Municipal

The President

The President
   The White House
     Washington 25, D. C.
Sir: *or*
Mr. President: *or*
My dear Mr. President:

The Vice-President

The President of the Senate
   United States Senate
     Washington 25, D. C.
Sir:
          or
Honorable ....
   The Vice-President of the United
     States
     Washington 25, D. C.
My dear Mr. Vice-President: *or*
My dear Mr. ....:

Cabinet Member

The Secretary of ....
   Washington 25, D. C.
Dear Sir:
         or
Honorable ....
   Secretary of ....
     Washington 25, D. C.
My dear Mr. Secretary: *or*
My dear Mr. ....:

Members of Congress

Senator:
Honorable ....
   United States Senate
     Washington 25, D. C.
My dear Senator: *or*
My dear Senator ....:

Representative:
Honorable . . . .
  House of Representatives
  Washington 25, D. C.
My dear Congressman (or Con-
  gresswoman): *or*
My dear Mr. . . . . (or Miss,
  Mrs. . . . .):

Chief Justice of the United States

The Chief Justice of the United
  States
  Washington 13, D. C.
My dear Mr. Chief Justice:
                or
Honorable . . . .
  Chief Justice of the United States
  Washington 13, D. C.
My dear Mr. Chief Justice:

*Associate Justice of the Supreme
  Court of the United States*

Honorable . . . .
  Justice, Supreme Court of the
  United States
  Washington 13, D. C.
My dear Mr. Justice:
                or
Mr. Justice . . . .
  Supreme Court of the United
  States
  Washington 13, D. C.
My dear Mr. Justice:

Ambassador

From Foreign Countries to the
  United States:
His Excellency
  The Ambassador of . . . .
  Washington 25, D. C.
Sir:

Of the United States in Foreign
  Countries:
The Honorable
  The American Ambassador
  Foreign Capital and Foreign
  Country
Sir:

Governor

The Governor of the State of . . . . .
  State Capital and State
Dear Sir:
                or
Honorable . . . .
  Governor of the State of . . . . . .
  State Capital and State
Dear Sir: *or*
My dear Governor . . . . :

State Senator

Senator from . . . . (District) . . . .
  The State Senate
  State Capital and State
Dear Sir:
                or
Honorable . . . .
  The State Senate
  State Capital and State
Dear Sir: *or*
My dear Senator . . . . :

*State Assemblyman, Representa-
  tive, or Delegate*

(According to official name of the
  lower house in the respective
  state)
Assemblyman (or Representative
  or Delegate) from . . . .
  District . . . .
  The State Assembly (or House of
  Representatives or House of
  Delegates)
  State Capital and State
Dear Sir:

or

Same as second form for State Senator, with appropriate changes.

Mayor

The Mayor of the City of ....
City, State
Dear Sir:

or

Honorable ....
Mayor of the City of ....,
City, State
Dear Sir: *or*
My dear Mayor ....:

Roman Catholic Clergy

Cardinal

His Eminence (given name) Cardinal (surname)
Street, City, State
Your Eminence:

Archbishop

The Most Reverend ....
Archbishop of ....
Address
Your Excellency:

Bishop

The Most Reverend ....
Bishop of ....
Address
Your Excellency:

Monsignor

The Right Reverend Monsignor ...

Address
My dear Monsignor:

Priest

The Reverend ....
Address
Dear Father:

Mother Superior

The Reverend Mother Superior,
with initials of order
Address
Reverend Mother:

Sister

Sister ...., with initials
of order
Address
My dear Sister:

Protestant Clergy

Protestant Episcopal Bishop

The Right Reverend ....
Bishop of ....
Address
Dear Sir: *or*
My dear Bishop:

Protestant Episcopal Dean

The Very Reverend ....
Dean of ....
Address
My dear Dean:

Methodist Episcopal Bishop

Bishop ....
Address
My dear Bishop ....:

Other Clergymen

The Reverend Mr. (or Dr., if entitled to a degree) ....
Address
My dear Mr. (or Doctor) ....:

Jewish Rabbi

Rabbi . . . .
Address
My dear Rabbi:

Military and Naval Personnel

Addresses. The addresses of both officers and enlisted men of the armed forces should include: (1) full title of rank or rating (as *Major, Sergeant, Ensign*), (2) branch of the service (as *Signal Corps, Ordnance Department*), and (3) some such abbreviation as *U. S. A.* (*United States Army*), *U. S. C. G.* (*United States Coast Guard*), which may follow either the personal name or the branch of the service.

Major General . . . ., U. S. A.
Commanding General, Third Corps Area

Commander . . . .
Medical Corps, U. S. N. R.

Sergeant . . . ., U. S. A.
First Tank Corps

Salutations. The formal salutation *Dear Sir* may be used for all ranks or ratings. For personal salutations, the following rules govern:

1. For Army officers above the rank of lieutenant, the title is used, as follows:

For generals, lieutenant generals, major generals, and brigadier generals: *My dear General* . . . . :
For colonels and lieutenant colonels: *My dear Colonel* . . . . :
For majors and captains: *My dear Major* . . . . : and *My dear Captain* . . . . :

2. For Army lieutenants, either first or second, and for all noncommissioned Army officers, the salutation is simply *My dear Mr.* . . . . :

3. For Navy officers of the rank of admiral (including vice-admiral and rear admiral) and of captain, the salutation is *My dear Admiral* . . . . . . :; or *My dear Captain* . . . . :

4. For all Navy ranks from commander down, the salutation is *My dear Mr.* . . . . :

Grammar Refreshers

Grammar Refresher 1

Make any corrections that are necessary and give the reason for each correction you make. These instructions apply to all Grammar-Refresher exercises.

1. Mr. Forbes is the man who managed the business and later rising to the position of president.
2. Whom can that be?
3. Please bring Samuel and him to the conference with you.
4. The goods was sold before ten o'clock.
5. The number of mistakes in the letters were small.
6. Not one of those complaints were received.
7. All the data is on my desk.
8. Was you at the meeting yesterday?
9. Nobody makes you do that work, do they?
10. Henry and myself are hoping to see you on Monday.
11. Who told you about my being late?
12. There will be a meeting of the girl's society today.
13. His secretary works harder than me.
14. Mr. King will sure like your work.
15. Having gained admission through the employees' entrance, John dashed up the back stairway.
16. I told Mary and she to go in the private office.
17. Please help we poor girls.
18. Who are you thinking about?
19. You cannot expect to sing like Robert and I.
20. Whom did you seem to be in your dream?

Grammar Refresher 2

1. Give the book to whomever comes to the door.
2. You will find the stylus lying on the long bench.

3. I wanted to see him win very badly.
4. The president of the company will be here inside of an hour.
5. Is that them in the corridor?
6. Miss Williams selected John to be he in the class play.
7. The new building sits on a hill near the village.
8. He has neither the personality nor has he the background for that job.
9. Whom did you think I was?
10. This is the most unique letter style I have ever seen.
11. We should like the candidates to be they.
12. David plans on going to lunch early.
13. Bryant & Bryant is owned by my brother-in-laws.
14. Everybody must remember to take their pencils with them this afternoon.
15. The information should be kept between we three men.
16. Give this telephone number to whomever calls me today.
17. Those girls, Alice and she, are wasting too much time.
18. I just couldn't help but like him.
19. Either the boys or Mary have to work overtime tonight.
20. He acts as if he was tired.

Grammar Refresher 3

1. I will be glad to see you any morning after nine o'clock.
2. Was Jane and her friend at the meeting yesterday?
3. I will leave you have that information inside of an hour.
4. I don't do so good at typing myself.
5. We have et in that restaurant many times.
6. Neither Frank nor George ever offer their services.
7. I haven't but one criticism to make.
8. I shall congratulate whoever he names for the position.
9. The boy was undecided whether he should take the test now or to wait until next week.
10. Is that him at the desk?
11. Careful study of the production methods of the most success- ful firms have shown that the expediter is a valuable man.
12. The assembly voted to change their meeting place.
13. Anybody in his senses would know that courtesy is a neces- sary basic quality.
14. There is two ways of looking at the matter.

15. James took a picture of Ruth and myself.
16. Neither of the girls had remembered to bring their notebook.
17. I wish you could tell me where that stenographer is at.
18. This is one of those fountain pens that needs to be filled every five years.
19. Your problem is no different than that of many others who do the same kind of work.
20. Will I lie the package on the floor?

Grammar Refresher 4

1. He will not hire either you or me.
2. Everyone of we typists are going to get salary increases.
3. Is that one of those sandwiches that is all bread and no meat?
4. The brief case was lain very carefully upon the table.
5. Mr. Olson wants either Agnes or I to take his dictation.
6. Who did they refer to in that bulletin?
7. I talked with whomever was present.
8. He confessed that he was wrong in his decision.
9. Did you think it was to be she?
10. It is difficult to get the office rug to lie straight.
11. It begins to look like our hopes will be realized.
12. Two-thirds of the village were submerged during the hurricane.
13. The rules provide that any member of the office force who is repeatedly tardy will be discharged.
14. Yesterday the trade journal laid on the shelf above the presidents' desk.
15. Whom did you find was at fault in the matter?
16. The boy who you thought to be me has left the employ of Johnson & Johnson.
17. Every one of those pencils is sharpened.
18. Both Robert and I are to be promoted.
19. Many a boy and girl is ambitious.
20. Mr. Blythe asked me to rise the window a few inches.

Grammar Refresher 5

1. Stonington lies about ten miles east of New London.
2. He could not remember who he was to see.

3. Either of the two men are eligible for a pension.
4. Either Samuel or he is to collect the mail.
5. The audience was very receptive this evening.
6. From so far away you seemed to be her.
7. To his typists, Sylvia and she, Mr. Stewart expressed his appreciation.
8. Those envelopes have laid here long enough.
9. The dough is not raising very fast.
10. Where was Mr. Allen going to in such a hurry?
11. Mr. Gordon wants you to quickly go to his office.
12. You haven't scarcely time to collect all the material.
13. Whoever Mr. Jones found was late, he reprimanded.
14. Whomever Mr. Jones found late, he reprimanded.
15. Who did you think I called?
16. Maryann has less friends than me.
17. Of the two positions offered me, I like that of secretary best.
18. More people are employed in New York than in any city in the United States.
19. If he were a foreigner, he might be more appreciative of his privileges.
20. You done your work good today.

Grammar Refresher 6

1. Is your mother and your father going to the banquet?
2. The womens' lounge is on the second floor.
3. Each of the girls have their own locker.
4. Leave me help you with them books.
5. Samuel seen his duty and he done it.
6. Hasn't anyone finished his work?
7. The teacher objected to their coming.
8. Will I make an appointment for Mr. Ferris?
9. Please take them papers off of my desk.
10. There are only two courses of action, but I cannot decide which is the best.
11. Mr. Andrews is better prepared to make the report than me.
12. There are two o's in *loose;* there is only one in *lose.*
13. There is no question about who will get the coveted position.
14. I wish I was able to work more than eight hours a day.

15. Handling the numerous details is time consuming.
16. The staff is enthusiastic about the elimination of several of those time-consuming details.
17. Time certainly don't matter to that girl.
18. We have our tires checked regular.
19. Who's eraser is that on the floor?
20. Her desk is just inside of the gate.

Grammar Refresher 7

1. It won't take you but a minute to address these envelopes.
2. Radio commercials sure do promote sales.
3. Albert does considerable more than his share of the work.
4. We have never bought our office supplies off that firm.
5. Mary is the girl who I always thought would do the best work.
6. Miss Critcherson will admit whoever has an appointment.
7. Everyone but Alice and she contributed to the fund.
8. Bookkeepers like they are assets to any organization.
9. For as long as I can remember, I have drank four glasses of milk every day.
10. I was asked to look for three stenographers, but I only could find Miss Stephens.
11. Production suffers when there are to many distractions.
12. I most always go to lunch before Jane.
13. Set the file on the table where the folders are lying.
14. Will you take this letter to Mr. Palmer's office?
15. Both of the girls are now doing better work.
16. We are calling your attention to a discrepancy in the debit and credit columns.
17. There is some question as to whom they intend to choose.
18. It could just as well have been she who received the notice.
19. There is many preparations to be made before presenting yourself for a personal interview.
20. Mr. Walker was to the bank this morning.

Grammar Refresher 8

1. In regards to the matter we discussed at our last meeting, the time is not right for immediate action.

2. The faculty expressed its opinions in a very frank manner.
3. It seems that the past winter has just flew.
4. George is not so industrious as he.
5. Beverly works in the building opposite to ours.
6. Whom do you plan to select as treasurer of the branch?
7. Where was you last night?
8. How is your mother and father today?
9. Here comes two of our best customers.
10. Neither of the men knows that his stock is sold.
11. Being that you have worked here longer, you should know the routine better than me.
12. Jessica is the most perfect example of a well-groomed lady.
13. Did you say that Mr. Wood is a more polished speaker than any salesman you have?
14. In her living room was a rosewood-and-mahogany piano.
15. The river has bursted through the opening in the dam.
16. Neither Donald nor the other boys admitted the possibility of a mistake in their figures.
17. This is one of those decisions that are certain to cause widespread dissatisfaction.
18. There are no elevators above the twenty-third floor.
19. This is all the farther I can walk in the time I have at my disposal.
20. Who shall I say is calling?

Grammar Refresher 9

1. I should never have taken the auditor to be him.
2. Nine-tenths of the girls were poor spellers.
3. Henry, together with a hundred others, is to take the examination.
4. Her knowledge of shorthand and of typewriting has enabled her to progress rapidly.
5. Mr. Zeller, whom I know is the best comptroller we have had, will resign his position this week.
6. The applicant said that her name was Mary Doe.
7. I do not recall who I saw in the lobby yesterday.
8. I have arose at the same hour every morning for the past five years.

9. A self directing person is of value in the business world.
10. All of the personnel will receive a bonus.
11. There is the machine with all the attachments.
12. Helen is one of those efficient girls who always does like she promises.
13. Every typist, stenographer, and secretary are supposed to have a good English background.
14. Who else could they have taken the messenger to be?
15. The consultant gave us boys a full hour of his time.
16. The successful person is he who takes advantage of his opportunities.
17. My pet aversion are time-wasting employees.
18. Neither Ruth nor I are ready to accept that position at this time.
19. Anthony seems real happy to be working with you.
20. Mr. Coombes promised me the promotion and to pay me $25 a week.

Grammar Refresher 10

1. Them records should be locked in the safe.
2. The editor-in-chiefs of all the New York newspapers met for a conference.
3. Eileen was chosen for advancement because she could take dictation faster than any girl in the office.
4. Who did you think I was?
5. Who did you take me to be?
6. How did you know the caller was I?
7. Between you and I, Barbara should receive more co-operation from the other girls.
8. I opened the door, and in come Ada.
9. The first carbon is some darker than the third.
10. This is one of the copies that were rejected because of untidy erasures.
11. Everybody in the office seemed to be busy at his desk.
12. Will you please help me? Sure.
13. It looks like we have a busy day ahead of us.
14. It must have been she whom he meant.
15. Us boys have organized a bowling league.

16. Is the president and his secretary going to Washington?
17. In back of them coats are the water cooler.
18. I think I am as reticent as she.
19. Did you see Miss Hunt and her at the theater last evening?
20. This time I have beat my own record.

Grammar Refresher 11

1. Both Suzanne and me can transcribe at the rate of forty words a minute.
2. That folder lay in plain sight all day yesterday.
3. While she was in our employ, Esther done very good work.
4. Our prices are the most cheapest in the city.
5. Roberta is one of the girls who was chosen because of good diction.
6. Arthur's enunciation is not as good as that of the others' in his class.
7. If I was you, I would insist upon a vacation.
8. Who's the person responsible for the incoming mail?
9. It is we who have to check all the articles, not they.
10. I laughed when Edward said that he would like to be I.
11. Mr. Cooper called both you and her to his desk.
12. The cartoons were thought to represent we girls.
13. Peter foolishly thought the inspectors to be us.
14. I felt as though I were walking on air.
15. A number of people were influenced by the fraudulent advertising.
16. Neither Dorothy nor Helen saw themselves as potential material for an executive position.
17. One species of the monkey is unable to live in captivity.
18. We owe Bay and Berry six month's interest.
19. What do you think of them resigning without giving the required notice?
20. There is no better people to work for than them.

Grammar Refresher 12

1. Mr. Sheffield said that in his opinion the number of accidents in industrial plants was too high.

2. I like to think of his retiring at an early age.
3. Their is too many lose ends in that project.
4. If this was another century, you would not be able to obtain all these conveniences.
5. The president added the names of his three son-in-laws to the payroll.
6. I think I would prefer to work with Eugene.
7. Yes, this is one of those machines that have weak draw bands.
8. Only us five girls are now members of the stenographer's pool.
9. My present typewriter has a more better action than the one I used formerly.
10. In fact, this typewriter has an easier action than any machine in the office.
11. I haven't scarcely but a single complaint.
12. Beside being a good penman, Robert is an excellent speller.
13. Mr. Chesebrough was in the building this morning when I went into his private office.
14. I have forgot all the shorthand I learned at school.
15. Be really sure that the final draft is correct.
16. Will you walk too work with me tomorrow?
17. This model is different to the one I have been using.
18. If your desk is in front of a window, your eyes will suffer undue strain.
19. I have never used these sort of pencils.
20. Well, what kind of a pencil do you want?

Grammar Refresher 13

1. I was right here when Mr. Allen took his correspondence off of her desk.
2. If you have to concentrate, you will find quite surroundings helpful.
3. Most all the workers are satisfied.
4. Anybody in his senses would know what a mailable letter is.
5. I did not learn that shorthand was the art of writing by sound.
6. The committee were divided as to their ideas about entrance requirements.

7. I naturally depended on you who are my friend.
8. The number of applicants for the positions was beyond all expectations.
9. Some of the audience have their coats ready for a quick exit.
10. A block and tackle are still a good machine for some types of work.
11. I give him his check last Friday.
12. I vow that I shall never again put myself in such a position.
13. The president travels by airplane, and the treasurer travels by train.
14. We could neither understand his telegram nor his letter.
15. This is not a matter for you and I to arbitrate.
16. The ocean looks smoothly tonight.
17. All except Donald and me have private telephones.
18. Whom did she refuse to admit to Mr. Bryson's office?
19. I should like to be him with all his money.
20. Was you the first clerk hired by this firm?

Grammar Refresher 14

1. I had began to think you were not feeling good.
2. Without you let me borrow the calculator, I shall be here all night.
3. Whom do you think Rosemarie resembles?
4. Industry is it's own reward.
5. Are you familiar with the operation of them new machines?
6. Who do you like best, Mr. Forbes or Mr. Egan?
7. You can depend on our selling only those goods that are of high-grade.
8. I am feeling somewhat better today.
9. The managing editor expects each of us boys to do their very best.
10. I have laid aside my work for the day.
11. This invitation is extended to yourself and your family.
12. The ship sailed proudly on his way.
13. A man who I think is the new mayor called today.
14. I neither like the work nor the salary.
15. Set up that letter like I showed you.

16. I intended to close the books this morning, and Mr. Bende needed me for some special work.
17. It was he who saved the day for us.
18. Kenneth, who I know is reliable, will finish the proofreading.
19. Is the house and the store for sale?
20. I was certainly glad I did not have to be he.

Grammar Refresher 15

1. If he were your employer, what would you do?
2. Mr. Mellon, may we discuss this question with you this afternoon?
3. If you work to the best of your ability, you hadn't ought to worry about being replaced.
4. I agreed to accept the increase and that I would try to be worthy of Mr. Walker's confidence.
5. Let him and her be the judges for the contest.
6. Mr. Harrison is the man who I think is an ideal executive.
7. Ruth's and Kathryn's mother will be pleased with this evidence of their progress.
8. Our inventory shows that we need more of those kind of material.
9. When you raise your voice, it sounds shrilly.
10. If you don't mind, I should like to set here.
11. What is the use of my studying history?
12. Lying on the floor was the paper, the carbon, and the envelope.
13. Every business person not only must be courteous but also tactful.
14. As soon as we receive the order, I will leave you know.
15. John does his work so good that i know he will be selected to take charge of the branch office.
16. Mr. Gordon? That is he whom you met in the hall.
17. They would like to be we, just for a week.
18. Mary wondered who the next principal would be.
19. Would it be alright for her and me to answer the telephone during the noon hour?
20. Her and I have a special reason for requesting this permission.

Grammar Refresher 16

1. The scissors is in the top middle drawer of the desk.
2. What kind of a fountain pen do you prefer?
3. Which of them would you promote, him or her?
4. Lay your magazine on the table and help me change this ribbon.
5. It was she, alright. I recognized her voice.
6. Do you know who would be capable of recording these transactions?
7. In my opinion, Michael is a better bookkeeper than he.
8. He does his work quickly, and he does it good.
9. Nobody should have their head turned by a little praise.
10. Does it always have to be I?
11. I did not know that Olga had hid the calendar.
12. That experience surely learned me a good lesson.
13. Will you take care of the incoming mail?
14. If this was Saturday, I would go with you.
15. Mr. Bunker asked Frank and me to clean the duplicating machine.
16. The three accountants and Eleanor was there before we arrived.
17. Did you lose your styli? Are these they?
18. I can type faster than her, but she can transcribe faster than me.
19. It was the other operator, not me, whom Mr. Ash blamed for the accident.
20. George is a boy who I think is going to succeed.

Grammar Refresher 17

1. What do you think caused the stock-market situation of the late 20s?
2. To use ones time to advantage is good business practice.
3. The hen sits on the eggs for hours.
4. The victims were they, Natalie and she.
5. One of the girls will give their blotter to Lois.
6. Gertrude seemed tired, and I could see no reason for her weariness.

7. Before I had a chance to remove my coat, the telephone had rang five times.
8. If your plan don't succeed, don't blame it on me.
9. The special permission for Lillian and me finally came.
10. Charles, whom were you talking to just now?
11. Idylhour was the place where I was at all during my summer vacation.
12. Mr. Clark will trust nobody but her and me to tidy his desk.
13. There is a splendid spirit of co-operation between all six members of the force.
14. Jane made more complaints than anyone at the conference.
15. Esther and she can read one another's shorthand notes.
16. Henry was told to give the key to Ellen or me.
17. Do you know who made the appointment for three o'clock?
18. You may take with you whomever you choose.
19. John speaks distinctly but not as correctly as you do.
20. Without you learn to control your temper, you will find that life can be very unpleasant.

Grammar Refresher 18

1. Can I use your dictionary for fifteen minutes?
2. Even if you have to omit your lunch, my orders are that you will have these letters filed before the day is over.
3. With the shorthand notes lying on the table before her, Ann began her report.
4. Was it he whom they called?
5. This data is to be kept confidential.
6. Which is the most important, enunciation or pronunciation?
7. Had I know you needed it, the check would of been sent last week.
8. It was she who addressed the last ten envelopes.
9. Us girls must present a united front on this question.
10. There will be a special sale of chintzs next Saturday.
11. You are not so good an office housekeeper as she.
12. Both David and I are taking courses leading to the degree of C.P.A.
13. Who did you say was chosen the person most likely to succeed?

14. Mr. Moody left word for Norman and me to balance all accounts.
15. I shall be glad to work for whoever makes me the best offer.
16. It looks like we shall have to work evenings during the Christmas rush.
17. It is important that you observe all them little courtesy rules.
18. Leave us your instructions before you go to Chicago.
19. Would you take this work home if you were me?
20. What kind of a job do you have now?

Grammar Refresher 19

1. Will we have the advertising copy ready by this afternoon?
2. Which of these three typewriters has the better action?
3. The matter has been laid before the council for its consideration.
4. This special privilege is for only James and yourself.
5. The news from the center of operations are better today.
6. Charles Perry and James Hunt's garages are closed on Sunday.
7. If you were I, would you speak to Mr. Olson about an increase?
8. Everyone has had sick leave except Joseph and me.
9. Let Alice and I attend to the ticker this week.
10. Which is the oldest, Mr. Fuller, Mr. Bunker, or Mr. Ames?
11. I am sure it could not have been she who mislaid the deed.
12. Both Margaret and she are competent medical secretaries.
13. Miss Fahey seems to think that Sarah is just as alert as she.
14. Do you remember who Mr. Curran told to take the switchboard?
15. Someone left their umbrella here yesterday.
16. The bus had went just before I reached the terminal.
17. There is ten people waiting to see you, Mr. Dolan.
18. I am happy to be of service to you last June.
19. Mr. Moody, as well as Barbara, Agnes, and Jean, is making remarkable improvement.
20. Neither of the contractors has submitted his specifications.

Grammar Refresher 20

1. I felt as if I was the one to correct the mistake.
2. Will John be glad to hear about the safe arrival of the consignment?
3. Our office is better furnished than that of any firm in the building.
4. By lying under the car, Henry was able to find the cause of all the trouble.
5. We dislike very much to lose an old customer like yourself.
6. Had it been he, nobody would have made any comment.
7. The office force quarrels among itself about every proposed change.
8. Can I use your name as a reference, Mr. Boynton?
9. Just outside the office doors were the elevator.
10. Who do you think will be the top-ranking salesman this year?
11. Neither of them was careful about checking his work.
12. When your account has been payed in full, we shall be glad to do business with you on a cash basis.
13. The sales and advertising department are on the top floor.
14. The slogan contest was won jointly by Bernard and me.
15. The tickets will be given to whoever asks for them.
16. Whom did they ask to entertain the client?
17. How many As did you get on your last report?
18. I always thought that Lawrence did his work satisfactory.
19. I wish I could spell like her.
20. Where did my dictionary go to?

Grammar Refresher 21

1. We were supposed to have completed that work yesterday.
2. Your desk looks very attractively.
3. We are rising our requirements for head bookkeeper.
4. William and myself are assigned to be your assistants for this month.
5. The Commonwealth and Northern Corporation have just declared a dividend.

6. Here are the Joneses, who I think have an appointment with Mr. Foley.
7. Them checks must be signed today.
8. We could not deny that the culprits were we.
9. There was to good reasons for his refusal.
10. When I left the office last night, the tabs were laying on the cabinet.
11. What was you doing here so early this morning?
12. Our employer insists on many things that is not required in other offices.
13. Who do you suppose would do such a thing?
14. Mr. Allen, can us men have permission to smoke during working hours?
15. Not one of his friends thinks he will fail to get the order.
16. Any one of you has the same chance as he.
17. I haven't been out of the city but once in the past year.
18. The envelope as well as the letter were smudged.
19. There go Mr. Brooks and his callers.
20. Only one of the twenty applicants knows how to answer the telephone.

Grammar Refresher 22

1. We will all have a holiday on Monday.
2. You will find the folder in back of the last guide card.
3. The production editor was very angry at Doris.
4. I was sure that I had laid the finished letters on his desk.
5. Shall he be forced to do that work?
6. If he was my own father, I could not make no other decision.
7. The number of correct answers was indeed amazing.
8. A number of applicants call at our office every working day.
9. Mary, together with her three sisters, is living in New York.
10. I am not certain for whom the letter is intended.
11. Is Patrick here? Why, I only saw him a few minutes ago.
12. I am just going out to eat myself.
13. Each of the boys insisted that he had not taken the letter from the file.
14. Our office manager praised everyone but me.

15. Why don't he say what he means?
16. There was only Christine and her left to attend to last-minute details.
17. The account of all his expenditures was checked by the cashier.
18. Each boy and girl in this office has the right spirit.
19. Everyone in the group was told to report at eight o'clock tomorrow morning.
20. Where is the list of accounts receivable?

Grammar Refresher 23

1. Mr. MacNeil sent a box of oranges to Virginia and myself.
2. We should very much appreciate your answering these questions.
3. I hope that there will be no repetition of these kind of errors.
4. I like to see a dog lie down at his master's order.
5. Neither Harriet nor her friends know how to write a good business letter.
6. Neither her friends nor Harriet knows how to write a good business letter.
7. Do Donald and him call you during office hours?
8. See, $10 was found on the floor behind the wastebasket.
9. The committee of ten men chosen from all the offices in the building is ready to hear complaints.
10. Three-fourths of the report was typed by Clara.
11. Perhaps it was her who forgot to turn off the switch.
12. The shades were adjusted to suit Mrs. Grossman and she.
13. What do you think of us, Peter and me, as candidates for the position?
14. Who was it whom they mentioned, he or I?
15. This sandwich tastes well.
16. The more louder he talked, the less could the man on the other end of the wire hear.
17. Most everybody has read the bulletin.
18. How my purchasing power has shrunk in the past few years!
19. The speaker said that Belgium was a small country.
20. If you wish, you may come with Evelyn and me.

Grammar Refresher 24

1. Isn't anyone going to have his lunch now?
2. Borrow the money off of Peter.
3. We see James going in the new restaurant this noon.
4. In an office, it is not necessary to rise every time the employer stops at the desk.
5. The Chamber of Commerce in this city is very active.
6. The administrators, Miss Fallon and us men, are pleased with the increased production.
7. Who but her is sure to remember the names of all customers?
8. For whom were these instructions meant, you or me?
9. Jeannette speaks better English than either you or me.
10. Are you sure you know who this woman is?
11. Whom did you take Mr. Baker to be?
12. I must say that I think the joke is on you and me.
13. I intended to have written you, but I have been unable to find the necessary time.
14. Are them the Browns who have a letter of introduction to the president?
15. It is evident that either Charles or Edward will have to submit his resignation.
16. Because of the annual renovating spree, our office is all tore up.
17. I wish I were in Bermuda.
18. Because of the maritime strike, many ships were laying idle in the harbor.
19. I have made requisition for a fifteen inch ruler.
20. Mr. King conducts his business like he did twenty-five years ago.

Grammar Refresher 25

1. Who told you about my being late?
2. I think she has more responsibility than any person on the staff.
3. The four boys you mention are all good mathematicians, but I think Fred is the better.
4. We pride ourselves on selling only high grade goods.

5. Great rocks raise out of the water at low tide.
6. I saw in the paper where Miss Higgins is taking another business trip.
7. Whom would you choose, him or me?
8. No one should boast about how well he knows his business.
9. You make your 3s and 5s too much alike.
10. Your data regarding income-tax reductions is incorrect.
11. I do not know whether either of the stenographers is ready to take your dictation now.
12. Can it be we whom they are blaming for the production lag?
13. It was she and I who shared the sales record.
14. Whom did they select to accompany Mr. Leahy to Philadelphia?
15. Mr. Hakes had a sort of a smile on his face.
16. Mr. Ellis thought it was we who were making all the noise.
17. Either you must support the policies of the company or resign your position.
18. We telephone operators have worked very hard today.
19. The applicant whom you praised so glowingly has justified your recommendation.
20. I should have stood in bed.

INDEX

INDEX TO VOCABULARY STUDY